PRA

Praise for

The Fortune at the Bottom of the Pyramid

"C. K. Prahalad argues that companies must revolutionize how they do business in developing countries if both sides of that economic equation are to prosper. Drawing on a wealth of case studies, his compelling new book offers an intriguing blueprint for how to fight poverty with profitability."

Bill Gates
Chairman and Chief Software Architect,
Microsoft

"The Bottom of the Pyramid belongs at the top of the reading list for business people, academics, and experts pursuing the elusive goal of sustainable growth in the developing world. C. K. Prahalad writes with uncommon insight about consumer needs in poor societies and opportunities for the private sector to serve important public purposes while enhancing its own bottom line. If you are looking for fresh thinking about emerging markets, your search is ended. This is the book for you."

Madeleine K. Albright
Former U.S. Secretary of State

"Prahalad challenges readers to re-evaluate their pre-conceived notions about the commercial opportunities in serving the relatively poor nations of the world. The Bottom of the Pyramid highlights the way to commercial success and societal improvement—but only if the developed world reconceives the way it delivers products and services to the developing world."

Christopher Rodrigues
CEO, Visa International

"An important and insightful work showing persuasively how the private sector can be put at the center of development, not just as a rhetorical flourish but as a real engine of jobs and services for the poor."

Mark Malloch Brown
Administrator
United Nations Development Programme

"Most people recognize that poverty is a major problem in the world, yet they throw up their hands and say, 'What to do?' Not so C. K. Prahalad. The Fortune at the Bottom of the Pyramid *gives us hope and strategies for eradicating poverty through profits that benefit all. Pass this book on to those who need to read it."*

Ken Blanchard
co-author of *The One Minute Manager*® and
The Secret: What Great Leaders Know-And Do

Ideas. Action. Impact.
Wharton School
Publishing

In the face of accelerating turbulence and change, business leaders and policy makers need new ways of thinking to sustain performance and growth.

Wharton School Publishing offers a trusted source for stimulating ideas from thought leaders who provide new mental models to address changes in strategy, management and finance. We seek out authors from diverse disciplines with a profound understanding of change and its implications. We offer books and tools that help executives respond to the challenge of change.

Every book and management tool we publish meets quality standards set by The Wharton School of the University of Pennsylvania. Each title is reviewed by the Wharton School Publishing Editorial Board before being given Wharton's seal of approval. This ensures that Wharton publications are timely, relevant, important, conceptually sound or empirically based, and implementable.

To fit our readers' learning preferences, Wharton publications are available in multiple formats, including books, audio, and electronic.

To find out more about our books and management tools, visit us at whartonsp.com and Wharton's executive education site, exceed.wharton.upenn.edu.

The Fortune at the Bottom of the Pyramid

C. K. Prahalad

Harvey C. Fruehauf Professor of
Corporate Strategy and International Business
The University of Michigan Business School

Wharton
UNIVERSITY of PENNSYLVANIA

Wharton School Publishing

A CIP record of this book can be obtained from the Library of Congress

Editorial/Production Supervision: Patti Guerrieri
Art Director: Gail Cocker-Bogusz
Manufacturing Manager: Alexis R. Heydt-Long
Manufacturing Buyer: Maura Zaldivar
Executive Editor: Tim Moore
Editorial Assistant: Richard Winkler
Development Editor: Russ Hall
Marketing Manager: Martin Litkowski
Cover Design Director: Jerry Votta
Cover Design: Chuti Prasertsith
Cover Photograph: Oriol Alamany, Corbis
Interior Design and Composition: Meg Van Arsdale

Ideas. Action. Impact.
**Wharton School
Publishing**

© 2005 Pearson Education, Inc.
Publishing as Wharton School Publishing
Upper Saddle River, NJ 07458

Wharton School Publishing offers excellent discounts on this book when ordered in quantity for bulk purchases or special sales. For more information, please contact:
U.S. Corporate and Government Sales, 1-800-382-3419, corpsales@pearsontechgroup.com. For sales outside of the U.S., please contact: International Sales, 1-317-581-3793, international@pearsontechgroup.com.

ISBN 0-13-146750-6

Pearson Education Ltd.
Pearson Education Australia Pty., Limited
Pearson Education South Asia Pte. Ltd.
Pearson Education Asia Ltd.
Pearson Education Canada, Ltd.
Pearson Educación de Mexico, S.A. de C.V.
Pearson Education—Japan
Pearson Malaysia SDN BHD

C. K. Prahalad
THE FORTUNE AT THE BOTTOM OF THE PYRAMID
Eradicating Poverty Through Profits

Yoram (Jerry)Wind, Colin Crook, with Robert Gunther
THE POWER OF IMPOSSIBLE THINKING
Transform the Business of Your Life and the Life of Your Business

Scott A. Shane
FINDING FERTILE GROUND
Identifying Extraordinary Opportunities for New Ventures

Contents

Preface

This book is a result of a long and lonely journey for me. It started during the Christmas vacation of 1995. During that period of celebration and good cheer, one issue kept nagging me: What are we doing about the poorest people around the world? Why is it that with all our technology, managerial know-how, and investment capacity, we are unable to make even a minor contribution to the problem of pervasive global poverty and disenfranchisement? Why can't we create inclusive capitalism? Needless to say, these are not new questions. However, as one who is familiar with both the developed and the developing world, the contrasts kept gnawing at me. It became clear that finding a solution to the problems of those at the bottom of the economic pyramid around the world should be an integral part of my next intellectual journey. It was also clear that we have to start with a new approach, a "clean sheet of paper." We have to learn from the successes and failures of the past; the promises made and not fulfilled. Doing more of the same, by refining the solutions of the past—developmental aid, subsidies, governmental support, localized nongovernmental organization (NGO)–based solutions, exclusive reliance on deregulation and privatization of public assets—is important and has a role to play, but has not redressed the problem of poverty.

Although NGOs worked tirelessly to promote local solutions and local entrepreneurship, the idea of large-scale entrepreneurship as a possible solution to poverty had not taken root. It appeared that many a politician, bureaucrat, and manager in large domestic and global firms agreed on one thing: The poor are wards of the state. This implicit agreement was bothersome. The large-scale private sector was only marginally involved in dealing with the problems of 80 percent of humanity. The natural question, therefore, was this: What if we mobilized the resources, scale, and scope of large firms to co-create solutions to the problems at the bottom of the pyramid (BOP), those 4 billion people who live on less than $2 a day? **Why can't we mobilize the investment capacity of large firms with the knowledge and commitment of NGOs and the communities that need help? Why can't we co-create unique solutions?** That was the beginning of my journey to understand and motivate large firms to imagine and act on their role in creating a more just and humane society by collaborating effectively with other institutions.

It was obvious that managers can sustain their enthusiasm and commitment to activities only if they are grounded in good business practices. The four to five billion people at the BOP can help redefine what "good business practice" is. This was not about philanthropy and notions of corporate social responsibility. These initiatives can take the process of engagement between the poor and the large firm only so far. Great contributions can result from these initiatives, but these activities are unlikely to be fully integrated with the core activities of the firm. For sustaining energy, resources, and innovation, the BOP must become a key element of the central mission for large private-sector firms. The poor must become active, informed, and involved consumers. Poverty reduction can result from co-creating a market around the needs of the poor.

We have to discard many of the "for and against" views of the world. For example, "are you for globalization or against it" is not a good question. Globalization, like all other major social movements, brings some good and some bad. Similarly, global versus local is not a useful debate. The tensions are real. Very early in my career, I learned that even within the multinational corporation (MNC) that is not a settled debate.

Similarly, the debate between small (e.g., microfinance) and large (e.g., multinational firms) is not a useful debate either. Large business can bring efficiency. NGOs can bring creativity to solve the problems that face us all. Certainly, I wanted to avoid the paternalism towards the poor that I saw in NGOs, government agencies, and MNCs.

This book is concerned about what works. This is not a debate about who is right. I am even less concerned about what may go wrong. Plenty can and has. I am focused on the potential for learning from the few experiments that are going right. These can show us the way forward. I do not want the poor of the world to become a constituency. I want poverty to be a problem that should be solved. This book is about all of the players—NGOs, large domestic firms, MNCs, government agencies, and most importantly, the poor themselves—coming together to solve very complex problems that we face as we enter the 21st century. The problem of poverty must force us to innovate, not claim "rights to impose our solutions."

The starting point for this transition had to be twofold. First, we should consider the implications of the language we use. "Poverty alleviation" and "the poor" are terms that are loaded with meaning and historical baggage. The focus on entrepreneurial activities as an antidote to the current malaise must be on an active, underserved consumer community and a potential for global growth in trade and prosperity as the four to five billion poor become part of a system of inclusive capitalism. We should commence talking about underserved consumers and markets. **The process must start with respect for Bottom of Pyramid consumers as individuals. The process of co-creation assumes that consumers are equally important joint problem-solvers.** Consumers and consumer communities will demand and get choice. This process of creating an involved and activist consumer is already emerging. The BOP provides an opportunity to turbocharge this process of change in the traditional relationship between the firm and the consumer. Second, we must recognize that the conversion of the BOP into an active market is essentially a developmental activity. It is not about serving an existing market more efficiently. **New and creative approaches are needed to convert poverty into an opportunity for all concerned. That is the challenge.**

Once the basic approach was clear, the opportunities became obvious. The new viewpoint showed a different landscape and a focus on early and quiet attempts by some firms to explore this terrain. Unilever and its Indian subsidiary, Hindustan Lever Limited, was one such early experimenter. Around 1997, I found a kindred spirit in colleague Professor Stu Hart at the University of Michigan Business School (UMBS), who was approaching similar problems from a sustainable development perspective. We produced a working paper called "The Strategies for the Bottom of the Pyramid." Needless to say, not a single journal would accept the article for publication. It was too radical. Reviewers thought that it did not follow the work of developmental economists. Nobody noticed that we were offering an alternative to the traditional wisdom of how to alleviate global poverty. Thanks to the Web, various revisions of the working paper circulated freely. Surprisingly, a number of managers read it, accepted its premise, and started to initiate action based on it. Managers at Hewlett-Packard, DuPont, Monsanto, and other corporations started a venture fund and dedicated senior managers' time and energy to examine this opportunity. Meanwhile, the Digital Dividend conference organized by Dr. Allen Hammond and the World Resources Institute in Seattle in 1999 provided a forum to examine these ideas in depth. I have not looked back. Since 1997, I have used every possible platform—academic, managerial, and governmental—to push the idea of the BOP as a market and a source of innovations. During the last five years, slowly at first but now more rapidly, a large number of NGOs, academics, and managers have started to discuss the need for an alternate approach to poverty alleviation and the potential role of the private sector and entrepreneurship as one of the critical elements.

The publication of the two articles, "The Fortune at the Bottom of the Pyramid," in *Strategy+Business* (January 2002) with Stu Hart, and "Serve the World's Poor, Profitably" in the *Harvard Business Review* (September 2002) with Allen Hammond, facilitated the process of widespread discussion within corporations. Today, the discussion is not about "whether" but how fast and where. We have come a long way.

In the fall of 2002, several MBA students at the UMBS came to me and said that they would like to work with me on BOP issues and that they were intrigued by the ideas they had seen in print as well as my message in numerous lectures on campus and outside. I was not easily convinced. I imposed extraordinary demands on them to convince me that they really cared. They convinced me overwhelmingly. They were ready to travel, explore opportunities, and endure the painful task of assembling convincing evidence. That was the start of the now widely accepted XMAP projects (a variant of International Multidisciplinary Action Projects [IMAP], which UMBS has long supported with faculty mentoring.) The X in XMAP stood for experimental. The enthusiasm of the students, especially Cynthia Casas and Praveen Suthrum, provided the glue and helped see the project through administrative difficulties. I am grateful to all the MBA students whose dedication made this book possible.

The book is in three parts. In Part I we develop a framework for the active engagement of the private sector at the BOP. It provides the basis for a profitable win–win engagement. The focus is on the nature of changes that all players—the large firm, NGOs, governmental agencies, and the poor themselves—must accept to make this process work. Part II describes 12 cases, in a wide variety of businesses, where the BOP is becoming an active market and bringing benefits, far beyond just products, to consumers. The cases represent a wide variety of industries—from retail, health, and financial services to agribusiness and government. They are located in Peru, Brazil, Nicaragua, Mexico, and India. They represent a wide variety of institutions working together—subsidiaries of MNCs, large domestic firms, startups, and NGOs. They are all motivated by the same concern: They want to change the face of poverty by bringing to bear a combination of high-technology solutions, private enterprise, market-based solutions and involvement of multiple organizations. They are solving real problems. The BOP consumers get products and services at an affordable price, but more important, they get recognition, respect, and fair treatment. Building self-esteem and entrepreneurial drive at the BOP is probably the most enduring contribution that the private sector can make. Finally, decision-makers do not often hear the voices of the poor. We tend to make assumptions about how they feel. Part III (video stories on CD) is an attempt to tell the story primarily from their perspective. Each of the research teams—MBA students—went with video cameras and recorded their conversations with the BOP consumers as well as with the company managers. We collected well over 100 hours of video as part of the research. We present 35 minutes of the story from the point of view of the BOP consumers, the so-called poor. They are the primary storytellers. They tell us in their language—from Portuguese to Hindi—their view of what the involvement of the private sector and the resultant transition have meant for them. The three parts—the rationale for and the approach to private-sector involvement, the in-depth case studies, and the voices of the BOP consumers—are all an integral part of the book. They are intended to focus not only on the intellectual but also on the emotional arguments for encouraging private-sector engagement.

No research of this nature can be done without the active support of firms and managers. They gave us open access, their time, and their insights. Their enthusiasm was infectious. None of us who was a part of the research need any more convincing. We do know that the entrepreneurship and inventiveness of dedicated managers can bring a sea of change rapidly. That is true across the world. We could not have documented the richness of the transformation taking place at the BOP through the efforts of dedicated management teams without an unstinting effort by the students. The names of the students who were involved in developing the cases stories are given at the end of the book.

Research of this nature, on the cutting edge, cannot take place in an academic institution without the active support of the dean. Dean Robert J. Dolan bet on the initiative. Associate Dean Michael D. Gordon remained a constant source of encouragement to me and to the students in all stages of the project, from obtaining enough video cameras to providing substantive inputs to the research. His deep belief and commitment to the research agenda were critical to the project. Several of my colleagues provided support. I owe special thanks to Associate Dean Gene Anderson, Associate Dean Izak Duenyas, and colleagues Andy Lawlor and Jan Svejnar, former Director of the William Davidson Institute.

It was fortuitous that Kofi Annan, Secretary General of the United Nations, constituted a special commission on Private Sector and Development under the auspices of the United Nations Development Program and its Administrator Mark Malloch Brown. As a member of the Commission, I had a chance to share my ideas with the members of the Commission and staff and found a very useful platform for dialogue. Nissim Ezekiel, Yann Risz, Sahb Sobhani, Jan Krutzinna, and Naheed Nenshi showed great willingness to debate and challenge many of the ideas presented in this book. I have benefited from their dialogue. It is my hope that the body of work represented in this book influenced the thinking of the Commission as well.

No project of this size can be done without the active support of a wide variety of people. Cynthia Shaw (UMBS) and Fred Wessells provided editorial assistance in reducing the mountain of data we had collected on each case story into a manageable document. Russ Hall provided additional editorial support and helped in considerably improving the case studies and the text. Many of my colleagues, including Prof. M. S. Krishnan, Prof. Venkat Ramaswamy, Prof. Michael Gordon, and Ron Bendersky (Executive Education, UMBS) helped with detailed suggestions for improving the text. Hrishi Bhattacharyya (Unilever), Allen Hammond (World Resources Institute), and Jeb Brugmann and Craig Cohon (Globalegacy) provided useful insights. The Wharton Business Publishing team has been exceptional in its support and belief in the message. Jerry Wind (Wharton) accepted the idea of this book with great enthusiasm. The editorial team led by Tim Moore and including John Pierce and Martin Litkowski was remarkable in their support. Their commitment to this book has been a source of strength. Patti Guerrieri was always willing to help and produced yet another revision of the manuscript with patience and quiet competence. Kimberly Ward (UMBS) oversaw the entire project, and Brian Greminger worked magic with the videos. Both of them, by their dedication to the students and to the overall project, were a source of inspiration. Finally, the students stayed with the project for over a year, always managing to do more and accommodating what must have appeared to be random demands on their time.

The biggest supporters of this project were my family. Our children, Murali Krishna and Deepa, and the latter's husband, Ashwin, kept me going when I was willing to give up the idea of writing a book-length manuscript. As always, my wife, Gayatri, was my source of strength. She deeply believed in the cause and accompanied me to a wide variety of on-site visits, be it Jaipur Foot or the Shakti Amma. She willingly created the space and time for me to work on this project.

It is my hope that this book will provide the impetus for a more active engagement of the private sector in building the marketing ecosystems for transforming the BOP.

C. K. Prahalad
San Diego

About the Author
C. K. Prahalad

*"...he may well be the most influential thinker
on business strategy today."*

BusinessWeek

Internationally recognized as a specialist on corporate strategy and value-added of top management in multinational corporations, he has consulted with many of the world's foremost companies. In addition to being the Harvey C. Fruehauf Professor of Business Administration at the University of Michigan, he serves on the board of Directors of NCR Corp., Hindustan Lever Ltd., and the World Resources Institute.

A prolific author as well, his book, *Competing for the Future* (co-authored with Gary Hamel), was a national bestseller and was the Best Selling Business Book of the Year in 1994. He also co-authored *Multinational Mission: Balancing Local Demands and Global Vision* (in 1987 with Yves Doz) and *The Future of Competition: Co-Creating Unique Value with Customers* (in 2004 with Venkat Ramaswamy).

He has been named among the top ten management thinkers of the world in every major survey for over ten years.

PART **I**

The Fortune at the Bottom of the Pyramid

The objective of this section is to *build a framework* for poverty alleviation. We start with a simple proposition. **If we stop thinking of the poor as victims or as a burden and start recognizing them as resilient and creative entrepreneurs and value-conscious consumers, a whole new world of opportunity will open up.** Four billion poor can be the engine of the next round of global trade and prosperity. It can be a source of innovations. Serving the BOP consumers

I

will demand innovations in technology, products and services, and business models. More importantly, it will require large firms to work collaboratively with civil society organizations and local governments. Market development at the BOP will also create millions of new entrepreneurs at the grass roots level—from women working as distributors and entrepreneurs to village-level micro enterprises. These micro enterprises will be an integral part of the market-based ecosystem. It will require organizational and governance innovations as well.

The vision that is presented in the following pages is the co-creation of a solution to the problem of poverty. The opportunities at the BOP cannot be unlocked if large and small firms, governments, civil society organizations, development agencies, and the poor themselves do not work together with a shared agenda. Entrepreneurship on a massive scale is the key. This approach will challenge the prejudices about the "role and value added" of each group and its role in the economic development at the BOP.

In these chapters the reader will find the opportunities for co-creation among the various players. More importantly, the poor themselves are willing to experiment, learn, and change. While we will focus on the role of the private sector, the importance of collaboration across the various groups will become obvious. The interconnectedness of the approach to economic development and social transformation as visualized below will become obvious.

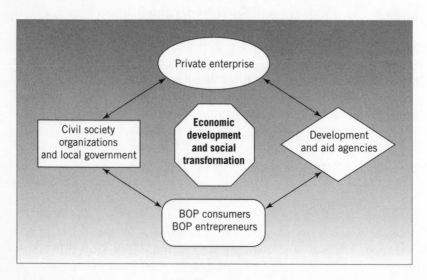

Part I outlines how that can be accomplished by isolating principles from successful, large-scale experiments involving the entire private sector ecosystem. Most of the examples of successful experimentation are taken from the case studies included in Part II of the book. The bottom line is simple: It is possible to "do well by doing good."

I

The Market at the Bottom of the Pyramid

Turn on your television and you will see calls for money to help the world's 4 billion poor—people who live on far less than \$2 a day. In fact, the cry is so constant and the need so chronic that the tendency for many people is to tune out these images as well as the message. Even those who do hear and heed the cry are limited in what they can accomplish. For more than 50 years, the World Bank, donor nations, various aid agencies, national governments, and, lately, civil society organizations have all fought the good fight, but have not eradicated poverty. The adoption of the Millennium Development Goals (MDG) by the United Nations only underscores that reality; as we enter the 21st century, poverty—and the disenfranchisement that accompanies it—remains one of the world's most daunting problems.

The purpose of this book is to change that familiar image on TV. It is to illustrate that the typical pictures of poverty mask the fact that the very poor represent resilient entrepreneurs and value-conscious consumers. **What is needed is a better approach to help the poor, an approach that involves partnering with them to innovate and achieve sustainable win–win scenarios where the poor are actively engaged and, at the same time, the companies providing products**

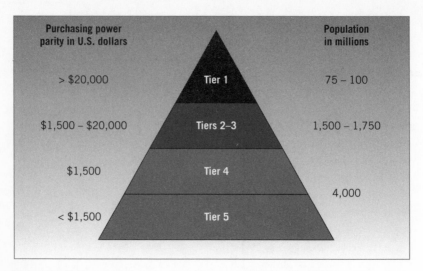

Figure 1.1   The economic pyramid. *Source:* C. K. Prahalad and Stuart Hart, 2002. The Fortune at the Bottom of the Pyramid, *Strategy+ Business*, Issue 26, 2002. Reprinted with permission from *strategy + business*, the award-winning management quarterly published by Booz Allen Hamilton. www.strategy-business.com.

and services to them are profitable. This collaboration between the poor, civil society organizations, governments, and large firms can create the largest and fastest growing markets in the world. Large-scale and wide-spread entrepreneurship is at the heart of the solution to poverty. Such an approach exists and has, in several instances, gone well past the idea stage as private enterprises, both large and small, have begun to successfully build markets at the bottom of the pyramid (BOP) as a way of eradicating poverty.

The economic pyramid of the world is shown in Figure 1.1. As we can see, more than 4 billion constitute the BOP. These are the people who are the subject matter of this book.

THE BOTTOM OF THE PYRAMID (BOP)

The distribution of wealth and the capacity to generate incomes in the world can be captured in the form of an economic pyramid. At the top of the pyramid are the wealthy, with numerous opportunities for generating high levels of income. More than 4 billion people live at the BOP on less than $2 per day. They are the subject matter of this book.

As you turn these pages, you will discover companies fighting disease with educational campaigns and innovative products. There are organizations helping the handicapped walk and helping subsistence farmers check commodity prices and connect with the rest of the world. There are banks adapting to the financial needs of the poor, power companies reaching out to meet energy needs, and construction companies doing what they can to house the poor in affordable ways that allow for pride. There are chains of stores tailored to understand the needs of the poor and to make products available to them.

The strength of these innovative approaches, as you will come to appreciate, is that they tend to create opportunities for the poor by offering them choices and encouraging self-esteem. Entrepreneurial solutions such as these place a minimal financial burden on the developing countries in which they occur.

To begin to understand how all of this is remotely possible, we need to start with some basic assumptions:

- First, while cases certainly can be found of large firms and multinational corporations (MNCs) that may have undermined the efforts of the poor to build their livelihoods, the greatest harm they might have done to the poor is to ignore them altogether. The poor cannot participate in the benefits of globalization without an active engagement and without access to products and services that represent global quality standards. They need to be exposed to the range and variety of opportunities that inclusive globalization can provide. The poor represent a "latent market" for goods and services. Active engagement of private enterprises at the BOP is a critical element in creating inclusive capitalism, as private-sector competition for this market will foster attention to the poor as consumers. It will create choices for them. They do not have to depend only on what is available in their villages. If large firms approach this market with the BOP consumers' interests at heart, it can also lead to significant growth and profits for them. These characteristics of a market economy, new to the BOP, can facilitate dramatic change at the BOP. Free and transparent private-sector competition, unlike local village and shanty-town monopolies controlled by local slum lords, can transform the "poor" into consumers (as we illustrate with examples). Poverty alleviation will become a business development task shared among the large private sector firms and local BOP entrepreneurs.

- Second, the BOP, as a market, provides a new growth opportunity for the private sector and a forum for innovations. Old and tired solutions cannot create markets at the BOP.

- Third, BOP markets must become an integral part of the work of the private sector. They must become part of the firms' core businesses; they cannot merely be relegated to the realm of corporate social responsibility (CSR) initiatives. Successfully creating BOP markets involves change in the functioning of MNCs as much as it changes the functioning of developing countries. BOP markets must become integral to the success of the firm in order to command senior management attention and sustained resource allocation.

There is significant untapped opportunity for value creation (for BOP consumers, shareholders, and employees) that is latent in the BOP market. These markets have remained "invisible" for too long.

It is natural for you to ask this: If all of this is so obvious, why has this not yet occurred?

The Power of Dominant Logic

All of us are prisoners of our own socialization. The lenses through which we perceive the world are colored by our own ideology, experiences, and established management practices. Each one of the groups that is focusing on poverty alleviation—the World Bank, rich countries providing aid, charitable organizations, national governments, and the private sector—is conditioned by its own dominant logic. Let us, for example, examine the dominant logic of each group as it approaches the task of eradicating poverty.

Consider, for instance, the politicians and bureaucrats in India, one of the largest countries with a significant portion of the world's poor. India is home to more than 400 million people who qualify as being very poor. The policies of the government for the first 45 years since independence from Great Britain in 1947 were based on a set of basic assumptions. Independent India started with a deep suspicion of the private sector. The country's interaction with the East India Company and colonialism played a major part in creating this mindset. The experience with the indigenous private sector was not very positive, either. The private sector was deemed exploitative of the poor. This suspicion was coupled with an enormous confidence in the government machinery to do what is "right and moral." For example, the government of India initiated a series of large industrial projects in the public sector (owned by the Indian government) in a wide variety of industries, from steel to food distribution and global trading in essential commodities. India's general suspicion of the private sector led to controls over its size and expansion. Some sectors of economic activity were reserved for small-scale industries. In textiles, for example, the "hand loom sector" dominated by small firms was given preference. There was no credible voice in public policy for nurturing market-based ecosystems that included the large and the small in a symbiotic relationship. The thinking was cleanly divided among the public sector (mostly large firms with significant capital outlay as in steel), the private sector with large firms strictly controlled by the government through a system of licenses, and a small-scale sector. The focus of public policy was on distributive justice over wealth creation. Because of the disparities in wealth and the preponderance of the poor, the government thought its first priority must be policies that "equalized" wealth distribution. Taxation, limits on salaries of top managers, and other such measures were instituted to ensure distributive justice. The discussion further polarized around the somewhat contrived concepts of rural poor and urban rich. The assumption was that the rural population was primarily poor and the urban population was relatively rich. However, the data increasingly does not support this distinction. There are as many rural rich as there are urban poor. Poverty knows no such boundaries. In the developing world, more than one third of the urban population lives in shanty towns and slums. These traditional views reflect the philosophy behind actions taken by bureaucrats and politicians. During the last decade, a slow but discernable transition has been taking place from the traditional to a more market-based outlook.

This much-needed and desirable transition is in its infancy. The dominant logic, built over 45 years, is difficult to give up for individuals, political parties, and sections of the bureaucracy. This is the reason why politicians and bureaucrats appear to be vacillating in their positions. Most thinking people know where they have to go, but letting go of their beliefs and abandoning their "zones of comfort" and familiarity are not easy. We also believe that it is equally difficult for a whole generation of BOP consumers to give up their dependence on governmental subsidies.

We have explicitly focused on ideology and policy and not on the quality of implementation of projects focused on the poor, be it building roads and dams or providing basic education and health care. The distinct role of corruption, which seems so endemic to developing countries in general, deserves separate treatment (see Chapter 5).

Private-sector businesses, especially MNCs (and large local firms that emulate their MNC competitors), also suffer from a deeply etched dominant logic of their own, which restricts their ability to see a vibrant market opportunity at the BOP. For example, it is common in MNCs to have the assumptions outlined in Table 1.1. These assumptions dictate decision and resource allocation processes for developing countries and BOP markets in particular.

These and other implicit assumptions surface in every discussion of BOP markets with managers in MNCs and those in large domestic firms in developing countries that fashion their management practices after those at successful MNCs. These biases are hard to eradicate in large firms. Although the dominant logic and its implications are clear, it is our goal in this book to challenge and provide counterpoints. For

Table 1.1   The Dominant Logic of MNCs as It Relates to BOP

Assumption	Implication
The poor are not our target customers; they cannot afford our products or services.	Our cost structure is a given; with our cost structure, we cannot serve the BOP market.
The poor do not have use for products sold in developed countries.	We are committed to a form over functionality. The poor might need sanitation, but can't afford detergents in formats we offer. Therefore, there is no market in the BOP.
Only developed countries appreciate and pay for technological innovations.	The BOP does not need advanced technology solutions; they will not pay for them. Therefore, the BOP cannot be a source of innovations.
The BOP market is not critical for long-term growth and vitality of MNCs.	BOP markets are at best an attractive distraction.
Intellectual excitement is in developed markets; it is very hard to recruit managers for BOP markets.	We cannot assign our best people to work on market development in BOP markets.

Adapted from C. K. Prahalad and Stuart Hart, The Fortune at the Bottom of the Pyramid, Strategy + Business, Issue 26, 2002. Reprinted with permission from *strategy + business*, the award-winning management quarterly published by Booz Allen Hamilton. www.strategy-business.com.

example, BOP markets enable firms to challenge their perspectives on cost. We will show that a 10 to 200 times advantage (compared to the cost structures that are oriented to the top of the pyramid markets) is possible if firms innovate from the BOP up and do not follow the traditional practice of serving the BOP markets by making minor changes to the products created for the top of the pyramid.

Most charitable organizations also believe that the private sector is greedy and uncaring and that corporations cannot be trusted with the problems of poverty alleviation. From this perspective, profit motive and poverty alleviation do not mix easily or well. Aid agencies have come full circle in their own thinking. **From aid focused on large infrastructure projects and public spending on education and health, they are also moving toward a belief that private-sector involvement is a crucial ingredient to poverty alleviation.**

Historically, governments, aid agencies, nongovernmental organizations (NGOs), large firms, and the organized (formal and legal as opposed to extralegal) business sector all seem to have reached an implicit agreement: Market-based solutions cannot lead to poverty reduction and economic development. As shown in Figure 1.2, the dominant logic of each group restricts its ability to see the market opportunities at the BOP. The dominant logic of each group is different, but the conclusions are similar. During the last decade, each group has been searching for ways out of this self-imposed intellectual trap. To

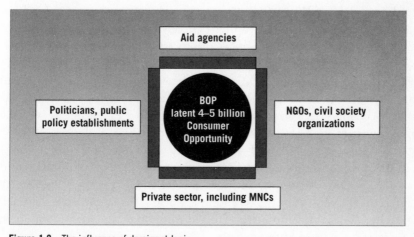

Figure 1.2 The influence of dominant logic.

eradicate poverty, we have to break this implicit compact through a BOP-oriented involvement of the private sector.

We have to change our long-held beliefs about the BOP—our genetic code, if you will. The barrier that each group has to cross is different, but difficult nonetheless. However, once we cross the intellectual barrier, the opportunities become obvious. The BOP market also represents a major engine of growth and global trade, as we illustrate in our subsequent stories of MNCs and private firms from around the world.

The Nature of the BOP Market

The nature of the BOP market has characteristics that are distinct. We outline some of the critical dimensions that define this market. These characteristics must be incorporated into our thinking as we approach the BOP.

There Is Money at the BOP

The dominant assumption is that the poor have no purchasing power and therefore do not represent a viable market.

Let us start with the aggregate purchasing power in developing countries where most of the BOP market exists. Developing countries offer tremendous growth opportunities. Within these markets, the BOP represents a major opportunity. Take China as an example. With a population of 1.2 billion and an average per capita gross domestic product (GDP) of US $1,000, China currently represents a $1.2 trillion economy. However, the U.S. dollar equivalent is not a good measure of the demand for goods and services produced and consumed in China. If we convert the GDP-based figure into its dollar purchasing power parity (PPP), China is already a $5.0 trillion economy, making it the second largest economy behind the United States in PPP terms. Similarly, the Indian economy is worth about $3.0 trillion in PPP terms. If we take nine countries—China, India, Brazil, Mexico, Russia, Indonesia, Turkey, South Africa, and Thailand—collectively they are home to about 3 billion people, representing 70 percent of the developing world population. In PPP terms, this group's GDP is $12.5 trillion, which represents 90 percent of the developing world. It is larger than the GDP of Japan, Germany, France, the United Kingdom, and Italy combined. This is not a market to be ignored.

Now, consider the BOP within the broad developing country opportunity. The dominant assumption is that the poor do not have money to spend and, therefore, are not a viable market. Certainly, the buying power for those earning less than US $2 per day cannot be compared with the purchasing power of individuals in the developed nations. However, by virtue of their numbers, the poor represent a significant latent purchasing power that must be unlocked. For example, all too often, the poor tend to reside in high-cost ecosystems even within developing countries. In the shanty town of Dharavi, outside Mumbai, India, the poor pay a premium for everything from rice to credit. Compare the cost of everyday items of consumption between Dharavi and Warden Road (now redesignated B. Desai Road), a higher income neighborhood in Mumbai. The poverty penalty in Dharavi can be as high as 5 to 25 times what the rich pay for the same services (Table 1.2). Research indicates that this poverty penalty is universal, although the magnitude differs by country. The poverty penalty is the result of local monopolies, inadequate access, poor distribution, and strong traditional intermediaries. Large-scale private-sector businesses can "unlock this poverty penalty." For example, the poor in Dharavi pay 600 to 1,000 percent interest for credit from local moneylenders. A bank with access to this market can do well for itself by offering credit at 25 percent. Although 25 percent interest might look excessive to a casual observer, from the point of view of the BOP consumer, access to a bank decreases the cost of credit from 600 percent to 25 percent. The BOP consumer is

Table 1.2 The Poor and High-Cost Economic Ecosystems

Item	Dharavi	Warden Road	Poverty Premium
Credit (annual interest)	600–1,000%	12–18%	53.0
Municipal grade water (per cubic meter)	$1.12	$0.03	37.0
Phone call (per minute)	$0.04–0.05	$0.025	1.8
Diarrhea medication	$20.00	$2.00	10.0
Rice (per kg)	$0.28	$0.24	1.2

Source: Reprinted with permission from *Harvard Business Review.* "The Poor and High Cost Economics Ecosystems." From "Serving the World's Poor Profitably" by C. K. Prahalad and Allen Hammond, September 2002. Copyright ©2002 by the Harvard Business School Publishing Corporation, all rights reserved.

focused on the difference between the local moneylender rates and the rates that a commercial bank would charge. The bank can make a reasonable profit after adjusting for risk (10 percent over its traditional, top-of-the-pyramid customers). We argue later that the BOP consumers do not represent higher risk.

These cost disparities between BOP consumers and the rich in the same economy can be explained only by the fact that the poverty penalty at the BOP is a result of inefficiencies in access to distribution and the role of the local intermediaries. These problems can easily be cured if the organized private sector decides to serve the BOP. The organized sector brings with it the scale, scope of operations, and management know-how that can lead to efficiencies for itself and its potential consumers.

The poor also spend their earnings in ways that reflect a different set of priorities. For example, they might not spend disposable income on sanitation, clean running water, and better homes, but will spend it on items traditionally considered luxuries. Without legal title to land, these residents are unlikely to invest in improving their living quarters, much less the public facilities surrounding their homes. For example, in Dharavi, 85 percent of the households own a television set, 75 percent own a pressure cooker and blender, 56 percent own a gas stove, and 21 percent have telephones. In Bangladesh, women entrepreneurs with cell phones, which they rent out by the minute to other villagers, do a brisk business. It is estimated that the poor in Bangladesh spend as much as 7 percent of their income on connectivity.

Access to BOP Markets

The dominant assumption is that distribution access to the BOP markets is very difficult and therefore represents a major impediment for the participation of large firms and MNCs.

Urban areas have become a magnet for the poor. By 2015 there will be more than 225 cities in Africa, 903 in Asia, and 225 in Latin America. More than 368 cities in the developing world will have more than 1 million people in each. There will be at least 23 cities with more than 10 million residents. Collectively, these cities will account for about 1.5 to 2.0 billion people. Over 35 to 40 percent of these urban concentrations will be comprised of BOP consumers. The density of these settlements—about 15,000 people per hectare—will allow for intense distribution opportunities.

The rural poor represent a different problem. Access to distribution in rural markets continues to be problematic. Most of the rural markets are also inaccessible to audio and television signals and are often designated as "media dark." Therefore, the rural poor are not only denied access to products and services, but also to knowledge about what is available and how to use it. The spread of wireless connectivity among the poor might help reduce this problem. The ability to download movie and audio clips on wireless devices might allow firms to access traditionally "media dark" areas and provide consumers in these locations with newfound access to information about products and services. However, this is still an evolving phenomenon restricted to a few countries.

The BOP does not lend itself to a single distribution solution. Urban concentrations represent a problem distinct from that of the distribution access to dispersed rural communities. Worldwide, the cost of reach per consumer can vary significantly across countries. A wide variety of experiments are underway in these markets to find efficient methods of distributing goods and services. One such experiment, Project Shakti at Hindustan Lever Ltd. (HLL) in India, is a case in point. HLL created a direct distribution network in hard-to-reach locales (markets without distribution coverage through traditional distributors and dealers). HLL selected entrepreneurial women from these villages and trained them to become distributors, providing education, advice, and access to products to their villages. These village women entrepreneurs, called Shakti Amma ("empowered mother"), have unique knowledge about what the village needs and which products are in demand. They earn between Rs. 3,000 and 7,000 per month (U.S. $60–$150) and therefore create a new capacity to consume for themselves and their families. More important, these entrepreneurial women are increasingly becoming the educators and access points for the rural BOP consumers in their communities. This approach is not new. Avon is one of the largest cosmetics operations in Brazil and has used a similar approach by leveraging more than 800,000 "Avon ladies" as distributors to reach even the most remote regions of Amazonia.[1]

The BOP Markets Are Brand-Conscious

The dominant assumption is that the poor are not brand-conscious. On the contrary, the poor are very brand-conscious. They are also extremely value-conscious by necessity.

The experience of Casas Bahia in Brazil and Elektra in Mexico—two of the largest retailers of consumer durables, such as televisions, washing machines, radios, and other appliances—suggests that the BOP markets are very brand-conscious. Brand consciousness among the poor is universal. In a way, brand consciousness should not be a surprise. An aspiration to a new and different quality of life is the dream of everyone, including those at the BOP. Therefore, aspirational brands are critical for BOP consumers. However, BOP consumers are value buyers. They expect great quality at prices they can afford. The challenge to large firms is to make aspirational products affordable to BOP consumers. These consumers represent a new challenge for managers with increased pressure on costs of development, manufacturing, and distribution. As a result, BOP markets will force a new level of efficiency in the MNCs, as we demonstrate in Chapter 2.

The BOP Market Is Connected

Contrary to the popular view, BOP consumers are getting connected and networked. They are rapidly exploiting the benefits of information networks.

The spread of wireless devices among the poor is proof of a market at the BOP. For example, by the end of 2003, China had an installed base of 250 million cell phones. India had an installed base of approximately 30 million. The Indian market is growing at about 1.5 million handsets per month. The expectation is that India will reach 100 million handsets by 2005. Brazil already has 35 to 40 million. Both the current market size and the growth rates suggest that the BOP market is a critical factor in worldwide wireless growth. Telecommunications providers have made it easier for BOP consumers to purchase handsets and service through prepaid cards. The proliferation of wireless devices among the poor is universal, from Grameen Phone in Bangladesh to Telefonica in Brazil. Further, the availability of PCs in kiosks at a very low price per hour and the opportunity to videoconference using PCs are adding to the intensity of connectivity among those at the BOP. The net result is an unprecedented ability of BOP consumers to communicate with each other in several countries. The technology of wireless and PC connectivity is allowing the BOP population to be actively engaged in a dialogue with each other, with the firms from which they wish to purchase goods and services, and with the politicians who represent them.

Connectivity also allows the BOP consumers to establish new patterns of communication away from their villages. With cell phones and TV, the BOP consumer has unprecedented access to information as well as opportunities to engage in a dialogue with the larger community. As a result, word of mouth among BOP consumers is becoming a very potent force for assessing product quality, prices, and options available to them. The spread of good bargains as well as bad news can be very rapid. For example, in India, it appears that some consumers found worms in chocolates sold by Cadbury, a large and very successful MNC. Ten years ago this would have been a nonevent, but with access to multiple and fiercely competitive TV channels, wireless, and Internet, the news spread so rapidly across India that not just managers within Cadbury but all managers involved in the "fast-moving consumer goods" industry were surprised and worried.[2]

BOP Consumers Accept Advanced Technology Readily

Contrary to popular belief, the BOP consumers accept advanced technology readily.

The spread of wireless devices, PC kiosks, and personal digital assistants (PDAs) at the BOP has surprised many a manager and researcher. For example, ITC, an Indian conglomerate, decided to connect Indian farmers with PCs in their villages. The ITC e-Choupal (literally, "village meeting place") allowed the farmers to check prices not only in the local auction houses (called *mandis*), but also prices of soybean futures at the Chicago Board of Trade. The e-Choupal network allowed the farmers access to information that allowed them to make decisions about how much to sell and when, thus improving their margins. Similarly, women entrepreneurs in southern India, given a PC kiosk in their villages, have learned to videoconference among themselves, across villages on all kinds of issues, from the cost of loans from various banks to the lives of their grandchildren in the United States.[3] Chat rooms are full of activity that none of us could have imagined. Most interestingly, in Kerala, India, fishermen in traditional fishing boats, after a day of productive work, sell their catch to the highest bidders, using their cell phones to contact multiple possible landing sites along the Kerala coast. The simple boats, called catamarans, have not changed, but the entire process of pricing the catch and knowing how to sell based on reliable information has totally changed lives at the BOP.[4] The BOP consumers are more willing to adopt new technologies because they have nothing to forget. Moving to wireless from nothing is easier than moving to wireless from a strong tradition of efficient and ubiquitous landlines.

The Market Development Imperative

The task of converting the poor into consumers is one of market development. Market development involves both the consumer and the private-sector firm. We consider the risks and benefits to the private-sector firm later. Here, we reflect on the incentives for the BOP consumer, who is so far isolated from the benefits of access to regional and global markets, to participate. What are the benefits to the BOP consumer? Our examples are drawn primarily from the stories that appear in the book.

Create the Capacity to Consume

To convert the BOP into a consumer market, we have to create the capacity to consume. Cash-poor and with a low level of income, the BOP consumer has to be accessed differently.

The traditional approach to creating the capacity to consume among the poor has been to provide the product or service free of charge. This has the feel of philanthropy. As mentioned previously, charity might feel good, but it rarely solves the problem in a scalable and sustainable fashion.

A rapidly evolving approach to encouraging consumption and choice at the BOP is to make unit packages that are small and, therefore, affordable. The logic is obvious. The rich use cash to inventory convenience. They can afford, for example, to buy a large bottle of shampoo to avoid multiple trips to the store. The poor have unpredictable income streams. Many subsist on daily wages and have to use cash conservatively. They tend to make purchases only when they have cash and buy only what they need for that day. Single-serve packaging—be it shampoo, ketchup, tea and coffee, or aspirin—is well suited to this population. A single-serve revolution is sweeping through the BOP markets. For example, in India, single-serve sachets have become the norm for a wide variety of products, as shown in Table 1.3.

The number of products sold in the single-serve format is rapidly increasing. The format is so popular that even firms producing high-end

ty to Consume: Single-Serve Revolution

ail

ypical Products
hampoo, confectionary, matches, tea
Shampoo, salt, biscuits, ketchup, fruit drink concentrate
Detergent, soap, mouth fresheners, biscuits, jams, spreads, coffee, spices
Biscuits, toothpaste, color cosmetics, fragrance, bread, cooking oil, skin cream

biscuits are shown under different price ranges because these items are
ple single-serve and low unit pack quantities.

merc... ise have to adopt it to remain viable long-term players in the growing markets. For example, in the shampoo business, the situation in the Indian market is shown in Figure 1.3.

Measured in tons, the size of the Indian shampoo market is as large as the U.S. market. Large MNCs, such as Unilever and Procter & Gamble (P&G), are major participants in this market, as are large local firms. Because the poor are just as brand-conscious as the rich, it is possible to buy Pantene, a high-end shampoo from P&G, in a single-serve sachet in India. The entrepreneurial private sector has created a large market at the BOP; the penetration of shampoo in India is about 90 percent.

A similar approach to creating capacity to consume is through innovative purchase schemes. More BOP consumers in Brazil are able to buy appliances through Casas Bahia because the firm provides credit even for consumers with low and unpredictable income streams. Through a very sophisticated credit rating system coupled with counseling, Casas Bahia is able to provide access to high-quality appliances to consumers who could not otherwise afford them. At the same time, the firm ensures that its consumers are not overstretched. The default rate is very low at 8.5 percent, compared to over 15 percent for competitor firms. Casas Bahia has also created a new pool of repeat customers. Cemex, one of the world's largest cement companies in Mexico, follows a similar approach in its "do-it-yourself" business focused on the BOP market. The idea is to help the consumers learn to save and invest. By creating a pool of three women who save as a group and discipline and pressure each other to stay with the scheme, Cemex facilitates the process of consumption by bundling savings and access to credit with the ability to add a bathroom or a kitchen to their homes.

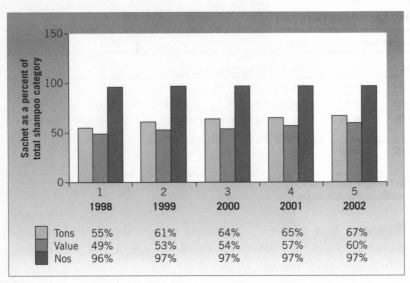

Figure 1.3   Single-serve sachet as a percentage of total shampoo market in India.

Creating the capacity to consume is based on three simple principles best described as the "Three As":

1. *Affordability.* Whether it is a single-serve package or novel purchasing schemes, the key is affordability without sacrificing quality or efficacy.
2. *Access.* Distribution patterns for products and services must take into account where the poor live as well as their work patterns. Most BOP consumers must work the full day before they can have enough cash to purchase the necessities for that day. Stores that close at 5:00 PM have no relevance to them, as their shopping begins after 7:00 PM. Further, BOP consumers cannot travel great distances. Stores must be easy to reach, often within a short walk. This calls for geographical *intensity of distribution.*
3. *Availability.* Often, the decision to buy for BOP consumers is based on the cash they have on hand at a given point in time. They cannot defer buying decisions. Availability (and therefore, *distribution efficiency*) is a critical factor in serving the BOP consumer.

Of course, the ideal is to create the capacity to earn more so that the BOP consumers can afford to consume more. The ITC e-Choupal story illustrates how farmers with access to the Internet and thereby access to the prices of commodities around the world can increase their incomes by 5 to 10 percent. These farmers can decide when and how much to sell based on their understanding of the likely price movements for their products. Modern technology not only allows them to realize better prices, but also to improve their logistics. The aggregation of food grains allows for efficiencies for both the farmer and the buyer.

By focusing on the BOP consumers' capacity to consume, private-sector businesses can create a new market. The critical requirement is the ability to invent ways that take into account the variability in the cash flows of BOP consumers that makes it difficult for them to access the traditional market for goods and services oriented toward the top of the pyramid.

The Need for New Goods and Services

The involvement of the private sector at the BOP can provide opportunities for the development of new products and services.

Amul, a dairy cooperative in India, has introduced good quality ice cream at less than $0.05 per serving, affordable by all at the BOP. This product is not only a source of enjoyment; the milk in it is also a source of nutrition for the poor. Now, Amul is planning to introduce a natural laxative-laced ice cream called "isabgol-enriched." It is too early to tell whether the product can be a success. However, the experimentation is what the game is about. Similarly, the popularization of pizza by the same company allows the poor to obtain an adequate quantity of protein.[5] PRODEM FFP, a Bolivian financial services company, has introduced smart automated teller machines (ATMs) that recognize fingerprints, use color-coded touch screens, and speak in three local languages. This technological innovation allows even illiterate BOP consumers to access, on a 24-hour basis, high-quality financial services.[6] Cemex, as we saw earlier, provides access to good quality housing. Through Tecnosol, the BOP consumers in rural Nicaragua have access to clean energy from renewable sources—solar and wind power. Previously, these consumers did not have access to grid-based electricity and were dependent on more expensive sources, such as kerosene and batteries. Now they have energy that is affordable enough to run their households. Casas Bahia not only sells appliances, but has also introduced a line of good quality furniture oriented toward the BOP markets. Furniture has become one of the fastest growing businesses for the company as well as a source of pride and satisfaction to its consumers.

Dignity and Choice

When the poor are converted into consumers, they get more than access to products and services. They acquire the dignity of attention and choices from the private sector that were previously reserved for the middle-class and rich.

The farmers we interviewed at an ITC e-Choupal were very clear. The traditional auctioning system at the government-mandated markets (mandis) did not offer them any choices. Once they went to a mandi, they had to sell their produce at the prices offered on that day. They could not wait for better prices or haul their produce back to their villages. More important, the local merchants who controlled the mandi were not very respectful of the farmers. One farmer remarked, "They make rude comments about my produce. They also raise the prices in the auction by $0.02 per ton. It is as if they have already determined the price you will get and they go through the motions of an auction. It used to be very demeaning." Not any longer. Now, the same farmers can access information on the Web across all the mandis and can decide where, when, and at which prices they want to sell. Similarly, women in self-help groups (SHGs) working with ICICI Bank in India also have had their dignity restored. As a group, they decide which borrowers and projects will receive loans. This involvement of women in leadership development and in learning about finances and bank operations has given them a new sense of personal worth. The single-serve revolution has created a revolutionary level of choice for consumers at the BOP. For example, the "switching costs" for the consumer are negligible because she can buy a sachet of shampoo or detergent or pickles; if she is not satisfied with her purchase she can switch brands the next day. Firms must continuously innovate and upgrade their products to keep customers interested in their brands, thereby improving quality and reducing costs.

Trust Is a Prerequisite

Both sides—the large firms and the BOP consumers—have traditionally not trusted each other. The mistrust runs deep. However, private-sector firms approaching the BOP market must focus on building trust between themselves and the consumers.

This is clearly evident when one visits a Casas Bahia store. BOP consumers here venerate the founder, Mr. Klein, for giving them the opportunity to possess appliances that they could not otherwise afford.

Although the shanty towns of Sao Paulo or Rio de Janeiro can be dangerous to outsiders, Casas Bahia trucks move freely around without worry. The same is true for Bimbo, the provider of fresh bread and other bakery products to the BOP consumers in Mexico. Bimbo[7] is the largest bakery in Mexico and its trucks have become symbols of trust between the BOP consumers and the firm. The truck drivers are so trusted that often the small store owners in the slums allow them to open their shops, stock them with bread, and collect cash from the cash boxes without supervision. Both Casas Bahia and Bimbo believe that the truck drivers who deliver their products to the BOP consumers are their ambassadors and neither company will outsource the delivery process. In fact, all managers at Bimbo must work as truck drivers for the company to become better educated about their customers .

MNCs often assume that the default rate among the poor is likely to be higher than that of their rich customers. The opposite is often true. The poor pay on time and default rates are very low. In the case of ICICI Bank, out of a customer base of 200,000, the default rate is less than 1 percent. The default rate at Grameen Bank, a microfinance pioneer in Bangladesh, is less than 1.5 percent among 2,500,000 customers. The lessons are clear. Through persistent effort and the provision of world-class quality, private-sector businesses can create mutual trust and responsibility between their companies and BOP customers. Trust is difficult to build after 50 years of suspicion and prejudice based on little evidence and strong stereotyping.

Benefits to the Private Sector

We have identified the immediate benefits of treating the poor as consumers as well as the poverty alleviation process that will result as businesses focus on the BOP. It is clear that the consumers (the poor) benefit, but do the private-sector businesses benefit as well? The BOP market potential is huge: 4 to 5 billion underserved people and an economy of more than $13 trillion PPP. The needs of the poor are many. The case for growth opportunity in the BOP markets is easy to make. However, to participate in these markets, the private sector must learn to innovate. Traditional products, services, and management processes will not work. In the next chapter, we discuss a philosophy of innovation focused on BOP markets.

Endnotes

1. Helen Cha, Polly Cline, Lilly Liu, Carrie Meek, and Michelle Villagomez "Direct Selling and Economic Empowerment in Brazil: The Case of Avon." Edited by Anuradha Dayal-Gulati, Kellogg School of Management, 2003.

2. Syed Firdaus Ashraf. "Worms Found in Chocolate Packet," *rediff.com*, October 3, 2003.

3. See multiparty video conferencing, *www.n-Logue.com*.

4. Saritha Rai. "In Rural India, a Passage to Wirelessness." *The New York Times*, August 4, 2001.

5. Harish Damodaran. "Try Amul's New Ice Cream and—Be Relieved." The Hindu Business Line, September 8, 2002.

6. Roberto Hernandez and Yerina Mugica. "What Works: Prodem FFP's Multilingual Smart ATMs for Micro Finance." World Resources Institute, Digital Dividend Website, *digital dividend.com*, August, 2003.

7. *www.bimbo.com*

2

Products and
Services for the BOP

As we saw in the previous chapter, the BOP can be a viable
growth market. During the last decade, many MNCs have approached
BOP markets with an existing portfolio of products and services.
Because these product portfolios have been priced and developed for
Western markets, they are often out of reach for potential customers in
BOP markets. More important, the feature–function set has often been
inappropriate. As a result, the promise of the emerging BOP markets has
been largely illusory.[1] At the same time, developmental agencies have
also tried to replicate developed country models at the BOP with equally
unsatisfactory results. The development assistance community has
invested billions in Western mechanical waste water treatment facilities
in the developing world. Many if not most of these facilities were no
longer operating within a year of their completion because the local
"markets" could not afford the electricity to operate them, did not have
a steady electricity supply, or lacked an adequate supply of chemicals and
spare parts.

MNCs do recognize that only 5 to 10 percent of the population of China or India can represent a new market of 50 to 100 million each. MNCs can more easily tap into the top of the economic pyramid in emerging economies such as China, India, or Brazil and these markets can be substantial. Although the affluent in these markets might appear to be similar to "traditional" consumers in developed countries, they are not. They tend to be much more value-conscious. Regardless, the goal is to reach the entire population base, including the BOP. How can MNCs capitalize on this emerging BOP opportunity?

A Philosophy for Developing Products and Services for the BOP

The BOP, as a market, will challenge the dominant logic of MNC managers (the beliefs and values that managers serving the developed markets have been socialized with). For example, **the basic economics of the BOP market are based on small unit packages, low margin per unit, high volume, and high return on capital employed.** This is different from large unit packs, high margin per unit, high volume, and reasonable return on capital employed. This shift in business economics is the first surprise to most managers. As we observed in Chapter 1, creating the capacity to consume—the single-serve and low unit pack revolution at the BOP—can be the first surprise for product developers trained in the West. "How can anyone make money at $0.01/unit price at retail?" is often the question. Similarly, in the West, product developers often assume that the required infrastructures for the use of products exist or that Western infrastructure can be made economically viable and will function properly in these markets. In a developed market, access to refrigerators, telephones, transportation, credit, and a minimum level of literacy can all be assumed. The choice of technologies is not constrained by the infrastructure. However, in BOP markets, the quality of infrastructure can vary substantially, especially within a country as vast as China, Brazil, or India. What is available in Shanghai or Mumbai is not an indication of the infrastructure in the hinterlands of China or India. For example, the supply of electricity can be quite erratic and blackouts and brownouts are very common. **Advanced technology solutions, such as a regional network of PCs, must coexist with poor and indifferent electrical and telecom**

infrastructures. Hybrid solutions that integrate backup power sources with PCs are a must, as are customer interfaces. For example, India boasts more than 15 official languages and 500 dialects, and 30 percent of the total population is illiterate. How then can we develop user-friendly interfaces for products that the poor and the illiterate can understand and utilize? Surprisingly, illiteracy can lead to acceptance of the state-of-the-art solutions. For example, illiterate consumers can "see and hear," not read. Therefore, video-enabled cell phones might be more appropriate for this market.

These challenges are not isolated conditions. Involvement in BOP markets will challenge assumptions that managers in MNCs have developed over a long period of time. A new philosophy of product development and innovation that reflects the realities of BOP markets will be needed. This philosophy must represent a different perspective from those that we have grown accustomed to in serving Western markets.

Based on my research, I have identified 12 principles that, taken together, constitute the building blocks of a philosophy of innovation for BOP markets. In this chapter, we discuss each of these principles with specific illustrations drawn primarily from the detailed case stories of successful innovations at the BOP included in this book.

Twelve Principles of Innovation for BOP Markets

1. Focus on price performance of products and services. Serving BOP markets is not just about lower prices. It is about creating a new price–performance envelope. Quantum jumps in price performance are required to cater to BOP markets.
2. Innovation requires hybrid solutions. BOP consumer problems cannot be solved with old technologies. Most scalable, price-performance-enhancing solutions need advanced and emerging technologies that are creatively blended with the existing and rapidly evolving infrastructures.
3. As BOP markets are large, solutions that are developed must be scalable and transportable across countries, cultures, and languages. How does one take a solution from the southern part of India to the northern part? From Brazil to India or China? Solutions must be designed for ease of adaptation in similar BOP markets. This is a key consideration for gaining scale.

4. The developed markets are accustomed to resource wastage. For example, if the BOP consumers started using as much packaging per capita as the typical American or Japanese consumer, the world could not sustain that level of resource use. All innovations must focus on conserving resources: eliminate, reduce, and recycle. Reducing resource intensity must be a critical principle in product development, be it for detergents or ice cream.

5. Product development must start from a deep understanding of functionality, not just form. Marginal changes to products developed for rich customers in the United States, Europe, or Japan will not do. The infrastructure BOP consumers have to live and work in demands a rethinking of the functionality anew. Washing clothes in an outdoor moving stream is different from washing clothes in the controlled conditions of a washing machine that adjusts itself to the level of dirt and for batches of colored and white clothes.

6. Process innovations are just as critical in BOP markets as product innovations. In developed markets, the logistics system for accessing potential consumers, selling to them, and servicing products is well-developed. A reliable infrastructure exists and only minor changes might have to be made for specific products. In BOP markets, the presence of a logistics infrastructure cannot be assumed. Often, innovation must focus on building a logistics infrastructure, including manufacturing that is sensitive to the prevailing conditions. Accessing potential consumers and educating them can also be a daunting task to the uninitiated.

7. Deskilling work is critical. Most BOP markets are poor in skills. The design of products and services must take into account the skill levels, poor infrastructure, and difficulty of access for service in remote areas.

8. Education of customers on product usage is key. Innovations in educating a semiliterate group on the use of new products can pose interesting challenges. Further, most of the BOP also live in "media dark" zones, meaning they do not have access to radio or TV. In the absence of traditional approaches to education—traditional advertising—new and creative approaches, such as video mounted on trucks and traveling low-cost theatrical productions whose job it is to demonstrate product usage in villages, must be developed.

9. Products must work in hostile environments. It is not just noise, dust, unsanitary conditions, and abuse that products must endure.

Products must also be developed to accommodate the low quality of the infrastructure, such as electricity (e.g., wide fluctuations in voltage, blackouts, and brownouts) and water (e.g., particulate, bacterial, and viral pollution).

10. Research on interfaces is critical given the nature of the consumer population. The heterogeneity of the consumer base in terms of language, culture, skill level, and prior familiarity with the function or feature is a challenge to the innovation team.

11. Innovations must reach the consumer. Both the highly dispersed rural market and a highly dense urban market at the BOP represent an opportunity to innovate in methods of distribution. Designing methods for accessing the poor at low cost is critical.

12. Paradoxically, the feature and function evolution in BOP markets can be very rapid. Product developers must focus on the broad architecture of the system—the platform—so that new features can be easily incorporated. BOP markets allow (and force) us to challenge existing paradigms. For example, challenging the grid-based supply of electricity as the only available source for providing good-quality, inexpensive energy is possible and necessary in the isolated, poor BOP markets.

It might appear that the new philosophy of innovation for the BOP markets requires too many changes to the existing approach to innovation for developed markets. It does require significant adaptation, but all elements of innovation for the BOP described here might not apply to all businesses. Managers need to pick and choose and prioritize. Although effective participation requires changes to the philosophy of innovation, I argue that the pain of change is worth the rewards that will be reaped from the BOP as well as from traditional markets. Further, once we recognize the issues involved, innovation can be quite an energizing experience. I also plan to illustrate with a large number of examples that a wide variety of organizations—MNCs, local firms, and NGOs—are successfully innovating with vigor in these markets, and are making a great difference in the quality of life of low-income customers and low-income communities. This is of particular importance to MNCs. Because innovations for the BOP markets challenge our established ways of thinking, BOP markets can become a source of innovations for the developed markets as well. **Innovation in BOP markets can reverse the flow of concepts, ideas, and methods. Therefore, for an MNC** that aims to stay ahead of the curve, experimenting in BOP markets is increasingly critical. It is no longer an option.

Making It Happen

Let us begin with each of the principles involved in innovation for the BOP, identify the rationale for it, and analyze examples that illustrate what can be done to incorporate it.

1. Price Performance

Addressing the market opportunity at the BOP requires that we start with a radically new understanding of the price–performance relationship compared to that currently employed in developed markets. This is not about lowering prices. It is about altering the price–performance envelope.

Price is an important part of the basis for growth in BOP markets. GSM handsets used to be sold for $1,000 in India. Not surprisingly, the market was quite limited. As the average price dropped to $300, sales started to increase. However, when Reliance, a cell phone provider, introduced its "Monsoon Hungama" (literally Monsoon Melee) promotion that offered 100 free minutes for a mobile, multimedia phone with an up-front payment of $10 and monthly payments of $9.25, the company received 1 million applications in 10 days. Of course, price is a factor. Equally important is the performance associated with the price. The applications available through the Monsoon Hungama offer, for a mere $10 downpayment, are quite incredible, including news, games, audio clips of movies and favorite songs, video clips, astrology and numerology, city guides, TV guides, stock quotes, and the ability to surf the Internet. The phone itself is very fashionable and state of the art, using CDMA technology.[2] Today, India is the fastest growing wireless market in the world. During the last quarter of 2003, India was adding 1.5 million new subscribers per month! Both GSM and CDMA technologies are readily available, as are a host of features and pricing options. The regulatory process is also rapidly evolving. This milieu can be confusing at best. However, most value-conscious consumers do not seem to be concerned. There are so many comparisons of the alternate technologies, features, and payment schemes that are debated in newspapers, on TV and radio, and in magazines, that consumers are well-informed. Even those who cannot read tend to consult with others who can. Word of mouth is so powerful that the consumers seem to have found an efficient process—combining analyses offered by journalists, companies, consumer reports, and their friends—for evaluating the price–performance options available to them.

How can we provide a high level of price–performance to a consumer population that exists on less than $2 per day? The changes in price–performance that are called for must be dramatic. Let me illustrate. Consider a cataract operation. It can cost as much as $2,500 to $3,000 in the United States. Even most of the poorest in the United States can get access to this surgery through health insurance (Medicare and Medicaid). In other developed countries such as the United Kingdom, the nationalized health services pay the cost. Now, consider the poor in India or Africa. For these mostly uninsured individuals to even consider cataract surgery, it would need to be priced around $50, a fraction of what it costs in developed markets (about 50 to 75 times less than in the United States), and the quality of surgery cannot be any less. Variation in quality in restoring eyesight is unacceptable. For a successful cataract operation in BOP markets, the quality of surgery must also include postoperative care of semiliterate patients in very unsanitary environments. Commitment to quality in BOP markets must be broad-based: identifying patients for surgery, most of whom have had limited medical care in the past, much less visits to the hospital; preparing them for the procedure; performing the operation; and postoperative care. The Aravind Eye Care System, the largest eye care facility in the world, is headquartered in Madurai, India. Doctors at Aravind perform more than 200,000 state-of-the-art cataract surgeries per year. Their price is $50 to $300 per surgery, including the hospital stay and any complications in surgery. However, over 60 percent of Aravind's patients get their surgeries for free with no out-of-pocket payments by patients, insurance companies, government, and so on. With only 40 percent of paying patients at such seemingly low prices, Aravind is nevertheless very profitable. The cost of the surgery, for all the patients taken together (paying and free) is not more than $25 for a basic cataract operation with intra-ocular lens (IOL).

Similarly, access to financial services for the poor provides a challenge to conventional wisdom. Saving with a bank is a new idea for most people at the BOP. They have hardly any savings to begin with and whatever they have they wear it on them (as jewelry) or keep under their mattresses. Simple steps such as saving $1 per week and starting an account with as little as $20 can provide the impetus to cultivating the savings habit among the poor. **Building the savings habit and giving** them access to the basic building blocks of financial services must precede providing them with access to low-cost loans or rain and crop insurance. How does a large global bank approach this market and provide world-class (if a limited range of) services starting with a $20 deposit? Citicorp started $25 deposit-based banking services, called Suvidha, in Bangalore, India. Suvidha was oriented toward the urban population and was entirely based on an ATM, networked, 24/7 model. In the first year, Citibank enrolled 150,000 customers. This was the first time a global bank approached consumers with a $25 deposit option. Now several Indian banks offer similar service, both branch-based and ATM-based, in both rural and urban areas.

BOP markets, be they in telecom, personal care, health care, or financial services, impose very interesting business design criteria. MNCs have to fundamentally rethink the price–performance relationship. Traditional approaches to reducing prices by 5 to 10 percent will not suffice. We should focus on an overall price–performance improvement of 30 to 100 times. This calls for a significant "forgetting curve" in the organization—an ability to discard traditional approaches to price–performance improvements. However, these efforts can be justified only if the markets are very large and global and the returns are more than commensurate with the risks. Although the margin per unit might be low, investor interest in BOP markets is based on expectations of a large-volume, low-risk, and high-return-on-capital employed business opportunity. BOP markets do represent an opportunity to create economic value in a fundamentally new way.

2. Innovation: Hybrids

The BOP market opportunity cannot be satisfied by watered-down versions of traditional technology solutions from the developed markets. The BOP market can and must be addressed by the most advanced technologies creatively combined with existing (and evolving) infrastructure.

More than 70 million Indian children suffer from iodine deficiency disorder (IDD), which can lead to mental retardation. A total of 200 million are at risk. IDD in many parts of Africa is equally daunting. The primary source of iodine for most Indians is salt. Indians do eat a lot of salt, but only 15 percent of the salt sold in India is iodized. Iodine is added by spraying salt with potassium iodate ($KIO3$) or potassium iodine (KI) during manufacturing. Salt, to be effective as a carrier of iodine, must retain a minimum of 15 parts per million of iodine. Even iodized salt in India loses its iodine content during the harsh conditions of storage and transportation. Indian cooking habits account for further iodine loss. The challenge in India (and similar markets in Africa) is clear: How do we create iodized salt that will not lose its iodine content during storage, transportation, and cooking but will release iodine only on ingesting cooked food?

In an effort to address the immense iodine loss in Indian salt, HLL, a subsidiary of Unilever, recognized that chemicals can be protected by macro and molecular encapsulation. HLL first attempted macro encapsulation (similar to coating medicine with a covering). Although this process kept the iodine intact, it was difficult to guarantee the exact amount of iodine as the miniscule size of the salt crystals complicated the process. HLL thus decided to try molecular encapsulation. Called K15 (K for potassium, 15 ppm), the technology encapsulates iodate particles between inorganic layers, protecting iodine from harsh external conditions. The inorganic layers are designed to only interact with and dissolve in highly acidic environments (i.e., a pH level of 1 to 2, as in the stomach). Here, iodine is released only upon ingesting food, only negligibly before that. The tests to validate this technology under the harsh conditions of Indian spices and cooking methods required that the researchers resort to techniques developed by the Indian Atomic Energy Agency, using radioactive tracers. The tracers did not alter the chemistry of the iodine but could detect it throughout the simulated cooking process. To be marketable, though, the iodized salt so developed must also retain its attractiveness (whiteness, texture) and, needless to say, must be priced comparable to iodized salt using the traditional methods (ineffective as a carrier of iodine) and noniodized salt. The technical breakthrough in applying molecular encapsulation of iodine in salt is now a patented process. Unilever is already leveraging this innovation from HLL to other countries such as Ghana, Ivory Coast, and Kenya, where IDD is a problem.

The concept of hybrids appears in strange places. Consider that the dairy industry in India, Amul, is organized around 10,675 cooperatives from which it collects 6 million liters of milk. Amul collects milk from the farmers in villages by providing village collection centers with over 3,000 Automatic Milk Collection System Units (AMCUS)—an integrated milk-weighing, checking (for fat content), and payment system based on electronic weighing machines, milk analyzers, and a PC-based accounting and banking system for members. Amul makes 10 million transactions and payments in the neighborhood of Rs. 170

million. Payments can also be made instantaneously. This integrated electronic system sits in the middle of the traditional Indian village in the milk cooperatives. Many of the farmers feel that, for the first time, they have been treated "right"—the weighing and testing are honest, they are paid without delays, and they can now become part of the national milk network without leaving their villages.[3]

3. Scale of Operations

It is easy to succeed in a limited experiment, but the market needs of 4 to 5 billion people suggest that the experiments must be commercially scalable.

NGOs and other socially concerned groups are by far the lead experimenters in BOP markets. For example, we can demonstrate that a combination of photovoltaic and wind-based energy systems can be built for less than $1,000, consistently deliver the necessary power, and be very acceptable as a single-family or village solution. However, how do you scale it to cover 1.5 billion people who live without access to grid-based electricity? What is involved in scaling these successful experiments? Can small local entrepreneurs and NGOs accomplish this transfer of technology across geographies?

Scale of operations is a prerequisite for making an economic case for the BOP. Given a stringent price–performance equation and low margins per unit, the basis for returns on investment is volume. Only a few BOP markets are large—China, India, Brazil, Mexico, and Indonesia. **Most of the markets, such as the African nations, are poor and small. The prerequisite for scalability of innovations from these markets is that they are supported by organizations that have significant geographical ambitions and reach.** MNCs are ideally suited for this effort. Further, size allows MNCs to make the necessary financial commitments behind potentially successful, innovative ideas. How can HLL leverage its learning, know-how, and "know-why" developed in marketing salt in India and take it to Nigeria, Chad, Ivory Coast, and China?

It is clear, therefore, that pursuing the promise of BOP markets will challenge the dominant logic of both MNCs and NGOs. MNCs will benefit from learning how to engage with NGOs and local community-based organizations to co-create new products, services, and business. NGOs will benefit from partnerships with MNCs, through which they can leverage MNC know-how and systems to scale innovations broadly.

4. Sustainable Development: Eco-Friendly

The poor as a market are 5 billion strong. This means that solutions that we develop cannot be based on the same patterns of resource use that we expect to use in developed countries. Solutions must be sustainable and ecologically friendly.

Consider the use of water. In the United States, domestic use of water per capita is around 1932 cubic meters per person per year. In China, it is 491 cubic meters and in India, 640 cubic meters, respectively. There is not enough water available in most parts of the world to support demand.[4] Even if it is available, the quality of water available varies from indifferent to poor. For example, in Chennai, India, there is an attempt to collect rainwater from rooftops and store it in wells. So far, scarcity has not altered usage patterns. Water usage continues to be a critical component of high standards of living in the Western world. The question that BOP markets will pose for us is this: Can we develop products that provide the same level of functionality with no or minimal use of water? For example, can we wash clothes without water? Can we refresh ourselves without a shower? Can we flush toilets without much water, as is done in airplanes? Can we recycle water for multiple uses within an apartment complex (in urban settings) and within a village (in rural settings) in a closed loop system? Can we conserve water in agriculture through innovative cultivation methods?

In the United States, each person generates 4.62 pounds of waste per day. If everyone in China adopted Western standards of waste per capita, there would be more than 5.5 billion pounds of waste per day.[5] There are not enough places to dump this amount of garbage! Packaging can play a crucial role in the sustainable development of markets in the BOP. With 5 billion potential users, per-capita consumption of all resources, including packaging materials, can be crucial. Even recycling systems might not be practical as the rural markets are dispersed and waste collection for recycling might not be economically viable. At the same time, packaged goods are one way of ensuring product safety. The dilemma is real. So far, MNCs and others have not suggested a practical solution to the packaging problem, nor do we have a comprehensive approach to energy and water use. Water might get the attention of MNCs sooner than energy as the availability of quality water, even for human consumption, is becoming difficult in BOP markets and, in some cases, developed markets as well. The growth of bottled water is an indication of this trend.

The goal here is not to be alarmist. The BOP will force us to come to terms with the use of resources in ways that we have not so far. Whether it is in the use of fossil fuels for energy and transportation, water for personal cleanliness, or packaging for safety and aesthetics, ecological sensitivity will become paramount. I believe that more innovative, sustainable solutions will increasingly emerge from serving the BOP markets than from the developed markets.

5. Identifying Functionality:
Is the BOP Different from Developed Markets?

Recognizing that the functionality required in products or services in the BOP market might be different from that available in the developed markets is a critical starting point. In fact, developers must start from this perspective and look for anomalies from their prior expectations based on their experiences with developed markets.

Take prosthetics as an example. The artificial limb, as a business and good medical practice, is not new. It has been around for a long time and every war, starting with the American Civil War, has given a boost to its usage. Lost limbs due to accidents, polio, or war, are common. India is no exception: There are 5.5 million amputees and about 25,000 to 30,000 are added each year. However, most of the patients needing prosthetics are poor and illiterate. For a poor Indian, regaining the ability to walk does not mean much if he or she cannot squat on the floor, work in the field, walk on uneven ground, and not wear shoes. As Mr. Ram Chandra, talented artist, sculptor, and inventor of the Jaipur Foot, the Indian alternative to traditional prosthetics, said, "Indians do not wear shoes to the temple or in the kitchen." Jaipur Foot's design considerations are based on unique functionality, specific to this market, and are easy to recognize, as shown in Table 2.1. The design requirements can be divided into two parts. Design must take into account the technical and medical requirements for various foot movements, but this is not enough. We can build a prosthetic that can perform all the functions required. However, if it is not within reach of the target customer—here the BOP patient—it does not help. Therefore, we need to superimpose the business requirements, not just appropriate prices, but how the individual is likely to use the prosthetic.

The design considerations isolated by the design team of the Jaipur Foot were uniquely oriented to BOP problems (e.g., in India,

Table 2.1 Jaipur Foot: Design Considerations

Activity	Technical Requirements Functionality 1	Business Requirements Functionality 2
Squatting	Need for dorsiflexion	
Sitting cross-legged	Need for transverse rotation	Work needs, poverty, lack of trained manpower, time for fitting
Walking on uneven ground	Need for inversion and eversion	
Barefoot walking	Need for natural look	

Source: Our synthesis of discussions with Jaipur Foot team.

Afghanistan, Bangladesh, Pakistan, Cambodia, Congo, and Vietnam) in fitting prosthetics and are not the problems that designers would have to contend with in the United States. Functionality 1 describes the technical requirements that are unique to BOP consumers in India. Contrary to popular assumptions, this set of design parameters increased the required functionality of prosthetics compared to what is available in the United States or Europe. Functionality 2 describes the additional unique requirements at the BOP level. For example, farmers in the BOP must work in standing water in paddy fields for about eight hours every day. Vendors in the BOP must be able to walk long distances (about 8–10 km per day). Therefore, prosthetics for consumers in the BOP must be comfortable, painless, and durable. The poor cannot afford frequent replacements or hospital visits. They travel from all over India with their families to get treatment at Jaipur Foot but cannot afford boarding and lodging, much less stay for an extended time in a new location. The prosthetics must be custom-fitted in a day. From the perspective of Jaipur Foot, the prosthetics must be fitted with less than fully trained physicians, as there is a shortage of doctors and hospital space. The job of fitting a custom-developed artificial leg must be "deskilled." On top of this, prices must be reasonable, as most clients are poor. They cannot afford the typical $7,000 to $8,000 per foot cost of prosthetics. At best they can afford $50.

This might appear to be a daunting and impossible task. How can one develop a prosthetic that is more advanced in functionality, for 1/200 of the cost, can be custom-fitted by semiskilled paramedics in one visit (one day at the clinic), and last for a period of four to five years? By accepting these prerequisites, the Jaipur Foot team, led by master craftsman Ram Chandra and Dr. P. K. Sethi, a trained physician, developed a prosthetic that meets all of the criteria for less than $30. This innovation has helped farmers to farm again and a renowned Indian classical dancer to perform onstage fitted with a prosthetic.

The needs of consumers in BOP markets might not be obvious either to the firms or to the consumers. Certainly, the consumers might not know what can be accomplished with new technology to improve their productivity. Managers need to invest the necessary effort to gain a granular understanding of the dynamic needs of these consumers.

India is a country with more than 1 million retail shops. Most of the shops are tiny (around 300–400 square feet) and cater to the immediate neighborhoods in which they operate. Despite space constraints, each might offer well over 4,000 stockkeeping units (SKUs). These stores stock unpackaged (e.g., rice, lentils, oils, salt) as well as packaged products that are both unbranded and branded. Most of the store owners are semiliterate and work long hours. The average sales volume per month is about Rs. 400,000 ($9,000) with very thin margins. Can these stores be possible targets for a state-of-the-art point-of-sale (POS) system? TVS Electronics, an Indian firm (and a part of the TVS group of companies), focused on this market as a potential opportunity for a POS system. To start, its engineers spent several weeks in the store observing operations and the store owners' approach to management. More than 1,000 hours of video ethnography and analysis by engineers preceded the design of the POS system. The specification of the system was set as follows:

1. Robust system (must accommodate heat, dust, poor training and skills).
2. Stock management with alerts.
3. Payment modalities (cash, credit card).
4. Identification of slow-moving items.
5. Bill printing in multiple languages (English and 11 Indian languages).
6. Power back-up (built-in uninterruptible power supply).
7. Handheld bar code reader.
8. Internet-enabled.

9. Easy-to-learn and -use interface.
10. Priced attractively for this market.

As of the end of 2003, TVSE machines were being field tested in more than 500 stores. The company already has on order more than 5,000 units in industries as varied as petrol stations, railway stations, and pharmaceutical outlets. The design of the POS and its cost structure allow TVSE to migrate this platform seamlessly to other applications.

6. Process Innovation

A significant opportunity for innovation in BOP markets centers around redefining the process to suit the infrastructure. Process innovation is a critical step in making products and services affordable for the poor. How to deliver is as important as what to deliver.

We referred to the Aravind Eye Care System, a profitable institution where 60 percent of the patients are nonpaying patients and the remaining 40 percent pay about $50 to $300 for cataract surgery. What is the secret? The visionary founder of Aravind Eye Hospital, Dr. Venkataswamy (Dr. V as he is affectionately called), says he was inspired by the hamburger chain, McDonald's, where a consistent quality of hamburgers and french fries worldwide results from a deeply understood and standardized chemical process. In-depth attention to inputs and process steps guarantees high-quality outputs. Dr. V has developed and standardized the Aravind process, in which the first step is more than 1,500 eye camps where the poor are tested for vision problems and those needing help are admitted. They are then transported to hospitals. This is different from the more popular on-site eye camps in villages and small towns in India. The conditions of sanitation and medical care in such camps cannot be controlled as well as they can be in specially designed hospitals developed for this purpose. In the Aravind process, technicians, often young women drawn from the local areas and trained in eye care only, supplement the work of doctors. Patient preparation and postoperative work are done by these technicians. Doctors perform only surgeries. The process flow allows a doctor and two technician teams to perform more than 50 surgeries per day. Because the process is so well developed, technicians and doctors are so carefully trained, inputs are fully controlled, and the system and values are rigidly enforced, Aravind boasts of an outcome rate that is among the best in the world. The IOL, part of the modern cataract operation, is manufactured at Madurai, the central hub of Aravind, and exported to multiple countries, including the United States.

Amul, the largest and best-known dairy in India, is yet another example. Amul, as a system, is one of the largest processors of raw milk in India. Milk collection is totally decentralized, yet Amul has innovated processes by which collection is reliable and efficient. Villagers, with a buffalo or two, bring their collection to the village collection center twice daily. The milk is measured for volume and fat content and the villager is paid every day. The collected milk is transported to processing facilities in refrigerated vans. Amul's centralized, large, and highly efficient world-class processing facilities pasteurize and package the milk for retail consumption. Amul also converts raw milk into primary products—milk powder, butter, and cheese—and secondary products such as pizza, ice cream, and Indian sweets. Amul handles marketing and promotion for a very heterogeneous customer base centrally.

The Aravind and Amul stories appear to be very different, but they have many similarities. At the heart of their extraordinary success lie the process innovations they made. These can be visualized as shown in Figure 2.1. The genius of these innovations is the way these two groups—in such different industries—have maintained the local infrastructure of the villages and brought to them the most advanced facilities in their respective fields. Amul connects the farmer with two buffaloes to the national and global dairy market and gives him or her an identity. Aravind brings the world's best technology at the lowest global cost to the poorest villager and gives him or her the benefit of eyesight and dignity. Neither starts with the idea of disrupting the lives of the poor. Both aim to improve the quality of the life of the poor profitably. Neither compromises on world-class quality. Both have, through careful consideration of process innovation, achieved the requirements we set forth for successful BOP innovations: price performance, scaling, innovative high-technology hybrids, and sustainable, ecologically friendly development.

7. Deskilling of Work

In most BOP markets there is a shortage of talent. Work must, therefore, be deskilled.

One of the major goals facing the developing world and, by implication, the developed world is active surveillance of the spread of infectious diseases. The spread of Severe Acute Respiratory Syndrome

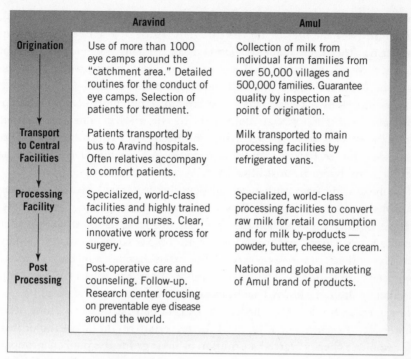

	Aravind	Amul
Origination	Use of more than 1000 eye camps around the "catchment area." Detailed routines for the conduct of eye camps. Selection of patients for treatment.	Collection of milk from individual farm families from over 50,000 villages and 500,000 families. Guarantee quality by inspection at point of origination.
Transport to Central Facilities	Patients transported by bus to Aravind hospitals. Often relatives accompany to comfort patients.	Milk transported to main processing facilities by refrigerated vans.
Processing Facility	Specialized, world-class facilities and highly trained doctors and nurses. Clear, innovative work process for surgery.	Specialized, world-class processing facilities to convert raw milk for retail consumption and for milk by-products — powder, butter, cheese, ice cream.
Post Processing	Post-operative care and counseling. Follow-up. Research center focusing on preventable eye disease around the world.	National and global marketing of Amul brand of products.

Figure 2.1   Process innovations for the BOP.

(SARS) all across Southeast Asia and from there to Canada is a case in point. The World Health Organization (WHO) and Centers for Disease Control (CDC) recognize that active monitoring of the origination of these diseases in remote regions of the world is critical. Voxiva, a startup in Peru, created a system to monitor disease patterns. Peru suffered a devastating attack of cholera in 1998 in which more than 11,000 people perished. Peru offers a challenge for the active monitoring of diseases in the remote and mountainous regions where access to the Internet and PCs is scarce. Voxiva created a device-agnostic system. Health workers in remote areas can contact health officials in Lima, Peru, through wireless devices, landlines, or the Internet using a PC. More important, each of the health workers in remote areas was given a card with pictures of the progress of the disease. For example, the symptoms of smallpox over a period of time were captured in photographs. Anyone looking at a patient could relate the actual lesions on the patient to the corresponding picture and make a judgment on how severe the disease was. He or she simply had to telephone the central health authorities in

Lima and identify the location and the severity of the case by mentioning the number of the picture on the card. The card, in a sense, was a way of capturing the knowledge of experts and identifying the stages of severity. With this simplified diagnostic process, health workers in the field need not be highly trained, nor do they need access to a complex communications network. They just need a telephone to call the health officials in Lima. Voxiva deskilled the diagnostic and surveillance problem in two ways: by reducing the need for a complex technology backbone for real-time communication as well as for diagnosis of the problem at the local, unskilled level.

Cemex, a Mexican multinational firm in the cement business, started a project called Patrimonio Hoy (Patrimony Now) to help the poorest people build their own homes. The poor in Mexico add, whenever they can, an additional bathroom, kitchen, or bedroom to their homes, endeavors that are very expensive. They often do not know exactly which materials are required. They often cannot afford to buy all the materials needed at the same time. For example, they might buy and store sand in the street, in front of their homes, until they can afford to purchase other materials. A significant amount of the materials would be wasted or lost. In response, Cemex started a program of savings for the poor. A group of three women could start the savings program and over 76 weeks they would save enough to buy a bathroom or a kitchen. The women knew before they started the savings program what kind of a room they could add, including its size, appearance, and materials needed to build it, including cement, steel, paints, tools, and so on. All of the necessities would come in a package and Cemex would hold it in storage until the customers were ready. Further, they provided technical assistance and advice on how to "do it yourself" with skilled technicians. Since the launch of this program, Cemex has helped more than 300,000 families build additions to their homes.

8. Education of Customers

Innovation in BOP markets requires significant investments in educating customers on the appropriate use and the benefits of specific products and services. Given the poor infrastructure for customer access, innovation in the educational process is vital.

More than 40 percent of India is media-dark, so TV- and radio-based messages are inappropriate methods to reach these consumers and educate them on product and service benefits. Not surprisingly, in BOP markets, education is a prerequisite to market development. Consider, for example, the incidence of stomach disorders among children, especially diarrhea. More than 2 million children die of this malady every year, a totally preventable cause of death. The cure is as simple as washing one's hands with soap before eating. HLL discovered that by this simple process, diarrhea-related fatalities could be reduced by at least 50 percent. Incidentally, HLL could also increase its volume of soap sold. However, the problem was how to educate people on the need for washing hands with soap and to convey the causality between "clean-looking but unsafe hands" and stomach disorders. HLL decided to approach village schools and educate children on the cause of disease and how to prevent it. HLL built simple demonstrations using ultraviolet dirt and bacteria detectors on "clean-looking hands." The point was that washing hands in contaminated running water might give the appearance of cleanliness, but such water harbored invisible germs that cause the damage. They co-opted teachers and NGOs and used their own "evangelists" who went to village schools and spread the messages of cleanliness, washing with (HLL) soap, and disease prevention. The children often became the most educated in the family on hygiene and, therefore, began educating their parents. The children became the activists and the advocates of good and healthy practices at home and HLL reaped new profits.

In order to access and educate consumers at the BOP, more than a single format and approach is called for. Often, collaboration between the private sector firms, NGOs, the public health authorities (Ministers of Health), and the World Health Organization can be of great value. However, collaboration is not without its attendant problems. Although all of these organizations might agree on the broad agenda of improving public health, each has a slightly different approach and mandate (i.e., politicians are also very concerned about public image). As HLL learned, collaborating with local authorities and the World Bank can cause innumerable and unforeseen problems. Although this multiparty collaboration is difficult, collaborating with the ministers (and their bureaucracies) who have as their mandate better health can be a positive step. NGOs, which are also focused on improving the lives of the poor and have deep local knowledge, can be a great help, once they can accept a commercial solution (as opposed to a charity-based or government-subsidy-based approach) to the problem.

The methods used for educating consumers will also vary. In media-dark zones, billboards painted on walls have been a staple in most developing countries, as are truck-mounted demonstration crews with catchy jingles that attract crowds in villages. In the case of Aravind Eye Hospital, well-publicized eye camps in villages conducted with the cooperation of local enterprises, NGOs, and schools, are a good way to educate people on eye care and access patients who need surgery. Aravind has developed a strict procedure for holding these eye camps. They are used for preliminary examination of patients. All surgery is performed in specially designed hospitals.

9. Designing for Hostile Infrastructure

The BOP markets exist in a hostile infrastructure. Design of products and services must take this into account.

Consider the design of PCs for a rural network application in northern India. ITC was building this network for connecting Indian villages in a seamless supply chain. E-Choupal, literally "the village meeting place," was designed to enable the farm community and ITC to collaborate and have a constant dialogue. The PCs placed in the village had to work under conditions unthinkable in the West. For example, the voltage fluctuated between 90 and 350 volts against a rated 220-volt transmission. Sudden surges in the current were quite the norm. Early installations were burned out and rendered useless in a very short time. Further, the supply of electricity was very uneven, often available for only two or three hours per day. ITC engineers had to add to the installation an uninterruptible power supply system, including surge protectors and a solar panel that would allow at least three to four hours of uninterrupted, quality electricity to operate the system. For communication, they had to depend on the satellite network rather than regular landlines. All this added to the cost. However, without this complete system that can operate in the "hostile" village environment, the entire project would have failed.

Consider the provision of good-quality water for the BOP market. Water treatment must eliminate particulate pollution, microbes, viruses and cysts, and organic and inorganic compounds. In addition, if we can supply improved taste and nutrition, it could be a welcome benefit. Systems have been developed to eliminate the "bad stuff" from water, including simple filters to complex systems. However, "purified" water from these systems can still be parceled out in unhygienic containers and touched by unclean hands. The benefits of water purification can be totally offset by what can best be described as the "last step" problem: the last step from the purifier system to consumption. Part of the system design must include the way water is dispensed and stored immediately before actual consumption.

10. Interfaces

The design of the interface must be carefully thought through. Most of the customers in BOP markets are first-time users of products and services and the learning curve cannot be long or arduous.

In designing the POS system for grocery stores, one of the main considerations was the nature of the interface. For example, each store had its own terminology and there were no set standards. Further, each store, based on its clientele, had a particular portfolio of fast-moving items. The software architecture, therefore, had to be designed so that the system could be customized easily and rapidly for each store.

Interface design can also provide some interesting and unexpected surprises. For example, in the case of rural agricultural kiosks, EID Parry found that its customers prefer an English-language interface to their PCs rather than the local language (Tamil). Wireless customers in India and Bangladesh were able to take to the new technology more rapidly than expected. Indian housewives—rich and poor alike—are avid users of SMS messaging; on average they send 60 messages per day. Farmers in the ITC e-Choupal network, in a very short period of time, were sufficiently knowledgeable to navigate the Web to check on soybean prices at the Chicago Board of Trade or the latest cricket score. The BOP can be a source of surprises on how rapidly new technologies are accepted and assimilated.

The PRODEM FFP interface in Bolivia is yet another case of creative interface design. The retailer Elektra in Mexico caters to BOP customers and has also introduced fingerprint recognition as a basis for operating the ATMs in its stores so customers need not remember their nine-digit ID codes. The opportunities for innovation—iconic, color-coded, voice-activated, fingerprint and iris recognition (biometric–based) interfaces— are more likely at the BOP than in developed countries. How we interpret the future of interface design is critical and significant research is necessary.

11. Distribution: Accessing the Customer

Distribution systems that reach the BOP are critical for developing this market. Innovations in distribution are as critical as product and process innovations.

ICICI started as an institutional lender and has grown to become the second largest bank in India. Its move into retail banking started in 1997. As such, it is a newcomer and has had to compete with banks such as the State Bank of India with more than 14,000 branches and a 200-year history in retail banking. To compete, ICICI redefined distribution access; by moving away from the approach of building branches as the primary source of access to retail customers, ICICI was able to innovate. ICICI defined access through multiple channels. Today it is the largest PC-based bank in India with more than 5 million active PC banking customers. ICICI also has the largest and fastest growing base of ATMs in India. As of August 2003, it had an installed base of 1,750 ATMs. Further, in acquiring The Bank of Madura (which had built a strong base of rural distribution through self-help groups in southern India), it gained access to 10,000 such groups involving more than 200,000 customers. In addition to its own initiatives in building retail access, ICICI also formed partnerships with large rural marketers such as ITC and EID Parry to access farmers through their networks. Over a period of six years, through this unconventional approach to retail customer access—PCs, ATMs, self-help groups, NGOs, microfinance organizations, large rural marketers and their networks, Internet kiosk operators, and some traditional branches of their own—ICICI has a retail base of 9.8.million customer accounts and is growing at a rapid rate.

HLL, a subsidiary of Unilever, is a very well-established marketing powerhouse in India. HLL serviced urban markets through dealers and suppliers and boasted the best distribution access in India. However, the company found that it was unable to access remote villages through the traditional system. As a result, HLL started a program whereby village women are involved in distributing their products in villages that were not fully serviced by HLL's existing systems of suppliers and dealers. The program, called Shakti, empowers women to become entrepreneurs. HLL's CEO, M. S. Banga, believes that this additional arm of distribution will eventually provide coverage in the 200- to 300-million-person market at the BOP currently not served by existing systems.

Avon has been extremely successful in using direct sales in Brazil. Avon has built a $1.7 billion business based on direct selling. Avon representatives become experts who provide guidance to customers, minisuppliers, distribution channels, and providers of credit.[6] Amway has had similar success in India and has built a direct distribution system covering more than 600,000 Amway representatives and a total revenue base of Rs. 500 crores ($110 million).

12. BOP Markets Essentially Allow Us to Challenge the Conventional Wisdom in Delivery of Products and Services

By its very nature, success in BOP markets will break existing paradigms.

All examples used in this book challenge conventional wisdom. They challenge the current paradigms in innovation and product and service delivery in fundamental ways.

For example, Jaipur Foot and Aravind Eye Hospital challenge the assumptions behind how health care can be delivered. By focusing on one disease and one major process, these great institutions have pioneered a way of gaining scale, speed, extremely high quality, and unbelievably low costs. Their systems are being replicated by others in India and around the world. For example, several hospitals in India are increasingly specializing in cardiac care. The cost of a bypass operation in India is now as low as $4,000, compared to $50,000 in the United States. In fact, Indian groups are now negotiating with The National Health System in the United Kingdom to fly British patients into Delhi and operate on them at lower costs, including travel, than they could in the United Kingdom without compromising quality of care.

BOP markets accept the most advanced technology easily. In the wireless market, CDMA coexists with GSM in India. Customers and operators see 3G as a viable alternative. Access to audio and video clips and news and stock quotes are considered basic services. These services are available at $10 down per handset and $0.02 per minute of long-distance calling. Building a customer base of 1 million new customers in 30 days also appears to be normal.

As the innovation for public health surveillance invented by Voxiva has demonstrated, innovations from the BOP can travel to advanced countries. Voxiva's solution is now being used by the U.S. Food and Drug Administration (FDA), Department of Defense, and the Centers for Disease Control (CDC).

Energy innovator E+Co is demonstrating that it is possible to develop hybrid systems that are local, economic, and sustainable. Although not yet a full-fledged commercial success, this experiment is challenging current thinking about reliance on grid-based electricity.

Enabling people to buy by accessing markets creatively and designing affordable products for them breaks the long-held assumption that BOP markets are not viable. A wide variety of firms—HLL, Cemex, ITC, Amul, and ICICI—are demonstrating that this can be done profitably.

BOP markets break our traditional ways of thinking and acting. This might be their biggest allure and challenge alike. Unless we are willing to discard our biases, this opportunity will remain invisible and "unattractive."

Conclusion

Getting the right combination of scale, technology, price, sustainability, and usability requires that managers start with a "zero-based" view of innovations for the BOP markets. Managers need a new philosophy of innovation and product and service delivery for the BOP markets. The 12 principles that constitute the minimum set of a philosophy of innovation are critical to understand and apply. Needless to say, they challenge the existing assumptions about product and market development. By forcing managers in large enterprises to rethink and re-examine their assumptions about form and functionality, about channels and distribution costs, BOP markets can serve as catalysts for new bursts of creativity. The biggest advantage is often in challenging the capital intensity and the managerial cost structures that have been assumed in MNCs.

Large firms, especially MNCs, can learn a lot from their active participation in BOP markets. It can help them improve their own internal management processes and bottom line. We examine how MNCs can benefit from their involvement in the BOP in the next chapter.

Endnotes

1. C. K. Prahalad and Kenneth Lieberthal, "The end of corporate imperialism." *Harvard Business Review*, July–August,1998.

2. Anil Kripalani, "Strategies for Doing Business in India." Lecture delivered at the TiE San Diego chapter, August 26, 2003. *akripalani@qualcom.com*.

3. "Amul: The Poster Boy of Rural IT." *www. Expresscomputeronline.com/20020916/ebiz1.shtml.*

4. World Watch, "State of the World, 2004," Chapter 3.

5. 4EPA. 2001 Municipal Solid Waste in The United States. *http://www.epa.gov/garbage/facts-text.htm.*

6. "Pots of Promise," *Daily News*, July 30, 2003.

3

BOP:
A Global Opportunity

We have described the process by which large firms can create products and services that are ideally suited for the BOP markets. It is natural to ask whether the managerial energy required for these innovations is justified. Although there are opportunities for growth in BOP markets, are these opportunities attractive enough for large firms (including MNCs) to go through the changes that are required in their internal systems and processes? To challenge their dominant logic? Similarly, will the social and developmental benefits of such business growth be substantial enough for NGOs and community organizations to give priority to market-based approaches?

I believe the answer is an unambiguous "yes." Based on emerging evidence, we can identify four distinct sources of opportunity for a large firm that invests the time and energy to understand and cater to the BOP markets:

   1. Some BOP markets are large and attractive as stand-alone entities.

2. Many local innovations can be leveraged across other BOP markets, creating a global opportunity for local innovations.
3. Some innovations from the BOP markets will find applications in developed markets.
4. Lessons from the BOP markets can influence the management practices of global firms.

The benefits of operating at the BOP, therefore, do not just accrue in local markets. We describe each one of these opportunities next.

Engaging the BOP

There are two ways in which large firms tend to engage the BOP markets. The traditional approach of many MNCs is to start from the business models honed in the developed markets—the top of the pyramid and their zone of comfort. This approach to the BOP market inevitably results in fine-tuning current products and services and management practices. There is growing evidence that this approach is a recipe for failure. MNCs and large firms have to start from a deep understanding of the nature and the requirements of the BOP, as outlined in Chapter 2, and then architect the business models and the management processes around these requirements. This approach to the BOP market will not only allow large firms to succeed in local markets but will also provide the knowledge base to challenge the way they manage the developed markets. Let us consider some examples.

BOP consumers in Latin America are careful in their use of diapers. They use one or two changes per day compared to the five or six changes per day common among the top of the pyramid consumers. Because they can afford only one or two changes, they expect a higher level of absorbency in the diapers and an improved construction of the diaper that will accommodate additional load. This means that the firms have to technically upgrade the quality of their diapers for the BOP consumers compared to the products they currently sell to the rich in those markets. Needless to say, the new product built for the BOP market is higher in quality and provides a better price–performance proposition. Similarly, detergent soap, when used by BOP consumers in India washing their wares in running water, becomes mushy. About 20

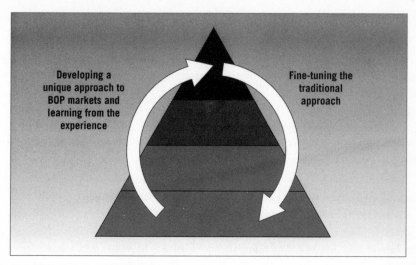

Figure 3.1 Learning from the BOP.

to 25 percent of the detergent soap can be lost in the process. Therefore, HLL developed a soap with a coating on five sides, which makes it waterproof. The coated soap saves 20 percent wastage even in a hostile user environment. The innovation is of interest to the rich as well. Access to clean water is a major concern at the BOP. Polluted water (particulate, bacterial, and viral pollutants) is common. Boiling water is the only current alternative to eliminating the bacterial and viral pollutants. A focus on solving this problem has to start with a cost target that is no more than the cost of boiled water. Further, the system has to create a quality level that is better than boiled water (removing sediments). The process is of interest to the rich as well.

The quality, efficacy, potency, and usability of solutions developed for the BOP markets are very attractive for the top of the pyramid. The traditional MNC approach and the approach suggested here—top of the pyramid to BOP and from the BOP to the top of the pyramid—are shown in Figure 3.1.

As the foregoing examples illustrate, the demands of the BOP markets can lead MNCs to focus on next practices. **The BOP can be a source of innovations for not only products and processes, but business models as well.** Let us start with the growth opportunities in local, stand-alone BOP markets first.

Local Growth Opportunities

Some of the local BOP markets are very large. Large population base is one indicator of the size of the market opportunity at the BOP, not necessarily the per-capita income. For example, China, India, Indonesia, Brazil, Mexico, Russia, South Africa, and Nigeria can potentially be very large emerging BOP markets. If an industry or a firm finds the "sweet spot"—meaning the right business model and the right combination of products and services—these markets could have explosive growth. Consider growth opportunities in China. China today is the world's largest producer of steel. The growth of the appliances, building, and auto markets has created an insatiable appetite for steel. China's steel capacity is estimated at 220 million tons compared to 110 million tons in Japan and 90 million tons in the United States. China has also an installed base of over 250 million cell phones. That is larger than the installed base of the United States. China is also one of the largest markets for televisions, appliances, and autos. The growth spurt in China is without parallel. Similarly, India is at the very early stages of a growth spurt in a wide variety of businesses such as two-wheelers (4.8 million during the fiscal year 2002–03), housing loans, and wireless. The housing loan business went from a low of Rs. 19,723 crores during fiscal 1999–2000 ($ 4.4 billion) to Rs. 51,672 crores ($ 11.5 billion) in 2002–2003. During the latter part of 2003, India was adding about 1.5 million telephone subscribers/month.

Needless to say, this growth was not all derived from the very poor. There are a lot of emerging "middle"-class customers here, but most of them earn less than $1,500 per capita ($6,000 per family of four). This growth is not funneled by the top of the pyramid. What is it that MNCs learn in these markets? The lessons for Samsung and LG (South Korean suppliers of cell phones to India), not just for Reliance and Tatas (Indian providers of service), is that they have to adjust to rapid growth, not 2 to 5 percent per year, but perhaps 50 to 100 percent per year.

Learning to Grow

BOP markets can collapse the time frames taken for products, technologies, and concepts to diffuse in the system. Many of the drivers of change and market growth—deregulation, involvement of the private sector in BOP markets, digitization, ubiquitous connectivity and the

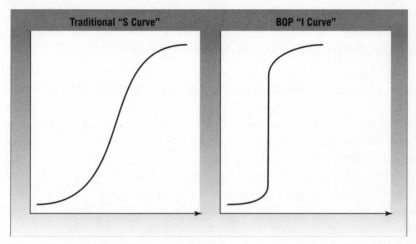

Figure 3.2   Traditional and BOP Growth Patterns. *Source:* M. S. Banga, CEO, HLL.

attendant change in the aspirations of people, favorable demographics (a young population), and access to credit—are simultaneously present in BOP markets. These drivers interact. The result is the challenge to the "S curve" that is the model for the diffusion of new products and services in the developed world. The changes that played out over 15 years in the developed markets are being collapsed into a short period of just three to five years in many BOP markets. M. S. Banga, CEO of HLL, suggests that the real challenge in BOP markets is that managers have to cope with the "I curve." The entire management process in most large firms is geared for slow growth, if at all. The I curve challenges the status quo. The S and the I curves, the two approaches to diffusion of innovations (products and services), can be conceptualized as shown in Figure 3.2.

This is good news and bad news. A cell phone today is a telephone, a camera, a watch, a computer, and a partial radio and TV. Why would one need a traditional watch (other than as an ornament) if one had a cell phone? The I curve can rapidly propel some innovations and can equally rapidly destroy some traditional markets.[1]

Rapid growth can also make new demands on firms. For example, HLL wants to build a network of 1 million direct distributors. This means the recruitment and training of about 30,000 to 40,000 people every month. Evaluating applicants; identifying those who could make good HLL distributors; training them in products, businesses models, and the values of the company; and inducting such a large number into the system create new demands on the process of management. Very few firms around the world have experience in inducting this many new recruits (independent distributors) per month.

Local Innovations and Global Opportunity

The micro encapsulation of iodine in salt to preserve the iodine in the harsh conditions of transportation, storage, and cooking in India has found market opportunities in Africa, especially in Ivory Coast, Kenya, and Tanzania. Iodine Deficiency Disorder (IDD) is common across the developing world, and the solution found in India has been transported across other similar markets with IDD by Unilever. Similarly, during the late 1980s, in response to the growing success of Nirma, a local entrepreneurial startup in the detergent business that created a new category, focused on the BOP markets, HLL launched Wheel, intended for the same market segment. Wheel today is one of the largest brands in the HLL portfolio in India ($150 million). The BOP market has grown rapidly. BOP markets in India account for a total of 1.0 million tons of detergents, compared with 300,000 tons for the top of the pyramid. More important, the lessons learned in India were not lost on Unilever. It wanted to protect BOP markets in countries such as Brazil, Indonesia, and China. It took the lessons from developing Wheel in India—from the formulation, manufacturing process, packaging, pricing, distribution, and advertising and promotion—to Brazil. It introduced a similar product oriented toward the BOP called Ala. The product was a runaway success. The product was available in 2,000 small neighborhood stores in less than three months. The detergent team that developed the new business model for the BOP in India also went to Brazil and China to help build the distribution systems that were critical for the success of the business. Today, India is seen as a laboratory for similar "India-like" markets within Unilever. Product ideas and concepts are tried out in India with a global BOP market in mind. Similarly, the idea of single-serve units has become a global phenomenon in the BOP markets. The growth in fast-moving consumer goods businesses in Bangladesh, Nepal, Pakistan, and China has been fueled by similar requirements.

The success of Grameen Bank in developing microfinance in Bangladesh as a successful commercial operation has led to global interest in the process. Grameen Bank was totally focused on BOP customers. The average loan size was less than $20 when it started. There are more than 17,000 microfinance operations that are variants of the Grameen concept around the world, including in the United States. The microfinance revolution now has its own global conference every year.

The success of Jaipur Foot is now exported to a wide variety of countries with similar requirements. The primary demand in all these countries for prosthetics is from BOP customers. They have been available in 19 countries, from Afghanistan to Vietnam. The Aravind Eye Hospital, in a similar vein, is training doctors to establish a low-cost, world-class delivery system for eye care in South Africa, Cambodia, and Vietnam. In an interesting twist of the traditional view of capabilities, the cost and quality advantages of cardiac care in India are allowing it to negotiate terms for the possibility of moving a portion of the patients from the National Health System in the United Kingdom to India. The total cost of the trip for the patient and an accompanying family member, the stays in India, and the cost of patient care will be less than the cost in the United Kingdom. More important, the quality of care is equally good or better. There are no delays in accessing care.

The Indian pharmaceutical industry had to learn to serve the BOP market. Prices were regulated by the government. Further, affordability of the public health system forced very low prices. It also forced them to develop methods for reverse engineering. Controversial as it is, the Indian pharmaceutical industry is able to deliver drugs coming off patents in the United States at a fraction of the cost charged by the established drug companies. However, the focus on the BOP has allowed these firms to invent cost-effective ways to manufacture, test, and distribute.

BOP Solutions for Developed Markets

In the rural areas of countries such as Peru, providing high-quality health care is difficult. More difficult is the surveillance of outbreaks of infectious diseases. These remote regions must be kept under constant surveillance to avoid the spread of disease, be it cholera or SARS. However, these locations are not well-connected for constant communications. PCs are rare, and telephone lines are a luxury. The question for public health professionals in such a situation is simple:

How do we connect remote areas to a real-time surveillance system so that the spread of infectious diseases can be monitored using devices that are currently available on location (often simple telephones)? This implies that the system must be simple and device-agnostic. Remote locations must be connected to a central node so that planners and policymakers are fully informed. Such a system, originally developed for Peru, is finding successes in the United States. The system, originally created by Voxiva, was based on three premises:

1. The system, to be robust, must be based on any device that is available: telephone (landline or wireless) or PC. The local community must know how to use the device. The telephone is the most widely used device for communications.
2. The remote populations were either illiterate or just moderately literate. The system had to deskill diagnosis at the point of patient contact. The chances of having a trained and experienced doctor in remote regions in the Andes are low. However, the quality of the diagnosis must be world-class.
3. The system must be reliable and available in real time so that senior members of the health care system are able to react immediately to emerging problems of infectious diseases. Early detection of health problems and rapid response (reaction time) are critical components of the system.

The system was first deployed in the remote regions of Peru and was a success. Similar problems confront the United States. The CDC and the FDA have to prepare to remotely monitor outbreaks of diseases caused by terrorists or problems in food quality that must be traced rapidly. Blood banks have to be monitored for stock and quality. When the FDA and CDC were looking for a system to help them with remote, real-time surveillance, they found the Voxiva system to be the best. Both of them are now Voxiva customers. Further, as the U.S. Department of Defense was inoculating soldiers with smallpox vaccine as a preventive measure, it needed a system for monitoring soldiers for possible adverse reactions to the vaccine. Voxiva, with its capabilities, was the obvious choice. Voxiva has moved on to sell its platforms for the detection of SARS, HIV, and other public health problems. The underlying platform is low-cost, robust, and simple, needs few skills, and can be grafted onto an existing telecom network.

Lessons for MNCs from BOP Markets

The most interesting lesson for MNCs from operating in the BOP market is about costs—for innovation, distribution, manufacturing, and general "costs of organization." **Because the BOP forces an extraordinary emphasis on price performance, firms must focus on all elements of cost.** Shortage and the cost of capital force firms in BOP markets to be very focused on the efficiency of capital use. MNCs tend to impose their management systems and practices on BOP markets and find that it is hard to make a profit. The choices are simple: Change the management systems to cut costs or lose significant amounts of money. The lessons learned from BOP markets by MNCs are covered in the following sections.

Capital Intensity

The judicious use of capital is a critical element of success in BOP markets. For example, HLL works with negative working capital. It focuses on reducing capital intensity in plants and equipment. By focusing on a judicious mix of outsourcing to dedicated suppliers, it not only reduces its capital intensity but creates several small and medium-size enterprises that can conform to the norms and standards set by HLL. HLL, as the only customer to these suppliers, can and does influence their operations. Second, a senior management focus on logistics and distribution is critical for reducing the capital needs of the business. HLL serves 850,000 retail outlets in one of the most difficult distribution terrains. The sales data from every retail outlet is collected and processed in a central processing facility. All the retail outlets are serviced frequently. Finally, a focus on revenue management allows for reducing the capital tied up in receivables. HLL is able to collect revenues in real time as the goods leave the warehouses of their suppliers. The suppliers might provide credit to the dealers and retailers. HLL as a manufacturer can reduce its capital intensity. The results can be compelling. For example, the system for focusing on capital first initiated with the introduction of the detergent Wheel to the BOP provided evidence of how many more opportunities for value creation can be unearthed by serving the needs of the BOP. A comparison of the financial performance of Nirma (the local competitor), HLL in the top of

Table 3.1   Economic Value Creation at the BOP

	Nirma	HLL (Wheel)	HLL (Surf)
Sales ($ Million)	150	100	180
Gross margin (%)	18	18	25
Return on capital employed (%)	121	93	22

Notes: The bottom line can be very profitable. Low margins/high unit sales. Game is about volume and capital efficiency. Economic profit vs. gross margins.

Source: John Ripley, Senior Vice President, Unilever PLC.

the pyramid market with Surf, and HLL in the BOP market with Wheel, is shown in Table 3.1.

It is important to separate gross margins from return on capital employed (ROCE). The real economic profit is in the effective use of capital.

A similar situation exists at the Aravind Eye Hospital. It uses the most modern equipment available in any facility in the world. It costs are dramatically brought down by its ability to use the equipment effectively, as it specializes only in eye care and every doctor and nurse team performs an average of 50 surgeries per day. Only 40 percent of its patients pay. A cataract surgery costs $50 compared to $3,000 to $3,500 in the United States. In spite of these differences, Aravind's ROCE is in the 120 to 130 percent range. Aravind is totally free of debt. The revenues for the year 2001–2002 were Rs. 388.0 million ($86 million) with a surplus (before depreciation) of Rs. 210.5 million ($46.5 million). This would be the envy of every hospital in the United States. The productivity and the volumes at Aravind are the basis for this level of profitability. Every doctor accounts for 2,000 operations per year, compared to a national average of 300 in India. The four locations in the Aravind system process more than 1.4 million patients (including 1,500 eye camps) and perform 200,000 surgeries. They operate with about 80 doctors and a total staff, including paramedics, counselors, and others, of 1,275.

With an ITC e-Choupal, it costs the company about Rs. 100,000 ($2,100) per kiosk installation. The company saves about Rs. 270 per ton on the acquisition of soybeans. The payback period can be as low as one full season. The recovery of that investment requires an acquisition target of about 4,000 to 5,000 tons from a single kiosk (a cluster of villages is supported by the kiosk). Adding additional services such as selling seeds, fertilizers, and crop insurance can enhance the profitability of the system. The economic returns can be significant.

Sustainable Development

BOP markets are a great source for experimentation in sustainable development. First, resources such as water, energy, and transportation are scarce and expensive. Automotive and two-wheeler manufacturers are learning that the BOP customers are very attuned to the total cost of ownership and not just the cost of purchase. The miles per gallon—the efficiency of energy use—is a significant determinant of market success. Similar demands are imposed on water use.

BOP markets can also represent an emerging problem. Single-serve packaging is advantageous to create the capacity to consume at the BOP but can also lead to a major environmental problem. More than 13 billion single-serve packages are sold annually in India and this trend is growing rapidly. Although plastic bags appear attractive, they are not biodegradable. MNCs involved in the BOP markets have the ability and the motivation to find solutions to the problem of packaging in emerging markets.

Innovations

As we discussed in depth in Chapter 2, the process of innovation for the BOP forces a new set of disciplines. First, the focus is on price performance. **Innovations must become "value-oriented" from the consumer's perspective. The BOP focuses attention on both the objective and subjective performances of the product or service.** Markets at the BOP also focus on the need for 30 to 100 times improvements in price performance. Even if the need is only for 10 to 20 times improvement, the challenge is formidable. The BOP can become a major source of innovations. Consider, for example, the need for user-friendly interfaces. Biometric authentication systems such as fingerprint and voice recognition are emerging from the BOP markets, as we saw in the case of PRODEM FFP in Bolivia and Elektra in Mexico. Logistics and distribution requirements are an integral part of the innovation process at the BOP.

Serving the BOP forces a new business model on MNCs. Management systems developed for a price performance level cannot be fine-tuned to cope with the demands of the BOP markets. Although MNCs are slowly adapting to the needs of the BOP, very few have consciously focused attention on examining the implications of their own operations in the BOP for their global operations. So far the attention has been on outsourcing from the more cost-efficient locations such as China, Taiwan, Thailand, the Philippines, and India. A $50 CD player is not just about wage rates, but a totally different way of approaching manufacturing.

The I curve has different implications for scaling. The timing of investments, investment intensity, and the pace of market and distribution development become crucial, as is the rate at which costs must be brought down to fuel growth of the market.

The Costs of Managing

ICICI Bank manages, with 16 managers, a portfolio of 200,000 customers at the BOP. The entire network of management consists of a hierarchy shown in Figure 3.3.

There are only 16 managers (employees) from the ICICI side. Each project manager oversees the work of 6 coordinators. Coordinators are women who are experienced in the development of self-help groups. They are identified and are asked to be coordinators. They helped project managers in approval of loans and help develop new SHGs. The coordinator oversees the work of promoters. The primary responsibility of the promoters is the formation of new SHGs. She must form 20 groups

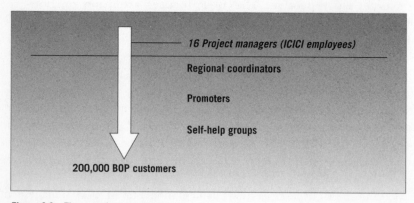

Figure 3.3   The cost of management.

per year. She is financially compensated for the successful formation of new groups. The promoters understand the village culture because they are part of it. They carry credibility because they have been part of a successful SHG. They speak the language of the groups that they deal with. They are also identified from the local communities. As a result, the organizational system that is built in this case is quite unique.

1. The basic unit of analysis is the SHG with 20 members. Loans are given to the SHG and the group decides how to partition the money it receives as loans. The SHG is responsible for paying back the loan and the interest. The bank does not lend to individuals. As such, the credit-worthiness of the SHG depends on how well it can enforce compliance among its members. They all understand that what is at stake is the access to cheap and reliable capital, compared to all the alternatives including the local moneylenders. Therefore, the SHG does credit analysis, project evaluation, monitoring of the use of funds, collection, and reinvestment. The control is totally local and the SHG is empowered. From this perspective, ICICI Bank takes little risk.

2. Market development is also handled by SHG veterans. The promoters are from SHGs and their territories are clearly demarcated. As a result, the person promoting the idea is closest to the community that the bank wants to reach. The promoters are paid an incentive based on the number of SHGs formed by them in good standing.

3. The regional managers or coordinators are also from local communities in which they work. Their work is primarily focused on training and supervising the promoters and evaluating the quality of the SHGs as they are formed.

4. The concept of the structure and the management process is built from the bottom up. There is distributed leadership. The role of the company employees in the day-to-day running of the SHG is minimal. The general sales and administration costs of this system are about 5 to 10 percent of the costs of a typical bank. That makes the system cost-effective and makes small transactions profitable. Further, this also allows for rapid scaling. ICICI increased from 2,000 SHGs in 2002 to 10,000 in 2003.

The SHGs and the direct distribution system we have described, such as Shakti Amma, represent an extraordinary innovation that both cuts costs and risks for the firm and at the same time creates an empowered group of new entrepreneurs with sustainable, rising income opportunities. **Business management skills, technology, and contacts are pushed down to the local grassroots level.** The SHGs perform several of the functions that the firm would have handled in the traditional approach to managing. For example, the SHG, by validating the individuals who will get the loan, by checking the nature and viability of the project, and by taking responsibility for monitoring the progress of the project is, in essence, an extension of the traditional firm. The SHG helps co-create value for the firm—in this case, ICICI. The bank does not have direct contact with the individuals, but monitors the loan indirectly through the SHG. This represents a new model of relationship between the firm and its consumers. The quality of the SHG is the guarantee of the investment. However, the SHG, being so close to its members—same village, same group, frequent meetings, visibility of progress of projects, and, most important, the ability to assess behaviors—is in a great position to alter the risk profiles of the loans. The large bank gains local responsiveness capability at low (or no) cost. The same is true of the Shakti Amma system. The local entrepreneur knows her village and its needs and can also influence the buying decisions of the villagers. She is at once the salesperson, the supplier, the trusted advisor, and the educator for the village. She is the one who can convince the villagers that iodized salt will be a healthy option for the family. HLL is now experimenting with connecting these individual distributors through an Internet network. The I-Shakti project will create the most dramatic opportunity for the BOP consumers to influence the firm and its decisions regarding product features, costs, availability, and the business model in general.

What we see here is the convergence of the traditional roles of the firm and the consumer and the distributor and the consumer. Functions such as advertising, credit management, risk analysis, and market development are assumed by the consumers-entrepreneurs and the consumer-entrepreneurial community (SHG). The boundaries of the firm expand beyond its legal parameters and begin to engage and empower the large and heretofore economically isolated segment of developing country societies known as the "informal sector." The resources that are available to the firm expand even more dramatically. Access to the 10,000 SHGs is, in its simplest form, a huge resource multiplier to the firm. Whether it is resource leverage through selective access, local knowledge, risk reduction, or reduction in capital needs, the firm benefits. This is at best a win–win situation. The local communities take charge of what they want. They make their own decisions and choices. They are accountable and therefore feel a sense of empowerment and self-esteem. They know they can deal with the large firm on an equal basis. Although the resources are limited for the SHG, the bank cannot unilaterally make decisions. In that sense, there is less asymmetry in power.

Learning to Live in a Network of Relationships

MNCs working at the BOP learn rapidly that they have to learn to live with a wide variety of relationships with a large number of institutions. For example, in the case of selling iodized salt, HLL learned very fast that its efforts would impact public policymakers and officials in the health department. NGOs focus on local communities and in many cases conflict with industry practices. HLL had to learn to cope with the agendas of the various parties that might be involved and work with them effectively in a cooperative mode. The case of soap, intended to reduce diarrhea, was more interesting. HLL had to deal not only with state governments and NGOs, but also with the World Bank, which wanted to partly fund the program of education and distribution. It also wanted to be involved in the evaluation of results. As such, the firm had to learn to cope with the differing priorities, time scales, decision cycles, and perspectives of both the causes of the problem and the nature and efficacy of the solution. The reactions of the various groups can vary from open hostility toward the MNC to a willingness to cooperate. At the end of the day, however, MNCs learn how to transform their ideals of good corporate citizenship and social responsibility into their core business of delivering value on a day-to-day business basis. Social sector organizations learn how to scale their still-marginal efforts at "social enterprise" into viable business models serving a mass market.

BOP markets represent 80 percent of humanity. It is reasonable to expect that 4 billion people in search of an improved quality of life will create one of the most vibrant growth markets we have ever seen. Private-sector involvement in development can be a win for both the BOP consumers and the private sector. All of us can learn. The flow of ideas, knowledge, and innovation will become a two-way street—from the developed countries to the developing as well as the reverse. MNCs can help BOP markets to develop. They can also learn from BOP markets.

In the next chapter, we discuss how the large firm can create a private-sector ecosystem and act as a nodal firm. This ecosystem is a prerequisite for developing markets at the BOP.

Endnote

1. Paul Glader. "China Feeds Desire for Steel Abroad," *Wall Street Journal*, March 31, 2004.

4

The Ecosystem for Wealth Creation

The need for building an ecosystem for wealth creation and social development at the BOP is obvious from the previous chapters. ICICI Bank with its 10,000 SHGs is an ecosystem. So is the HLL system with Shakti Ammas or ITC with sanchalaks in the e-Choupal. However, traditionally, the focus of both business and social developmental initiatives at the BOP has been on one aspect of the ecosystems for wealth creation at a time—social capital or individual entrepreneurs (the focus of so much of the microfinance efforts), small and medium enterprises (SMEs), or large firms (market liberalization or foreign direct investment). **There have been few attempts to focus on the symbiotic nature of the relationships between various private sector and social institutional players that can lead to a rapid development of markets at the BOP.**

Let us digress a moment to understand the thinking behind poverty alleviation and economic development. This thinking has influenced the pattern of private-sector involvement in development in many countries. We must start with the historical roots of the debate. The focus of public policy on the private sector as a possible instrument of poverty reduction is of recent vintage. Not surprisingly, there is no consensus on what "private sector" means. Public policy positions tend to shift from microfinance (individual entrepreneurs), to SMEs, to large domestic firms and MNCs. These trends tend to follow well-publicized successes in specific situations. The success of the Grameen Bank in Bangladesh, for example, spawned a spate of interest in microfinance. Similarly, there is a growing interest in SMEs fueled by the fact that they contribute a disproportionate percentage of jobs in poorer countries. The importance of SMEs correlates negatively with GDP per capita.[1] However, it is not clear why low GDP per capita coexists with SMEs. Is the dominant role of microenterprises and SMEs a result of an underdeveloped market system? Does the dominant role played by SMEs reflect poor enforcement of commercial contracts outside the neighborhoods in which they operate? Can an underdeveloped and poorly implemented legal system condemn countries to microprivate enterprises that cannot flourish beyond local communities? Development of SMEs cannot then become the sole basis for policy. The role of MNCs gets attention only as a vehicle for foreign direct investment (FDI). The role of the MNC (and large private-sector firms) in the development of solutions at the scale of the BOP neighborhood and the infrastructure needed for such a market economy are often not fully understood either by the MNCs or the development community.

Increasingly, the role of cooperatives is being debated. The successes of the milk cooperatives in India are a case in point. Cooperatives are an integral part of the private sector. They are inclusive. Amul, the showcase for the cooperative sector in developing countries, encompasses the poor farmer with two buffaloes and world-class processing facilities and a distribution system with a national and increasingly global reach. What cases like Amul and ICICI illustrate is the need for a more holistic understanding of the wealth creation process. Wealth creation at the BOP does not result from isolated public investment programs, from NGO self-help groups, or from FDI. Shifting the focus of debate from public investment to private sector, and vice versa, does not create the preconditions for wealth creation. Our cases demonstrate the fundamental role played by the private sector. **The private sector in the BOP context includes social organizations of different kinds that interact to create markets and develop appropriate products and services and deliver value. A business system is at the heart of the**

ecosystem for wealth creation. In this chapter, we want to change the focus of the debate from a preference for one form of private sector (say, SMEs) at a time to a focus on a market-oriented ecosystem that is a combination of multiple forms of private enterprises coexisting in a symbiotic relationship.

Market-Oriented Ecosystem

A market-based ecosystem is a framework that allows private sector and social actors, often with different traditions and motivations, and of different sizes and areas of influence, to act together and create wealth in a symbiotic relationship. Such an ecosystem consists of a wide variety of institutions coexisting and complementing each other. We use the concept of the ecosystem because each constituent in the system has a role to play. They are dependent on each other. The system adapts and evolves and can be resilient and flexible. Although there will always be distortions at the margin, the system is oriented toward a dynamic equilibrium. What then are the constituents of the market-based ecosystem? We can conceptualize it as shown in Figure 4.1.

Every developing country has the components of this portfolio. However, the relative importance of the various components of the ecosystem is different across countries. For example, the extralegal (those who exist outside the legal system) vegetable sellers in the slums of Sao Paulo or Mumbai coexist with global firms such as Ford and Unilever. The chicken cooperatives and processors such as Sadia in southern Brazil and a local fast-food chain such as Habib's coexist with Kentucky Fried Chicken and McDonald's. Whether it is Brazil, Mexico, South Africa, or

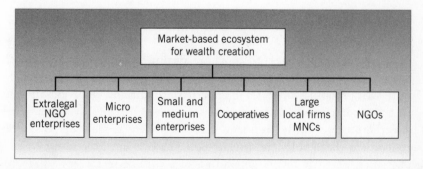

Figure 4.1 Components of the market-based ecosystem.

India, a portfolio of these constituents of various ecosystems exists. Needless to say, if the portfolio is totally skewed toward extralegal entities, the economy cannot advance and the private sector cannot contribute to poverty reduction. If it is skewed toward large local firms and MNCs, then it probably is a well-developed economy with a well-functioning private sector but is not oriented towards the creation of wealth among those living at the BOP.

Historically, the evolution of the large firm was a symptom of a maturing economy focused on system efficiencies through scale and scope. For example, the development of the large firms in the United States at the turn of the 20th century fueled by electricity, the telegraph, refrigeration, and the railroads is well-documented. There is a paucity of similar studies that document the evolution of ecosystems in developing countries. We do not have good studies on the underlying driving forces that create different compositions of private-sector firms in various countries. Further, we lack systematic evidence of triggers that shift the composition of an ecosystem in any direction.

It should be clear that a focus on any one component of the ecosystem to the negligence or detriment of others is not desirable. **The dilemma for public policymakers is clear: If we can't pick one sector for special attention, how do we mobilize the whole ecosystem?** Alternately, how do we move the composition of the ecosystem toward large firms? Both are legitimate questions. This is the state of the debate. I believe that the debate must shift towards building market-based ecosystems for broad-based wealth creation. Only then can we tap into the vast, dormant, and trapped resources, purchasing power, and entrepreneurial drive at the BOP. This will allow for new growth opportunities for the large corporations and a better quality of life for those at the BOP.

Ecosystems for a Developing Country

The evolution of the U.S. economy during the late 19th and 20th centuries might not be a good basis for prescriptions on how Brazil or South Africa should evolve. The competitive conditions, the availability of new technologies, the nature of resource endowments, and the educational infrastructure are vastly different. Are there new models of ecosystem development that public and private policymakers must focus on?

Let us start with an understanding of a private-sector ecosystem by considering the fast-moving consumer goods (FMCG) industry in India.

The largest FMCG firm in India is HLL, a subsidiary of Unilever. HLL is a Rs.100 billion ($2.3 billion) company with a wide portfolio of personal care and food products. The ecosystem of HLL consists of six components:

1. HLL (MNC) operates 80 manufacturing facilities.
2. A dedicated supplier base of 150 factories (SMEs) that employs anywhere between 30,000 and 40,000 people.
3. Exclusive stockist (7,250) who distribute HLL products nationwide.
4. Wholesalers (12,000) and small retailers and shop owners (300,000) who are either SMEs or microenterprises.
5. A growing direct distribution system (HLL net) and a rural direct distribution system called Shakti that cover 250,000 individual entrepreneurs in urban and remote villages who sell HLL products. This number is likely to grow to 1 million by 2005.
6. An advisory relationship with the government of the Indian state of Madhya Pradesh to help it brand local produce from villages and tribal areas, such as natural honey collected from forests in the state. It touches 35,000 to 40,000 tribals.

The ecosystem that this represents is shown in Figure 4.2.

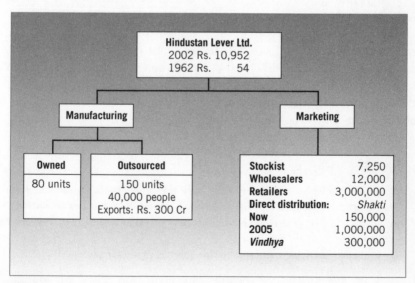

Figure 4.2 HLL's ecosystem for wealth creation.

HLL does not have legal control over the entire ecosystem, nor does it have direct influence on all the elements of the system. However, HLL provides the framework, the intellectual direction, and the processes by which the system is governed and operated. The Shakti Ammas are independent, but they must follow simple rules to be part of the system. In this sense, HLL is a *nodal firm* that facilitates the entire functioning of the network. Ownership is not the issue. Access and influence without ownership are more important factors, as are quality standards, mutual obligations, commitment to contractual relationships, and a shared set of values. As a nodal firm, HLL provides expertise and establishes technical standards for a wide variety of private-sector enterprises, from supplier factories to indiidual entrepreneurs in remote villages. Quality levels in the system are prescribed by HLL and are consistent with global standards and local needs.

What is the value of a private-sector ecosystem? Who benefits from the standards and quality requirements demanded by the nodal firm from the constituents to participate in the network? How does this transform the basis for commercial transactions within a developing economy?

Learning the Sanctity of Contracts

Underpinning this ecosystem is education across all levels. The individual entrepreneur in the village—the Shakti Amma, for example—is being educated to be a responsible entrepreneur. She is a wealth creator in her village. She learns about products, prices, returns, and being an advisor and helper to her customers in the village. When I interviewed one Shakti Amma, who had been an entrepreneur for less than six months, the impact of being part of the ecosystem became obvious. The conversation went something like this:

Q: If you could have any wish you want granted, what would your top three wishes be?

A: I want a telephone so I can order only the products that I can sell fast (inventory control). I want a scooter for my husband so that he can go and sell in villages close by (market expansion). I have no other wishes at this time.

Q: What is the biggest difference this job has made for you?

A: I am somebody now. People look up to me. They ask me for advice. I can help them.

The training she received from the representatives of the company on products and business certainly helped her. She and a million other entrepreneurs will help HLL get distribution reach to 200 million to 300 million people whom they could not cost-effectively reach through established distribution channels. This type of symbiotic relationship in the ecosystem creates a win for all. Better informed, educated, and financially successful, these independent entrepreneurs seek the same type of transparency and access to information on products and features (what is unique about these compared to similar products from other firms operating in the same market, with similar prices, promotional schemes and advertising). For example, the Shakti Amma that I interviewed had clear and unambiguous answers to all questions about product features and benefits. Market-based ecosystems can be a source of informing the poor of the benefits of transparency in transactions. She is also learning to respect contracts, be they implicit or explicit with the company. The mutual obligation between her and the parent company, HLL, which is just a concept for her, is real. Respect for contracts binds her to the company and allows her to make a profit. She recognizes that violating the contracts will dry up the source of her economic and social success. Transparent transaction governance is an integral part of the ecosystem. She is a local entrepreneur. She is a one-person company, but she does not operate as an extralegal entity. She is bound to the national and global system and is less beholden to the local system of moneylenders and slum lords. The social collateral of open and honest entrepreneurship that the market-based ecosystem provides will be significant. The ecosystem can provide the tools for the poor and the disadvantaged to be connected seamlessly with the rest of the world in a mutually beneficial and non-exploitative way. It provides them with skills and opportunities that are often denied by the informal sector.

Reducing Inequities in Contracts

Consider ITC's initiative, the e-Choupal (literally, the "electronic village meeting place"). ITC is the Indian subsidiary of British American Tobacco. ITC has branched out of its traditional and primary focus on tobacco to include hotels, paper, and food. The International Business Division (IBD) of ITC was concerned about its ability to source soybeans from widely scattered and subsistence farmers in Madhya Pradesh, India. The traditional system focused on the *mandi*, the place where the farmers brought their produce to be auctioned. The buyers in the mandi aggregated the produce and sold it to firms like ITC for further processing. The farmers got a raw deal in the mandi and the large processors like ITC were beholden to the intermediaries. ITC decided to use advances in digital technologies to reduce the inefficiencies in the system and to ensure a steady supply of good-quality soybeans for its processing plants. The approach depended on building a network of PCs in villages around the soya belt. ITC picked a successful farmer called the *sanchalak* in each village. He was given a PC that could be used by all the farmers in the village. The sanchalak took a formal oath in the village to be impartial and make access to the PC available to all the farmers in his area. The farmers could check the prices of soybeans in the neighboring mandis and decide when and where to sell their crops.

ITC decided to build a system that changed many of the existing practices. The farmers could check prices and decide at what prices they wanted to sell. They were not at the mercy of the auctioneers at the mandi on a particular day. The produce was weighed accurately, unlike the previous practice with the traditional aggregators in the mandi. Under the old system, farmers lost about two to three kilograms per ton in inaccurate weighing. Under the old system, farmers were also expected to pay for the bagging of their produce, about Rs. 3 per bag. IBD's system allowed for better and accurate weighing, immediate payment, and reduction of transportation and bagging costs for the farmer. The new system efficiencies compared to the traditional mandi system resulted in savings of Rs. 270 per ton for the farmer. The composition of the savings is shown in Figure 4.3.

ITC also saved Rs. 300 per ton. This is a win–win situation for both the farmer and the company.

The real benefits of the e-Choupal are more than cost reduction in the system. There were four sources of friction in the system:

1. There was significant *asymmetry in the access to information* between the farmer, the traders in the mandi, small local processors, and the large processors such as ITC. By providing the farmer access to information about prices not only in his mandi but around the world, the e-Choupal system dramatically eliminates the asymmetric information that confines the subsistence farmer to a helpless bargaining position.

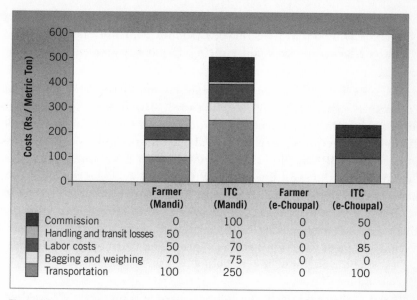

	Farmer (Mandi)	ITC (Mandi)	Farmer (e-Choupal)	ITC (e-Choupal)
Commission	0	100	0	50
Handling and transit losses	50	10	0	0
Labor costs	50	70	0	85
Bagging and weighing	70	75	0	0
Transportation	100	250	0	100

Figure 4.3 Savings for farmers compared to the traditional mandi system.

2. There was an *asymmetry in choice* between the farmer and the trader under the old system. The new system reduces the logistical problems of moving soybean crops from the village to the mandi and the costs incurred by the farmer in doing so. The farmer also had to deal with the procedural requirements imposed on him by traders, such as paying the costs of bagging the produce. The inaccuracies in weighing the product are eliminated. These logistical and procedural inefficiencies (as seen from the farmer's perspective) were built into the traditional system. It reflected the lack of choice for the farmer. He was for all practical purposes a semi-indentured supplier to the mandi close by.

3. There was an *asymmetry in the ability to enforce contracts* under the old system. The moneylenders and traders had the upper hand. The farmer could not alienate them. Therefore, the traders could take advantage of their strong bargaining position and delay payments. The farmers had no official recourse. The current system changes this dramatically.

4. Finally, under the old system, there was an *asymmetry in the social standing* of the farmer (the producer), the buyer, and the trader. Although all social inequities are unlikely to be solved, farmers do

not have to face the indignity of a rigged auction in the mandi. They can be assured that what they get paid for their work is a fair market price that can be verified by them without any distortions.

ITC's e-Choupal takes the idea of explicit contracting and transaction governance capacity a big step forward. **By providing access to information that the farmers can independently obtain, the system changes the inequities that the extralegal and the quasi-legal systems impose on BOP consumers and producers in developing countries.** ITC still pays the taxes due to the government as if the trade did take place in the mandi. The government is happy with revenues. The traders are likely to be unhappy, as their ability to coerce farmers into selling at the price that they decided in the auction is getting eroded. The most telling comment was from a farmer captured on video by the researchers:

"I did not even know how to hold a mouse."

Four months later:

"Even if they take away the computer, we will buy one. We need net connectivity."

That summarizes it all.

Building Governance Capabilities Among the Poor

There is a third phase of building transaction governance capacity. This entails building the capacity for self-governance. The Bank of Madura initiated a model of village development in southern India that has shown great promise. It was based on three assumptions:

1. Microsavings must precede microlending. BOP consumers must learn to save and there were no institutions to support microsavings.
2. BOP consumers must start trusting themselves. They must be actively involved in solving their problems. Outside help (financial and other) can go only so far. The village must break its cycle of dependency built by more than 40 years of subsidies and government handouts, NGO interventions, and the like. Private-sector development (in this case, banking based on commercial principles) and subsidies do not mix.
3. There is no dearth of latent leaders in the villages. Given the opportunity, they will emerge and will influence the start of a transparent and commercially viable system. This group will then

become the custodians of transaction governance instead of lawyers or the local slum lords.

These were bold assumptions, but the work started with a clear position. Dr. Raj Thiagarajan, who was the CEO of Bank of Madura, initiated this project in the rural areas of Tamil Nadu, India. He had difficulty, initially, getting the very best managers to work in the area of rural development. Once it became obvious to the bank employees that he was personally involved and it was going to be his initiative, the perceptions of the value attached to this work changed. There is a lesson for large firms here: Unless BOP work is seen as central to the firm, the very best managers are unlikely to sign up. Carefully selected bank employees were assigned to villages where their primary focus was to build confidence and trust among local groups. They interviewed and picked a woman in each village who could be a potential leader. The SHG consisted of 20 women in each village who formed the core group. They had no prior familial relationship, no formal participation or experience with the financial sector, and no incentives to trust each other. All were from the same village but could be strangers. The officers of the bank continued to visit these SHGs, organizing them and creating a sense of cohesion. The women who formed the SHGs were taught the disciplines of holding a meeting, developing an agenda, writing the minutes, keeping records, and saving. The team had to jointly guarantee any financial dealings with the bank. The SHGs understood the basic dimensions of transaction governance capacity—transparency, access, explicit contractual obligations, penalties for violating contracts, the connection between the cost of capital and the track record of performance of contracts, and most important, the need to take charge of their community and protect their newfound access to capital at reasonable rates.

The Bank of Madura paid a lot of attention to the maturation of the SHGs. As they matured and became a working group with a clear understanding of each other's obligations and the process by which conflicts of interest and ideas would be settled, the bank progressed them to the next stage, making capital available as microloans for building a common village facility (e.g., a toilet in the village) or expanding a member's agricultural operations.

The maturation model for SHGs is shown in Figure 4.4. The first three steps often took more than a year.

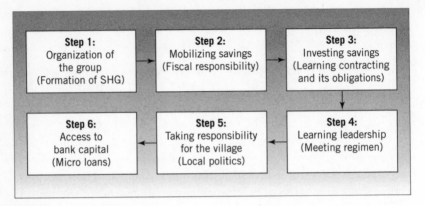

Figure 4.4 The evolution of SHGs.

As SHG leaders became more confident and capable of articulating the basic premise of the approach and could demonstrate how SHGs had helped their own communities, they became evangelists. They went to adjoining villages and recruited other women to form SHGs, providing both the motivation and the training.

At the time of the merger of Bank of Madura with ICICI, the second largest retail bank in India, there were 1,200 SHG groups. During the next two years the number expanded to 10,000 SHGs covering about 200,000 women and therefore 200,000 families. The default rates have remained, as of writing, at less than 1 percent. The model is scalable because the preconditions for the success of SHGs can be identified. The key criteria are as follows:[2]

1. Is the group between 15 and 20 members?
2. Are all of the members considered very poor?
3. Was there a fixed amount of savings collected each month?
4. Is there more than 20 percent literacy?
5. Have they used their savings for internal lending purposes?
6. Have the members kept a high level of attendance?

The second criterion is not critical. However, this was part of the policy adopted by the government of India. The concept of SHGs can work quite effectively with the other principles.

The lending from the bank is quite safe. The marketing ecosystem—the private sector—left to operate in a commercially responsible way, can create transaction governance capacity at all levels of society, from the very poor individuals in the villages to microentrepreneurs (like Shakti Ammas), to SMEs. Governments tend to overregulate the private sector (assuming that such overregulation will protect the poor) or tend to use public-sector corporations as a way of creating a culture of subsidies disguised as commercial operations (e.g., loans from banks that are not returned and where no enforcement is possible). Nonperforming assets are not only a problem with large borrowers but also with small borrowers at the village level.

In this chapter, we tried to illustrate the three steps in creating a transaction governance capacity based on the marketing ecosystem:

1. Help the poor understand that there is a win–win situation for them and the firm by respecting contracts. The Shakti Amma wants to be within the system and can respect the contract with a large firm such as HLL. Respect for the contract must transcend people you see every day. A contract with another legal entity, large or small, seen or unseen, is critical.

2. The private sector can reduce the asymmetries in information, choice, ability to enforce contracts, and social standing. The use of information technology to build a network can create a powerful motivation to be part of the system. The farmers know the difference between the old system and the system introduced by the ITC e-Choupal. It is more than just a win in terms of savings. It provides a social basis for becoming an insider.

3. The ICICI-supported SHGs take it one step further. They start with understanding the rationale for the contacting system: how and why it reduces transaction costs and therefore reduces the cost of capital as well as increases access to capital. Further, governance cannot be just between ICICI and the individual. By creating a collective commitment to accountability to contracting conditions, SHGs continually reinforce in the local community the benefits of being within the system.

Ultimately, the goal in development is to bring as many people as possible to enjoy the benefits of an inclusive market. Transaction governance capacity is a prerequisite. The market-based ecosystem might provide us an approach to building the basic infrastructure for inclusion of BOP consumers. It also allows large firms to build new and profitable growth markets.

The impact of the market-based ecosystem and the role of the nodal company can be very important in developing the disciplines of the market—respect for contracts, understanding mutuality of benefits, being local and at the same time getting the benefits of being national and global, and most important, recognizing the benefits of transparency in relationships. **The private sector, in its desire to leverage resources and gain market coverage, will invent new systems depending on the nature of the market. That is precisely what we need. We need the capacity to bring more people into the market system.** This means not only gaining the benefits of globalization, but also accepting the disciplines that it imposes. Opaque, local moneylender-based contract enforcement and participating in a national or regional private-sector ecosystem are not compatible. Again, this is a positive situation for both the large firm and the BOP consumers. MNCs and small-scale enterprises and entrepreneurs can co-create a market and the BOP consumers can benefit not only by the quality and choice of products and services available to them, but also by building local entrepreneurship.

In the next chapter, we address the ever-present but seldom openly discussed topic of corruption. Corruption and poverty go together. However, given the advancement of technologies, we can mitigate corruption rapidly. This is what governments can do to facilitate the rapid development of market-based ecosystems and the active involvement of large firms and MNCs in the BOP market.

Endnotes

1. Meghana Ayygari, Thorsten Beck, and Asli Demirguc-Kunt. "Small and Medium Enterprises Across the Globe: A New Database," World Bank, 2003.
2. NABARD. "Banking with Self-Help Groups: How and Why," p.5.

5

Reducing Corruption: Transaction Governance Capacity

The private sector, as we saw in the previous chapters, can be a major facilitator of poverty alleviation through the creation of markets at the BOP. Although managers might be convinced about the opportunity, it is likely that there are lingering doubts about the ability of large firms to operate in these markets. The primary source of this concern is corruption. In many cases, the impact of micro regulations and local customs that are opaque to MNC managers may be interpreted as corruption. For example, the criticality of relationships in Japanese and Chinese business, opaque to the Western MNCs, can appear to be corruption. So will local customs and the set of mutual obligations in rural societies. We must understand the difference between corruption and local practice. Alliances with local firms and NGOs can provide visibility to these "understood but not explicit" local practices. **Transaction governance capacity is about making the entire process as transparent as possible and consistently enforced. We** must reduce the frictional losses in doing business at the BOP. The focus of this chapter, however, is overt corruption. Corruption in various forms adds to this cost burden and business uncertainty. In the previous chapter, we examined how MNCs and large firms (nodal firms) can create transaction governance capacity (TGC) within their ecosystems.

Most developing countries do not fully recognize the real costs of corruption and its impact on private-sector development and poverty alleviation. The capacity to facilitate commercial transactions through a system of laws fairly enforced is critical to the development of the private sector. I call this a nation's TGC as opposed to TGC within an ecosystem we considered in the previous chapter. In this chapter, we examine the need for and the process by which countries can develop their TGC. Again, as in the last chapter, we digress and consider the accumulated thinking on corruption and poverty alleviation.

Are the Poor Poor?

Some basic assumptions have been at the core of the thinking on poverty reduction and developmental assistance during the past 30 years.

- First, poor countries are poor because they lack resources.[1] Aid was, therefore, seen as a substitute for locally generated resources.
- Second, aid from rich countries to the governments of the poor countries for specific projects (typically infrastructure) would reduce poverty.[2]
- Third, investments in education and health care might have the largest multipliers per dollar of investment in economic development. Therefore, aid must be skewed to these sectors.
- The record of aid and loans from the various donor countries and the World Bank, International Monetary Fund, and other institutions is at best mixed. More recently, the development community is paying attention to the role of the private sector in building markets.

There have been few voices of dissent to the dominant logic of the development community. Hernando De Soto, in his path-breaking book, *The Mystery of Capital*, challenged the assumption that poor countries are poor.[3] Poor countries could often be asset-rich but capital-poor. Assets cannot become capital unless the country guarantees a rule of law—primarily the law of contracts—whereby the ownership of assets is clear; and because of clear legal title, these assets can be sold, bought, mortgaged, or converted into other assets. It is this concept of legal ownership that converts assets into capital. This is a compelling argument. De Soto also demonstrated in his work that the trapped resources—assets that cannot be converted into capital because of underdeveloped legal framework and institutions—can be significant. For example, he estimated that the trapped resources of Mexico are about $300 billion. In Egypt, the estimate is about $198 billion. This perspective suggests that poverty is, at least partially, a self-imposed problem in most of the world. Local capital formation and the functioning of markets are stymied by the lack of appropriate institutional arrangements.

We can derive several conclusions from this:

1. All forms of foreign investment in poor countries—whether aid, FDI by multinational firms (the private sector), or philanthropy—are but a fraction of the potential for capital that is trapped in these countries.
2. In the absence of enforceable contract law, local commerce is conducted by a vibrant extralegal or informal sector (or the black market). This is the primary face of the private sector in most developing countries.[4] These firms in the informal sector are unable to grow because they cannot attract capital. They remain small, local, and often inefficient.
3. There are contract enforcement systems that are local. Each slum might have its own unwritten but clearly understood rules. Enforcement might be the privilege of the local "strongmen."

This is the ultimate paradox. Poor countries might be rich if we consider trapped assets. They might have a vibrant private sector and a market economy, although this private sector is informal, fragmented, and local. Ironically, these economies tend to be high cost with poor access to credit and inefficient systems of management.[5] However, not all poor countries have a poor legal structure. Some merely lack the ability to enforce the laws. India, for example, is not Congo. In India, contract law is well-developed but enforcement mechanisms are not. What, then, is the problem?

The consultants from McKinsey & Company believe that the laws on the books are not enough. It is how laws are implemented at the ground level through a system of microregulations that matters. In a study jointly conducted with the Confederation of Indian Industries (CII), the McKinsey consultants found that the cost of microregulations in the areas of import–export, labor laws, and transactions involving land can be as high as 2 to 3 percent of GDP growth.[6] Microregulations result from bureaucratic interpretation of the laws. The proliferation of regulations can make the system opaque to anyone but the very savvy. De Soto argued that his country, Peru, enacts more than 28,000 pieces of legislation per year at the rate of more than 100 per day. No one can keep pace with that rate of change.[7] Interpretation of the regulations can compromise the timely execution of contracts and the clear establishment of ownership. As a result, corruption at all levels of bureaucracy can become endemic. The consequence of proliferation of microregulations can be the same as not having laws in the first place. An informal sector emerges outside the law of the land. The private-sector businesses remain small and local. For large firms, corruption becomes the cost of doing business.

Yet another variant of the same phenomenon is that the laws are underdeveloped. As a result, bureaucrats have a significant influence on the interpretation of the law (or the desires of the state). In spite of this, business can flourish. China represents a case in point. Oddly enough, in China, the bureaucrats are also the entrepreneurs. It is in the interest of the bureaucrats to guarantee a level of "certainty" in the interpretation of the contract—implicit and explicit. In the absence of laws and institutions that govern contracts, aligning the interests of the private sector and bureaucracy seems to have worked in building a vibrant economy in China. However, the poor in villages might be paying a price. For example, in the absence of institutions and laws, farmland can be appropriated for other uses by bureaucrats without a legal recourse for the farmer.

Given these variations, what is the secret for the evolution of a market economy in the BOP markets? What are the essential requirements for active private-sector involvement in development? I believe that the key lies in a nation's TGC.

TGC

Fundamental to the evolution of capital markets and a vibrant private sector is the need for a transparent market for capital, land, labor, commodities, and knowledge. **Transparency results from widely understood and clearly enforced rules. Transactions involving these rules must be clear and unambiguous.** Ownership and the transfer of ownership must be enforced. Under such a system, assets can become capital. Investors will seek the best opportunities. TGC is the capacity of a society to guarantee transparency in the process of economic transactions and the ability to enforce commercial contracts. This is about reducing uncertainty as to ownership and transfer of ownership. Transparency in the process reduces transaction costs. Clearly developed laws, transparent microregulations, social norms, and timely and uniform enforcement are all part of TGC. My argument is that TGC is more important than laws that are not enforced.

BOP consumers live in a wide variety of countries with varying degrees of TGC. Consider the spectrum:

1. Countries that are arbitrary and authoritarian. Laws do not exist and the laws that do exist are not enforced. Congo is an example of this situation. Private-sector development, in the Western sense, is very unlikely here. The only FDI that is likely is focused on the extraction of mineral wealth.
2. Countries where laws and institutions of a market economy exist. The private sector is vibrant. Still, the country does not reach its potential. India is a case in point. Alternatively, the GDP growth is great, but the underlying legal systems are not fully developed. China is an example.
3. Countries with well-developed laws, regulations, institutions, and enforcement systems. The United States is an example.

We can look at the spectrum of TGC as shown in Figure 5.1.

TGC captures the dilemma that the BOP consumers and the private sector face. A country like Congo will have a long wait before an active private sector will propel the economy. However, both China and India

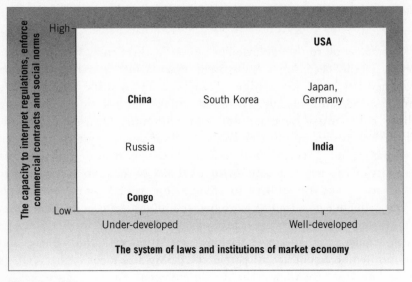

Figure 5.1   TGC.

are growing rapidly. They are the only two large countries showing more than 5 percent GDP growth over a decade. Both countries have significant corruption. Estimates of nonperforming assets on the books are as high as 50 percent of GDP for China and 20 percent for India. However, they have to travel different roads to become full-fledged market economies. As commercial transactions become large, complex, and multiyear, traditional approaches to bureaucratic interpretation and enforcement in China become problematic. China must develop laws and institutions. India must become more aggressive in enforcement. Political and bureaucratic intransigence will hurt investments and growth.

There is a need for us to recognize that economic growth fueled by the market economy around the world is not a single, monolithic problem. Each country has its own road to travel. Easy prescriptions that suggest that enacting laws will suffice are as naive as suggesting that contract enforcement even without laws provides adequate protection. The migration path toward the goal of a fully functioning market economy will be different depending on the point of departure for each country. Private-sector investors seek certainty— enforcement—over laws on the books. Enforcement allows firms to compute the cost of doing business in a system. That is the reason that most MNCs continue to prefer China over India: a clear preference for enforcement capacity over the legal system on the books. In China, corrupt as they are, the bureaucrats and politicians can enforce a contract. However, the corrupt in India cannot necessarily enforce contracts consistently. The checks and balances built into the Indian polity, especially the press and the multiparty political system, continually unearth corruption in contracts.

Building TGC

TGC is about creating transparency and eliminating uncertainty and risk in commercial transactions. The specifications for TGC are fourfold:

1. A system of laws that allows for ownership and transfer of property.
2. A process for changing the laws governing property rights that is clear and unambiguous. Democracies provide a safety net from idiosyncratic changes. For example, in the United States, the process by which new laws are enacted is clear and unambiguous. The process in democracies is arduous and open. This provides a share of voice to all the affected in shaping the laws.
3. As societies become more complex, a system of regulations that accommodates complex transactions.
4. Institutions that allow the laws to be implemented fairly, in a timely fashion, and with transparency.

TGC is more than laws or regulations. For example, de Soto found that there are 71 procedures and 31 agencies that are involved in legally acquiring and registering land in Egypt. The situation is no different in other developing countries. However, to come to the conclusion that microregulations are the problem would be premature. The United States is full of microregulations, as anyone who has tried to build a new factory can testify. The regulations are even more complex if it happens to be a chemical factory. In addition to regular procedures involved in building a factory, additional regulations for a chemical factory can add to the difficulty of getting a license. Microregulations are an integral part of any complex legal system.

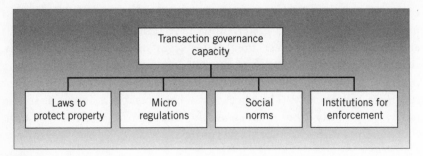

Figure 5.2 Components of TGC.

TGC consists of laws, regulations, social norms, and institutions. We need to think of the various components of TGC as a portfolio, shown in Figure 5.2.

Each country and economy might need a different portfolio of the elements of the TGC: One size might not fit all. The goal is to increase the TGC of a society in such a way that a vibrant private sector can flourish. We need to recognize that each country is at a different starting point.

I believe that the real problem is how bureaucracies deal with citizens. Consider a farmer in India, a semiliterate person approaching government officials to register his land. He will be approached by "brokers," who are the facilitators of the transaction. They fill out the forms for the farmer, lobby with the authorities, and ostensibly make the process easy. The total cost of the transaction for the farmer consists of the fee paid to the broker for his services (an uncertain percentage of the value of the transaction), the registration fee, and the bribes paid to corrupt officials. The process is so opaque to the farmer that the broker and the officials have opportunities to be arbitrary about the quality of the title and the value of the land. More important, they have the ability to decide how long the process will take. They can give this particular case the level of priority that they think is appropriate. Corruption is about providing privileged access to resources and recognizing the time value of money. *Corruption is a market mechanism for privileged access*. Bureaucrats use microregulations to control access, transparency, and therefore time.

TGC is about eliminating the opaqueness in the system and providing ease of access. Changing laws and regulations does not help the ordinary citizen if the system is not transparent or if access is not easy. From the point of view of the citizen, TGC must fulfill four criteria:

1. Access to information and transparency for all transactions.
2. Clear processes so that selective interpretation by bureaucrats is reduced, if not eliminated.
3. Speed with which the processes can be completed by citizens.
4. Trust in the system (with its faults). Trust is a result of the first three criteria, and is a crucial component of TGC.

I prefer to start with building ease of access and transparency, even before the regulations and the laws are changed to reduce selective interpretation. How?

The Andhra Pradesh e-Governance Story[8]

Let us look at one bold move by the Chief Minister of Andhra Pradesh, Nara Chandrababu Naidu. Andhra Pradesh is a state in India with 75 million people, 48 percent of whom are illiterate. Seventy percent are involved in agriculture. The GDP per capita is a low $600. Fifty percent have no electricity and 69 percent have no running water. Five distinct languages are spoken in the state. There are an estimated 15.6 million households and 2 million farms. Citizens depend on the state for a wide variety of services, from admission to schools to birth and death certificates, paying utility bills, taxes, driver's licenses, and registering property. The role of the government is pervasive. Therefore, a large bureaucracy has evolved to administer the various laws and regulations. There are more than 1 million government employees servicing 75 million citizens, a ratio of 13 to 14 government employees per 1,000 citizens. The system is opaque and the opportunities for corruption are high. This appears to be an unlikely place for a world-class experiment to develop good TGC.

Naidu decided in 1998 to make his state the model state in India. His approach was unique: He wanted to use digital technologies and the Internet as the basis for making his government responsive and citizen-centric. The goal was to reverse the process from an institution-centric civil service (citizens adjust to the requirements of the bureaucracy and government) to a citizen-centric system (a bureaucracy that is accountable to the citizens who elect the government). This concept was a 180-degree turn from the prevailing norm. The intended transformation is visualized in Figure 5.3.

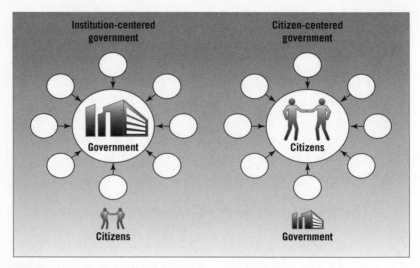

Figure 5.3   Intended transformation to citizen-centric governance.

Over a period of five years, a wide variety of governmental systems and services was brought online. Let us continue with the land registration process as an example. What has changed? The work flow has not changed. However, the quality of interaction between the citizen and the system has changed in the following ways:

1. All the steps that are required are now transparent and easy to access. The sequence of steps to be followed is also clear. All interdependent steps are completed automatically.

2. In the old system, the officials calculated the value of the land and the associated fees for registration. There were opportunities for selective value assessment. Now the entire process of calculation is automated with market value assessment algorithms built in. The documents are scanned and stored digitally, reducing the opportunities for them to be lost or misplaced.

3. The entire process of registration of land now takes one hour (from initiation to completion), compared to 7 to 15 days in the old system. Title searches over the past 20 years from 50 different offices can be done in 15 minutes versus three days. Certified copies of documents can be obtained in 30 minutes against the three days in the conventional system.

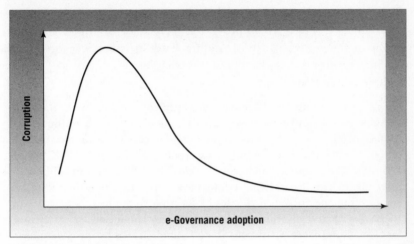

Figure 5.4 Corruption and e-governance.

No laws have changed here and no regulations have been eliminated. However, the transparency, access, and time to transact business have changed dramatically. Andhra Pradesh has more than 2.8 million land records on digital files that can be accessed by citizens on the Internet from their homes or through Internet kiosks set up by the government.

Land registration is one of the key areas in which TGC can help. However, the transition to an all-digital, Internet-enabled system will not be without glitches. Actually, it might increase corruption before it reduces it dramatically as shown in Figure 5.4. The logic is fairly straightforward. E-governance[9] requires the education of the citizen as well as bureaucrats and politicians. Citizens who have grown up with a system of bribes to get things done are unlikely to believe that this is different. They need to experience the difference. Officials who recognize that this will dramatically alter their ability to wield power and extract "speed money" will extract bribes to get the records properly digitized. The opportunity for altering the records before digitizing is high. Finally, all officials do not see that the system will be reducing opportunities for corruption immediately. Some will persist and must be prosecuted. Therefore, in the initial stages of implementation of the system, we should not be surprised if the level of corruption increases. However, the shape of the corruption curve, over time, is not in question.

This schematic is important to bear in mind as countries move toward e-governance as a way to improve the TGC. For example, the initial reaction to the e-governance in Andhra Pradesh is best captured in the following excerpt taken from our research on e-governance reported elsewhere in the book:

Using a sophisticated document management system with imaging technology, the land registration department digitized 2.8 million land records dated from 1983 onward and implemented the project in 387 offices around the state. A pilot was conducted in 1996 at a cost of $55,000. The project, which was launched in 1998, cost $6 million to implement. The department is integrating all 148 offices in the state, empowering the citizen to choose the location where he or she wants to transact with the government. A recent survey conducted by the Center for Good Governance (CGG), the think tank instituted by the government of Andhra Pradesh and the Department of International Development, uncovered disappointing insights into the current registration process. Eighty-seven percent (90 percent rural and 80 percent urban) of all those registering land went to the CARD office with the help of a document writer or a middle man. The average bribe paid was an additional 7.95 percent (2.85 percent urban and 25.81 percent rural) of the actual fees due. Eighty-three percent (60 percent urban and 94 percent rural) of citizens share the view that the registration officer is corrupt and 85 percent (64 percent urban and 96 percent rural) feel that the land department is corrupt. One hundred percent do not feel that the government of Andhra Pradesh has done anything to tackle corruption in the registration department. The study also observed that citizens and document writers consistently underdeclare the actual transaction price and real market values are far higher than those kept on the CARD systems. Rural transaction prices (Rs. 550,000) are underdeclared on average by Rs. 48,000 each. Urban transaction prices (Rs. 450,000) are undeclared by Rs. 36,000 each. This adds up to a potential annual revenue loss to the government of Andhra Pradesh of Rs. 4.5 billion. The think tank recommends privatization of the front office as one of the ways to reduce corruption. This would mean providing land registration services through the zero-corrupt Internet kiosk environment.

The survey confirms the logic of the corruption curve; corruption is bound to increase in the near time, peaking and then steadily declining to near-zero levels. Once the system is fully operational, it is difficult to change the data in the system. Further, all entries will leave a trail, indicating who as well as when. This level of scrutiny and openness will reduce the opportunities for corruption.

Last Name (Print) _____ First Name _____ Initial _____

Street Address (Mailing address also, if different) _____

City or Post Office _____ State _____ Zip Code _____ Area Code-Phone Number _____

Alternate Address (College or Out-Of-State Residence) _____ E-Mail Address _____

Please Circle Age Group:

1) AG00 Pre 1919   2) AG01 1919-1928   3) AG02 1929-1938   4) AG03 1939-1948

5) AG04 1949-1958   6) AG05 1959-1968   7) AG06 1969-1978   8) AG07 1979-1988

9) AG08 1989-1998   10) AG09 1999-2008

BIRTH DATE _____

I agree to abide to Library rules and understand that I am liable for all materials checked out on my card in accordance with the rules of the Greenville Library and the laws of the state of Rhode Island. I have read, and understand, the law regarding overdue materials which is printed on my library card. I understand that when I use my CLAN (Cooperating Libraries Automated Network) card in another library which accepts it, I must abide by the library's rules and regulations. If I am signing for a minor (anyone under the age of 18) I will be held responsible for the use of the minor's card until he/she reaches the age of 18, or until I, in writing, notify the Greenville Library that I no longer wish to be responsible for the card holder.

We comply with ADA requirements.

Signature of Applicant _____

R.I. Lic# _____ CLAN Barcode _____ Date _____

Signature of parent or guardian for minor _____

TGC is not just about large, one-time transactions that people engage in, such as buying land or property. Every citizen depends on the government for much of his or her day-to-day existence. Paying utility bills, getting a license for opening a shop, and getting admission to a college using birth and caste certificates are all part of a citizen's dependence on government. That is where the government of Andhra Pradesh turned next.

eSeva

The government of Andhra Pradesh has now set up eSeva (literally, "e-service") to provide ease of access to services from the government and its agencies. eSeva centers are operated through a public–private partnership model. This is outsourcing of government functions to the private sector. The government of Andhra Pradesh is trying several models, including build-own-operate (BOO) and build-own-operate-transfer (BOOT).

eSeva can be accessed via the Internet or through the kiosks[10] set up by the government. Citizens can pay water and electricity bills through eSeva. They can get their driver's license. They can pay their property taxes. There are more than 45 integrated state and federal services currently available to citizens through this system. The list of services is given in the Appendix. Imagine the losses that this approach to government service can eliminate. It used to take a minimum of half a day for a worker to go to the Electricity Department and pay his or her monthly bill, and 3.5 million bills are paid per month in the city of Hyderabad alone. If we compute the frictional cost at a meager wage rate of Rs. 50 per half day (U.S. $1.00) per person, it totals a staggering Rs. 2.1 billion per year. The cost to the citizens of just paying electricity bills is a staggering collective wage loss of about U.S. $45 million in one city. There is also a host of other bills to be paid and services that require the citizen to go to government offices and wait. Again the paradox is that the poor pay a heavy price for basic services. In the eSeva system, a citizen can, in one trip to the kiosk, transact all routine business with the state at the same time without "speed money."

A wide variety of ordinary citizens was interviewed for our research on what they thought of these services and they reacted favorably. Here are some citizens' reactions in their own words:

"There is absolutely NO corruption in eSeva."

"We needn't stand in long lines in the hot sun and waste time."

"All transactions are visible and it is easy for us to pay all bills in a single location."

" eSeva system is beautiful."

"We are not harassed anymore at the hands of government employees."

"I can get back to work to earn my hourly wages."

Unlike most government establishments, the eSeva centers[11] are clean and citizens receive the same levels of service regardless of their economic class. The services are used by an average of 1,000 citizens per day, ranging from 400 to 2,000 people. The software system is cleverly designed to prevent corruption and create accountability at every level. More important, every detail in a transaction is permanently recorded into a database in Telugu, the local language. Of the 750,404 transactions in March 2003, the number of transactions that had a rupee value below Rs. 100 ($2.00) contributed 11 percent (presumably the poor), greater than Rs. 20,000 ($400) about 1 percent, and the middle segment, Rs. 100 to Rs. 20,000, about 80 percent. Considering the amount collected during the period, the middle segment contributed 73 percent of the Rs. 4.3 billion.

It is important to recognize that an Internet-based system such as eSeva can be of great help to a large number of educated citizens, be they rich or poor. The educated can access their own records, pay their bills online, and get the benefits of the system. How about the illiterate and poor? By providing the urban poor with access to the kiosks and help from the kiosk operators, the long waits and trips to multiple agencies can be eliminated. The intermediary is still needed. He or she is not a broker but is the operator, a private-sector employee, in the kiosk. The satisfaction scores from the citizens with eSeva services are high, even with an intermediary, with no opportunity to be corrupt. The access to eSeva for the rural poor is still to be implemented at the time of this writing. The goal of the government of Andhra Pradesh is to have 100 percent access throughout the state by 2005.

Center for Good Governance

Although the governance initiatives set up by Andhra Pradesh are praiseworthy, it is important that the direction of change, the quality of implementation, and progress are measured. With this in mind, the government of Andhra Pradesh, in collaboration with the International

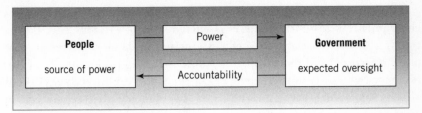

Figure 5.5 Good governance model.

Development Institute of the United Kingdom, has set up an independent watchdog agency called the Center for Good Governance (CGG). The role of the CGG is to monitor the implementation of the ICT approach to citizen-centric governance and publish independent and periodic reports of how the entire process is proceeding. The CGG is authorized to challenge the government agencies. Further, it makes recommendations to the Chief Minister on what needs to be changed.

The CGG approach is based on the simple premise that power in a democracy is derived from the people and government must be accountable to them (see Figure 5.5).[12] Obvious as this is, the basic premise of an elected government is often lost in the bureaucratic and regulatory maze.

Needless to say, good governance, as shown in Figure 5.5, cannot be achieved without a clear set of guiding principles, performance indicators and measurements, and constant attention to improvement of the underlying processes.

The guiding principles of CGG in Andhra Pradesh are listed in Table 5.1.

Table 5.1 Guiding Principles of the CGG in Andhra Pradesh

Guiding Principles	Explanation
Consultation	Public consulted regarding service level and quality.
Service standards	Educate public on level of service entitled.
Access	Equal access regardless of societal position.
Courtesy	Treat people with courtesy and consideration.
Information	Give public full and accurate information about service.
Openness and transparency	Inform public about government operations and budget.
Redress	Apologize and redress if promised service is not given.
Value for money	Public services provided economically and efficiently.

A performance management system (PMS) for the efforts of the government of Andhra Pradesh is introducing a citizen-centric view through a wide variety of schemes, including land registration (2.8 million records) and monitoring of public spending programs. The Chief Minister (who calls himself the CEO of the state) can directly access any village, bypassing the usual layers of bureaucracy that separated the ministers from their constituencies. The chief minister of Andhra Pradesh started town meetings (via videoconferencing facilities) with the villages randomly chosen. That further cemented the transparency and access available to ordinary citizens.

> According to Dr. P.K. Mohanty, Executive Director of the Center for Good Governance, the PMS was developed as a "hexagonal model." In other words, it can be used to rate a department on six variables: 1) relative performance compared to last year, 2) relative performance compared to peers now, 3) relative performance compared to peers last year, 4) relative performance to benchmarks, 5) relative performance to targets, and 6) relative performance compared to government as a whole. This model presents a complete picture of a particular department over time, allowing senior officials to get to the root cause of problems that arise.

How does the performance system work? Is the transition to the system smooth and without tensions? Do bureaucrats believe in the system? What is the role of political leadership in making this system work? TGC cannot be enhanced without a deep commitment from the top. The researchers witnessed the monthly meeting of the Chief Minister (CM) with the district collectors. These monthly meetings were one of the tools used to implement the system and identify problem areas. Here is an excerpt from the case story on the government of Andhra Pradesh:

Researchers witnessed firsthand the PMS in action. The CM holds monthly, sometimes weekly, video teleconferences with all 26 district collectors. The CM is located in Hyderabad, and each district collector is located in his or her respective district headquarters. Each district collector was joined by 50 other personnel. Interesting to note was that the press was given full and open access to this meeting; in fact, they recorded the entire five-hour meeting.

> Various subjects were covered throughout the meeting, with the CM driving the discussions. Significant time was spent on the issue of drought remediation actions taken by the districts. The CM was using data from the PMS and forcing the district collectors to explain any negative trends.

It was very evident when a particular employee was not familiar with the data that had been entered. What the reader needs to realize is that this was taking place live in front of more than 1,000 government employees across the state, plus the press. The pressure to perform in front of peers is a huge motivational factor for the district collectors.

The CM also used this forum to discuss public opinion numbers. Each district collector was again asked why things were going poorly in his or her area and what he or she planned to do about it. It was evident during the meeting that many of the figures that had been input in the system were not the "actual" numbers, but simply placeholders that were entered by the cut-off time, four hours before the meeting. Staff scrambled to present the CM with appropriate numbers, especially, when the new numbers were better than the fictitious ones. Transparency such as this, in front of the press, is forcing government officials to embrace the PMS. Also, they must now pay attention to the citizens and perform only actions that are really important.

During these meetings, the CM chooses a random subject to scrutinize. At this particular meeting, commodity prices were picked. The officer in charge of this was caught, and subsequently embarrassed, because he had entered data simply to enter data. Quite often his commodity prices were off by a factor of 10 or 100! There is no doubt this particular individual will input proper data from now on. No doubt seeing one's peers publicly embarrassed will encourage district collectors to make sure that proper data are input by their staffs.

Although the systems are in place, they are still works in process. E-governance increases the TGC of a society through increased transparency, accountability, speed, and accessibility. Such citizen-centric governance creates a better economic climate by reducing risk. However, the concept, the approach to implementation, and the initial results suggest that it can lead to improved TGC. Further, improved TGC can lead to development. Conceptually, the virtuous cycle is shown in Figure 5.6.

Impediments

One should not conclude that this experiment is a done deal. There are significant impediments to the entire process, the most important being the education of the citizen. For decades, the citizens associated

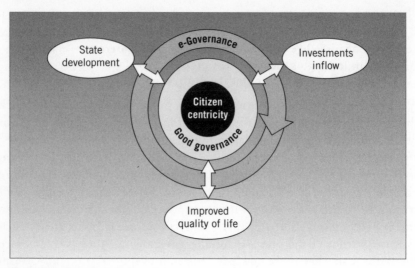

Figure 5.6   The virtuous cycle.

corruption, sweat, long lines, and humiliation with government, so they are likely to look at these initiatives with skepticism. Only consistent performance can convince the skeptics. The bigger problem is with the employees—the functionaries within the government. Initially, they accepted these initiatives because no one was displaced by the e-governance initiatives. No changes were made to the underlying processes. As might be expected, in the initial stages, the potential for "speed money" was not severely compromised. However, in the second phase of implementation this will start to change. The regulations and governmental business processes can be simplified. Interconnected systems will be able to identify pockets of graft and corruption. Records cannot be easily altered or lost. The change will not come easily. It is the support of the citizens and the pressure from them for change that can reduce the political price for moving forward with these initiatives. The benefit of TGC is worth the risk.

Lessons from the Andhra Pradesh Experiment

There are several lessons to be learned from the experiment in Andhra Pradesh. Transformation of a well-entrenched system takes not only building an IT system, but also building trust. Citizens must feel that changes are taking place. The experience with eSeva is therefore critical. The services offered by eSeva allow citizens to experience streamlined services, not just once in their lifetimes (as in buying or selling land and property) but frequently (as in paying electricity and water bills every month). Furthermore, confidence-building requires that citizens experience a high quality of service with no corruption in a wide variety of services such as getting a driver's license or a birth certificate. TGC is about communicating a consistency in the behaviors of the bureaucracy and governmental institutions. Citizens must convince themselves that it is cheaper to be within the system than outside it. The shift from the informal sector to the formal sector will take place if ordinary citizens can be confident that:

$$\frac{\text{The cost of being } inside \text{ the system}}{\text{The cost of being } outside \text{ the system}} \leq 1$$

Ordinary people instinctively recognize that there are costs to being within the system. They have to declare their assets and pay taxes. They also recognize that there are costs to being outside the system. They have to be beholden to local politicians and a cruel system of enforcement of local practices with no legal recourse. The cost is high and difficult to predict. Bureaucratic corruption had made the cost of being inside the system too high for most citizens and the benefits too low. Poor access to the formal system and its lack of transparency compared to social norms force people to seek a higher cost option, but one where the rules are clear (even if cruel).

Corruption, as we said, is a market for privileged access. It thrives in a system that allows for opaque decision-making. The cost of being inside the system will decrease only if governments tackle the issues of access and transparency and recognize the changes needed in both the regulations and the laws. The experiment in Andhra Pradesh is one example of how digital technologies can be used to creatively enhance TGC through better access and transparency.

Building TGC is not only the job of the government. It does play a significant role in ensuring that corruption is reduced, but market-based ecosystems that large firms can create, as we saw in Chapter 4, can also increase TGC in a society. The combination of the two, with the use of digital technologies, can rapidly transform the TGC of a country.

Endnotes

1. Some would argue that development assistance was based on the belief that although resources might exist (e.g., Nigeria), they might have a bottleneck in some of the critical ingredients to development. In this sense, development assistance was a "complement," not a substitute.

2. The focus of development aid has also shifted from infrastructure, education, and structural adjustments over the decades.

3. Hernando de Soto. *The Mystery of Capital: Why Capitalism Triumphs in the West and Fails Everywhere Else*. Basic Books, New York.

4. It is important to distinguish the informal, extralegal sector from the private sector even though the informal sector is about entrepreneurship under very hostile conditions.

5. C. K. Prahalad and Allen Hammond. "Serving the World's Poor, Profitably." *The Harvard Business Review*, September 2002.

6. CII-McKinsey Report on Learning from China to Unlock India's Manufacturing Potential, March, 2002.

7. Hernando De Soto. Presentation at the World Economic Forum, Davos, Switzerland, 2004.

8. Supportive case written by Praveen Suthrum and Jeff Phillips under the supervision of Professor C. K. Prahalad. Copyright © The University of Michigan Business School, 2003.

9. The World Bank defines e-government as the use of information and communications technologies to improve the efficiency, effectiveness, transparency, and accountability of government (*http://www1.worldbank.org/publicsector/egov/*). I prefer to use the term e-governance, as it refers to a broader relationship between the political system and society. The terms e-governance, e-government, and e-democracy are used interchangeably in the literature.

10. Available only in towns and cities in Andhra Pradesh. Kiosks will cover the entire state in two years.

11. Our researchers visited three eSeva centers in Andhra Pradesh's capital city, Hyderabad, and one in the village of Nagampally.

12. This view is accepted in a vibrant democracy. How about countries that are not democratic (even if they hold "mock elections")? The idea of ultimate accountability to the citizen is fundamental to good governance.

Appendix: List of eSeva Services

Payment of utility bills	Renewal of trade licenses
Electricity	Change of address of a vehicle owner
Water and sewerage	Transfer of ownership of a vehicle
Telephone bills	Issue of driving licenses
Property tax	Renewal of driving licenses
Filing of CST returns	(nontransport vehicles)
Filing of A2 returns of APGST	Registration of new vehicles
Filing of AA9 returns of APGST	Quarterly tax payments of autos
Collection of examination fee	Quarterly tax payments of goods
Filing of IT returns of salaried class	vehicles
Sale of prepaid parking tickets	Lifetime tax payments of new vehicles
Permits and licenses	

Certificates	Reservations and other services
Registration of birth	Reservation of APSRTC bus tickets
Registration of death	Reservation of water tanker
Issue of birth certificates	Filing of passport applications
Issue of death certificates	Sale of nonjudicial stamps
Internet services	Sale of trade license applications
Internet-enabled electronic payments	Sale of National Games tickets
Downloading of forms and government orders	Sale of entry tickets for WTA
	Sale of EAMCET applications

Business to Consumer (B2C) services
Collection of telephone bill payments
Sale of new AirTel prepaid phone cards
Top up/recharge of AirTel Magic cards
Sale of entry tickets for Tollywood Star cricket
Sale of entry tickets for Cricket match (RWSO)
Filing of Reliance CDMA mobile phone connections

- Railway reservation
- Sale of movie tickets
- Payment of traffic-related offenses
- Payment of degree examination fees of O.U.

- Sale of I-CET applications
- Online reservation of Tirupati Temple tickets
- Collection of bill payments of Idea Cellular
- Collection of bill payments of HUTCH
- Issue of encumbrance certificate
- Market value assistance
- General insurance
- Reservation of tourism tickets for accommodation
- Reservation of tourism bus tickets
- Call center
- Indian Airlines ticket reservation
- Life insurance premium payment
- Issue of caste certificates
- Sale of Indira Vikas Patra
- ATM services
- Collection of bill payments of Air Tel
- Renewal of drug licenses
- Issue of bus passes
- Collection of trade licenses of Labor Department

6

Development as
Social Transformation

We have looked at the BOP as a viable and profitable growth market. We have also understood that treating the BOP as a market can lead to poverty reduction, particularly if NGOs and community groups can join with MNCs and local companies as business partners. The development of markets and effective business models at the BOP can transform the poverty alleviation task from one of constant struggle with subsidies and aid to entrepreneurship and the generation of wealth. **When the poor at the BOP are treated as consumers, they can reap the benefits of respect, choice, and self-esteem and have an opportunity to climb out of the poverty trap.** As small and micro-enterprises, many of them informal, become partners to MNCs, entrepreneurs at the BOP develop real access to global markets and capital and effective transaction governance. MNCs gain access to large new markets, developing innovative practices that can increase profitability in both BOP and mature markets.

National and local governments have an important role to play in this process. They have to create the enabling conditions for active private-sector involvement in creating this BOP market opportunity. TGC is a prerequisite. Governments now have new tools to create TGC in a short period of time. Further, new technologies and new approaches to reaching the BOP such as SHGs and direct distribution (creating millions of new entrepreneurs) can also create a respect for the rule of law and commercial contracts among the BOP consumers (e.g., as they access credit through the microfinance route) and local entrepreneurs. **The capabilities to solve the perennial problem of poverty through profitable businesses at the BOP are now available to most nations, as we have illustrated. However, converting the poor into a market will require innovations.** The methodologies for innovation at the BOP are different from and more demanding than the traditional approaches, but so is the opportunity for significant profitable growth. Finally, BOP markets represent a global opportunity. Lessons learned at the BOP can transform MNC operations in developed countries as well. BOP can be the engine for the next round of global expansion of trade and good will. If we follow this approach, what impact will it have on the BOP consumers? How will their lives change?

Development as Social Transformation

We have come full circle. We have made three transitions in our thinking. First, we demonstrated that the BOP—the poor—can be a market. Second, once we accept the BOP as a market, the only way to serve that market is to innovate. The BOP demands a range of innovations in products and services, business models, and management processes. Third, these innovations must be accompanied by increased TGC, making the government accountable to the citizens and making it accessible and transparent. Market-based ecosystems can also facilitate the process of making transparency, access, and respect for commercial contracts a way of life. The intellectual transitions that are the substance of this book and its implications are visualized in Figure 6.1

How will these changes impact life at the BOP? **As BOP consumers get an opportunity to participate in and benefit from the choices of products and services made available through market mechanisms, the accompanying social and economic transformation can be very rapid.** The reason for this is that BOP consumers are very entrepreneurial and can easily imagine ways in which they can use their newly found access to information, choice, and infrastructure. Let us look at some examples:

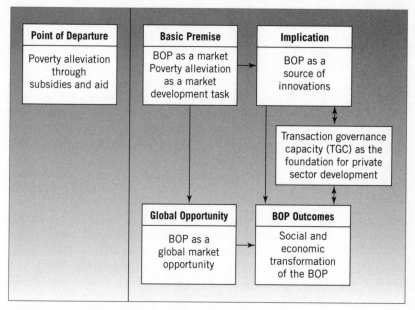

Figure 6.1 The Private sector and the BOP: Transitions.

The ITC e-Choupal infrastructure was created for farmers to have access to information regarding prices as well as agriculture-related information, as shown in Table 6.1. The system was configured to make them productive farmers and to make the supply chain for soybeans more efficient so that there was a win for both the farmer and ITC. That was the intent.

It took farmers fewer than three months to understand the strength of the Internet and they started using the system for a host of other, non-business-related and socially beneficial tasks. They found that they could connect with each other and chat about a whole range of issues, not just agriculture and prices. They found that the PC could be an entertainment device. It could be used to play movies, listen to songs, and watch cricket (a sport that is a national obsession in India). They could print out the classroom grades of their children. They also became very sophisticated in tracking prices, not just at the local mandi or ITC prices, but also for futures at the Chicago Board of Trade. They were able to correlate intuitively the futures prices with the prices they should expect in selling to ITC or others. They were establishing a clear link between global price movements and the prices in remote villages of northern India. Just three months earlier they were "hostages" to the

Table 6.1   Intended Uses of ITC e-Choupal System

Features	Description and Operational Goals
Weather	Users can select their district of interest by clicking on the appropriate region of a map. Localized weather information is presented on regions within a 25-km range. Typically, 24–72-hour weather forecasts are available along with an advisory. The advisories are pieces of information directly related to the farmer, which he can put to use. For instance, during the sowing season, a weather forecast for days following rains might include the advisory that instructs the farmer to sow when the soil is still wet. Weather data is obtained from the Indian Meteorological Department, which has a presence even in small towns and can provide forecasts for rural areas.
Pricing	The e-Choupal Web site displays both the rate at which ITC offers to procure commodities and the prevailing mandi rates. ITC's next-day rates are published every evening. The prices are displayed prominently on the top of the Web page on a scrolling ticker.
News	For the soyachoupal Web site, relevant news is collated from various sources and presented. Aside from agriculture-related news, this section also includes current affairs, entertainment, sports, and local news.
Best practices	Here, best farming practices are documented (by crop). Here again, the information presented is actionable. For instance, in this section the farmer would not only find what kind of fertilizers to use, but also how and when to use them.
Q & A	This feature enables two-way communication. Here a farmer can post any agriculture-related question he needs answered.

vagaries of the local merchants in the mandi. They also became experts at e-mail and chat capabilities. The list of dominant, unplanned activities that evolved in three to six months among the villages connected by the system is shown Table 6.2.

Breaking Down Barriers to Communication

ITC worked hard to create interfaces in the farmers' native language, Hindi. It also provided software that made it possible to type Hindi characters using a standard English keyboard. The preferred language for writing e-mails and other electronic communication, however, is "Hinglish," or Hindi typed with English characters. The reason for this is that combining vowels and consonants to create Hindi letters is a very

Table 6.2   Unplanned Activities at e-Choupal: The Social Transformation

News	Dainik jagran, Web Dunia
Market prices	One sanchalak actually followed Chicago Board of Trade prices for a month and arrived at a correlation with the local market prices. He used this information to help other farmers decide when to sell.
Entertainment	Movie trivia.
	Rent CDs to watch movies on the computer.
	Music downloads from the Internet.
Sports	Cricket-related news.
Education	Students use the Internet to check their results and grades online.
Communication	E-mail.
	The sanchalaks have e-mail accounts on Yahoo! Chat.
	Some sanchalaks frequent chat rooms and chat with other sanchalaks and ITC managers.
General interests/other	Information about cell phones.

cumbersome affair on a keyboard. It sometimes takes three keystrokes to render one letter. All the sanchalaks we spoke to agreed that this was the only aspect of computer usage they had not yet been able to master.

Undeterred, the sanchalaks started to use the English keyboard to write e-mails in Hindi. They were able to move fast in building both the capacity to communicate with the outside world and the ability to make themselves well-understood. The creativity in building communication patterns can be illustrated by one of the e-mails between a sanchalak in a remote village in northern India and the researcher in Ann Arbor, Michigan. There appear to be no barriers. The student in the United States was educated, rich, sophisticated, and well-traveled. The farmer probably never traveled beyond a cluster of villages, was poor and uneducated. All those boundaries were broken by the possibility of asynchronous communication through e-mail. We do not know how long it took to compose this e-mail, but suspect probably not long. It is very straightforward and to the point. The e-mail is shown in Figure 6.2.

The use of the infrastructure in creative ways is not confined to the sanchalaks. Across the board, BOP consumers are able to use the systems they have access to in ways unimagined by those providing the systems. What is the real change for those at the BOP? The real advantages of a private-sector network can be captured as shown in Table 6.3.

Date: Sunday, May 18, 2003 11:01 PM

From: arun nahar

To: <sachinr@umich.edu>

sachin ji namaste

aapka mail padkar khushi hui aapki english meri samajh mae aati hai agribusiness mae jaivik khad(bio-fertilizer) ke bare mae aapke kyaa vichar hai present polution ko dekhate hua future plan ke bare mae socha ja sakta hai public chemical less product khana pasand karte hai aane wale 10 years organic product ke honge organic product bio-fertilizer se taiyar hote hai village mae organic product taiyar kiye ja sakte hai in product ko sahi market dene ke liye aap network bana sakte ho

thanks

The English translation of this e-mail is as follows:

Date: Sunday, May 18, 2003 11.01 PM

From: arun nahar

To: sachin@umich.edu

Mr. Sachin, greetings

I was delighted to read your mail. I was able to understand your communication in English. What is your opinion about bio-fertilizers in agro-business? Considering current pollution, we can develop trends. People prefer meals, which are prepared with "chemical less products." For the next 10 years, markets will be dominated by organic products. Organic products can be produced with bio-fertilizers in our village. ("We can do it"). In order to market this product can you develop the distribution network?

Figure 6.2   E-mail from a sanchalak.

The simple case of the ITC e-Choupal, if repeated 1,000 times, can transform a country. We find increasingly that women from different villages who have never met each other are in chat rooms discussing complex issues like interest rate fluctuations and political positions to take with respect to specific issues. They also use it for more family-oriented topics. In one chat room on the n-Logue network in southern India, the women were discussing the status of their grandchildren or

Table 6.3   The Drivers of Social Transformation

Dimension of Social Transformation	Traditional	Emerging
Access to information	Limited	Unlimited; large firms, government, and bureaucracies in areas of interest to them.
Community	Locationally bound, typically a cluster of villages	Could be regional, national, and global.
Patterns of interaction and access to knowledge	Limited	Infinitely more; word of mouth "turbocharged."
Ability to make independent choices	Low	High and can get very sophisticated through dialogue and interaction.

other relatives living abroad. The newly found advantages are the building blocks of a market economy: transparency of information, universal access, dialogue among various thematic communities that form autonomously, and a discussion of the risks and benefits of various courses of action such as "Should I sell my corn today or hold back?" These four building blocks are dialogue, access, risk benefits, and transparency (DART). These are the same building blocks that are leading to more consumer activism in developed markets.[1]

BOP Consumers Upgrade

Contrary to popular belief, BOP consumers are always upgrading from their existing condition. MNCs and large firms oriented toward the top of the pyramid sometimes look at what the BOP consumers use and think of it as downgrading from the products they are selling. These products are seen as cheap. On the other hand, for the BOP consumers, the newly found choice is an upgrade from their current state of affairs. For example, when Nirma, a startup, introduced a detergent powder in India, the established firms in that business—both MNCs and large Indian firms—considered the product as low end and not of interest to them. At that time the total tonnage for high-end products was about 25,000 tons. Nirma was a new category, upgrading the BOP consumers from poor-quality, locally made soaps, and the brand built an impressive market of 300,000 tons. The lessons were not lost on the incumbents. The size of the market at the BOP is significant (300,000 tons vs. 25,000 tons at the top of the pyramid), but more important, Nirma was a product uniquely fashioned for the poor who wash clothes under a tap or in a running stream rather than in a washing machine.[2] The same process is evident in a wide variety of businesses, including financial services. When the BOP consumers opt for a loan from a bank, as opposed to a local moneylender, they are upgrading. When they use iodized salt over the locally available unbranded salt, they are upgrading. When they get access to good-quality building materials and a design for how to add an additional room from Cemex, they are upgrading. The examples can be multiplied. The message is simple: **For the BOP consumer, gaining access to modern technology and good products designed with their needs in mind enables them to take a huge step in improving their quality of life.**

Gaining Access to Knowledge

We have already examined the benefits of access and transparency and how that impacts the asymmetric information that was (and is) the norm in most BOP markets. However, once BOP consumers get access to digital technologies, the pattern of access to knowledge changes. For example, in the EID Parry Agriline example used in the book, the farmers had a concern about the quality of a particular crop: betelnut. They used their PCs and the attached cameras to send pictures of the affected leaves to a central agronomy center 600 miles away. They received advice from the agronomists at a remote location. That certainly improved their ability to solve the problem. Examples such as this one are proliferating by the day. It is becoming well-accepted in some parts of India that telemedicine is the way to go to get remote diagnostics based on PCs. Shanker Netralaya, for example, brings world-class eye care to rural India. It has vans fitted with optometric equipment that are connected via satellite hook-up to the hospital. Senior doctors can review complex cases on a two-way videoconferencing hook-up and discuss with the patients their problems. They can also offer a diagnosis based on images presented on a split screen. They can then recommend a course of action. This incredible access to very high-technology solutions is changing the way we think about the BOP consumers. Increasingly sensitized to what is possible, they are also demanding high-technology solutions to their problems.

Identity for the Individual

One of the common problems for those at the BOP is that they have no "identity." Often they are at the fringe of society and do not have a "legal identity," including voter registration, driver's license, or birth certificate. The instruments of legal identity that we take for granted—be it a passport or a Social Security number—are denied to them. For all practical purposes, they do not exist as legal entities. Because they do not have a legal existence, they cannot be the beneficiaries of a modern society. Voter registration in vibrant democracies, such as India, provides one form of identity. Erstwhile communist regimes had a system of documenting everyone, including the location to which they belonged. In Shanghai, for example, all the migrant workers were undocumented for a long time. They did not officially belong to Shanghai and therefore could not participate in programs such as government-assigned housing.

This picture starts to change as a private-sector ecosystem emerges. The individuals in an SHG have an identity. They are recognized as legal by the ICICI Bank. They all have a name, a designation, a group to which they belong, and a scheme in which they participate. The same is true of the eSeva service provided by the government of Andhra Pradesh. Now all citizens who pay their utility bills or register births and deaths have an identity. In fact, many BOP consumers are elated to see their names on a computer screen. This is universal. The poor in Brazil, when they shop in Casas Bahia, get an identity. They get a card from the company and that tells the world who they are. Consumers proudly display their Casas Bahia cards as proof of their existence as well as their creditworthiness. A similar situation exists in Mexico. When Cemex organizes women, it not only gives them the tools and the materials required for them to build a kitchen; it also gives them a legal identity. The women are bound to the firm and vice versa. Neither party can break the contract without penalty. That is a proof of legal identity.

The importance of legal identity cannot be underestimated. Without it, BOP consumers cannot access the services we take for granted, such as credit. Hernando de Soto documented the problems of a lack of legal identity at the BOP. The status of a "nonperson" in legal terms can confine people to a cycle of poverty.

Women Are Critical for Development

A well-understood but poorly articulated reality of development is the role of women. Women are central to the entire development process. They are also at the vanguard of social transformation. For example, Grameen Bank's success is based on lending only to women. The entrepreneurs who were able to use the microfinance made available were women. The Grameen phone "ladies" are the entrepreneurs. In the cases in this book, there is adequate evidence of the role of women in building a new society at the BOP. The SHGs at ICICI Bank are all women, as are the Shakti Ammas at HLL. These women are entrepreneurs responsible for saving and accessing credit. In the case of Cemex, the company works only with women. Amul, a milk cooperative, depends on women for their milk origination in villages. Women also collect the "cash" for the milk, and therefore have achieved a new social status. Access to economic independence can change the long tradition of suppression of women and denial of opportunities. The success of Avon, Mary Kay, and Tupperware in the United States and other parts of the world is also based on the role of women entrepreneurs. Although the evidence is overwhelming, very little explicit attention has been paid to actively co-opting women in the efforts to build markets and lead the development process. MNCs and large firms will do well to keep this in mind in their efforts to create new markets at the BOP.

Evolving Checks and Balances

It is natural for us to ask, "If the involvement of the private sector in BOP markets can have such a significant impact on social transformation, do we need checks and balances?" Yes. **We need to make sure that no organization abuses its power and influence, be it corrupt governments or large firms.** Fortunately, checks and balances are evolving rapidly. The spread of connectivity—wireless and TV—makes it impossible for any group to abuse its position for long. Further, civil society organizations are always on alert. However, the most important protection is informed, networked, and active consumers. The evolution of the BOP consumer is ultimately the real protection.

The social transformation that is taking place in markets where the public and the private sectors have been involved at the BOP is quite impressive. BOP consumers have constantly surprised the elite with their ability to adapt and their resilience. As we described in this chapter, they do the following:

1. They adapt to new technology without any difficulty and are willing to experiment and find new and "unforeseen" (by the firms) applications for the technology. Nobody thought that the farmers from the middle of India would check prices at the Chicago Board of Trade.
2. Technology is breaking down barriers to communication. Given that BOP consumers can increasingly enjoy the benefits of dialogue, access, risk benefit analysis and transparency (DART) and make informed choices, the chances of change in tradition will be improved.
3. BOP consumers now have a chance to upgrade and improve their lives.
4. By gaining access to a legal identity, they can participate more effectively in society and gain the benefits of the available opportunities. They do not have to remain marginalized.
5. Finally, the emancipation of women is an important part of building markets at the BOP. Empowered, organized, networked, and active women are changing the social fabric of society.

Taken together, these changes will lead to significant social change and transformation.

The Real Test: From the Pyramid to the Diamond

Although we have discussed the nature of social transformation that is possible at the BOP, the real test of the entire development process of development is poverty alleviation. How will we know it is taking place? Simply stated, the pyramid must become a diamond. The economic pyramid is a measure of income inequalities. If these inequalities are changing, then the pyramid must morph into a diamond. A diamond assumes that the bulk of the population is middle class. The morphing that we must seek to accomplish is shown in Figure 6.3.

There will always be "the rich," but a measure of development is the number of people in a society who are considered middle class. **More important, social transformation is about the number of people**

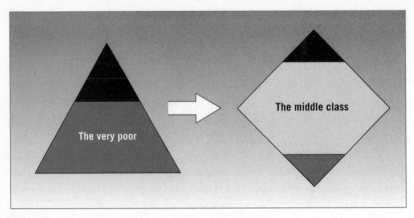

Figure 6.3 The morphing of the pyramid into a diamond.

who believe that they can aspire to a middle-class lifestyle. It is the growing evidence of opportunity, role models, and real signals of change that allow people to change their aspirations. Our goal is to rapidly change the pyramid into a diamond. To be confident that this transformation is occurring rapidly, we should be able, at a minimum, to measure the changing patterns of income inequities in a society. This is a relative measure. We can also measure the income levels over a period of time. This is an absolute measure of change in that society. Needless to say, modeling this change requires reliable measures of income, appropriate sample size, and longitudinal data. These are hard to come by.

An interesting study by the National Council of Applied Economic Research (NCAER) in India suggests that there might be some weak but clear signal that this change is emerging. During the last decade, India has liberalized its economy, promoted private-sector development, and allowed each state to experiment. As a result, instead of one monolithic approach to economic development, there are multiple models of development being implemented. The various states are also growing at highly differentiated rates. NCAER modeled the changing patterns of income distribution by states and projected the inflation-adjusted income pyramid for 2006–2007. It is easy to see that in some states such as Bihar and Orissa, the shape of the income distribution does not change. It is still the pyramid. However, in other states, such as Assam, Maharashtra, Gujerat, Haryana, and Punjab, the pattern is shifting noticeably. The projections of income distribution from NCAER are shown in Figure 6.4.

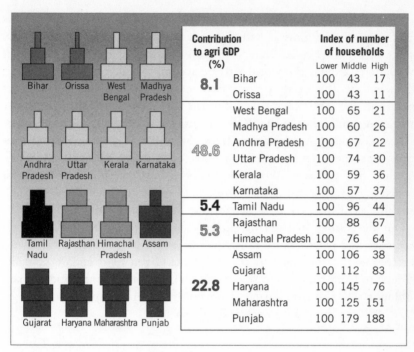

Figure 6.4 The shape of rural income distribution.

Contribution to agri GDP (%)		Index of number of households		
		Lower	Middle	High
8.1	Bihar	100	43	17
	Orissa	100	43	11
48.6	West Bengal	100	65	21
	Madhya Pradesh	100	60	26
	Andhra Pradesh	100	67	22
	Uttar Pradesh	100	74	30
	Kerala	100	59	36
	Karnataka	100	57	37
5.4	Tamil Nadu	100	96	44
5.3	Rajasthan	100	88	67
	Himachal Pradesh	100	76	64
22.8	Assam	100	106	38
	Gujarat	100	112	83
	Haryana	100	145	76
	Maharashtra	100	125	151
	Punjab	100	179	188

This pattern will repeat itself in both rural and urban India. This has several implications. First, we can measure the patterns of income distribution over time and can develop both relative and absolute measures of change. Second, the changing nature of the income distribution creates a virtuous cycle. The demand for products and services increases domestic economic activity, creating more jobs and wealth. The changing patterns of consumption of durables in India—in both rural and urban markets—are well-documented.[3] Third, as the BOP morphs from a pyramid into a diamond, the distinction between the BOP consumer and the top-of-the-pyramid consumer disappears. There is only one consumer group.

The pattern of changes in income distribution seen in India is an early signal of what is possible. A measure of success is when the debate about BOP consumers becomes irrelevant as they become part of the mainstream market.

I have tried to depict a picture of the possibilities. I am sensitive to the fact that the illustrations that I provide are but islands of excellence in a sea of deprivation and helplessness. The important question for us is, "Do we see the glass as half full or half empty?" There is a long way to go before the social transformation leading to the elimination of inequalities around the world will be accomplished. The private sector, as shown by the examples we have examined, can make a distinct contribution. The changing patterns of income distribution, the increasing confidence of the BOP consumers, and their ability to become activists in changing their own lives through entrepreneurship give us hope. But the examples that we have examined challenge all of us, whether our primary obligation is boosting shareholder returns or reducing poverty and social injustice, to bring the resources and capabilities of the private sector to bear in pursuit of that goal.

Our best allies in fighting poverty are the poor themselves. Their resilience and perseverance must give us courage to move forward with entrepreneurial solutions to the problem. Given bold and responsible leadership from the private sector and civil society organizations, I have no doubt that the elimination of poverty and deprivation is possible by 2020. We can build a humane and just society.

Endnotes

1. C. K. Prahalad and Venkat Ramaswamy. *The Future of Competition: Creating Unique Value with Customers*. Harvard Business School Press, 2004.

2. "Hindustan Lever Limited: Levers for Change." Case study, INSEAD, Fontainebleau, France, 1991.

3. Rama Bijapurkar. "The New, Improved Indian Consumer." *Business World*, December 2003.

PART II

Innovative Practices at the Bottom of the Pyramid

In this section, we present detailed case stories of successful innovations at the BOP. These cases span a wide range of industries—health care, financial services, housing, energy, personal care, and agriculture. Each case details innovations in business models. They represent a wide variety of country settings: Peru, Brazil, Mexico, and India.

Global firms, large domestic firms, nongovernmental organizations (NGOs), and startups are all represented. This collection of cases is intended to demonstrate that the opportunities for innovation at the BOP are not limited to a locale, an industry, or a certain type of business entity.

These stories of innovation were written with three goals in mind. First, we want to give the reader enough information to make an assessment of how to innovate at the BOP. The cases, therefore, are rich in detail. Second, we want to demonstrate that there is no mystery to unlocking the potential of these markets. It requires vision, leadership, a new perspective, and a new approach. Finally, we want you to know the potential of this opportunity—how big it is. Each one of these innovations can be turned into a global opportunity. As you read these cases, think of the people behind the cases, their motivations, the innovations that allowed them to create new markets, the obstacles they had to face (and in some cases continue to face), and the social transformation to which they have contributed. Each case represents a "win–win" scenario: a win for the BOP consumer as well as for the firm. The relationship between the consumer and the firm at the BOP market is symbiotic. They co-create value.

The Market at the Bottom of the Pyramid

The first question that most people ask is this: Is there a market at the BOP? The answer is a resounding "Yes." The two stories that follow represent the potential of this market.

Casas Bahia is a Brazilian retailer. Started by Samuel Klein in 1952, Casas Bahia has become one of the largest retailers in Brazil. It employs 20,000 people, operates 330 stores, and has a current customer list of over 10 million consumers. Yet it only operates in the deprived areas of Brazil. Its customers are primarily from the *favelas*—the shanty towns. It is a case of a big business, one with sales of R$4.2 billion (US $1.2 billion), built on converting the BOP into consumers. Samuel Klein learned very early that there is a market at the BOP and the key to that market is creation of a "capacity to consume." He therefore initiated financing as a way to get the BOP consumers to buy. In the process, he invented the combination of retailing and financial services: retailing products and financing the very poor with irregular work and, therefore, irregular income streams. He had to invent the basis for credit analysis and risk management at the BOP, where most customers do not have a credit history or a regular job. Casas Bahia provides the credit. To cut costs of brand name appliances, Casa Bahia has invested in world-class logistics, operating some of the largest warehouses and one of the largest delivery fleets in the world.

Cemex is one of the largest manufacturers of cement in the world. Cemex, with its origins in Mexico, started Patrimonio Hoy (patrimony now), a scheme to allow BOP customers to add on to their homes—a kitchen, a bathroom, or a bedroom—one room at a time. Cemex organizes BOP customers, typically women, into groups of three. The group can start saving every week toward payment for the addition of their choice to the house. They have to save for a period of six weeks before the company releases materials worth 10 weeks of savings. The process is based on a simple formula: The more the customers demonstrate their willingness to be disciplined and save, the more the company is willing to provide them credit. This is another variation of credit and risk management. This allows the very poor to start small, and over a period of 76 weeks to save enough to pay for the addition of their choice. The company guarantees good-quality materials delivered when the customers want it, with advice and technical help in building the addition. The BOP customers feel empowered and very proud of their own accomplishment.

Casas Bahia and Cemex are not exceptions. They are just the examples we chose to use.

Variations of the recipe for accessing the BOP and creating the capacity to consume can be traced in several parts of the world. For example, Elektra in Mexico is very similar. Elektra is one of the largest retailers, with revenue exceeding US $2.0 billion in 2003. It sells brand name appliances to the BOP. The Elektra clientele is very similar to that of Casas Bahia. Elektra also provides credit; in fact, it operates its own bank. Habibs, a fast-food chain that provides healthy, family-oriented meals for the BOP markets in Brazil, is now a 220+ branch chain and growing rapidly. A full meal per person can cost as low as US $1.50, about one hour's wage for a Brazilian construction worker in Sao Paulo. Habibs is moving rapidly to expand into Mexico, where it already operates six stores. Bimbo is the largest baked goods manufacturer and distributor in North America. Bimbo's revenue was US $3.7 billion in 2003. Bimbo is focused on the BOP customers in Mexico that are not served by the big supermarkets. It provides good-quality, fresh bread, and the company is appreciated by its customers. It operates a fleet of 25,000 trucks that take fresh bread to 690,000 points of sale across the BOP markets throughout Mexico. It operates in most difficult neighborhoods, but its trucks are never robbed. Bimbo employs 72,000 people. It has expanded, based on their success in BOP markets in Mexico, into the United States. It owns famous brands such as Thomas's English muffins, Orowheat, Tia Rosa, and Mrs. Bairds in the United States.

In India, Reliance, one of the largest firms, is building a huge wireless franchise by focusing on the capacity to consume. By making available a full-color, Internet-enabled wireless device for less than $12 down and about $7 per month for 36 months, Reliance has spawned a connectivity revolution. Overall, India is adding more than 1.5 million cell phone subscribers per month. This growth is totally driven by the access to credit.

These cases illustrate the reality of the market at the BOP and how large it is. It needs to be activated by creating the capacity to consume, which in most cases translates into low-cost, high-quality products and access to credit. The two cases that follow demonstrate how it can be done.

Casas Bahia:
Fulfilling a Dream

Through a unique approach to customer service, Casas Bahia has developed an innovative business model that successfully serves the bottom of the pyramid (BOP) population throughout Brazil.

THE INNOVATION...

The poor represent a large, lucrative, and sustainable market with the right financial approach in countries where even Sears and Wal-Mart have failed.

It is all about fulfilling the customer dream. My sales agent has to be very well-dressed, shaved and always smiling. If he has a personal problem, he cannot come to work. I will never allow him to transmit to my customer anything but perfection.

Michael Klein,
Chief Financial Officer,
Casas Bahia

In 1952, after surviving two years in a Nazi concentration camp, Samuel Klein left his homeland to start a new life in Brazil. To support his family, Klein sold blankets, bed linens, and bath towels door to door in São Caetano do Sul. Fifty years later, Klein has transformed his door-to-door business into the largest retail chain in Brazil, selling electronics, appliances, and furniture. Casas Bahia's figures are significant: R\$4.2 billion in revenues (the Reais is the Brazilian currency), 330 stores, 10 million customers and 20,000 employees.

Klein has built Casas Bahia into a successful and sustainable business serving Brazil's poor.

> *When my father arrived in Brazil, he realized the average population was not wealthy. Thousands of people were migrating from the northeast region to work in São Paulo. That is why our name is Casas Bahia (Bahia is the largest state in the northeast region). This population needed all kinds of basic goods, such as linens, towels, and sheets. My father's vision was to fulfill the needs of the poor population. But how could they pay for it? The answer was simple: financing.*
>
> —Michael Klein

Today, Samuel Klein's two sons, Michael and Saúl, manage the day-to-day operations at Casas Bahia. Michael is responsible for finance, stores, distribution, fleet, technology, and employees. Saúl oversees suppliers, customer sales, and marketing. Although Samuel no longer visits stores, due to security concerns, he is always at the headquarters and is considered the "mind of the company." Moreover, his son Michael states, "He [Samuel] understands this business better than anyone else in the world. I would be foolish if I did not use this invaluable resource."

Casas Bahia believes in staying true to its customers. As an example of the company's ability to both reflect and support the communities they serve, Casas Bahia's headquarters have remained in the blue-collar city of São Caetano. The atmosphere and attire are casual. Samuel Klein has set the tone and philosophy of Casas Bahia. His deceptively casual attire masks an intense head for business and passion for his customers and employees. This passion for total dedication to service has led to an atmosphere of reverence from both employees and customers. When you enter the headquarters of Casas Bahia, a large caricature portrait of Samuel leaning over a Casas Bahia store greets you. A grateful employee, who, despite having no formal art training, wanted to show his appreciation to the man who had changed his life painted it. One of Casas Bahia's most successful regional sales managers has a life-size painting of Samuel in his office to serve as a reminder of the traditional values the charismatic founder instilled within Casas Bahia. When Michael attends store openings, lifelong customers approach him to show their appreciation and ask how his father is doing.

The culture and philosophy are important to the continued success at Casas Bahia. Maintaining control over culture is one reason Samuel Klein is adamant about not selling a stake to outside investors. "Partners boss you around," he says. This deceptively simple approach to business is at the heart of Samuel Klein's direct, old-world style of management. He does not like surprises and follows his instincts. Klein believes in iron-fisted control over spending. Only four Klein family members have the authority to sign checks. Although Michael and Saúl continue to perpetuate their father's beliefs and management style, they have begun to modernize the business. The current emphases in marketing and information technology (IT) are the clearest signals of this modernization.

Scope and Size of Opportunity

Brazil maintains a standard that stratifies individuals into one of five basic economic classes: A, B, C, D or E. C, D, and E are considered to be the "bottom of the pyramid (BOP). In 2002, the population in Brazil was 176 million, 84 percent of whom were considered to be at the BOP. The economic stratification is illustrated in Table 1.

Table 1 Brazilian Stratification Breakdown

Familar Income (MW*)	Economic Segment	Population (Million)	Household (Million)	Inhabitants per Household
0-2x	E	54.3	7.6	7.1
2–4x	D	44.2	9.4	4.7
4-10x	C	48.9	12.6	4.0
10-25x	B	21.6	5.4	4.0
>25x	A	7.3	2.5	2.9

*MW = minimum wage (R$200/month)

The BOP represents significant purchasing power in Brazil's economy, at 41 percent of total spending capacity. This US $124 billion accounts for only the formal, reported economy. It is estimated that the informal market in Brazil for the BOP reaches an additional 50 percent. Specifically, 45 percent of total appliance and furniture spending is done by the BOP (see Figures 1 and 2).

Of particular interest is the high penetration of major appliances, such as television sets and refrigerators, at the BOP in Brazil (see Table 2). It is not uncommon to find households with a television or refrigerator yet lacking basic infrastructure, such as toilets and telephone lines. Those at the BOP in Brazil spend based on their needs and desires. In a tropical climate, a refrigerator is a necessity. Everyone, regardless of class, feels the need for entertainment. For the poor in Brazil, that comes in the form of television or radio.

Typical Customer

Seventy percent of Casas Bahia customers have no formal or consistent income. Casas Bahia customers are primarily maids, cooks, independent street vendors, and construction workers whose average monthly income is twice the

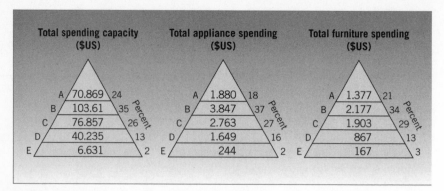

Figure 1 Total spending in Brazilian economy by economic group (in U.S. $ millions). *Source:* Target, Braisil Em Foco, 2002.

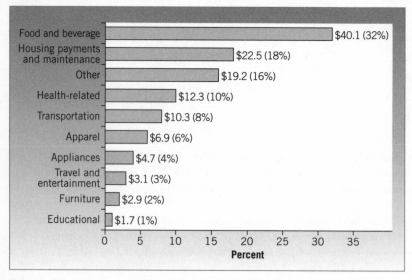

Figure 2 Total spending outlays by population categorized as C, D, and E (in U.S. $ billions).

minimum wage (R$400). Customers typically live in concentrated areas called *favelas*. The average size home in a favela can be as small as 215 square feet and house up to seven family members. As a result, these communities are densely populated, with approximately 37,000 people per square kilometer. In comparison, according to the U.S. Census Bureau, five of the most densely populated cities in the United States are Union City, NJ (17,962); Guttenberg, NJ (16,569); West New York, NJ (14,480); Hoboken, NJ (10,133); and New York City (9,151).

Table 2 Penetration of Selected Goods by Economic Status

	SegmentE	Segment D	Segment C	Segments A and B
Households	33%	21%	28%	18%
Number of toilets/household				
0	36%	14%	5%	1%
1	60%	77%	74%	39%
2	4%	8%	18%	34%
3	0%	1%	3%	18%
>4	0%	0%	1%	8%
Garbage pickup	60%	80%	90%	96%
Electricity	87%	96%	99%	100%
Phone	11%	28%	51%	86%
Microwave	3%	9%	22%	58%
Refrigerator/ Freezer	62%	88%	96%	99%
Radio	78%	88%	93%	97%
Television	72%	90%	96%	99%

Competitive Landscape

Casas Bahia has operations in three Brazilian regions and eight states: Southeast (São Paulo, Rio de Janeiro, and Minas Gerais), South (Santa Catarina and Paraná) and Central West (Distrito Federal, Goiás, and Mato Grosso do Sul).

The competitive landscape of the retail industry in Brazil is constantly changing based on product offerings, geography, and target population. For example, Ponto Frio offers a wide range of products, but primarily serves the medium- to high-income population. Marabrás is focused on the BOP, but carries only furniture. Casas Bahia's competition also varies by region. In the Southeast region top competitors include Ponto Frio, Lojas Cem, Magazine Luiza, Marabrás, and Kolumbus. Lojas Columbo is the only serious threat in the South region.

Due to difficult economic conditions, the retail landscape over the past several years has seen many competitors exit the industry and considerable consolidation. With no new entrants, a large portion of the market share is concentrated with only a few companies. The top five competitors comprise 45 percent of total retail sales. Casas Bahia remains the leader with approximately 15 percent to 20 percent of the market. The top competitors continue to grow; Casas Bahia, Ponto Frio, Marabrás, and Lojas Cem averaged 10 percent growth per year over the past several years. Others, such as Magazine Luiza, experienced 20 percent growth per year in the last decade.

With average net margins in the retail sector at a modest 2.5 percent, competition is fierce and volume-based. As such, it is doubtful that many new companies can afford to enter the market. Thus, the remaining 55 percent of the market, which is comprised of small- to medium-sized regional stores, should provide the opportunity for further consolidation within the retail market.

Until now, Casas Bahia has concerned itself only with "traditional" competitors. Recently, large hypermarts, such as Carrefour, Extra, and Big, have begun to enter into the appliance and furniture business. The entrance of these companies into the market represents an increasing threat to Casas Bahia. Hypermarts generate high customer traffic and have strong brand recognition. They have the physical size to accommodate additional merchandise as well as an existing distribution network of locations. Moreover, the difficult economic times are forcing hypermarts to find new ways of increasing the amount of each customer's purchase. Despite this emerging threat, Michael Klein believes the Casas Bahia business model is distinct and that "our customer service is far above the competition."

Casas Bahia Business Model and Positioning
Management Style

Although his father's management style is the basis for Casas Bahia's culture, the moment you walk into Michael Klein's office and see the large flat-panel monitor sitting on his desk, you begin to notice how Casas Bahia is leveraging Samuel Klein's traditional ideals with modern concepts. As Michael taps on his keyboard, the monitor pops to life and the modern manifestation of Casas Bahia's traditional values appears. The screen displays a large array of real-time information: total unit sales, total revenues, total financed value, average down payment, average interest paid, average payment period, percentage use of own resources to finance, use of third party for financing (borrowing), and total sales to customers who enter the store to pay an installment (cross-sale).

All stores are linked and monitored in real time. Casas Bahia has developed a system that can analyze data from multiple points of view: individual store, groups of stores, region, city, and even product category, individual product line, or stockkeeping unit (SKU). From his desk, Michael can track the results of the 6 million people who enter his stores every month. Those 6 million customers generate an average of 900,000 new sales per month, and 7 percent take advantage of a cross-selling opportunity. The people comprising this 7 percent have an average balance of R$11.7 million and purchase an additional R$31 million. The percentage of cross-selling seems relatively low because customers are eligible to make additional purchases only after they have paid at least 50 percent of the original purchase price.

Currently, the average finance term is six months, the average interest rate is 4.13 percent per month (ranging from 2.5 percent for four-month-term sales to 6 percent for 12-month-term sales), the average ticket is R$440 and the default rate is 8.5 percent. Default rates vary by product. For example, furniture has a default rate of 4 percent. Because Casas Bahia delivers and installs the merchandise in the customer's home, it is much easier to collect. Conversely, portable items such as mobile phones and bicycles have default rates of up to 10 percent. Casas Bahia does not monitor default rates by length of loan.

All major projects, capital or otherwise, are under Michael's supervision and direction. Although each project varies based on particular circumstance, Casas Bahia maintains general guidelines. A new store must have at least 100,000 potential customers. Casas Bahia also will examine the number of inquiries made to the Service of Credit Protection (Serviço de Proteção ao Crédito, or SPC). This provides a rough estimate of the commercial activity in a particular area. Additionally, the cost of logistics is examined; that is, how close the facility will be to any of the three distribution facilities or the six cross-docking centers or if a new cross-docking center would be warranted.

Michael gives a significant amount of freedom to store and region managers. The only requirements are predetermined revenue and profit targets. Knowing their stores' cost structure, managers have the discretion to manage their operations as they see fit. A store manager has the ability to reduce the price of any product up to 10 percent to match the competition. If more negotiations are required, the regional manager can authorize a price reduction up to 25 percent. For anything greater than a 25 percent reduction, the regional manager must call Michael Klein directly. With more than 20,000 employees, there are only three levels from the store manager to the top executive. This autonomy does not equal a lack of control. An internal audit system is one of the important management tools for Michael.

We are always auditing our operations. I have an internal audit team. They show up unexpectedly in one store and check everything: the money on the cashiers, the inventory, the cleanliness, and the quality of in-store advertising. Everything is checked.

—Michael Klein

One of the most important managerial tools at Casas Bahia is the daily Director lunch. Every day, the Klein family and key executives sit down over lunch to discuss current issues. Tuesdays are reserved for discussions with key suppliers. Occasionally, an outside guest is invited to lecture about a specific topic. The conversations are quick and informal. Typically, the food is served only when all the guests have arrived. The environment is very relaxed and lighthearted. When an attendee introduces an important topic, the atmosphere in the room changes slightly. For example, Saúl asks his Sony supplier about a price increase. After 15 minutes of negotiation, an agreement is reached.

A recent change in interest rates is brought up. The change is analyzed based on the impact to final installment prices. Every executive sitting around the table knows his or her specific business down to the lowest level and what impact an interest change will have. For instance, the marketing director begins to discuss how a change will affect his current and scheduled promotions. In such a relatively flat organization, it is easy to pass decisions down through all levels of the organization. While still in the meeting, executives will be on the phone with store managers to better understand the impact. The fast-paced decision-making does not mean that decisions are uniform or made hastily. The determination of rates and terms for Casas Bahia merchandise takes into consideration the negotiation in the buying process (purchase power), market interest rates, product default rates, and sales volume (seasonality, etc.). Once all issues have been finalized, the lunch is finished. All executives leave the room knowing what to do and sharing a broad vision of Casas Bahia operations.

Casas Bahia maintains a simple culture dedicated to serving the customer by undertaking an aggressive style when it comes to other areas of its business. For example, when Casas Bahia enters a market, it wants to gain market share quickly. The goal is always to be first in every market. "We enter the market to be the leader, to be the best. When we arrive, we want to attract everybody, and then we clean the base and cross-sell," says CIO Frederico Wanderley. This mentality is not without a significant cost. When a store is opened, its default rate averages 16 percent, almost double the company average. It takes a couple of years for that rate to come down to the average of 8.5 percent (see Figure 3). The cost of customer acquisition is considered a cost of doing business at Casas Bahia.

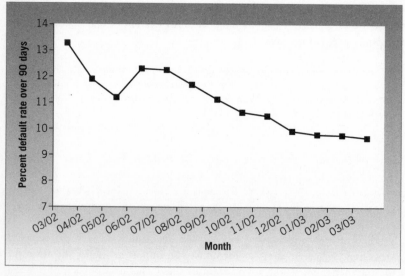

Figure 3 Default Evolution in New Stores: Sobradinho, DF.

This aggressiveness also applies to Casas Bahia suppliers. Due to its size, Casas Bahia purports to be able to buy from suppliers at lower costs than the competition while still being able to sell for about the same price. "The secret is not to pass our margin on to the final product price. Thus, we respect suppliers' brands, remain competitive, and maintain our profitability," says Allan Barros, Director of Furniture.

Finance

Brazilian Overview

Finance here is totally different from what one learns in school. First, the informal market is twice as big as the formal market, especially in the lower income population. Most of my customers do not declare income. I have to believe what they are telling me. Here, several multinational retailers did poorly because they were not able to understand local needs, for example, Sears and Wal-Mart.

—Michael Klein

Retail banks in Brazil are "universal banks," with wide national presence and complete product offerings such as credit, savings, insurance, and finance products. Client information is very important because the credit bureau in Brazil, SPC, provides only positive or negative information on customers. Any disclosure of credit information is illegal. Based on historically high interest rates, the banking system is highly profitable. Maintaining this profitability has made banks' credit policies conservative toward the low-income population. Consequently, access to current accounts varies significantly with economic level (see Table 3).

Table 3   Current Account Penetration by Economic Segment

Segment	Current Account Penetration (%)
A	>90
B	~60%
C/D/E	<40%

Because traditional banks would not serve the poor population, *financeiras*, consumer credit companies, emerged to serve unmet consumer credit needs. Their core business is granting credit to low-income people who do not have access to a bank account. Additionally, a significant amount of current account holders rely on financeiras because traditional banks cannot fulfill all their credit needs. Financeiras typically have very high interest rates—up to 14 percent per month on personal loans—and origination fees that keep a significant share of this population away from credit products (see Figure 4).

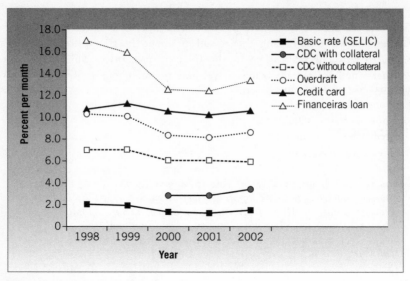

Figure 4 Evolution of distinct interest rates.

Casas Bahia's Role

Casas Bahia emerged by fulfilling this untapped financing need. Since joining the company 27 years ago, Celso Amancio, Director of Credit, has helped the company perfect a unique financing model that has enabled Casas Bahia to successfully serve BOP customers, customers previously ignored by the retail industry. "Casas Bahia's motto is, 'Total Dedication to You.' This dedication is evident since Casas Bahia has created a culture whose sole purpose is to fulfill the dreams of its customers," says Amancio. Whereas many companies considered Casas Bahia customers undesirable, Casas Bahia saw an opportunity.

To serve the poor population, Casas Bahia developed an innovative approach. Part of the solution is the now famous *carnê*, or passbook, that allows its customers to make small installment payments for merchandise. Payment schedules range from 1 to 15 months. The passbook is payable only at Casas Bahia stores, and every month consumers must enter a store to pay their bill. This method also helps to maintain relationships with clients. The financed sales are responsible for 90 percent of all sales volume: 6 percent are cash payments and 4 percent are credit card sales.

All customers who wish to finance their purchase must submit to an SPC credit check. If the customer has a negative SPC score, Casas Bahia will not be able to complete the transaction until the customer resolves his or her credit problem. If the customer has a positive score, there are two alternatives. If the merchandise costs less than R$600, no proof of income is required; a valid permanent address will suffice. If the merchandise costs more than R$600, Casas Bahia has developed a proprietary system to evaluate the prospective client. The client receives a credit limit based on total income, both formal and informal, occupation, and presumed expenses. This scoring process takes less than one minute. If the system approves the prospect, the salesperson can continue with the sale. If the client is rejected by the system, he or she is directed to a credit analyst for further evaluation. This is where the importance of building a relationship is prominent. Based on training, the credit analyst will ask a series of questions to determine a client's creditworthiness. The entire process typically is finished in 10 minutes or less.

The proprietary system that determines the creditworthiness of new clients also evaluates existing clients for potential new purchases. Based on the same drivers already noted, in addition to payment history, the system will automatically produce a new credit limit. This ability is key in the cross-selling process. When customers come into the store to pay their monthly installment, a new credit limit is available to the Casas Bahia salesperson. This salesperson has the opportunity to make a tailored cross-sale in the amount of the new credit limit.

Many outsiders argue that Casas Bahia is simply exploiting the poor and charging them exorbitant interest rates because the poor do not know any better. Quite the opposite seems to be true. To maintain low default rates, salespeople must "teach" consumers to buy according to their budget. For instance, a customer enters the store and wants a new 27-inch television. A salesperson will sit down with the customer (a Casas Bahia Regional Manager mentions that you always discuss price sitting down, so it is harder for the customer to walk away) and discuss multiple payment options. If it becomes clear the customer cannot afford the 27-inch television, the salesperson will work with them to "tweak" their dream to temporarily include a 20-inch TV.

The consumer education process is a key component for Casas Bahia's default level of 8.5 percent. To put it into perspective, the average for the entire retail sector, which serves all income levels, is 6.5 percent (see Figure 5). Casas Bahia's competition at the BOP has a default rate that reaches 16 percent.

If you look at the default rate for furniture at Casas Bahia, it averages 4.5 percent. Marabrás, our main competitor in the furniture industry, has an average default rate of 15 percent to 16 percent. One of the driving factors of the higher default rate is that they don't finance the customers themselves. In the [competitor's] store you have a number of kiosks from various financeiras. The customer simply chooses a kiosk. This creates a large disconnect between the salespeople and customer. The salesperson has no incentive to build a relationship with customers or understand their abilities and needs because they are at no risk.
—Michael Klein

Although Casas Bahia has become the largest retailer in Brazil by focusing on financing BOP customers, it has also faced several challenges. Identifying and overcoming these challenges have strengthened the vision Samuel Klein had more than 50 years ago. If you ask any customer, they will state, "At Casas Bahia, it is easy to get credit." Samuel Klein believes that customer needs are paramount and it should be as easy as possible for customers to fulfill their dreams. To make a seamless and efficient customer-facing process requires rigorous and strict planning by Casas Bahia. It starts with the training of its credit analysts.

Training

The credit analyst plays a vital role in the success of Casas Bahia. As such, the company has devoted significant time and resources to train its credit analysts. With an average of 750,000 customers requesting financing every month (1.4 million in December), Casas Bahia's 800 credit analysts are the linchpin, not only in maintaining a default rate below industry average, but also in fraud detection. In 2002, 35,000 cases of fraud representing $440 million were averted.

Many at the BOP have never applied for or been granted credit, rendering the formal SPC system useless. Without a steady or reported income and a personal economic status that can change daily, it is up to the credit analyst to

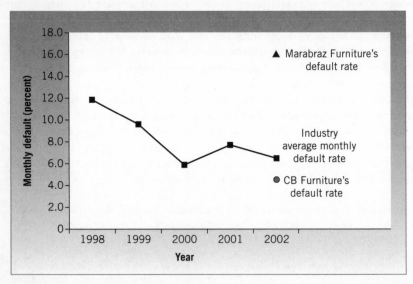

Figure 5 Monthly average default rate in retail.

decide if his or her customer is honest, sincere, and will be able to make the necessary payments. Every customer who presents himself or herself has a unique situation. The training the analysts receive prepares them to make decisions that enable the continued success of Casas Bahia.

Training is a combination of classroom and informal techniques. The first step takes place in the classroom. Employees learn the basics, ranging from the importance of personal grooming to the necessity of having a positive attitude toward the customers. It is in the classroom where Casas Bahia employees begin to understand the importance of building a long-lasting relationship with the customer. When people, especially the poor, walk into the store, they want a friendly face, someone to whom they can talk about their day. Customers want to ensure that the person they are talking with understands their background and can help them fulfill their dream. According to Celso Amancio, many customers "come in as a client and leave as a friend."

The relationship between the analyst and customer creates a virtuous cycle. For instance, a customer enters Casas Bahia in need of an oven to replace her current oven that is no longer working, yet she is currently unable to pay. Based on either an existing relationship or one that is developed in the short time she is in the store, a credit analyst can approve a loan even if the customer does not currently have the necessary proof of income. The customer is grateful that the analyst is taking a chance and trusting she will make the payments. Then, when things turn around for the customer, she is willing to buy more from Casas Bahia and she also tells family and friends about her positive experience.

It is also in the classroom where analysts learn the importance of asking the right questions. Depending on the store location, the analysts will learn about their customers' primary livelihood. For example, if a customer comes in and says he is a construction worker, the analyst will begin to discretely "size up" the customer. The analyst will notice if the customer has calluses on his hand or wrinkles around his eyes from working outside all day. The analyst also might ask a few technical questions in the context of a project he or she might be involved with at home. This interaction serves two purposes: It begins to filter out fraud potential, but more important, it helps build the relationship with that customer. Analysts are taught to always ask questions and be creative in trying to understand the customer.

After completing classroom training, new employees "shadow" an experienced employee for two weeks in a store. Trainees learn firsthand how to implement classroom teachings and the importance of cross-selling at Casas Bahia. Cross-selling is an important part of the company's success because 77 percent of clients who open an account make repeat purchases.

Another important aspect of Casas Bahia training is teaching the analyst the art of saying "no" to the customer. An estimated 16 percent of customers applying for credit are denied. What is a seemingly basic concept has a long-lasting importance to Casas Bahia customers. When customers enter a Casas Bahia store, they are hoping to fulfill a dream. When you tell a potential customer "no," you are effectively destroying his or her dream. Samuel Klein has fostered a culture in which this is unacceptable. Analysts always work to maintain the relationship. Customers should be viewed for their long-term potential as lifetime customers. Although they can't afford something right now, their situation will improve and then they can buy that new TV.

Rejection is sometime necessary and appropriate. The main reasons for rejection are threefold: negative SPC rating, credit limit, and third-party acquisition. With a negative SPC rating, there is nothing Casas Bahia can do. The analyst tells the customer that if it were up to Casas Bahia, the company would do business, but cannot due to the score. The analyst apologizes and mentions that as soon as the "little problem" is resolved, he or she will welcome the customer back and finish the transaction. An insufficient credit limit is handled with offers of similar products or different brands or models. Third-party acquisition is when the actual customer has a bad credit rating or cannot afford the merchandise himself or herself, and has another person purchase it. The customer would then pay the third party. However, this arrangement usually leads to default. First, there is a reason the customer could not afford the merchandise in the first place; second, the third party who purchased the merchandise has no vested interest in paying Casas Bahia. Third-party purchase is the leading cause of default at Casas Bahia. The second is unemployment, and the third is simply spending beyond one's means.

Cash Management

Casas Bahia's dependence on banks is very low. According to Michael Klein, Brazilian law does not permit Casas Bahia to fund the interest portion of its consumer loans. Therefore, that portion is packaged and sold to banks or financeiras. Casas Bahia used to have its own financeira. The company dissolved this entity because it was not the core business for Casas Bahia. Now, the company's policy is to borrow as little as possible and finance the customer while funding the expenses internally.

Additionally, Casas Bahia does not hold to external currencies. This is especially important in the Brazilian economy, where local currency devaluations have caused prices to increase dramatically. Casas Bahia believes that because it does business in Brazil, the company's currency and exposure should be within Brazil. Moreover, minimal exposure to banks for external debt is beneficial.

Products

Casas Bahia carries and sells top-quality brands: Sony, Toshiba, JVC, and Brastemp (Whirlpool). There is a misconception that because customers are poor they do not desire quality products. In Brazil, C, D, and E customers desire the same merchandise as A and B customers. They want the dream they see on TV, not a cheapened version of that dream. The difference is that individuals at the BOP cannot afford to walk into a store and pay $500 cash for a new refrigerator. They can, however, afford to make small installment payments to pay for that new refrigerator.

Currently, furniture is Casas Bahia's top-selling product category, at 31 percent of total sales. Televisions place second at 14 percent, and audio products are third with 10 percent of total sales. Remaining sales are spread among phones, computers, electronic accessories, and appliances.

Casas Bahia's purchasing power is one of its key success factors. In 2002, Casas Bahia sold 18 percent of the 4.5 million televisions produced in Brazil. Consequently, the company can determine the success or failure of a supplier in local markets. Allan Barros, Director of Furniture, related the story of a Casas Bahia supplier: "Last year Mitsubishi was out of our stores from June through December. In six months they fell from third to the 15th position in Brazilian television sales."

Due to the pursuit of higher margins and an increasingly difficult market for appliances, Casas Bahia has shifted focus and plans to increase furniture sales in 2004 to 40 percent of its total revenues (up from 15 percent in 2001). To keep up with demand, Casas Bahia has built its own production facility, a wholly owned subsidiary called Bartira. Producing the furniture internally also will help ensure that the company can continue to provide customers great-looking furniture while controlling costs. Casas Bahia produces only large pieces of furniture, such as kitchen cabinets and room wardrobes. The remaining furniture is purchased from several suppliers.

When designing its products, Casas Bahia utilizes a reverse engineering process. First, the company determines the terms it will pass along to the customers, both price and number of installments. Based on experience and research, Casas Bahia understands what the customer is willing to pay. The product then is developed. In addition to the cost, product size and appearance are considered. An example of focusing on the importance of customer research can be seen with the success of the recently released "Top Line" wardrobe product. Traditionally, wardrobes in Brazil were 2.2 meters high. However, Casas Bahia observed that many customers had houses that would allow only furniture that was 2.0 meters high. Casas Bahia designed a product that matched the customer needs. "Top Line" products have been a tremendous success. In the first month, 7,000 units were sold, with an average price of R$1,035. Customers pay up to 15 installments of around R$70 (about US$20). In addition to the commercial success of the new wardrobe, Casas Bahia developed a manufacturing process for the product that virtually eliminated all the waste previously associated with the manufacture of wardrobes.

The production schedule is based on sales forecasts, which are derived based on historical sales, targets, and product availability at the warehouse. Typically, Casas Bahia maintains 30 days of inventory for furniture and 45 days for all other products.

In an attempt to fully realize the benefits from the growing furniture segment, Casas Bahia brought a second furniture production facility online in the second half of 2003, at a cost of R$25 million. This will increase production from 100,000 to 230,000 pieces per month. In 2002, Casas Bahia had to purchase up to 60 percent of its furniture from external suppliers. The chain will have special promotions to continue the growth in furniture sales. For example, Casas Bahia offers interest-free financing for furniture for up to 15 months. Typically, at Casas Bahia, interest-free financing is allowed only up to the first six months.

Distribution

The poor are requiring more. Five years ago, giving the customer a seven-day delivery window was sufficient. Now they require the specific day. The main reason for this change is that now, more than ever, both the man and woman of the household are working. As a result, we are always looking for new technology to better serve the customer. Our next step will be to be able to schedule the actual time of delivery.

—Gilberto Duarte, Distribution Director

Unlike its competitors, Casas Bahia does not strictly focus on streamlining the supply chain, minimizing working capital, or increasing its inventory turnover ratio. Casas Bahia differentiates itself by placing a large emphasis on the supplier negotiation process. The company strives to make the best possible deal with its suppliers, negotiating huge volumes at very low prices. Casas Bahia claims this strategy works best both financially and in terms of customer service. For example, Casas Bahia typically sells 1,000 units of an item per month and a supplier comes with a great offer on 6,000 units. For the right price, the deal will be executed. One reason why Casas Bahia has built the largest warehouse in South America (and one of the largest in the world) is to give management the freedom to make deals the company deems good for business. The large warehouse also allows Casas Bahia to hold large inventory positions. This can be important because the supplier and production system in Brazil can be much less reliable than that in more developed countries. Casas Bahia cannot afford to be out of stock.

To support operations Casas Bahia has three distribution centers. The largest is in São Paulo (230,000 m^2), then Rio de Janeiro (100,000 m^2) and Ribeirão Preto (27,000 m^2). Additionally, the company has six cross-docking facilities: Brasília, Goiânia, Campo Grande, Belo Horizonte, Curitiba, and Itajaí. Due to its strategic position, the main distribution center for São Paulo is located in Jundiaí. The facility is located on several major freeway access points that provide multiple entryways into São Paulo in case of traffic problems. It also allows for easy access to the roads to Rio de Janeiro and Minas Gerais. There are more than 1,800 employees at the São Paulo distribution center alone.

Casas Bahia owns and maintains a fleet of approximately 1,000 trucks: 90 long-haul trucks, 700 standard trucks, 200 medium trucks, and 10 small trucks. The small trucks can maneuver difficult deliveries in the small streets that run throughout the "shantytowns." The fleet is entirely comprised of Mercedes trucks. This enables efficiency and cost reduction when it comes to maintenance. Casas Bahia, at its São Paulo distribution center, does all maintenance, cleaning, and care on the vehicles.

Delivery Drivers

Our business is not only sales, but also the delivery. If I sell the merchandise and the delivery is not well done, the customer is not happy and the dream is broken
—Gilberto Duarte

A successful delivery can determine whether the customer makes a second purchase at Casas Bahia. Casas Bahia employs and trains approximately 2,500 drivers and crew. All trucks for customer delivery go out with one driver and two crew members to help with delivery.

To reduce training costs, Casas Bahia focuses on employee retention; current driver turnover is very low, approximately 3 percent to 4 percent. The company has developed a number of programs and incentives to target retention. Casas Bahia pays its drivers more than the competition. The company offers subsidized cafeterias in each of its three distribution centers. In São Paulo, Casas Bahia provides free transportation (park-and-ride bus system). Finally, no one can be fired without director approval.

Drivers go through a formal training process. Drivers must always be respectful, clean, well-groomed, and must wear a clean uniform. The majority of people they deal with are female. Drivers are taught how to properly load and unload a truck. They always must be courteous and never bump or drag the merchandise. If they are there to replace the refrigerator, for example, the crew will dispose of the existing appliance if desired. This is all a part of respecting the customer.

Once the delivery is complete, customers are given a phone number to call if they have any complaints. If a driver or crew member receives two complaints, he is typically let go. Additionally, 3 percent of all customers are randomly sampled to report on their delivery experience with Casas Bahia.

Delivery Process

Do you know why I do not outsource delivery? Because I cannot permit the delivery person arriving at a client's house without a uniform, or that he doesn't have enough care and causes damage at my customer's house. If he is my employee, my client knows where to complain.

—Michael Klein

All major appliance deliveries are made from one of the three distribution centers or six cross-docking facilities and are guaranteed by a specific date. No deliveries are made from the stores. If customers want an item that day, they must carry it out themselves. In some instances when the customer really wants that stove or refrigerator that day and has no way to get it home, Casas Bahia will, at their own expense, hire a local service to deliver the merchandise. Other than that rare occasion, the merchandise in the store is mainly for display purposes. Once the display items begin to get old, they are moved to the clearance section for sale as an "open item." These items will be delivered by Casas Bahia the next time a truck from the warehouse arrives to replenish the store. In this instance, there is no guaranteed delivery time. Stores utilize a system that automatically reorders their inventory based on predefined reorder points. On average, each store has 15 days of merchandise on hand for small appliances.

In general, a long-haul truck that carries an average of 120 orders delivers to one of the six cross-docking facilities. At the cross-docking facilities, the orders are broken down onto four "urban" trucks that each carry 30 orders. The urban trucks also can deliver directly from the distribution center. In December alone, Casas Bahia averages 24,000 deliveries per day, six days a week.

Customers can pick the date they wish to have the merchandise delivered. In general, deliveries are made within 48 hours of purchase. However, a customer can make the purchase and have it delivered six months later. Also, a customer can purchase any item at any store and have it delivered to any location in Brazil where Casas Bahia operates.

Stores and Storefronts

When a customer walks in the store, they are not buying a stove or television, they are buying a dream. It is the job of salespeople to help them fulfill that dream. This aspect of the business is what many competitors, especially foreign, do not understand

—Michael Klein

All stores have roughly the same configuration, product offerings, and brands. Each store will differ slightly based on the local client needs. In São

Caetano, more appliances are sold. In São Paulo, televisions and electronics are the biggest sellers. The layout of the stores is decided by the store and regional managers based on local needs. Generally, layouts and product mix will be adjusted over time, especially at new stores.

Training is a very important part in the success of fulfilling the customers' dreams. Salespeople become experts in their particular department, and are allowed to sell only in their department. If the customer wants something from another department, the salespeople will team-sell with a representative from that department. The only people in the store who can sell across departments are those located at the cashier, whose sole purpose is to focus on cross-selling. Several sales representatives are dedicated to this function. When customers come in to pay their monthly bill, salespeople gather all the feedback on the purchase, delivery, and process. This information is then passed on to the store manager. As long as the customer has paid off 50 percent of his or her bill, that customer is eligible for cross-selling.

One strategy that Casas Bahia has undertaken is building several stores close together. This strategy serves two distinct purposes. In an area like São Paulo that is very densely populated, traveling can be difficult. Bringing the store to both the customer and employee is crucial. Many customers must walk to the store. A customer can take the bus, but that costs money and takes a lot of time. Stores must be accessible to be successful. Also, having several stores located in close vicinity effectively saturates the area, making it difficult for outside competition to enter. One megastore is not the same as four or five smaller stores serving the same population. Some cannibalization has taken place. Although individual store sales have decreased, the overall sales of Casas Bahia have increased dramatically.

To better understand the size, scale, and profitability of a Casas Bahia store, we have selected a few examples. For instance, in the southern part of São Paulo, there are 15 Casas Bahia stores serving more than 4 million people. In one large neighborhood in this region, there are seven stores in a four-block radius. In a large nearby shantytown, Jardim Angela, 350,000 people are served by one store. Despite this variation, all Casas Bahia stores average 25 to 30 percent gross margins.

Marketing

Marketing has always been very important to Casas Bahia and is one of the key components of its success. Casas Bahia strives to always be foremost in the minds of its population because potential customers tend to research prices at one of the chain's stores prior to making a purchase.

Today, fierce competition in the retail industry has increased the importance of marketing. Because most products do not differ significantly, competition is fierce. The lack of product differentiation reinforces the importance of marketing within the retail sector. Today, Casas Bahia invests approximately 3 percent of revenues in advertising. It maintains one of the largest advertising budgets in Brazil. In 2003, the advertising budget for Casas Bahia totaled R$200 million, equal to the combined advertising budgets of McDonalds and Pão de Açúcar (the largest Brazilian hypermarket chain) for the same period. Casas Bahia's total airtime is larger than that of the most famous Brazilian soap opera. The company's strategy to attract customers to the stores is to announce its low prices with brand-name products. Michael Klein believes that, "Once in the store, the well-trained sales rep has to make the sale."

Casas Bahia's main advertising venue is television, which reaches more than 90 percent of all Brazilian households. The company also uses significant radio time. According to Crowley Broadcast Analysis, Casas Bahia led the ranking of the 10 most invested companies in radio advertising. The survey covered 15 São Paulo-based radio broadcasters and 16 Rio de Janeiro-based stations over the second half of 2002 (July–December). The chain accounted for 17,438 radio spots in São Paulo and 11,106 in Rio de Janeiro. In Belo Horizonte, Casas Bahia ranked 10th with 1,843 ads. Throughout Brazil, Casas Bahia has moved to the number two position in advertising.

Because there is little product differentiation, sales are often made on the basis of emotion, leveraging famous singers, actors, and television personalities. In 2002, Casas Bahia used a campaign utilizing client testimonials for the first time, which intended to show the emotional relationship between the company and its consumers. Casas Bahia advertisements are broadcast on main television channels, including premium programs at prime time. Advertising messages range from pure price advertising and notification of clearances to a company belief that "If the competition has a better price or better payment plans, we will beat them."

Every month, Datafolha/M&M Research publishes a summary of the marketing impact on the Brazilian consumer. In May 2003, the research reported the following information: Casas Bahia ranked fifth in the overall favorite advertisements by television viewers. The top three were beer sellers and the fourth a cleaning sponge. The closest competitor was Marabrás at number 11. Additionally, Casas Bahia ranked as the fourth most recognized brand that is on consumers' minds (see Figure 6).

Casas Bahia also relies on special promotions to both maintain its current customer base and attract new customers. In 2002, the company pardoned the debt of consumers who had defaulted on payments prior to 1997. As a result, thousands of previously inactive clients were able to purchase again. Not only did this promotion generate significant sales flow, it also provided Casas Bahia with a tax break. The company also created "unemployment insurance" for appliance sales. If a client lost his or her job, Casas Bahia would forgo the first six installments.

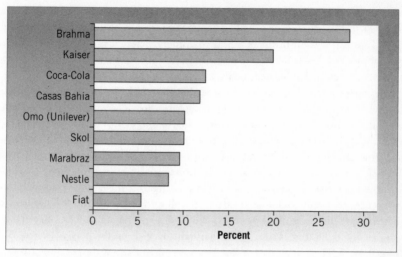

Figure 6 Top brands in Brazil, May 2003.

Other promotions include the Casas Bahia yellow preferred-client card. The card, which gives punctual payers automatic credit approval, is considered a status symbol among customers. Another marketing tool is a form letter that is generated when a customer has had no activity on his or her account for several months. It serves as a subtle reminder to customers that they have not purchased anything for some time and their business is valued. The letter, from Michael Klein, "thanks the customer for paying on time." As witness to the seeming success of this campaign, while visiting a store we noticed customers proudly displaying their letters as they waited in line to pay for their new purchases.

Technology

The role of technology at Casas Bahia is to enable three guiding principles: productivity, low-cost operations, and client satisfaction.

On April 21, 1994, while competitors were scaling back technology spending, Casas Bahia upgraded its systems. This has effectively enabled Casas Bahia to take full advantage of the economic regeneration in Brazil. The company has grown sixfold in nine years. On July 1, 1994, Brazil introduced its economic turn-around plan, effectively halting its massive inflation. This improved the everyday life of those at the BOP, triggering a consumption explosion. Today, Casas Bahia has more than 10 million customers. This figure does not include those individuals who have not been active in the past two years.

Technology has been a key enabler of the growth of Casas Bahia. Prior to upgrades in technology, Casas Bahia required an average of 30 credit analysts per store. Every customer was treated as new whether he or she had been a loyal customer for 30 years or just walked in off the street. The average wait time for credit approval was 30 minutes for all customers. There was no purchase history or documented behavior for the customers. There were numerous clerical mistakes and considerable redundancy.

The entire process is now automated. Stores require only four or five credit analysts. For purchases under $600, customers experience virtually no waiting time. If the purchase is greater than $600, average wait time is one to two minutes. If there is a new customer or a credit limit extension is required, the wait time can be up to 10 minutes. Because all information is only entered once, processing time and related mistakes have essentially been eliminated.

Technology also has helped to greatly reduce fraud. All customer information is now centralized and available to all stores. Information is stored regardless of whether a purchase was made or not. In addition to personal information, purchase history, and credit score, Casas Bahia maintains records on the personality traits of its customers. These include the questions asked and the corresponding answers. Technology also has allowed for a centralized database of all names and companies associated with fraud or attempted fraud at all their stores.

Example of Technology at Casas Bahia

One important aspect of the Casas Bahia customer relationship is that every month the customer must enter the store to pay his or her bill. Until 1995, customers and salespeople would complete a form by hand and then turn it in to the credit department to have it typed. In addition to errors, customers were forced to wait for extended periods of time.

The first significant change came in 1995, when Casas Bahia developed a system that would print the passbook from a computer. The company also decided to make it easier on the customer by sending the bill directly to the customer's home. The speed and accuracy of the customer ticket increased dramatically and the waiting time decreased. However, the customer default rate and associated costs increased dramatically. Disturbed and surprised by the two negative side effects, Casas Bahia quickly began to investigate the root cause.

The problems stemmed from two simple issues. First, the new computer generated a passbook that could not fit into a shirt pocket. Until then, customers carried the passbook in their pocket as a reminder to pay their bill. Now, customers would simply forget to pay their bills. Customers also claimed they never received the passbook or it took too long to arrive at their house. Although some customers actually did not receive the book, others were tempted to default. Within a year, Casas Bahia had developed a new system that solved these problems. The new passbook could fit into a shirt pocket and people remembered to pay. Also, all paperwork was completed at the store, and the customer would provide a signature confirming receipt of the passbook and an understanding of the terms. Moreover, costs decreased due to the lack of postage and handling. With the modifications in place, default rates returned to their normal levels.

The new system significantly increased customer satisfaction. Every time a customer made a new purchase, his or her information was already in the system. There was effectively no waiting time associated with receiving a passbook. This system saved Casas Bahia over $4 million in annual labor and printing savings.

The next evolution of this idea is currently in process. All customer-related materials will be optically scanned and digitized. Casas Bahia will be able to examine any information by customer, store, contract number, credit analyst, and so on, at the source document level. With an average of 800,000 tickets printed per month, any incremental efficiency has a significant impact.

History with IBM and Linux

In 1994, Casas Bahia was running on an IBM 3090. It was the first company in South America, and second in the world, to run IBM 2074 OS 1.2 and 1.4. From 1994 to 2002, Casas Bahia used IBM OS/2 for its point-of-sale (POS) terminals. The technology was solid and stable and no serious problems occurred. In 2002, IBM announced it would no longer support OS/2.

Initially, the only option for Casas Bahia was to migrate to a Microsoft Windows environment. The migration worried the company for several reasons. First, it would cost more than $20 million. Second, it would effectively change the systems and processes to which employees were accustomed. Retraining thousands of employees would require a significant investment in time and resources in addition to the cost of software. Moreover, it would be difficult to quantify the effect on sales and customer relationships that would result from the distraction of a major systems implementation. (Casas Bahia would switch to smart terminals.) Finally, the expense associated with ongoing maintenance and individual site licenses was significant.

Casas Bahia was not satisfied with a Windows solution, so it began to investigate alternatives. Casas Bahia researched Linux. Because Linux is an open-source system, Casas Bahia developed a solution that closely matched its existing setup but with more flexibility and scalability. The company would be able to remotely boot and utilize frame relay and dummy terminals. The end user would never know the difference. Casas Bahia was the first to transition from the IBM OS to Linux. The company was the first in the world to come up with this POS solution.

Recently, IBM contracted with Casas Bahia to become strategic partners, helping IBM sell this solution to other companies looking for an alternative to

Windows. As of March 31, 2003, Casas Bahia was one of three companies worldwide to have this agreement with IBM. Effectively, IBM can use Casas Bahia as an example and Casas Bahia gets 24/7 tech support from IBM and access to their development labs. When asked if Casas Bahia is concerned about opening up its solution to the competition, the Director of IT responded, "We are already two steps past that. Competition is good and gives you perspective as to what others are doing."

Technology Today

Casas Bahia spends 0.8 percent of its revenues on technology, including capital and maintenance spending. It is estimated that competitors spend an average of 3 percent of revenues on similar expenditures. The key to cost savings is really threefold. First, Casas Bahia employs a relatively low number of employees: 30 developers, 50 technicians, and 50 relatively inexpensive support staff. Second, Casas Bahia does not utilize third-party vendors. As seen with the Windows example earlier, licensing third-party software for an entire company is expensive. Finally, Casas Bahia invests its resources in infrastructure. In partnership with CISCO and Telefonica, Casas Bahia installed an Internet Protocol (IP) network that connects all stores, warehouses, and cross-docking facilities. Casas Bahia also worked with Telefonica to develop state-of-the-art frame relay with voice and data over IP, the first for both companies. Because this was a new venture for both Telefonica and Casas Bahia, Casas Bahia was able to lock into a long-term contract with a low rate. Finally, IT constantly focuses on reducing costs and improving productivity.

The majority of work today is focused on maximizing the customer experience. The new POS and passbook system enable the customer to have a very satisfactory in-store experience with minimal waiting. The POS terminals and related system also enable the salespeople to cross-sell more effectively. They instantly have the ability to know where the customer is in his or her payment stream and how much more the customer can afford. Casas Bahia utilizes an integrated warehouse system to ensure that customers receive the product they want when they want it. Also, the integration between the front and back offices enables management to be more responsive to customer needs.

Currently, Casas Bahia has no plans to integrate with its suppliers. The model in Brazil is much different from that in more developed countries. The economy is not as stable and the vendor mix changes quickly. Also, Casas Bahia focuses on personal negotiations for every major purchase. It would be inefficient to maintain a system that would have to keep up with constantly changing terms. It is easier for Casas Bahia to leverage its purchasing power without an automated system.

In the Store

Every month, the Casas Bahia system handles an average of 800,000 contracts. Thirty percent are new clients who must be set up in the system for the first time. Approximately half of all returning customers are automatically approved, whereas the remaining half are rejected by the system and must be approved by an analyst. There are several reasons why the system will reject a customer. One reason a customer may be rejected is if he or she has an outstanding bill that is less than 50% paid off. For a majority of those reasons, though, the credit analyst will override the system and, based on his or her relationship with the client, grant the credit. The system does not capture if the customer has had a change in circumstance, such as a new job. It is up to the analyst to take a risk based on the relationship with the customer. Although overrides increase the default rate, the increase in sales greatly outweighs the corresponding risk. If a customer is new and has no history, the analyst must determine if the customer is a good risk. For perspective, the default rate resulting from clients of whom the computer system automatically approves is 3%. Once you consider new customers and those customers whom the salespeople override the average default rate increases to 8%. The ability of the analyst to override, the system and provide customers what they require is vital in earning the trust of the customers. Once customers trust Casas Bahia, the virtuous cycle can begin.

Uniqueness

According to Casas Bahia, no competitor has developed, or is in the process of developing, a comparable IT backbone or infrastructure in Brazil. This unique network infrastructure is important to the company's ability to respond quickly to the unforeseen problems that arise. All stores have remote connectivity. Approximately one-third of the stores are connected via 256 kps. The remaining stores are connected at a rate of 128 kps. The warehouse is at 512 kps. Whether it is due to the lack of creativity or funding, the competition does not invest in technology. "Our competitors rely on third-party vendors that do not develop specific solutions, but rather a generic solution that can fit anyone's problem. It doesn't work," says Frederico Wanderley, CIO.

Ongoing IT Projects

Casas Bahia has four major initiatives. The first, which is currently being implemented, is linking sales with marketing at the POS. The company will be able to custom-design, roll out, and track promotions by store and customer. All stores will track the productivity and profitability of each campaign. This initiative took only four months from concept to implementation. The second major initiative is to improve deliveries. As customers become more demanding, Casas Bahia must find a way to meet their needs. The current process requires manual entry of the customer's address for all deliveries and leads to wasted time and errors. The third is the switch to optically scanning and digitizing all customer-related documents and collecting them together in one electronic file. Soon, all customer-related information will be centralized and viewable at the POS. Casas Bahia has invested in a six-terabyte hard drive to house all the data. The fourth initiative is to develop a desktop managerial tool based on the new Linux infrastructure.

Future

The project next on the horizon is wireless in the stores. We see this as a better way to serve the client. It will provide an easy and cost-effective way to change the layout of the stores to meet changing customer demands. Our main concern here is the security [encryption] issue.

—Frederico Wanderley, CIO

The future of technology at Casas Bahia can be described as "day by day." Although the behavior of A and B customers is predictable, the behavior of C, D, and E customers is not. Casas Bahia must remain flexible enough to react to quick changes. I see a problem, I create a solution. It has to be creative. My development teams are constantly in the stores talking with the users trying to understand current issues and determine future needs. We are constantly evaluating requests to see if they make sense for Casas Bahia and are feasible. Casas Bahia works very hard to foster an environment of trust where people feel safe to share their ideas.

—Frederico Wanderley, CIO

Human Resources Management

Casas Bahia has approximately 20,000 employees. The company employs an additional 2,500 contract installers. Until 1996, all human resources (HR)-related decisions, including training, hiring, and firing, were made at the corporate level. After rapid expansion began in 1996, all HR-related functions, except for specialized training and the administrative aspect of the function, moved to the local stores. All policy decisions are still centralized at headquarters.

Most employees spend their entire career at Casas Bahia and believe they have good jobs. Average employee turnover is only 1 percent. Most middle managers and above have been with the company for more than 20 years. They start at the bottom and work their way up. For example, the typical path in the sales function is salesperson, manager trainee, classroom training, manager, regional manager trainee, and regional manager. All along the way they are taught and come to believe that the better Casas Bahia does, the better off they will be personally and professionally.

Prior to 1994 there was no formal training. Training is now a two-step process that includes formal classroom training as well as two weeks of on-the-job shadowing. The actual shadow time can vary according to the specific job requirements. This system enables employees to quickly learn and become comfortable with their functions. Casas Bahia developed specialized teams in finance, sales, and management to assist in the training process. Additionally, suppliers now come to Casas Bahia to train employees in the uses and benefits of their respective products. This is a relatively new and welcome occurrence. The centralized HR department occasionally will sponsor small, specialized training courses or contract out to a third party if specific skill training is required.

Compensation for salespeople is based on performance. Although salaries are based on commission, salespeople are guaranteed a salary of R$500 per month (2.5 times the minimum wage). Brazilian labor laws do not allow for 100 percent commissioned salaries. The base salary is set well below the employees' sales targets. Casas Bahia employees believe the labor law is just to protect bad sales reps. Salespeople make an average of 2-percent commission on all their sales. However, as soon as the employee's salary from his or her commissions exceeds R$500, he or she switches to 100 percent commission only. The average salesperson makes R$1,500 per month (7.5 times minimum wage); high performers can reach R$3,500. Michael Klein says:

If I let them, some of them would work for hours and hours without stopping. They know they can make a lot of money at Casas Bahia. Any person has to have a motivation, an ambition in his life. Nothing is better than giving my employees the freedom to pursue their ambitions.

Casas Bahia prefers to hire locally for its stores for several reasons. First, local hires tend to be more familiar with the neighborhood and the customers. Second, hiring employees who live close to the store minimizes the impact of bus and train strikes. The rainy season in São Paulo also results in major traffic problems. Finally, hiring locally helps both the employees and customers feel a sense of pride and ownership. In the southern region of São Paulo, there are typically 100 applicants for every sales opening. Due to expansion and turnover, Casa Bahia hires an average of 20 to 30 salespeople every month.

On average, according to José Roberto Fernandes, HR Director, Casas Bahia pays better than direct competitors. People love working for Samuel Klein. They believe in his philosophy of valuing and respecting the individual. Fernandes believes, "Samuel Klein has planted a seed in every store and person that is now growing." That seed is most evident in Klein's belief that the more he makes, the more he needs to share. For example, Brazil requires that companies pay employees one extra pay period in the month of December. At Casas Bahia, if business goes well, the company often will pay employees a 14th period. Also, travel incentives for achieving business goals and targets are commonplace. If a region or store meets a particular quarterly goal or special promotional target, they are rewarded with several days at Disney World in Orlando, FL. Even now, when the overall economy is suffering, Casas Bahia continues its rewards practice; trips now are focused on local or in-country resorts.

Futures Challenges

The most important factor in the continued success of Casas Bahia is the belief system and values that Samuel Klein has instilled in all the employees. A strong and continuing relationship with customers is paramount. Also, within the company, every department believes the success of Casas Bahia is more important than the success of an individual department or group. Unlike in many organizations where the sales and credit departments have different objectives, this is not the case at Casas Bahia. Employees believe that as long as the customer is happy and Casas Bahia does well, then they will be personally better off.

Looking forward, there are several challenges to maintaining success. In the short run, the introduction of credit cards poses a threat of losing the important client relationship as well as decreasing cross-selling opportunities. General acceptance of credit cards with C, D, and E customers forced Casas Bahia to accept credit cards in September 2002. Casas Bahia was the last major retailer in Brazil to accept credit cards. In six months, credit card sales have reached 4 percent of Casas Bahia's total sales. On a positive note, when the credit card sale is made, the risk of default transfers to the credit card company. Credit card companies in Brazil offer an installment payment option without interest on a product-by-product basis. There is some concern that an increase in credit card sales might decrease customer loyalty due to the lack of in-store traffic. Currently, all customers must come in to a Casas Bahia store every month to make their monthly payments. This is the main traffic that facilitates the 77-percent cross-selling ability. This situation will be enforced only with the stabilization of the Brazilian economy and evolution of the financing market. Little by little, banks are targeting the BOP in Brazil with accounts and credit cards. This will be an issue Casas Bahia must learn to deal with.

Additionally, Casas Bahia has opened a few stores in neighborhoods that cater to A and B customers. Over the past 10 years, several retail chains that focused on serving the A and B segment have been forced to leave the market (Sears, Mappin, G. Aronson, and Casas Centro). Also, in parallel with these companies going bankrupt, Casas Bahia was undergoing a major modernization. Due to the purchasing power of Casas Bahia, the company could offer better prices on the brands that A and B customers desired on a cash basis. This combination has allowed the company to capture some of the A and B segment. Although store locations are in nicer areas of the city, the configuration and products offered remain the same. That said, A and B customers tend to purchase more appliances and electronics than furniture.

There are two significant differences when serving the A and B segment: decreased profitability and differing needs. First, A and B customers typically pay in cash (C, D, and E customers are 90-percent financed), so Casas Bahia receives no interest revenue. The company also must offer discounts to entice A and B customers into the stores. Also, A and B customers are much more demanding. Unlike those at the BOP, A and B customers require an exact delivery date and time. They also have a high propensity to complain. Moreover, as a low-cost operator, paying for real estate in more expensive markets will decrease the company's profitability. Casas Bahia must learn how to deal with high-income customers or risk taking the same path of its bankrupted competitors.

Expansion poses three major challenges. First, Casas Bahia must quickly learn the behavior of an entirely new customer base. This will be increasingly difficult as Casas Bahia continues its rapid expansion of 25 stores per year. Second, the rapid growth also creates new distribution demands. Monitoring thousands of drivers, damages to merchandise, turnover, and attending to customer demands for more accurate delivery time forecasting are not trivial. Finally, controlling the default level might be the key challenge for Casas Bahia. The company opened a centralized call and collection center to address this challenge. Since consolidating more than 300 call center employees from all stores, collections recovery has increased 100 percent. Casas Bahia must develop a process whereby it can maintain or reduce its current default rate while continuing with its plan of rapid expansion.

Another threat is the increasing competition of large hypermarts. It is unclear whether or not those chains will develop the capability to serve the BOP with any significant presence. This competition poses the biggest worry to Michael Klein.

One of the most significant issues Casas Bahia faces is a long-term plan for succession. Samuel Klein's two sons, Michael and Saúl, have successfully transitioned the daily operations from their father, convincing both employees and customers that they can continue the belief system their father instilled. As Samuel reaches his 80s and his sons get older, the plans for succession are either unknown or not publicly stated.

Endnotes

- Associação Comercial de São Paulo, Boletim do Instituto de Economia Gastão Vidigal (ACSP/IEGV)
- United States Census Bureau
- Banco Central do Brasil
- Casas Bahia
- Datafolha/M&M

This report was written by Sami Foguel and Andrew Wilson, under the supervision of Professor C. K. Prahalad. This report is intended to be a catalyst for discussion and is not intended to illustrate effective or ineffective strategies.

CEMEX:
Innovation in Housing
for the Poor

CEMEX is a multinational cement manufacturing company operating out of Mexico. It is the largest cement manufacturer in Mexico, the second largest in the United States, and the third largest in the world. The company has operations on four continents and recorded global revenues of $6.54 billion in 2002 with a gross margin of 44.1 percent.

THE INNOVATION...

CEMEX leads the paradigm shift of companies profitably providing housing for the poor, the Tier 4 population, instead of governments or not-for-profit organizations.

CEMEX manufactures and sells raw cement, ready-mix concrete, aggregates, and clinker (used to make cement) under different brand names. As the largest cement company in Mexico, CEMEX operated in a highly protected legal environment with little competition until the 1990s. It competed mainly on price and controlled 65 percent of the market share in Mexico. However, during the 1990s, the legal barriers in Mexico broke down, paving the way for international competition. CEMEX found itself operating in a highly competitive open environment.

Starting in 1987, under the leadership of Mr. Lorenzo Zambrano, CEMEX experienced explosive growth, mainly through acquisitions and global expansion. Today, the company has 235 cement and ready-mix plants in Mexico, 60 in the United States, 85 in Spain, 45 in Venezuela, 4 in Indonesia, and 4 in Egypt.

In the new competitive arena and under new leadership, CEMEX fundamentally changed its ways of conducting business. The company's strategy emphasized improving profitability through efficient operations. The company also shifted from selling products to selling complete solutions. With this new strategy, CEMEX has established a very strong brand and has managed to translate it into extraordinary profits from a commodity-driven business.

According to CEMEX, the following are the sources of its competitive advantage, many of which have been widely acknowledged in business circles:

- Continued innovation
- High level of commitment to customer service and satisfaction
- Proven postmerger integration expertise
- Digital evolution: efficient production, distribution, and delivery processes through sophisticated information systems
- Ability to identify high-growth market opportunities in developing economies

CEMEX: Mexico

CEMEX has 15 cement plants and 220 ready-mix plants spread throughout Mexico. The company sells cement to two main customer segments: the informal or self-construction segment and the formal construction segment. The formal segment consists of traditional large-scale customers, middle- and upper-income individuals, whereas the informal segment consists of the do-it-yourself homebuilders and low-income customers.

The company has invested considerably in information technology (IT) over the years to boost productivity and manage its operations more efficiently. CEMEX takes pride in its operations and was recently the winner of the CIO-100 from IDG's CIO magazine.[1] The company has gained a significant competitive cost advantage over its competitors by setting up an excellent distribution infrastructure and centralized, computerized delivery network in which every movement of every truck is monitored in real time, enabling on-time delivery of cement and ready-mix to customers. The operation in Guadalajara boasts a 97.63-percent on-time delivery of cement.

Patrimonio Hoy

Patrimonio Hoy means "savings/property today." In 1998, CEMEX launched an innovative experiment called Patrimonio Hoy that enables very poor people to pay for services and building materials to upgrade their homes. This program blends the pursuit of profit and social responsiveness at CEMEX. The key objectives of the program are as follows:

- Generate business that represents competitive advantages

- Represent an accessible option for poor families looking for a better quality of life through households by offering good-quality cement and raw material at reasonable and frozen prices (i.e., no price changes reflecting time and inflation)

- Offer access to credit (by providing materials in advance) not available to the poor otherwise

- Position CEMEX as a responsible corporate citizen that is committed to society

- Build social capital

During the Mexican economic crisis in 1994–1995, CEMEX experienced a significant drop in domestic sales. Sales in the formal segment dropped by as much as 50 percent, but sales in the informal and self-construction segment dropped by only 10 percent to 20 percent.[2] The company realized that its high level of dependency on the formal segment left it very vulnerable to business cycle swings in Mexico.

According to an estimate by CEMEX, the do-it-yourself segment accounted for almost 40 percent of cement consumption in Mexico and has a market potential of $500 to $600 million annually. Realizing the potential in this segment, CEMEX expanded its presence in the retail channel by setting up 2,020 kiosks or *construramas* to establish closer relationships with the informal segment. At the same time, CEMEX was looking for business opportunities to distinguish itself in the industry and establish a competitive advantage. The company also was keen to develop corporate citizenship and become a more socially responsive company.

CEMEX as a firm was known for identifying potential opportunities and turning them into profitable ventures. Realizing the huge potential in the do-it-yourself segment, the company embarked on a new venture to capture that untapped segment. This laid the foundation for Patrimonio Hoy.

The company realized the key difference between the formal segment and the informal segment was in the average revenue per customer. Whereas fewer big-ticket customers could generate most of the company's revenues, the situation is reversed for low-income customers (see Figure 1). It is estimated that 60 percent of the population in Mexico earns less than $5 per day. CEMEX learned that by converting the low-income population (which forms a majority) into customers, the steady revenues from this segment could be very impressive.

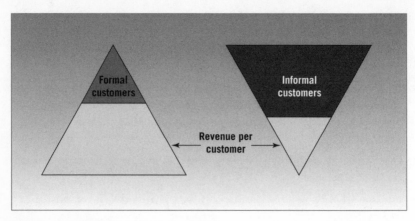

Figure 1 Customer/Revenue Contribution models

The management team headed by Francisco Garza Zambrano and a consulting team from Business Design Associates performed in-depth market research to gain a good understanding of this low-income market in Mexico. The research was an eye-opening experience (see Table 1) for the CEMEX management from a business and social perspective. Project Patrimonio Hoy was conceived.

Before actually entering the market with this program, CEMEX had to overcome a few fundamental and critical challenges that were specific to the low-income market. First, CEMEX had to build trust and convince the poor they would indeed be able to build a house with CEMEX. Second, CEMEX had to make the poor understand that credit was not a stumbling block for the poor as part of Patrimonio Hoy. The team had to work with a different mindset that did not include sale of cement as the sole objective of the program.

Mexican Society

Mexican society, like many other societies in developing countries, possesses certain characteristics specific to that society.

Savings

Low-income families in Mexico (and in many other parts of developing and underdeveloped countries) follow a different savings method from that of middle- and upper-income families. Because low-income families don't receive regular paychecks and don't receive any government subsidies or grants, they don't have access to banks and credit. Within a community, neighbors, families,

Table 1 Comparison of Formal and Informal Market Segments

Attributes	Formal Segment	Informal Segment
Sales	Higher revenue per customer	Low revenue per customer
Payments	Financing generally not required	Financing is important
Demand	Depends on economy	More or less steady demand
Price sensitivity	Driven by bargaining power	Convenience-driven (such as credit, delivery, etc.)
Brand equity	Recognized and trusted	Should build trust to deliver as promised
Growth	Slow growth	Very high potential for growth
Customer location	Usually located in places of easy access	Mostly located in remote areas
Relationships	Stops at the distributor level	Requires close ties with end customers

and friends get together and form *tandas* or "pools." The members of the tanda pool in money as and when they receive paychecks and if they have any money left to save. Once a week (or at some predetermined interval), one of the members can bid for the pool by deep discounting or can win the pool through a lottery. Typically this pool is used for unanticipated family emergencies, education, and sometimes housing. The only factor that enforces discipline in the tanda system is the social capital—the trust, reputation, and participation in the community.

However, the tanda system was not nearly as effective for housing. Even before money found its way to such pools, families (usually the men) spent it on various other non-primary activities—drinking, partying, and so on. Also, there were too many members in pools, and it was difficult to manage and enforce discipline. People often backed out of the pools and this led to many problems.

Women and Entrepreneurism

Women are the key drivers of savings in families. In Mexican society (and most other societies), women are very entrepreneurial in nature, and they very actively participate in the tanda system. Regardless of whether they are home-makers, working women, or small-business owners, they are responsible for any savings in the family. Research conducted by the Patrimonio Hoy team revealed that 70 percent of those women who were saving were saving money in the tanda system to construct homes for their families.

The men in the society considered their job done if they brought in their paycheck at the end of the day. The women actually manage expenses with the limited "allowance" that they receive per day from the men. They have to find very creative ways to allocate money from the allowance as savings to build a house, spend on their children's education, and so on.

Housing

The poorest people in the city live in settlements made of raw cinder blocks, and in worse cases cardboard and corrugated sheet metal. Most houses have one or two rooms per family, and the size of a family ranges from 6 to 10. The homes are overcrowded and this causes its own set of social problems, including friction within the family and children taking to the streets.

Initial Market Research: Guadalajara, Mexico

A research team of eight people selected Guadalajara in the province of Jalisco as the first city to implement the program. Guadalajara has been considered a traditional test market in Mexico for many reasons. First, the social and economic profile of low-income communities was very representative of most of the populated areas in Mexico. Over 50 percent of the population lives in homes that hug a network of pitted, unpaved roads in unplanned settlements surrounding the city and blending into the countryside. Second, CEMEX was gradually losing its stronghold in the second-largest city in Mexico. Nearly all the houses appear to be under construction. The third very subtle reason was that the construction methods in Guadalajara were different from that of other places. Traditionally, for every 100 pesos spent on construction raw materials, 52 pesos were spent on cement. In Guadalajara, the southwestern region of Mexico, only 22 pesos were spent on cement. Instead, clay and limestone were used in the construction of houses. CEMEX thus had to find new opportunities for growth in Guadalajara.

Market Eye-Openers

The team conducted a three-month study based on various demographic factors—social, religious, political, and financial. The study also analyzed the various construction practices and methods, brand perception, and image of various cement brands.

The team realized that financing was the most important and most difficult challenge to overcome for low-income customers. Unless the poor obtain access to credit, it would be difficult to sell the idea of constructing a complete house in the near future. The second challenge was that most families employed local semiskilled or unskilled masons who built rooms without any planning. The lack of technical expertise resulted in a lot of raw material waste. Often the masons did not order the right amount of material, and families didn't have a safe place to store the excess raw materials. They had to leave the material outside their houses at the mercy of nature and theft.

The team identified three keys areas of improvement and change for CEMEX before launching Patrimonio Hoy:

- Identify innovative ways to provide access to credit for the poor
- Improve the brand perception of CEMEX as a socially responsive company to earn trust among the people, especially the poor
- Change and improve distribution methods and construction practices to make it cost-effective for CEMEX, its distributors, and the low-income customers

Patrimonio Hoy: Program Design

Identification of Offices or Cells

A special research team set out to explore neighborhoods in and around the city of Guadalajara to identify high-growth opportunities. In a broad sense, the team identified potential pockets or cells based on income, construction progress, housing development, concentration of poor people, distributor network, and population growth.

The team identified target communities where the average family (5–6 people) earned around 50 to 150 pesos (US$5 to $15 approximately) per day. The target population for Patrimonio Hoy is not the absolute bottom of the economic pyramid, wherein the average per-capita income is less than $5 per day.

Cell Setup

Once a neighborhood was identified, Patrimonio Hoy set up a cell for that neighborhood. A typical cell is set up to target a customer group of 5,000 or a community with a population of between 50,000 and 100,000 (or 20,000 families). There are one to five employees per cell: a general manager or chief, an engineer, a technical advisor or an architect, a supplies manager, and a customer service representative or administrative clerk.

The chief works in identifying "promoters" within the community who go door-to-door selling the new savings–credit idea to the poor. The supply manager works closely with corporate CEMEX in the negotiation of prices for raw materials, interacts with the distributors for the delivery, and monitors the quality of suppliers and distributors in terms of delivery time, customer treatment, quality of materials, and so on.

Customer Enrollment

Recognizing the inefficiencies inherent in the original tanda system, Patrimonio Hoy has strict rules and standards for the program.

Socios or Partners

Socios are the actual customers who enroll in Patrimonio Hoy. The socios get together and form a group, restricted to three people. The reason for such a small group size is that it is easier to enforce payment discipline in a smaller group, and the group tends to form stronger relationships to help each other out during an emergency.

Promoters

Promoters play a key role as ambassadors for Patrimonio Hoy. Ninety-eight percent of the promoters are women. They work on a commission basis that is dependent on the number of socios they help enroll and on the duration of the stay of the socio within the program.

Savings—Credit Payment Cycle

CEMEX made improvements to the existing tanda system by offering a combination of savings and credit. In this system, poor people not only save their money, but also obtain access to credit based on their savings and payment discipline—a new model that moved away from a savings-only or a credit-only system to a savings-credit system. By introducing the savings-credit system, Patrimonio Hoy might have revolutionized the idea of savings by changing the basic spending pattern of the poor in Mexico.

The enrollment of a socio ensures a consistent and steady source of revenue in the pipeline (for x number of weeks) for Patrimonio Hoy and the distributors. The predictability of revenue has huge implications across the value chain from the suppliers to the end customers.

When a socio group is formed, the group goes to the nearest cell and completes an application. This application is completely informational and does not require any credit history or collateral. Also, the prices of raw materials are "frozen" throughout the payment period. The only requirement is a commitment from each socio in the group to pay 120 pesos per week for a definite period of time (at least 70 weeks).

After enrollment, each socio in the group sets up an appointment with the technical advisor or architect (for a low fee) for an interview. Through an interactive process, the technical advisor helps the socio decide the following:

- Types and quantities of the needed materials for the first room
- What the next room will be in his or her home and its placement in the current layout
- The sequence of the following rooms to be constructed in the future

The personal visits of architects make the socios feel like important customers, and have helped Patrimonio Hoy build trust among the socios.

Each socio in the three-member group takes a turn every month to collect money from the other two members and remits a weekly payment of 360 pesos (120 pesos per head). For every 120 pesos a partner pays per week, Patrimonio Hoy charges 15 pesos as a membership fee per socio.

Phase 1 (First 10 Weeks)

Each socio pays 105 pesos (120 pesos net of 15 pesos) for the first five weeks, totaling 505 pesos. At the end of the fifth week, Patrimonio Hoy makes its first delivery of raw materials for construction worth 1,050 pesos (equivalent of payment for 10 weeks). By advancing five weeks worth of raw materials, Patrimonio Hoy is effectively extending credit to its customers. The extension of credit by delivering raw material to partners in advance helps Patrimonio Hoy establish credibility with the socios by proving that it has lived up to its promise of delivering raw materials. This phase also serves as a pilot to test the commitment of the socios.

Phase 2 (11–70 Weeks)

If socios stay committed beyond the first phase, they gain from the program even more. During the subsequent phases, socios receive raw materials worth 10 weeks at the end of the second week; that is, advance worth eight weeks. They receive raw materials worth 10 weeks at the end of the 12th week. Deliveries are made during Weeks 12, 22, 32, 42, 52, and 62.

Material Distribution and Delivery

CEMEX offers socios two choices of delivery: receive delivery right away for immediate construction or receive a delivery voucher now that can be exchanged for raw material delivery at a later time when they are ready to start construction. However, they will never receive cash in hand, unlike the original tanda system wherein pool members could receive cash.

If the partners choose to receive their raw material, Patrimonio Hoy coordinates with its distributors to arrange for delivery of the material. If partners choose to receive delivery vouchers for delivery at a later date, the inventory is stored at the distributors' warehouses.

Interviews with socios revealed that the first delivery made after just five weeks of payment and consistent on-time delivery played a large role in earning the trust of the partners. The supply managers also play the role of an audit manager, ensuring that the distributors deliver good-quality materials on time and provide good service to the socios.

Value Analysis

CEMEX was quick to realize it had to position itself as a complete solutions provider at low cost and not as a cement seller competing on prices, in order to tap into the huge low-income market. It also realized if it tried to sell just cement, it wouldn't take too long for competitors to enter the arena. Hence, the company's strategy for the low-income market was to do the following:

- Position itself as a company committed to society by offering housing at a low cost to the poor and enabling a better quality of life.
- Sell cement and other raw materials as a package such as *pacquet tolteca*. (Tolteca is a CEMEX brand of cement sold in Guadalajara.)
- Offer value-added services such as credit access, technical advice, architect visits, storage space for raw material, and customer service.

Patrimonio Hoy had to offer a strong value proposition for customers to overcome their resignation to life as the ignored population segment, and also change certain fundamental and cultural spending (on nonbasic events such as parties, drinking, bars, etc.) patterns. It also had to ensure that its suppliers and distributors were enthusiastic about the new business model.

Value to Promoters

Promoters are the ambassadors of Patrimonio Hoy who identify prospective customers, sell the idea of savings–credit to them, and motivate them to enroll in the program. Hence, it is important that they are very enterprising and have active ties with the local community.

The reason for promoters to participate in the program is twofold: They do it for a social cause to build social capital (According to Patrimonio Hoy's general manager, "Social capital is very important for people with little economic capital.") and also to earn money. Patrimonio Hoy rewards their efforts on a commission basis (points system). A promoter earns 48 points (1 point = 1 peso or in U. S. $0.10) for every enrolled socio for whom she is responsible. To ensure that she brings in committed socios, the system rewards her with more, depending on the commitment of the socio to the program. On the 30th week of the socio, she gets 32 points, and from the 30th week on, she gets one point per week per socio. For example, if a socio is enrolled in the program for 70 weeks, the promoter who is responsible for the socio's enrollment earns 120 points (48 + 32 + 40).

The system implicitly encourages promoters to bring in as many committed socios as possible. Many promoters are socios themselves. At the end of the 70-week period, the promoters can convert the accumulated points on a one-to-one ratio to receive either cash or raw material (if the promoters are socios themselves).

Patrimonio Hoy offers initial training to promoters and they start with a target enrollment in the range of 80 to 90 (per cell) socios per calendar period (28 days). Typically, each cell has eight or nine promoters.

Value to Socios and Partners

The biggest challenge for Patrimonio Hoy is to build trust with the people. The poor people are resigned to the fact they will not be able to build a house in less than two to three years. Typically, it takes 16 years for a family to build a four-room house and an average of four years just to complete one room.

To lure the customers, Patrimonio Hoy offers the following proposition:

- Offer access to credit by providing materials in advance
- Offer good-quality cement and raw material from a trusted national brand at reasonable and frozen prices (i.e., no price changes reflecting time and inflation) up to 70 weeks
- Build a typical room in 1.5 years (instead of four years)
- Provide technical support and service such as architect visits and technical advice
- Provide skilled masons for construction for a reasonable fee by opening a school for masonry training
- Provide excellent customer service and good treatment
- Provide storage space for raw material and reduce waste
- Offer accelerated payment options for ambitious and aspiring customers
- Offer similar programs for schools (Patrimonio Hoy Escolar) and other infrastructure such as pavements (Calle Digna) for families and neighborhoods

- Reduce cost of construction by reducing waste and offering technical training for self-construction.
- Offer training to socios interested in masonry
- Build social capital

Patrimonio Hoy helps the poor build homes that might have been a distant dream otherwise. By offering such value-added services, Patrimonio Hoy has been successful in earning the trust of the socios. The general manager of Patrimonio Hoy claims the reduction in costs for the socios are as high as 30 percent, and the reduction in time reaches as high as 60 to 70 percent.

Value to Suppliers

CEMEX is the largest cement manufacturing company in Mexico and, by virtue of its size, it has significant bargaining power with its suppliers and distributors. Patrimonio Hoy collaborates with CEMEX in negotiating prices of raw material such as bricks, steel, clay, limestone, and so on, with suppliers. The company exerts collective bargaining power over its suppliers by negotiating on three key factors: generating a steady demand for materials, creating a consistent revenue stream, and ensuring zero-risk collection of money.

According to Patrimonio Hoy's general manager, the suppliers are very happy to supply materials to Patrimonio Hoy because of the steady demand for their materials and the quick growth in sales (as high as 30 percent annually) in locations of operations of Patrimonio Hoy.

Value to Distributors

Traditionally, the company has "pushed" its products and services through the distribution channels, and hence it was a very price-driven market. Distributors operated on a 15-percent average margin from the sale of building materials.

However, in the new business model, Patrimonio Hoy manages the distributor relationships on its own. Although it works with the existing CEMEX distributor network, the margins in the new channel are slightly different. Distributor margin on the sale of building materials sometimes drops to 12 percent. However, the slight drop in margins is more than offset by a steady demand for cement and other high-margin raw materials such as sand and gravel where the margin could be as high as 45 percent. Patrimonio Hoy has effectively created a pull for cement, and CEMEX on the supply side pushes it, enabling the push–pull strategy for cement sales. Patrimonio Hoy has seen a very enthusiastic response from distributors who are willing to participate in this program.

Operating Model of Patrimonio Hoy

The objective of Patrimonio Hoy is not only to serve a social cause, but also make it a profitable, self-sustainable business. Patrimonio Hoy also recognizes that volume is very important for it to be a success, and hence has based its revenues on a per-transaction basis. These revenues are in addition to the sale of cement by CEMEX.

Revenues

The revenue streams are as follows:

- Membership fee of 12.5 percent per socio per payment of 120 pesos
- Intermediation fee in the form of a 7-percent margin from distributors

Costs

The average initial investment per typical cell is 400,000 pesos. The operational cost per cell, including salaries, is around 85,000 pesos per month. An average cell needs approximately 700 enrolled socios to break even on operations. According to Patrimonio Hoy's general manager, the program generates approximately 2,000,000 pesos in cash flows from operations. The goal of this program is to operate as a standalone, break-even unit, because the initial objective is to increase customer awareness, change consumer behavior, and establish a competitive position in the market.

Marketing

The traditional methods of marketing communication, advertising, and promotion are not effective in this operating model. Patrimonio Hoy realized early on that mass media advertising through television, newspapers, and other outlets would not convey a personalized message and would not help build trust among the low-income people.

The Mexican people believe in leaving something behind for the next generation. Mostly, the families believe in leaving immovable property or wealth for their sons and daughters. That, in Spanish, is called *patrimonio*. The Patrimonio Hoy program tries to convey the message by motivating the public to "save today." In addition, the idea of being part of a family or a group, with a clear set of values, benefits, and so on, is extremely important in Mexican society. Patrimonio Hoy conveys this message in its marketing communications and encourages socios to enroll with Patrimonio Hoy.

Community Outreach

Among the poor, the best way to establish ties with the local communities is through personal interaction. Perhaps this explains the significance of the role of promoters for Patrimonio Hoy. The promoters go door to door in the neighborhood communities and talk about the benefits of the program. Patrimonio Hoy provides literature and pamphlets that contain relevant information, and provides preliminary training for the promoters. The main objective is to generate interest in the community. The sales officers and promoters periodically hold meetings and public gatherings to educate the customers. One can find messages and contact information painted on the walls of neighborhoods as bills or graffiti.

Word of Mouth

Word of mouth is the single most important broadcast mechanism that has proved to be successful in the expansion of the program. People in the neighborhoods tend to have very close-knit ties within the community that again reflect the importance of social capital. Anything good or bad spreads very effectively through the word-of-mouth channel, which is often underestimated or ignored.

Pricing

Patrimonio Hoy has adopted "the CEMEX way" to conduct profitable business. Although Patrimonio Hoy tries to offer cost-effective solutions to customers, it does not offer low-price or lower quality products and services. The company has been reasonably successful in convincing distributors of the same and has avoided a price war. In fact, CEMEX sells its cement at a slightly higher price than that of its competitors. The socios are aware of this. Interviews with socios reveal that the higher price charged by CEMEX is more than offset by the value-added services that Patrimonio Hoy offers to the socios.

Patrimonio Hoy negotiates a volume-based discount of up to 7 percent from its distributors. The salary structure of the supply manager is based on how well he manages to negotiate discounts with the suppliers and distributors. To ensure that the materials, including cement, are reasonably priced, Patrimonio Hoy conducts a market study that publishes prices of competitors and calculates an average price for each calendar month. The socios who sign up in a particular month enjoy the same prices through the 70-week payment cycle. For example, if the price of a ton of cement is 100 pesos when a socio signs up, Patrimonio Hoy commits to sell cement at 100 pesos for the rest of the 70-week period. By offering this price commitment, Patrimonio Hoy is able to charge a slight premium over its competitors. Each cell maintains its own list of prices.

Promotion

Patrimonio Hoy offers small-scale promotional events such as fee waiver for the first installment or a few installments for new enrollees, a raffle event wherein a socio receives a room essentially for free, and free "back-to-school" items for new enrollees. Some promotions have included seasonal offers such as vacation getaways and Christmas offers. However, these promotions are new, and Patrimonio Hoy doesn't have enough data to verify if promotions are a good way to increase enrollment.

Distribution

In the traditional distribution network and supply-chain model, bargaining power and market dominance had played a key role in the determination of prices and selection of distributors. The distributors primarily cared about prices and discounts. The industry was driven by price wars. However, the new model takes a very different approach. Not all the traditional distributors are part of Patrimonio Hoy. In fact, a new strategy is adopted for establishing a distribution model that would work for the program. Certain prerequisites are established for distributors and resellers to be part of the program:

- Good understanding and appreciation of the new business model
- Excellent delivery capabilities with trucks to deliver to the local neighborhoods with not-so-accessible roads and infrastructure
- Capacity for storage of raw material inventory
- Exclusive relationship with CEMEX

When the program originally started, only one-tenth of the distributors qualified under the rigorous selection process. For example, in the Mesa Colorada neighborhood in Guadalajara, of the 30 or so distributors that sold CEMEX products, 10 distributors were exclusive CEMEX distributors; among those 10 distributors, only 3 to 4 distributors were selected to participate in the project because of the capabilities.

Risk Management

Conducting business with the low-income population with no regular stream of paychecks seems riskier than the traditional lending models. Patrimonio Hoy claims the risks are actually low. According to the general manager of Patrimonio Hoy, the default rate so far has been an impressively low 0.45

percent. The huge rate of success can be attributed to three important factors: group commitment, social capital, and the penalty fee structure.

When a group of three socios walks into a cell and completes an application, the only commitment they are expected to make is the regular payment of 360 pesos per week per group on time. If for any reason one of the team members doesn't turn in his or her payment portion on time, the group as a whole will pay a late fee of an additional 50 percent (60 pesos) per late socio. Not only is there a late-fee penalty, but the delivery for the entire group is delayed by one week as well. This also is recorded as a black mark, and the group members will have problems later if they decide to apply for a new credit.

If one of the members defaults for some reason, news simply spreads by word of mouth and he or she is more or less ostracized from the whole process. He or she will lose credibility and will have problems finding a group later.

Strategic Importance of Patrimonio Hoy to CEMEX

After three years of operations, Patrimonio Hoy has 36,000 customers and over $10 million in credit. It operates through 49 cells in 23 cities across 19 states in Mexico. The customer base is growing at a rate of 1,500 to 1,600 per month.

It might be too early to use financial profits as a measure of success. As a standalone operation, Patrimonio Hoy might not be generating as high a margin as corporate CEMEX is through sale of cement. However, the project has strategic implications for CEMEX. According to the general manager of Patrimonio Hoy, the operation is generating positive cash flows from operations of 2 million pesos per month as of February 2004.

However, the more important and critical factor is that Patrimonio Hoy has successfully created an entirely new channel for selling cement and other construction materials. Patrimonio Hoy has helped CEMEX triple its cement sales in places where the operations of Patrimonio Hoy are set up. This has increased from 2,300 pounds of materials consumed once every four years per family, on average, to the same amount being consumed in 16 months.

Sustainable Growth Strategy and Innovation

By offering a complete and comprehensive solution for housing, Patrimonio Hoy has made it difficult for consumers to let go of this opportunity, and has fundamentally changed consumer behavior, even if on a small scale. Patrimonio Hoy is trying to find ways to keep the growth sustainable. It has introduced various innovations around Patrimonio Hoy: Patrimonio Hoy Escolar, Patrimonio Hoy Te Impulsa, and Patrimonio Hoy Calle Digna.

Patrimonio Hoy Escolar (School) is a variation of the original program in that it helps improve infrastructure of the local schools. Four percent of the membership payment of socios is allocated toward improvement of school facilities.

Te Impulsa is an accelerated version of the original program where raw materials are delivered to customers earlier. The materials are delivered in three installments—in Weeks 6 (30 percent), 14 (30 percent), and 22 (40 percent). By the 22nd week, 100 percent delivery is promised to the socios, although they make their usual weekly payments until the 70th week. This program is available to returning socios who have established credibility by making regular payments on time the first time they enrolled in the program.

Calle Digna ("Worthy Street") was created in response to the request of socios who wanted to move on from building their homes to improving infrastructure in their neighborhood. This is a classical example of how Patrimonio Hoy has changed the consumer outlook and how it has changed customers from people in despair to people with hope. This project brings people even closer to work together for the cause of their communities.

Patrimonio Hoy has partnered with the Mexican government to work on public infrastructure projects, many of which the local government hasn't been able to implement for various reasons. The local government provides drainage facilities, and Patrimonio Hoy provides the materials for paving the streets. The payment structure is slightly different. The weekly payments are 150 pesos for x number of weeks, depending on each family. Patrimonio Hoy provides ready-mix or raw materials starting on the 18th week of the payment cycle.

Challenges

Although customer enrollment is increasing at a rapid pace, customer retention is a huge problem for Patrimonio Hoy, not because of poor quality of products and services, but by virtue of the nature of the business. After a room is done, the probability of customers returning to build another room is not 100 percent. Many take a break from the rigors of payment. The biggest challenge for Patrimonio Hoy is to retain those customers for a longer period of time and motivate them to return for additional rooms or other expansions.

In many cases, the socios cannot afford weekly payments for raw materials and mason fee for construction at the same time, so they first buy raw materials over 70 weeks, build houses later, and then might return to save for the next room. To facilitate the continuity of the socios with the program, Patrimonio Hoy has established masonry training facilities for self-construction where socios can obtain technical training to build homes on their own. The socios not only get to build their own homes, but also gain a new competency.

Key Lessons from Patrimonio Hoy to CEMEX

Patrimonio Hoy has helped CEMEX gain a good understanding of the low-income population. It has helped CEMEX clear the misconception it originally had about the poor, and realize they could indeed form a good and profitable segment of the market. CEMEX also learned that traditional methods of operation would not work. However, it remains to be seen if CEMEX can provide housing for the poor to serve a social cause, and at the same time remain profitable in the long run by expanding this program globally.

Leveraging This Learning Through Contrumex

Having successfully launched Patrimonio Hoy in Mexico, CEMEX turned to another possibility. It was common knowledge that a large number of Mexican immigrants lived and worked in the United States. They sent remittances home every week. These total remittances were on the order of $10 billion. Although the size of the average remittance transfer was miniscule ($200–$300) in the world of international finance, the cumulative sums were significant. Further, an estimated 10 percent of these funds were intended to build additions to homes of the family members of the immigrants.

CEMEX saw an opportunity to capture a share of the remittance market to Mexico. This would further its business of helping the poor build good-quality houses.

Evolution of the Business Idea

CEMEX knew a significant portion (about 10 percent) of remittances to Mexico are used for construction of houses. Most of the Diaspora remit money using traditional money transfer companies like Western Union. This process is fraught with inefficiencies:

- The money transfer firms (oligopoly) charge high flat fees for transferring money.
- The exchange rate offered is less than the market rate.
- Relatives back home could spend a significant portion of the remittance meant for building the house for other purposes.
- There is a risk of theft when collecting money from money transfer agencies in Mexico.

CEMEX identified the need for an easier and cheaper way to help the Diaspora build houses back in Mexico. A subsidiary, Construmex, was formed to serve this need. Following a small-scale market research effort, Construmex set up its first experimental office in Los Angeles in July 2001. The significant Mexican population of Los Angeles made it the natural choice for trying out this business model.

The Business Model

In short, Construmex allows Mexicans living in the United States to send their money directly to cement distributors in Mexico. Distributors receive the order and the money, and deliver cement and other building materials to the site of the person's future home or business (see Figure 2).

Broadly, there are two types of customers:

- Individuals remitting money for building their homes in Mexico.
- Home town associations (HTAs) remitting money for public service projects in their home towns in Mexico.

Construmex USA

The express purpose of Construmex is to channel as large a share of the remittance flows to CEMEX as possible. It is not a profit center and has little revenue. Hence the primary activities of Construmex center around generating customer awareness, offering customer education, building trust in the Mexican community, spreading through word of mouth, and working with HTAs to capture a share of the HTA remittances. Not surprisingly, 60 percent of Construmex's budget is dedicated to marketing.

Construmex offices typically have one or two sales representatives. These sales representatives are multifunctional in that they do the following:

- Answer customer queries.
- Consult the customer about the architecture and plan of the house (they are trained Mexican architects).
- Estimate building material requirements based on the house plan.
- Help customers do price comparisons and choose the best distributors.
- Register customers in the Construmex database.

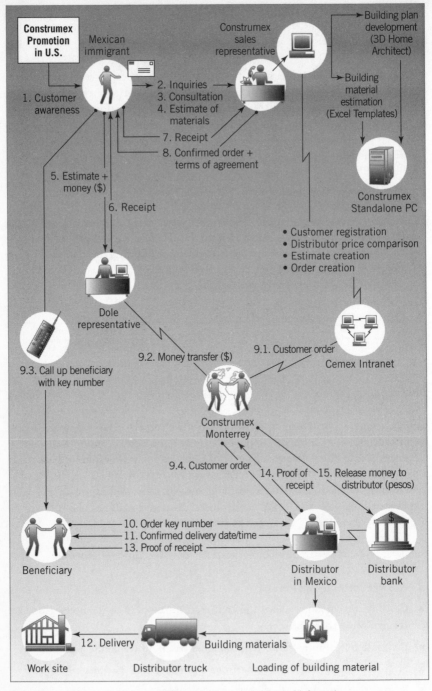

Figure 2 Construmex business model: Flow of money, materials, and information

Dolex USA

Dolex is the money-transferring agency that transmits the money from the customer to the Construmex account in Monterrey, Mexico. The money is transferred in dollars, and there is no exchange of currency. Construmex is still trying to define the perfect business model, according to General Manager Luis Enrique Martinez. However, it has tried two variants to this point:

1. The Construmex sales office has a Dolex counter within it. When a customer comes into this sales office, he or she has the option to remit money through Dolex or to send building materials through Construmex (e.g., Broadway office, Linwood Office, Fresno Office, Santa Ana office).
2. Construmex sets up a simple kiosk explaining the value proposition in a Dolex sales office. The customer has the option to send building materials through Construmex instead of remitting cash (e.g., the Huntington Park office).

Dolex started its U.S. operations in 1998 and is still a very young player in the money transfer business. Dolex has 600 sales offices in the United States, and Construmex wants to scale up its operations by using this existing network. Construmex will try out the second model in Chicago where Dolex has about 25 counters. There will be one Construmex sales office to answer any questions and provide consultation. The lean cost structure in the later model is obviously very appealing for an organization that has no revenues, so controlling costs is critical, because that is the only variable that is under the company's control.

Construmex Mexico

The Construmex office in Mexico does the following:

- Selects distributors for the Construmex program.
- Receives money from Dolex and processes the accounting of the money transferred.
- Transfers the order to distributors.
- Verifies delivery of material to the beneficiary.
- Releases money to the distributor.

Construmex Distributors in Mexico

According to the general manager of Construmex, the quality of service provided in the United States as well as Mexico is critical for generating trust and acceptance. Because of this, Construmex carefully selects distributors for its program. The different criteria applied are (a) accuracy of materials delivered, (b) adhering to the five-day delivery guarantee, and (c) prompt service. Now 1,600 of the 6,000 CEMEX distributors are part of the Construmex program. They cover all states of Mexico except Tijuana. These distributors are typically known to the beneficiaries and hence help in building trust with the clientele. They are happy to work with Construmex because this means more business for them.

International Growth

In 2002, a team from CEMEX Philippines visited Los Angeles to study the operations of the Construmex program. There is strong interest in CEMEX Philippines in replicating this model. This has great potential because Filipinos send much more money home than do Mexicans.

Endnotes

1. http://www2cio.com/info/releases/08150212_release.html.
2. www.vision.com: Media Coverage 2002: Enabling the poor to build housing: Pursuing profit and social development together.

This report was written by Ajit Sharma, Sharmilee Mohan, and Sidharth Singh under the supervision of Professor C. K. Prahalad. The report is intended to be a catalyst for discussion and is not intended to illustrate effective or ineffective strategies.

Known Problems and Known Solutions: What Is the Missing Link?

The most interesting and, at the same time, the most disturbing aspect of the BOP market is that the problems are known; so are the solutions. Often, the missing link is the need for investments in the education of customers, technology to develop that solution into an affordable product, and the distribution channels to make it widely available. Because BOP markets are often under the radar screen of large firms, these opportunities do not attract the necessary technical or market development investments.

Iodine Deficiency Disorder (IDD) affects more than 200 million children in developing countries, of which over 70 million live in India. IDD is one of the principal reasons for mental retardation and disabilities such as goiter. It is well-known that iodine in common salt is the easiest way to get the required daily dose. It is also well-known that only 20 percent of the salt in India is iodized, and even iodized salt loses its iodine content during the harsh conditions of storage, transportation, and Indian cooking. The solution that is needed is clear: Get enough iodine in salt so that children will get an adequate dose with their food in spite of the losses in storage and cooking. However, it must be affordable, meaning that the price cannot be much over the regular, untreated salt that is easily available and currently consumed by the BOP consumers.

The technical, distribution, and education effort required can be difficult. The Annapurna Salt story from Hindustan Lever Ltd. (HLL) illustrates the process by which a large firm with a global reach can create the connection between a known problem and a known solution. HLL had to investigate why iodine dissipated from iodized salt and invent an advanced technology solution called microencapsulation to retain iodine. Because of microencapsulation, HLL can guarantee that the iodine will not be dissipated during storage or cooking, but will be released only after the food is ingested. HLL called this K_{15} (Potassium, 15 parts per million). However, technology is only one part of the solution. HLL had to educate BOP consumers on why K_{15} was better than regular salt as well as iodized salt in which iodine is not encapsulated. HLL took multiple approaches to education. The company used regular information-oriented advertisements on national TV. More important, to reach the villages where TV coverage is limited, it created a direct education and distribution effort involving local village women. Selected village leaders were appointed Shakti Ammas (empowered women) who acted as educators of the local village on nutrition as well as distributors of the product. These women distributed all HLL products, not just salt. As a result, HLL found an innovative way to educate the rural BOP consumers and gain access to a new distribution system.

Treating diarrhea is an equally important problem for developing countries. More than 2.2 million children die of diarrhea every year. India accounts for 30 percent of these needless deaths. The poor do not wash their hands with soap. Contaminated water is the cause of most cases of diarrhea and the problem can be substantially contained by washing hands with antibacterial soap before feeding children, cooking, or eating. Again HLL used its distribution and reach to promote the idea of "safe hands" as distinct from "clean-looking hands" and the use of soap to get "safe." The idea is that washing hands in running water is not enough. The hands might appear to be clean, but they are not safe from disease-causing bacteria.

Both cases, IDD and diarrhea, represent major public health concerns. It is also a business opportunity for selling fortified salt or more bacterial soap. Further, the educational effort involved in helping the BOP consumers recognize the health risk and change their ways is the responsibility of not just the firm but that of the governments and nongovernmental organizations (NGOs) that are working in this area. The World Bank and other international organizations interested in improving public health might also be involved. Further, it is an industry responsibility to create awareness of the problems, not just the responsibility of one firm within that industry. As a result, a three- or four-way consortium is a logical outcome. Civil society organizations, governments (both local and federal), aid givers, and the industry group must work together. As the cases reflect, this partnership, although logical and obvious, is not easy to put together. Each member of this consortium starts with distinctly different agendas, even though they might all agree on an overall problem. Building a consensus can be a very difficult and time-consuming process. These cases illustrate how to navigate these difficult barriers to collaboration and details when going it alone might be a more cost-effective solution.

The Annapurna Salt Story: Public Health and Private Enterprise

I odine Deficiency Disorder (IDD) is the world's leading cause of mental disorders, including retardation and low IQ. Research indicates that 30 percent of the world's population is at risk for IDD. Well-balanced diets provide the required amount of iodine, making the poor particularly susceptible to IDD. In India, almost 90 percent of the population earns less than $3,000 per year;[1] more than 70 million are already inflicted with IDD and another 200 million are at risk.[2] Because even the poorest eat salt, it is globally recognized as the best vehicle for supplementing diets with iodine.

However, many still do not receive the required amount of iodine from salt because:

- Only about 25 percent of edible salt in India is iodized.

- Many consumers are not educated on the human body's requirements for iodine, despite the availability of iodized salt in the marketplace.

- Even those who understand the importance of iodine might be reluctant to pay the premium for iodized salt over the cost of noniodized salt.

- Traditionally, iodized salt loses a significant amount of iodine in storage, transportation, and Indian cooking. Even consumers who purchase iodized salt for its health benefits might not actually receive the recommended daily allowance of iodine.

THE INNOVATION. . .

The paradox of IDD, the leading cause of mental disorder among the poor, is that the solution is known and is inexpensive. The issues are how to reach and educate the poor while getting salt producers to innovate inexpensive methods to guarantee a minimum level of iodine concentration in salt. In developing countries such as India, traditional methods of iodizing salt are no guarantee that the salt will retain its iodine content as it reaches the consumer.

Nongovernmental organizations (NGOs) and governmental organizations are traditionally called on to solve problems pertaining to the poor and public health crises such as IDD. Nonprofit organizations often benefit from grassroots links, long-term commitment to a single cause, cost-effectiveness, and political influence.[3] According to Dr. C. S. Pandav, India's Regional Coordinator for the International Council for the Control of Iodine Deficiency (ICCIDD), NGOs have critical strengths:

> *NGOs serve as an interface between people, especially those who are poor and needy, and the private sector/governments. In other words, they form a link between those who have and those who do not have. The strength of an NGO such as ours is competence, commitment, credibility, collaboration and advocacy.*[4]

Conversely, multinational corporations (MNCs) typically limit their involvement with the poor to corporate social responsibility. Although many MNCs have tapped into India's wealthy, urban populations, few have attempted to reach the poor. MNCs have key capabilities, such as technological know-how, distribution networks, marketing experience, and financial backing, that enable them to combat public health problems such as IDD at a profit. Although nonprofit organizations are competent in dealing with such issues, it is rare for any one to have the same breadth as an MNC. The key to tackling epidemics such as IDD is collaboration between nonprofits and MNCs.

Hindustan Lever Ltd.'s (HLL) technological innovation, Annapurna salt with stable iodine, demonstrates how, together, nonprofits and a large, for-profit corporation can bridge the gap between:

- IDD and a healthier population.
- The poor as a problem and the poor as a source of innovation and profits.

As Rehka Balu of *FastCompany* magazine describes:

Poor people, [HLL's] executives believe, can become just as discerning about brands as rich consumers. And if brands exist as a store of value—a promise about a product's distinctive qualities and features—then offering poor consumers a real choice of brands means offering them a slightly better quality of life. Marketing well-made products to the poor isn't just a business opportunity; it is a sign of commercial respect for people whose needs are usually overlooked.[5]

The Public Health Crisis: Iodine and IDD

Iodine is a chemical element that is most prevalent as iodide (I-), iodate (IO_3-), and elemental iodine (I_2). *Iodine* (Greek for violet) was named for violet vapor that was isolated during gunpowder production. Iodine has been known to have medicinal purposes since the fourth century A.D. when a Chinese physician, Ko Hung, prescribed an alcoholic extract from iodine-rich seaweed to patients suffering from goiters.[6] In 1819, Jean-Baptiste Dumas, a prominent French chemist, proved that iodine was present in natural sponge, a standard treatment for goiters at that time.

Iodine, produced in the thyroid gland at the base of the neck, is critical for the production of two thyroid hormones, thyroxine (T4) and triiodothyronines (T3), that optimize physical and mental development, aid with cellular metabolism, and allow cells to manufacture proteins. When the body does not have sufficient iodine, this results in IDD.[7] Research has been done to estimate the proper dosage of iodine required and common ways of consuming the essential nutrient.

Iodine Deficiency

IDD is the world's leading cause of mental defects, including severe retardation, deaf-mutism, and partial paralysis. It can adversely affect the entire human body, including the muscles, heart, liver, kidneys, and developing brain. IDD can also cause growth retardation, reproductive failure, childhood mortality, physical sluggishness, and other defects in the development of the nervous system.

One of the most visible signs of IDD is a goiter. This painful growth occurs when the thyroid enlarges in an attempt to compensate for inadequate hormone production. In a healthy body, the pituitary gland sends the proper amount of thyroid stimulating hormone (TSH) to the thyroid to stimulate the production of T3 and T4, both of which require a certain level of iodine in the body. When the thyroid does not receive enough iodine, the T3 and T4 hormones are not produced in adequate quantities. The pituitary gland reacts to the low levels of T3 and T4 hormones in the body by sending more TSH to the thyroid, causing the thyroid to enlarge. This enlargement leads to goiter. Approximately 750 million people in the world were diagnosed with this painful growth during the 1990s.

Children living in iodine-deficient areas have an average IQ that is 13 points lower than that of children in areas with sufficient iodine. The most severe form of IDD is hypothyroidism, which is prevalent among young children in remote areas where the daily iodine intake is less than 25 micrograms (mcg).[8] Hypothyroidism causes cretinism, gross mental retardation, and short stature.

Iodine levels are relatively constant and abundant in seawater, so ocean fish and seaweed are good sources. In most parts of Asia, IDD is less prevalent in coastal regions, but continues to be problematic in mountainous interior provinces. The Japanese, who not only eat a great deal of fish and seaweed but also fertilize crops with seaweed, are not affected by IDD as much. Poor populations, for whom consistent, well-balanced diets are not available, must obtain iodine from another source. The incidence of IDD around the globe illustrates the disparity between rich and poor countries. Along with Vitamin A and iron deficiency, IDD can decrease the economic wealth of a nation by up to 5 percent.[9] The ICCIDD is a nonprofit NGO formed in 1985 with support from UNICEF and the World Health Organization to apply knowledge about IDD to help eradicate the disease worldwide. The ICCIDD has become the most significant nonprofit organization dedicated to iodine deficiency in India.

Excess Iodine

Excess iodine can also cause health afflictions, including thyroid underactivity, in which large amounts of iodine block the thyroid's ability to produce T3 and T4. Individuals' tolerances for iodine vary; those with a tendency toward autoimmune thyroid diseases (e.g., Graves' disease or Hashimoto's thyroiditis) and those with a family history might be more sensitive. Some research has indicated that excess iodine can also lead to papillary thyroid cancer, although this has not been proven. (Papillary thyroid cancer is usually mild and rarely causes death.[10]) Although excess and deficient iodine are both undesirable, the latter is worse because it can cause permanent brain damage.[11]

Iodine Supplementation

The prevention, control, and elimination of IDD depend on increasing iodine intake. Intervention measures designed to cover entire populations include iodizing salt, water, bread, and oil. Iodized salt is the best vehicle because salt is one of the few commodities that is universally consumed across socioeconomic and geographic segments. Further, iodizing salt is inexpensive, costing approximately 10 cents (U.S.) per person per year (see Table 1).[12] Other supporting factors include salt's wide production and distribution network, and the fact that adding iodine to salt does not alter salt's color, taste, or odor. Properly iodized salt will rarely add more than about 300 mcg of iodine daily to the diet. Therefore, concern about iodine excess is not a reason to stop or avoid consumption of iodized salt.

Table 1 Production Cost of Iodizing Salt (Assumes Indian Population of 1 Billion)

Description	Estimates
Desired level of iodine in salt	30 parts per million = 30 mg/kg
Total requirement of iodized salt	6 million tons
Total requirement of iodine	180 tons
Cost of iodine per ton	Rs. 60,000
Total cost of iodine per year	Rs. 10.8 crores
Cost of iodine per person per year	Rs. 0.108
Total lifetime cost for a person (70 years)	Rs. 7.56 ($0.16)

Note: 1 crore = 10,000,000.

Needless to say, the postmanufacturing investments required to provide iodized salt to customers and educate them on the benefits of consuming it entail additional costs.

Salt Market

India's salt market is dominated by more than 300 local players producing unbranded products of varying quality. A few branded manufacturers produce 500,000 to 600,000 tons per year, and most local producers sell less than 1,000 tons (see Figure 1).[13]

Unlike other parts of the world, in the Indian salt market, mineral salt comprises only 5 percent because India's topography does not lend itself to salt mines. Ninety-five percent of Indian salt is obtained by *salt farming*, a lengthy evaporation process whereby seawater is pumped and stored in man-made inland pans. High temperatures along these coastal pans evaporate the water, leaving behind unrefined salt. In India alone, about 10 million tons of natural evaporated salt are farmed yearly, of which 40–45 percent is for industrial use and 55 percent is for edible consumption. Of the edible salt, 25 percent is refined and 75 percent is purchased unrefined, unbranded, and unpackaged. Each year 800,000 tons of salt are iodized and packaged for consumption.

The salt market attracts a large number of producers, despite being a low unit-price business. Salt margins can be quite high and although the absolute values of

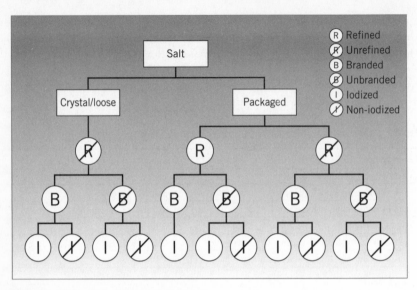

Figure 1 Edible salt varieties available in India.

revenues and profits are not as high as some consumer products, such as soaps and detergents, the return on capital employed makes for an attractive business.

Because it is virtually impossible to differentiate refined salt on the basis of taste, smell, or color and because honest packaging laws are inadequately enforced, Indian consumers face unique challenges:

- Imitation brands such as Captain Hook in place of Captain Cook or Tota for Tata lead confused consumers to purchase the wrong product.

- Many manufacturers print iodized salt on packaging when, in fact, the salt is not iodized.

Diverse Markets

Diverse tastes and cultural variations further complicate the demand for salt in India. For example, South Indians tend to prefer crystal salt, especially in the salt-producing states of Tamil Nadu, Andhra Pradesh, and Karnataka. Many Gujaratis purchase loose salt and use a large iron to pound it into smaller crystals themselves, making it more difficult to sell refined salt to these consumers. Small packs of refined salt are popular in the west, whereas in the north and east, where salt is not readily available, 1-kilogram packages drive penetration.[14]

Iodized Salt in India

Under pressure from the world health community, China (1995) and India (1997) banned the sale of noniodized salt. India's Universal Salt Iodization law mandated that all salt manufacturers add at least 15 parts per million (ppm) of iodine to edible salt.[15] The health community hailed the law. However, it was vehemently protested by independent salt producers who accounted for nearly one-third of India's salt production, which was consumed by 200 million people. These producers argued they could not afford the additional cost of purchasing iodine, machinery, and packaging to iodize salt.[16] Salt industry employees continued to consume noniodized salt. (This population is now afflicted with some of the highest incidences of IDD.) Succumbing to intense lobbying by the producers, many of whom operated manual 10-acre coastal plots that were leased from the government, the government of India repealed the Universal Salt Iodization law in July 2000.

Although a few manufacturers voluntarily added iodine, most uneducated consumers continued to purchase the lower priced uniodized salts, perpetuating IDD. Since 2000, a few individual states, including Gujarat, have reversed the federal government's repeal and forced manufacturers to iodize salt.

Iodine Characteristics and K15 Technology

Chemicals can be protected with macro or molecular encapsulation. Macroencapsulation is the most common approach and can be compared with medicine coated with a synthetic covering. In most iodized salts, iodine is added to salt by spraying a solution of KIO_3 (potassium iodate is the most common iodizing agent in India and other tropical regions) or of KI (potassium iodine is an iodizing agent used in most Western countries and is less stable than potassium iodate). Next, the salt–iodine mixture is dried and forms a homogeneous coating on the salt's crystal surface.

Hindustan Lever Research Center (HLRC) experimented with this method for salt, where a protective coating surrounded iodized salt particles to keep the iodine from escaping due to environmental conditions. However, because of the small size of salt crystals, it was difficult to guarantee a specific amount of iodine in each particle. Although macroencapsulation protected iodized particles from the external environment, this technique did not allow for iodine to be released in the stomach and so HLRC persisted with its research.

Dr. Pramanik then considered how iodine could be protected at a molecular level rather than macroencapsulating the entire salt particle. He eventually succeeded with HLL's stable iodine technology (see Figure 2). Stable iodine is also known as K_{15}, where K represents the element potassium and 15 represents 15 ppm of iodine. A patent was filed in India for this technology in 2001.

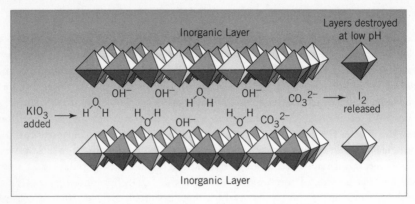

Figure 2   Structure of stable iodine (K_{15}).[17]

1. 15 ppm of iodate particles are inserted between two inorganic layers, protecting iodine from the external environment, including chemical reactions during storage, transportation, and cooking.

2. The inorganic layers are designed to primarily react under extremely acidic conditions where the pH is between 1 and 2 (the pH of the human stomach), allowing iodine to be released into the body. (The pH of typical Indian food being cooked is between 5.5 and 6.0.)

HLRC demonstrated that, unlike macroencapsulation, K_{15} technology would release iodine only in very acidic environments (low pH) such as that of the human stomach. (The pH of the human stomach is between 1 and 2.)

Iodine Loss in Indian Salt

Potassium iodate is very stable on its own and the iodine is retained even in varying ambient conditions; however, this compound becomes unstable when it interacts with salt. Research indicates that environmental factors such as air moisture, high temperatures, poor quality of raw salt, impurities in salt, low environmental pH, and time before consumption can all exaggerate the instability of salt iodized with potassium iodate, resulting in excess iodine loss. Most Indian salt is farmed in desert areas near India's coastline and must be transported long distances to reach consumers, adding storage time and exposure to external conditions. According to the National Institute of Nutrition (NIN) in Hyderabad, India, "Under Indian climate and storage conditions, iodine loss in fortified salt has been observed to be 25% to 35% in the first three months and 40% to 70% by one year."[18]

Indians' unique cooking style leads to further iodine loss. Traditional Indian cooking calls for salt to be added before food is fully heated, boiled, fried, or cooked; this contrasts with most Western cooking where salt is added for taste after food has been completely cooked. In addition, the varying pH levels of Indian spices interact with salt and result in further iodine loss. "The loss of iodine in Indian culinary practices ranges from 20% to 70%."[19]

A 1995 study at the All India Institute of Medical Sciences estimated the iodine lost in cooking 50 common Indian recipes that called for steaming, pressure-cooking, roasting, deep frying, or boiling. The results are displayed in Table 2.[20]

Table 2 Iodine Loss in Salt Due to Indian Cooking

Type of Cooking Procedure	Mean I_2 Content of Uncooked Sample (mcg/100 g)	Mean I_2 Content of Cooked Sample (mcg/100 g)	Mean % Loss of I_2
Pressure-cooking	6.68	5.31 mcg	21.92
Boiling	6.71	4.55	36.60
Shallow frying	5.74	4.89	26.74
Deep frying	8.51	6.89	19.55
Roasting	14.58	13.72	5.94
Steaming	6.8	5.5	20.62

The study concluded that the cumulative effect of heat, storage, and cooking can result in an almost complete loss of iodine by the time the consumer eats salt. Because salt is the primary carrier of iodine and a typical adult consumes 10 g of salt per day, iodized salt must be able to deliver 15 ppm of iodine on consumption to achieve the recommended daily allowance of 150 mg of iodine per day. Acknowledging that iodine is lost during storage and transport, the Indian Prevention of Food Adulteration law of September 2000 mandated that manufacturers of iodized salt add at least 30 ppm of iodine to ensure that 15 ppm is delivered to the consumer at retail. This law, however, did not take into account the iodine lost during Indian cooking.[21]

The Business of Salt In India

A few national players dominate the salt market, which is saturated with numerous local players. Although many brands of salt are also iodized, Annapurna (marketed by HLL) was the first to be marketed on the iodized and healthy platforms.

Tata Salt

Tata Sons Ltd. is a $10 billion conglomerate with 80 companies serving its seven business sectors. With unmatched breadth, from automobile engineering to information technology communications to hotel services, Tata is the most recognizable brand in Indian business.

Tata has been the dominant player in the salt market for more than 20 years with a focus on the 1-kg package in the urban market. Tata markets its salt as pure and as *Desh ka namak* (the country's salt) to upper-income segments.

Tata salt is a by-product of sodium bicarbonate, or soda ash. The company produces nearly 50 percent of India's total capacity for soda ash. Consumers are comfortable with Tata's household name and the quality of the salt, but the company has not exerted a strong salt branding campaign, relying instead on the strength of its name.

Dandi Salt

In 2001, Kunvar Ajay Foods Private Ltd. introduced Dandi salt as high-quality, triple-refined, and reasonably priced.[22] Leveraging the historical importance of Mahatma Gandhi's 1931 Salt March to Dandi Beach, Dandi salt was purposely named as such to evoke patriotic and emotional attachment to the brand. Dandi's aggressive advertising resulted in high first purchases; however, consumer complaints about its poor taste and appearance adversely affected repeat purchases.

Other Competitors

- Conagra entered the market with its Healthy World brand of salt.
- Cargil entered the branded staples market with wheat flour and subsequently introduced the Nature Fresh brand of iodized salt.
- Nirma Ltd. introduced Nirma salt with severe discounting and caused disruption and losses for Annapurna in the wholesale channel. Promotions included giving customers salt for free with the purchase of Nirma Washing Powder, its popular line of detergents.
- Pillsbury entered the branded staples segment with Pillsbury Atta and might be a future entrant into the salt market.
- ITC, which was originally limited to the tobacco business, entered the *atta* (milled wheat flour) and salt markets with its Aashirvad brand.

- Numerous manufacturers produced unrefined, unwashed salt that has iodine added right at the salt pan areas and sells for as little as Rs. 2 per kg.

- Hundreds of local players vie for market share in various areas of the country. From a cost perspective, local producers save on transport by selling only in areas close to salt farms.

HLL Company Profile

Unilever is a Fortune 500 multinational corporation, selling food and home and personal care brands through 300 subsidiary companies in more than 100 countries. Unilever products are available for purchase in 50 additional countries. In 1931, Unilever created its first Indian subsidiary, Hindustan Vanaspati Manufacturing Company, followed by Lever Brothers India Limited (1933) and United Traders Limited (1935). These three companies merged to form Hindustan Lever Ltd. in November 1956. Today, HLL is one of Unilever's largest subsidiaries with the parent company holding 52 percent equity.

HLL is India's leading fast-moving consumer goods company with 32,400 employees (40,000 including group employees) in both the Home & Personal Care Products and Foods & Beverages segments, and it is India's largest exporter of branded consumer products. This industry giant continues to win accolades for its innovative business strategies and uncanny ability to adapt to diverse markets in India and around the world. Forbes Global has rated HLL the "best consumer households company *worldwide*."[23] HLL's corporate vision is engrained in its employees from the outset of their careers:

> To meet everyday needs of people everywhere to anticipate the aspirations of our consumers and customers and to respond creatively and competitively with branded products and services, which raise the quality of life.
>
> —HLL Vision Statement

HLL's Entry Into Branded Staples

In the mid-1990s, foods comprised a Rs. 4.7 trillion market in India, of which 78 percent was unprocessed (see Figure 3). Of the unprocessed, 38 percent was food grains and staples (Figure 4). The Popular Foods division recognized a market potential and entered branded staples.[25]

According to Vishal Dhawan, Head of Popular Foods, HLL made the decision to enter the branded staples business with salt and atta by assessing the branding potential of these commodities:

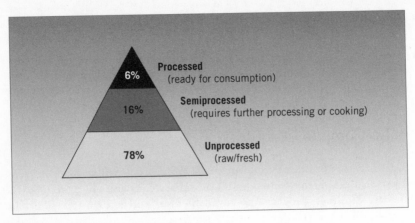

Figure 3 Food market structure in India.[24]

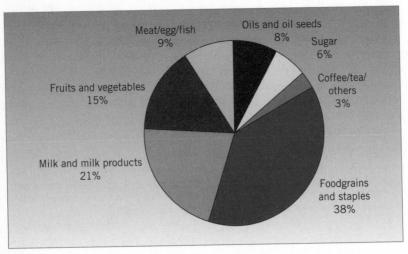

Figure 4 Unprocessed food market in India.[27]

Which products have the best potential for branding? How can we develop the undeveloped food staples market? People want the assurance of a high-quality, hygienic food product, which is often difficult to differentiate in something like salt. Consumers are looking for a brand to provide them with that trust. We decided we could provide that with salt and atta.[26]

HLL created the Annapurna brand for its new line of salt and atta. Annapurna (*an* means food or grain; *purna* means to prepare) is also the name of the Hindu goddess of abundance.

The Evolution of Annapurna Salt

The following timeline details the product evolution of Annapurna salt over its eight-year history.

- **1995:** Annapurna salt was launched in the southern state of Andhra Pradesh in a test market and positioned as a pure salt. This entry had limited success because most salts appeared pure, and Tata salt was already established under this platform.

- **1997:** As the government of India and the ICCIDD increased attention on the problems of iodine deficiency and the role that salt could play to combat IDD, HLL seized the opportunity to become the first to market salt on an iodized platform. Although other branded salts was iodized, none were advertised as such. HLL became the first corporation to address IDD-related health concerns such as mental retardation and goiters and to earn an endorsement from the ICCIDD. Meanwhile, additional reports by groups such as the World Health Organization revealed that unacceptable amounts of iodine salt were lost during manufacturing, storage, transport, and the "Indian" cooking process.

- **2000:** Annapurna's new line of iodized crystal salt was launched in southern India as the cleanest, whitest, most evenly sized on the market. The launch was successful and inventories were quickly depleted.

- **2001:** Annapurna was relaunched with HLL's proprietary stable iodine (K_{15}) technology, which limits iodine during storage, transportation, and "Indian" cooking. By now, the granularity and other features of Annapurna salt were much better as well, although advertising did not reflect these improvements. Marketing for the new product included the hiring of a public relations company to educate consumers on how K_{15} could help diminish the prevalence of IDD in India. Soon thereafter, Annapurna overtook HLL's other branded salt, Captain Cook, and became a close second to Tata salt in market share.

- **January 2003:** Annapurna Platinum salt was launched on a "mineral balance" platform. Platinum contains the same level of stable iodine as Annapurna; however, it has less sodium than most salts in order to appeal to consumers with high blood pressure.

- **April 2003:** After Unilver merged with Knorr in October 2000, the Annapurna brand was merged with Knorr to form Knorr-Annapurna. Knorr-Annapurna focused on authentic Indian cuisine in three segments:

soupy snacks, cooking aids (pastas, spices, etc.), and branded staples, which was headed by Dhawan's team. The new Knorr-Annapurna salt packaging had the key message of stable iodine printed on the front more prominently than the old package.

Dhawan justified the Annapurna evolution as necessary:

Annapurna needs to give reasons for the market to expand and that has happened. The number of re-launches is not too frequent in this market. The life of a product is usually 18 months. Because the name has remained the same throughout, each launch has had us going back with the strongest, most relevant perspective. We have gained market share each time. Who knows what benefits may be ahead with salt?[28]

Hindustan Lever Research Center

Unilever operates five research facilities worldwide: one in the United Kingdom, one in Holland, one in Edgewater, NJ, and two HLL laboratories with 95 scientists between them in Bangalore and Andheri (a suburb of Mumbai). HLRC in Andheri opened in 1958 to anticipate and meet the demands of Indian consumers. HLRC's innovation is recognized globally and has evolved to service other Unilever subsidiaries as well.

HLL scientists work closely with their business counterparts to anticipate and understand market demands. Dr. A. S. Abhiraman, a former chemical engineering professor at Georgia Tech, is HLL's Director of Research and actively recruits researchers from the top technical schools around the world who aim to set standards in marketable science:

The difficulty in research is what to innovate, not how to innovate. Research must be business relevant. Business occasionally only sees the reality of today but sometimes society does not articulate need for a product before it is created.[29]

HLRC and Annapurna Salt

The 1997 launch of Annapurna salt forced HLL to compete at the lowest price point of any product in the history of HLL; the brand team realized the need to differentiate the commodity in the increasingly competitive salt market. In 1995, Dr. Amitava Pramanik, an HLRC research scientist, developed the composition for the first Annapurna, which would be marketed as the most "pure" salt. After the launch, sales and market research indicated that consumers were more interested in the appearance and taste of salt than its chemical properties. Pramanik's team continued to search for a differentiator for Annapurna salt:

> *I remember reading an article by the Central Salt and Marine Chemicals Research Institute that mentioned the stability of iodine in salt is poor and can be lost in storage. That article, published in late 1992, was followed by a variety of publications that claimed that up to 70% of iodine can be lost during Indian cooking. This publicity gave us the idea we could differentiate Annapurna on the iodized salt platform—a recognized deficiency in other branded salts.[30]*

As the public health community, including the World Health Organization, ICCIDD, and the government of India, called IDD the leading preventable ailment in India, Pramanik and his team narrowed their focus to developing a technology that could guarantee that substantial iodine would not be lost during storage, transport, and cooking, and that 15 ppm were actually delivered to customers. Their reasons were twofold:

1. To provide the brand team with a differentiator no competitor could match.
2. To help combat IDD in India.

HLL Salt Target Market

HLL defines its various customer segments based on family income, with A being the richest and D being the poorest. The Knorr-Annapurna salt target group (TG) is young mothers in socioeconomic segments C and D, between 25 and 40 years of age, who are responsible for their household cooking and purchasing decisions. HLL believes these mothers' priorities include keeping their families healthy and ensuring that their children grow up bright in an increasingly competitive society. In a recent HLL poll of women in the TG, 56 percent indicated they had seen a message about stable iodine at least four times in the last one and a half years. The administrators of the survey did not inquire about the percentage that retained the message.

Knorr-Annapurna Platinum is targeted to the A and B socioeconomic segments. Although Platinum is a low-sodium salt solution for consumers with high blood pressure, its positioning is "mineral balanced" to convey an image of an established lifestyle. The marketing team believes the communication around Platinum must be updated. The larger cities have the greatest churn in the market, so the greatest focus for Platinum has been on urban markets.

HLL Product Line and Pricing

Indian law mandates that retail products must be sold at a maximum retail price (MRP), which is printed on the packaging. Some retailers charge less than this amount to draw customers. Annapurna salt packaging is printed in numerous vernacular languages; even if a consumer is literate, he or she might speak one of India's 14 official languages or 500 dialects. Annapurna's best-selling stockkeeping unit (SKU) to date is priced at Rs.7.50 for a 1-kg pack, the same as that of Tata salt (see Table 3).

HLL recognized the bottom of the pyramid's (BOP's) inability to afford large packages of salt. Annapurna responded by introducing 200-g and 500-g low unit price (LUP) packs to appeal to these consumers. Although the proportionate cost of manufacturing LUPs is currently higher than that of the 1-kg bag, HLRC is researching technologies that would drive the cost down. To this, Ram Narayan, Innovation Brand Manager for Annapurna, adds:

> The average consumption in India is 1.6 kg per month per family; so, if this is the average and if people are paid weekly, then they will buy smaller packages. We believe there is a huge potential in the low unit price packs, which are 200 g.[31]

Table 3   SKUs of Branded Salts

Brand	Size	Price (Rs.)	Target Market
Knorr-Annapurna	200 g	1.50	BOP
Knorr-Annapurna	500 g	3.75	BOP, middle class
Knorr-Annapurna	1 kg	7.50	middle class
Knorr-Annapurna Crystal	200 g	N/A	BOP, regional
Knorr-Annapurna Crystal	500 g	N/A	Regional
Knorr-Annapurna Platinum	1 kg	10.0	Urban upper income
Captain Cook	1 kg	7.0	Urban upper income
Dandi Salt	1 kg	7.5	Middle and upper income
Tata Salt	1 kg	7.5	Urban upper income
Tata Salt	500 g	4.0	Urban middle class

Annapurna retails at the same unit price, regardless of the package size purchased. As Annapurna targets BOP consumers more aggressively, this strategy could be an advantage against competitors who charge premiums for small packs. LUPs have been slow to penetrate mass markets; however, they have been successful in surprise niche markets such as college students living in hostels.

HLL Market Strategy

In determining which part of the salt market to enter, HLL considered which segments offered the greatest potential. In 1995, after considering input from brand managers and executives, Gunender Kapur, Director of Foods Division, led his team to enter the refined salt market with the primary goal of upgrading the 75 percent unrefined market (BOP consumers) to Annapurna and the secondary goal of converting branded consumers to Annapurna. Dhawan stands by the decision and this continues to be the order of focus for the HLL salt team.

Annapurna's Message

Annapurna salt is being marketed in two phases; the first message is that iodized salt, in general, helps prevent IDD and goiters. To urban and upper income markets that are more aware of the importance of iodized salt, Annapurna's message is that K_{15} specifically helps increase mental agility and IQ. HLL campaigns continue to emphasize that Annapurna's iodine is different: It does not get lost. The second phase involves advertising and marketing to this diverse group.

Advertising

The salt team believes all mothers are motivated by the same dreams of bright, healthy children. All of Annapurna's advertisements convey this message. This strategy is similar to that of most HLL products, except ice cream, which is a luxury purchase in India and is marketed only to urban high-income groups.

During the 2001 launch of Annapurna with K_{15}, HLL aired a puppet show about IDD on Doordharshan, an Indian government-run television network, sharing costs equally with the network. The infomercial was extremely successful, winning awards from Unilever for its effectiveness in delivering a retainable message. According to HLL market analysis, the target group viewed the Annapurna advertisement an average of four times. Although the long-term retention is unknown, the immediate recollection of the advertisement's message was about 90 percent. In the future, Annapurna's advertising will be tracked more carefully. An advanced tracking process (ATP) is typically used four times per year on established brands and was to be used for the first time on Knorr-Annapurna salt after the 2003 launch.

Market Fragmentation

Annapurna team members all share valuable insights into the challenges the salt market presents to the brand.

Zarius Master, a regional sales manager for HLL, said:

Everyone must consume some form of salt (therefore salt itself has 100 percent penetration); however, this makes the channels even more complex. For example, Annapurna has 20,000 to 30,000 outlets in Mumbai alone. So we need to put our products where the infrastructure supports them; we also need to look at culinary, seasonings, snacks, etc. in the foods business; basically manage categories well and make sure we have the infrastructure in place to support them.[32]

Dhawan said, "We must make the value proposition very clear to consumers. At an average of 400 gm per month of consumption, even if the consumers pay Rs.2/kg premium, it translates into just 2 to 3 paise per day for a major health benefit!"[33]

According to Narayan, "Salt is consumed at 2 kg per month in a household of four people. Annapurna costs Rs. 7.50 while the local product they can buy is Rs. 3 to Rs. 4. Annapurna offers full iodine without loss. The impact is not only on goiters but also on mental development. Our challenge is to communicate the larger picture so consumers connect that Annapurna can help them realize their aspirations and dreams."[34]

Market Share

Although unbranded local manufacturers still dominate the salt market, branded salts are slowly increasing shares. Tata salt remains the leader with 19 percent market share in a Rs. 130–140 crore business. HLL is a close second with 14 percent market share and a Rs. 100 crore business of which Annapurna is 11 percent and Captain Cook is 2 percent. Other players, each with 1.5 percent to 2 percent market share, are Nirma, Shudh, Dandi, Nature Fresh, Sprinkle, and Tota. In South India, where HLL has a strong presence, Annapurna is the dominant salt. Northern India also has mined salt available (Kala Namak), which takes some of the branded salt business.

Narayan believes the slowdown in sales the prior year is not indicative of Annapurna salt's future:

Neither the overall salt market nor Annapurna grew in 2002 because discounters such as Nirmas and Dandi waged price wars. They seem to have wiped themselves out of the market now. Nirma was riding on the back of its existing distribution network; the company tried to sell salt with detergent so traders got higher margins. But they did not have enough advertising Rupees behind it; and, of course, Nirma is known for detergents and toilet soaps and not foods. They did not realize that food is a different business. Dandi had tax evasion issues.[35]

In its advertising for Annapurna salt, the focus was primarily on iodine education. In fact, in the Doordarshan infomercial, the Annapurna name was mentioned only in the last few seconds. The brand team believed if the consumers were first educated on the importance of iodine, they would be more inclined to purchase salt positioned on iodine.

HLL Manufacturing and Distribution

In natural evaporation salt farming, seawater is pumped into flat manmade salt pans. Conditions for salt farms are very particular and include flat land between water and mountains, a coastline, and plenty of fresh air and wind so the water can evaporate naturally, leaving behind unrefined sea salt. Land that has been used for salt farming becomes barren and cannot be used for other purposes. After salt has been produced and packaged, distribution to the end consumer adds another level of complexity. Transport times can be very long due to India's poor road infrastructure. Because the shelf life of salt is only one year, minimizing storage time in the *godowns* (storage areas), decreasing transport distances, and increasing the number of consumer purchase points are vital.

HLL's Salt Production

HLL procures raw salt from privately owned salt farms and contracts with four third-party refineries to take advantage of underutilization in the refining industry and to minimize investment in manufacturing facilities. These refineries are strategically located near salt farms to minimize inbound transport (see Table 4). At least one HLL employee works with each refinery to ensure that the salt is manufactured per Unilever guidelines.

Table 4 HLL Third-Party Salt Refineries

Factory	Location	% of Production Volume	Supply Chains Serviced
Gandhidam	Near Bhuj, Gujarat	49	Northern, Eastern, Western
Jambusur	Near Baroda, Gujarat	29	Northern, Eastern, Western
Chennai	Tamil Nadu	29	Southern
Tuticorin	Tamil Nadu	12	Southern

Gandhidam Factory

The Gandhidam refinery, located in a vast desert close to the Arabian Sea, is the largest of the four. This region, where wind and sun are plentiful and rainfall is rare, was the site of the 2000 Oscar-nominated film *Lagaan*. Its numerous salt pans are renowned for excellent-quality raw salt, which is pure, white, and abundant, drawing many manufacturers to the region. The purer the raw salt is, the less washing it needs, resulting in cost savings.

Western India Ltd. is one of the largest manufacturers of raw salt from sea brine, owning 8,000 acres of land near Gandhidam and producing 6 million tons of raw salt per year. The company was formed in 1992 and produced three tons of salt in its inaugural year. In 1995, HLL approached Western India with a proposition to procure and manufacture salt for the Annapurna brand. Production began in 1997. Although HLL contracts with other salt manufacturers to produce Annapurna at the three other refineries, Western India can produce salt only for HLL. HLL forecasts sales at the start of each month and informs J. G. Natta, Managing Director of Western India Ltd., of the required amounts.

Birin Mehta is Western India's Quality Control Manger at Gandhidam and is responsible for ensuring raw salt and brine quality. Mehta has 15 chemists under him who work as inspectors to ensure that HLL standards are being met for salt quality and ingredients, weight, and packaging. This team conducts tests every hour and has the authority to reject nonconforming batches. Most batches do conform, however, because rejects are typically discovered during processing. HLL has its own quality control group in Mumbai that tests random samples obtained from all four refineries.

Production Costs and Western India's Role in Decreasing Them

Industry costs for refined salt production include materials (40 percent), transport from farms to factories (40–45 percent), and materials and packaging (15–20 percent). Western India has taken cost-cutting measures to decrease labor requirements at Gandhidam. Because oil companies and the Indian government determine fuel costs, the company is focusing on reducing fuel requirements.

Transport

The Annapurna salt supply chain varies significantly from region to region and takes between 1.5 and 6 months (from natural evaporation of sea salt to a customer's purchase), the bulk of which is during the salt farming stage. Table 5 shows postmanufacture times in the supply chain for southern and western India.[36]

Table 5   Example of Time in Annapurna Salt Supply Chain for South and West India

Activity	Time
Transport from Gandidham or Chennaii refinery to wholesaler on 10-ton truck	4–5 days in transit
Held in wholesaler inventory	2–3 weeks
Transport from wholesaler to retailer	2–3 hours
Held in retailer inventory	1–1.5 weeks

Unlike Annapurna, which is cleaned and packed prior to transport, Tata salt (produced in bulk from vacuum evaporation) is transported to depots where it is cleaned and packed. Although Tata loses economies of scale with higher packaging costs (each depot must have packaging capabilities), consumers benefit with a fresher product. Gopal Mishra, Business Manager Food Staples, strives to optimize distribution: "I am always looking for ways to minimize the cost and width of distribution. Salt is not a high-value product so distribution costs are almost equal to production costs. We must minimize salt handling."[37]

Innovations in Transport

Through 2000, most salt was distributed on trucks, a method that was not optimal in North and East India for the following reasons:

- Salt is produced in Gujarat (west) and Tamil Nadu (south) and must be transported over long distances to reach North and East India, resulting in high transit costs.
- Freight costs are high due to the large number of trucks required.
- Indian road conditions are poor, especially near hilly regions, causing long transit times.
- There is danger from political extremists, who control many roads in the northeast.

In response to these concerns, HLL successfully executed a salt supply chain innovation in the beginning of 2001. HLL began to use rail, mitigating some of the problems with trucking and earning an edge on competitors. With this system, salt is transported on *rake*-sized rail carriages (12 carriages carrying up to 2,200 tons), vastly increasing the amount of salt that can be transported in one shipment. Rail transport adds a "salt buffer depot" step to the process, in which salt is loaded onto trucks for delivery to the wholesaler or retail outlet (see Figure 5).

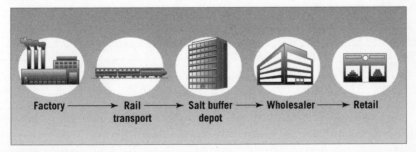

Figure 5   Rail distribution.

Rail has significantly improved efficiencies and decreased costs for salt distribution to locations far from HLL refineries and has replaced trucks as the primary mode of distribution for the north and east (see Table 6).[38]

Table 6 Distribution Percentages for Rail and Truck (Approximated)

Region	Type of Transport	% of Annapurna Sales
North	Rail	15
East	Rail	15
South	Truck	40
West	Truck	20

Although rail was an improvement, HLL's distribution team still found it difficult to service customers and believed that costs could be further decreased.
—Gopal Mishra, HLL

Retail Price Schemes

One way HLL aims to increase consumer demand for Annapurna salt is by aggressively increasing volumes in retail outlets. Although wholesalers educate retailers on HLL brand differentiation, most retail outlets are driven primarily by margins and schemes (promotions). Most dealers sell brands from a variety of companies, many of which offer competitive schemes (see Table 7).

Table 7 Retailer Margins Based on Rs. 7.5/Package; 1 Bag = 50 1-kg Packages

Annapurna Salt	Tata Salt
Without Schemes	Without Schemes
Rs. 6.86/package	Rs. 6.86/package
Direct to wholesaler Scheme #1: Buy 5 bags, get 3 free:	Direct to wholesaler Scheme (only one offered): Buy 5 bags, get 1 free:
Rs. 3.21	Rs. 1.78
Direct to wholesaler Scheme #2: Buy 25 bags, get 22 free	
Rs. 3.85	
Direct Dispatch–Direct to Retailer Scheme: 200-bag purchase	
Rs. 3.70	

Annapurna salt successfully penetrated many retail chains and converted shopkeepers with superior promotions. These schemes have spawned price wars among manufacturers and resulted in even less brand loyalty from store owners.

Direct Distribution to Reach Rural India

One of the greatest challenges with rural India is that the media only reaches 50% of the population. This leaves over 500 million people that don't see your message. The population lives in 600,000 villages and over half don't have motorable roads, so we needed unique means to communicate to them. This challenge is the same in other emerging markets.

—Vindi Banga, Chairman and CEO, HLL[39]

Project Shakti Background

A 1999 project identified six new growth opportunities for HLL:

- Confectionaries and sweets (since its launch, candy marketed to the BOP has become HLL's fastest growing product).
- Consumer health care (this resulted in the creation of HLL's "Ayush" brand).
- SANGAM, an e-tailing program for daily ordering and delivery. A pilot is being tested in Navi (New) Mumbai.
- Addressing the needs of top-end consumers (efforts in this area have been met with limited success so far).
- Water.
- *Shakti* (meaning strength in Sanskrit), a direct-to-consumer initiative targeted at individuals at the bottom of the pyramid in rural India.

Project Shakti was launched under the umbrella of New Ventures, a department created as a result of the work. Shakti utilizes women's self-help groups (SHGs) for entrepreneur development training to operate as a rural direct-to-home sales force, educating consumers on the health and hygiene benefits of HLL brands and nurturing relationships to reinforce the HLL message. New Ventures contends this direct-to-consumer initiative not only will stimulate demand and consumption to earn huge profits for HLL, but also change the lives of people in rural India, something that mass-marketing alone cannot accomplish. Sharat Dhall leads Project Shakti:

We have four goals for Project Shakti. First, we plan to increase our reach to the rural market. Then we will attempt to increase awareness and change attitudes regarding usage of the various product categories. Finally, and most important, catalyze rural affluence and hence drive growth of the market.[40]

In a typical SHG, 15 women invest Rs. 1 each daily into a joint account. These monies are loaned internally to group members at interest rates between 2 percent and 3 percent. Peer pressure often influences SHG members to have higher repayment than more "credit-worthy" lendees in urban and affluent areas, encouraging banks to loan money to them. This enables the members to start new business ventures and gain economic empowerment. They also can receive lending using cows, sheep, and other property as collateral.

SHGs were started five years ago in Andhra Pradesh and two years ago in Karnataka with the support of the state governments. HLL uses SHGs as a medium to transmit HLL brand awareness and sales and to empower the citizens of rural India.

Dhall continues:

Self-help groups present an enormous "Rural Direct to Home" opportunity for us. We are offering an opportunity to create meaningful incomes for the people at the bottom of the pyramid. It also can be very profitable for HLL. In December 2000, a pilot in one district resulted in a significant increase in household consumption expenditure on HLL brands and an overall increase in market share. In addition, the women were creating stable, sustainable, risk-free earnings. As a result of these promising figures, the corporate office approved the official launch of Project Shakti. Even now, the venture is low risk for HLL, and the potential increase in demand and consumption is astounding.[41]

Shakti Business Goals

Project Shakti has caught the attention of many within HLL who have recognized the venture as an exciting opportunity to penetrate the rural BOP, while finding double-digit savings in costs as compared to using independent rural sales agencies.

HLL executives also believe Shakti offers intangible benefits, including increasing brand awareness, developing new channels, and social impact. They assert that HLL's role in the empowerment of rural women is more important than sales alone.

Implementation Approach

Regions where HLL distribution networks are already established (e.g., Kerala and Tamil Nadu) and where the roads are already in good condition might not be as successful for Shakti, because they are within easy reach of traditional distribution. A viable village for Shakti is a function of many demographic factors, including current purchase patterns, population, and per-capita income.

Site Selection

Rural sales promoters (RSPs) go door to door to obtain demographic information about a potential village and enter it into Shakti Century, a tracking database. Promising villages have minimum populations of 3,000 (600 homes with an average of five residents per household). The population is divided into four economic segments with potential villages having at least 10 percent in Segment A and 15 percent in Segment B:

- **Segment A:** *Jamindars* (land owners) and other wealthy people earning over Rs. 3,000 per month.
- **Segment B:** Middle-class citizens whose employers pay them weekly. Monthly salaries are between Rs. 1,000 and Rs. 3,000.
- **Segments C and D:** C might be viable but the D segment is not viewed as a potential market. These individuals earn less than Rs. 1,000 per month and hardly purchase one bar of soap per month.

The Shakti team also identifies satellite villages, typically within 8 km of the dealer, with populations between 1,000 and 2,000. Satellite villages are not large enough to justify a separate dealer.[42]

Leveraging Government Relationships in Site Selection

Pradeep Kashyap, known as the "father of rural India," is head of the Marketing and Research Team (MART) consulting firm and was retained by HLL to help build strong government relations for Project Shakti. HLL and MART partner with state and local government departments such as Rural Development and Women's Empowerment to learn where SHGs exist and to obtain information about optimal locations and dealers.[43]

In Andhra Pradesh, up to 70 percent of women belong to SHGs. Nationwide, about 1 million groups already exist. HLL sales managers and MART communicate the potential benefits to local officials and are usually successful in obtaining support and information. Andhra Pradesh's Women's Empowerment Commissioner is so impressed with Project Shakti that she requests monthly updates. Going forward, A. Balasubramanian, Rural Sales Officer for Project Shakti, teaches his subordinates to communicate the following message:

> *We are offering economic opportunities for your community. It will be easier for you to convince them now since we have a proven track record. Andhra Pradesh typically had a 3% success rate with self-help groups. With Project Shakti, they have a success rate over 90%.*

After agreeing on a plausible location for a Shakti dealership, local government officials invite enterprising women from SHGs to an initial meeting. HLL conducts the meeting and invites women who express an interest in Project Shakti to learn more about the opportunities. Convincing the women and their families usually takes significant effort on the part of the HLL team.

Gender Considerations

At the onset of the program, the Project Shakti team discussed and experimented with the optimal profile of a Shakti dealer and Shakti communicator. Although the Indian population has a larger number of men and young boys for whom these positions could be an opportune career path and for whom the training and lifestyle required might be an easier fit, the team determined that women were the best conduits of education and influence. Conversely, the management team is currently comprised of men only, with only a handful of women having held these positions.

Many local retailers, mostly men, have asked to become Shakti dealers. However, HLL rejected their requests, explaining that retailers can still benefit from Shakti dealers who can supply them more regularly, saving shop owners long trips to obtain new inventory.

Project Shakti Local Organization and Process

Because most rural distributors own only one delivery vehicle, HLL limits the number of Shakti dealers to 20 per district so distributors are not overburdened. As Shakti grows, so will distributors' guaranteed income from each dealer, at which time HLL will increase the density of dealers.

Shakti Dealer

A Shakti dealer or Shakti Amma (mother) works as an HLL direct-to-consumer distributor, selling primarily to individuals from her SHG. She also relies on smaller distributors, retailers, and consumers in 6 to 10 satellite villages to supplement her business. She must invest between Rs. 15,000 and Rs. 20,000 at the onset for inventory and training, often borrowing to do so.

The Shakti Amma works toward having 500 customers on her roster and grossing between Rs. 15,000 and Rs. 20,000 per month. Most dealers gross between Rs. 10,000 and Rs. 12,000 and net about 7 percent (approximately Rs. 700–1,000 per month), often doubling their household incomes.

In the first few months, a RSP visits 30 homes in a new dealer's village with her. A dealer's learning curve is usually three months before she begins to perform like other HLL distributors. According to Dhall, the three most important factors for a Shakti dealer's success are as follows:[44]

- Dealer's entrepreneurial skills to seek out business instead of passively waiting for customers.

- Incentives and loyalty programs she offers to generate new and repeat business (e.g., if a customer purchases Rs. 50 of a product, then she receives a free sachet of another product).

- Dealer's willingness to service the retail trade in addition to her direct-to-consumer channel.

Dealer Evaluation

The Total Transactions (TT) or number of times a dealer is supplied during one journey cycle (JC) is usually one per month, with stronger dealers having up to three TT. HLL awards motivational prizes such as Best Performer to dealers as a part of a state-run Women's Day and other similar activities.

Although performance varies among dealers, over 60 percent are currently generating Rs. 12,000 per JC (see Table 8).[45] The disparity in dealer performance and income can lead to tensions in the villages. As one dealer in Rajapoor who grosses Rs. 22,000 per JC described, there is some jealousy between other dealers and customers in her village, but it is still not enough to affect the success of her business.

Table 8   Gross Revenues per Journey Cycle

Gross Revenue (in Rs.)	% of Shakti Dealers
15,000+	20
12,000–15,000	40
8,000–12,000	30
Sporadic or none in 3 months (inactive)	10

Most training is in a market setting (vs. a classroom) with dealers learning selling, business, and record-keeping skills. Dealers also are educated about HLL brands through communication with RSPs. Although sharing success stories with other dealers in a classroom could be beneficial, HLL has found the logistics difficult to manage. Not only is it difficult for the dealers to leave their villages, but it also is a logistic burden for RSPs to make the arrangements.[46]

Shakti Pracharani

The Shakti Pracharani or communicator is a person hired on a fixed-monthly-sum basis and typically earns less than a Shakti dealer. An ideal Pracharani is confident and outspoken, with excellent communication skills. Unlike the dealer, whose travel is limited to her village and a few satellite villages, the

Pracharani must travel throughout the district. She is paid bonuses of about Rs. 30 for attending more than her required number of SHG meetings. At such meetings, she facilitates games and tests members' knowledge with questions such as how to identify Annapurna salt from an imitation product. The Pracharani is required to call the area coordinator at the end of every day to update him on her progress.

The travel requirements for Pracharanis have proven to be a challenge. Most of the women have family responsibilities, which make it difficult for them to be out of their homes for long periods of time. Also, local cultural fears for a woman's safety when she travels alone from village to village. For these reasons, HLL is also experimenting with a model where two communicators represent each district to minimize travel and which, as necessary, allows them to travel together.[47]

Market Strategy

Similar to the Annapurna salt team's strategy, New Ventures aims to increase the range of HLL products in rural markets by taking market share from local players and establishing brands that are not currently in the market. Although New Ventures does not yet receive pressure from other HLL business units to push a particular unit's products, Dhall expects and hopes this will happen once Project Shakti proves itself.

Project Shakti was initially launched with personal products only; soaps and detergents and popular foods (including Annapurna salt) were added to the product offering in 2003. Personal products currently comprise 16 percent of sales. Beverages were also added in 2003.

HLL already has a strong presence in the rural markets with soaps, talcs, and shampoos and is now focusing on dental products (Colgate-Palmolive's Colgate is the leading toothpaste), fabric cleaners, and foods. The Shakti team is instructed to delicately balance the push between brands generating higher margins with those the market dictates.

Marketing Annapurna Through Project Shakti

True to HLL's vision of eventually converting Captain Cook customers to Annapurna, Captain Cook is not sold through Shakti.

- A picture of a laughing sun (i.e., the universal symbol for iodine) is printed on all Annapurna salt packaging so that those speaking other languages or even the illiterate can recognize the symbol and identify Annapurna salt.

- The Pracharani distributes pamphlets and other educational material on IDD during SHG meetings.

- Other educational marketing initiatives such as a two-week Annapurna salt drive and Iodine Day (as a part of World Health Day) further the stable iodine message in rural markets.

Stimulating Demand Through Linkages

Dhall believes that Shakti's long-term success will be dependent on dealers' ability to sell enough volume to earn substantial revenues. To this end, the team is exploring "linkage" or referral relationships with noncompetitive partners selling complementary products including insurance (crop insurance for farm communities) and financial services (loans from lenders such as ICICI Bank). Partnerships with battery, bulb, and other commodity manufacturers were considered; however, relationships where investment and inventory are not required look the most promising because it is difficult to share synergies for commodities without having common distributors.

Dealers stimulate business in their shops by selling products such as saris, bangles, and rice. HLL is supportive of Shakti dealers' selling noncompetitive products to encourage one-stop shopping for village customers; a formal linkage pilot is underway in the Nangonda District in Karnataka.

Stimulating Demand Through Education

The Shakti team sponsors festivals and value-added events to promote HLL brands:

- *Arogya (Health) Day:* HLL brings a physician to villages to discuss health issues and answer patient questions.

- *Shakti Family Packs:* The Shakti dealer creates a basket of health and hygiene products for the betterment of a family. She discounts the basket by leveraging her margins on various HLL brands to create perceived value for her customers. Specific products depend on her particular market and often include soap (Lifebuoy, Breeze), detergent powder or bars (Wheel, Super), coconut oil (Nihar), salt (Annapurna), talc (Ponds), cream sachet (Fair and Lovely), and shampoo (Clinic Plus). Most family packs retail for Rs. 100 with the purchaser receiving a 5 percent to 10 percent discount.

- *Shakti Day:* An artificial festival with product giveaways, songs, and opportunities to purchase HLL brands at discounted prices. The primary purpose of the day is to promote the dealer and this accounts for approximately 20 percent of a dealer's average monthly sales.

- *Newsletters:* Monthly updates written by the rural sales officer including success stories, schemes, and motivations are sent to dealers and communicators.

- *Project Iodine:* Educates children, parents, and schoolteachers on the importance of iodine through direct contact.

- *Promotional Video:* A famous Mumbai filmmaker, Adi Poacha, was commissioned to create a video to showcase Project Shakti to the media, government, and other organizations.

- *i-Shakti:* An information-technology-based initiative aimed at providing solutions to rural information needs. A six-month pilot was rolled out in 12 villages in May 2003. If successful, each Shakti dealer eventually will have a computer at her home with Internet and e-mail access. Villagers will be able to use the computer to learn about crops, health solutions, and hygiene solutions that HLL brands and its partner companies offer.

Shakti Sales and Margins

The Shakti dealer earns different margins based on to whom she sells. On average, she earns a 7 to 8 percent margin on her sales, higher than the 5 percent average margin gained by most HLL distributors (see Tables 9 and 10). She visits retailers twice monthly to pitch products and drop off inventory.[48]

Table 9 Shakti Dealer Margins

Sale From	Dealer's Margin on MRP
Dealer's home store	11%
Home to home	11%
Group meetings	6%
Village shopkeepers	3% (dealer's regular competitive rate)

Table 10 Shakti Dealer Margins, 200 g Annapurna Salt Example

	Price Paid by Customers	Dealer's Margin
Shakti dealer pays 0.90 for supply from HLL		
Sold at home	Rs. 1.50	Rs. 0.60
Sold at group meeting	Rs. 1.30	Rs. 0.40
Sold to shopkeepers	Rs. 1.20	Rs. 0.30

Competition

Most competitors have been following a watch-and-wait policy; however, new entrants such as Procter and Gamble and Brittania are expected by 2004. Local players have already started to feel a pinch in sales and have begun to fight back with consumer promotions and product giveaways.

Whereas HLL must pursue Shakti to grow, Dhall asserts that the other MNCs will first try to take business from the top of the economic bucket. Dhall asserts that HLL holds a competitive edge and others face fierce barriers to entry:

> They must first build a portfolio of brands that will generate enough sales so it will be worthwhile for dealers since the turnover is too low in any one product line. HLL is unique in its ability to generate such large rural turnover. Other companies may offer a higher margin to potential dealers, but HLL is shielded with brand depth followed by our familial spirit. Also, HLL can leverage its distribution system across India better than any of our competition.[49]

2002 Results

The 2002 goal for Project Shakti set by HLL executives was to have 500 dealers in its operating states with sales of Rs. 2.5 crore. This goal was surpassed with sales of Rs. 2.54 crore.

Shakti was rolled out across 21 districts in Andhra Pradesh and Karnataka each, with 375 and 324 dealers, respectively, covering 4,756 markets where regular distribution had not yet reached. This resulted in a 28 percent increase in the rural population reached by HLL.

2003 Performance

Project Shakti generated Rs. 294 lakhs through the first four JCs of 2003 (see Table 11), and the company targeted a year-end goal of Rs. 16 crore in sales. Sales officers compile districtwide sales reports every JC, which is about 28 days.[50]

Table 11   Project Shakti Sales (Lakh Rs.) for Journey Cycles 1–4 in 2003

State	JC1	JC2	JC3	JC4
Andhra Pradesh	22	31	52	67
Karnataka	25	29	35	33

The company's sales growth in Andhra Pradesh and Karnataka was 10 percent higher than that of non-Shakti areas. Of the almost Rs. 300 lakh generated, nearly half was earned from customers who switched from local, unbranded products. The team has not determined whether sales are incremental or just replacing other channels because some districts can grow more quickly than others for many unrelated reasons.

Project Shakti planned to have 1,000 dealers by May 31, 2003. Management hoped that by the end of 2003, every dealer will have at least 100 houses in each village purchasing Rs. 100 of HLL products each month.

In addition to sales revenues, Dhall is proud of Shakti's impact on the standard of living of people in rural markets through:

- Business consultancy to SHGs.

- Agricultural intermediation (i.e., castor seeds procurement in Mahboobnagar, Andhra Pradesh).

- Entrepreneurship training for more than 1,000 women in Andhra Pradesh.

Challenges

From the corporate perspective, Shakti's greatest challenge is distribution with India's underdeveloped infrastructure. For the sales managers on the front line, training rural women to work on their own for the first time poses the primary hurdle. For dealers and Pracharanis, educating rural consumers about the quality of HLL products continues to prove difficult because most villagers are accustomed to less expensive, unbranded, local products. Even if they are convinced of HLL's marketing message, many imitation products cloud the market and confuse consumers.

Long-Term Vision

In 2003, New Ventures plans to extend into 58 additional districts in Andhra Pradesh, Karnataka, Uttar Pradesh, Madhya Pradesh, and Gujarat. The team plans to drive sales of leading brands by leveraging health and hygiene ventures with NGOs. In the long term, Dhall hopes:

> *Shakti will broaden the scale of economic affluence via information. For example, i-Shakti could help increase crop yield. This creation of rural wealth can be an enabler to drive economic growth on a large scale in India. The vision for Shakti is that we will have 10,000 Shakti dealers covering 100,000 villages, selling to 100 million consumers. This is a vision we expect to achieve over the next three years. In my mind, it can become the biggest rural operation in the history of Indian business and change the way companies look at reaching the consumers at the bottom of the pyramid.*[51]

Leveraging Know-How Globally

Annapurna salt already has started to bridge the gap between the health needs of the 30 percent of the world's population that is at risk of IDD and Unilever's needs for sustained growth and profitability. After initial success with Annapurna salt in India, Unilever divisions sought to scale HLRC's patented technology to other markets. Research was conducted to determine which markets would be the best to explore. The team decided to focus on countries that were most similar to India in terms of climate, overall health of the population, cooking habits, and potential of branded staples. Based on these factors, Annapurna salt was launched in Ghana in December 2001 and, along with other products in the Knorr-Annapurna line, is now marketed, sold, and distributed as an international brand.

Africa represents an untapped market of 700 million people, the majority of whom live on less than two dollars a day. The Annapurna team has proven that, despite the perceived limited buying power of these people, the African market is still attractive. In some countries, Annapurna salt was profitable and met its gross margin target in just 18 months, nearly three years ahead of schedule.

Unilever established a Popular Foods Division in Ghana, under which Annapurna salt captured a 35 percent market share only two years after entering the market. In Ghana, a 250-g bag of Annapurna salt sells for 600 cedis, equivalent to about seven cents (compared with the 200-g Annapurna pack in India, which sells for Rs. 1.5, or just over three cents). This pricing is advantageous in the Ghanaian market because at 600 cedis, the price of Annapurna salt is about the same price as raw salt and half the price of other refined salts on the market, which are typically marketed to a small number of upper-income Ghanaians.

Unilever has also launched Annapurna in Kenya and the Ivory Coast, where the brand provides the poor with needed nutrients such as vitamin A, iron, and iodine. The success of Annapurna is mostly attributed to low-cost production and a pricing strategy geared toward low-income consumers. Annapurna's African expansion continues. In 2003, Annapurna salt was launched in Nigeria, Africa's largest salt market, which consumes nearly half a million tons per year. Under the umbrella of a new company, West African Popular Foods Nigeria, resulting from a joint venture agreement between Unilever and the Dangote group, Annapurna eventually will launch other basic food products. After Nigeria, Unilever plans to bring the Annapurna salt solution to West Africa's $150 million salt market, including Mali and Niger.

In Africa, Annapurna has become profitable by attracting and retaining consumers from the bottom of the economic pyramid. Annapurna's successful entry into Africa demonstrates that significant expansion is still possible; HLL can sell a product with breakthrough technology that promotes improved public health at competitive prices. This model can be applied to other Unilever brands to achieve similar results.

Conclusions

HLL is demonstrating that for MNCs, the BOP can serve as a profitable impetus of innovative technology and marketing savvy, and that corporations, together with NGOs, can address social problems at affordable costs. Annapurna salt's K_{15} (stable iodine) technology is uniquely positioned to combat IDD, a worldwide health problem, while delivering substantial profits to HLL. Similarly, Project Shakti is proving to be a repeatable model that can empower the BOP to enhance their quality of life and help pave a road from the bottom of the neglected social strata to a sought-after market. Although these accomplishments are admirable, several questions still remain. It is unclear whether Annapurna consumers truly appreciate the breakthrough technology embedded within the salt and purchase it because of K_{15}, or if most sales are a result of margin-driven shopkeepers who push Annapurna over other brands. HLL has not yet determined whether consumers are willing to pay a price premium for Annapurna based on the technology alone. Only time will tell; until then, HLRC is working to decrease costs, which in turn can lead to a price decrease in Annapurna salt if the market demands it.

Should HLL keep the K_{15} technology proprietary? If K_{15} (stable iodine) alone is not a differentiator in the sale of the product, would HLL earn higher profits by licensing the technology to other salt manufacturers and, at the same time, battle the IDD endemic on a larger scale?

HLL acknowledges that for Project Shakti to be a significant part of the company's rural penetration, dealers and communicators must be well-trained. It is unclear how dealers will perform in an expanded infrastructure. Also, HLL will need to determine whether the Project Shakti model is repeatable in other countries. Indian family structure and village interaction provide a unique diffusion mechanism that is an effective vehicle for Shakti. Whether this model will be successful in Africa, South America, or other parts of Asia due to cultural differences in village structures must be further explored.

Even though these questions remain unanswered, HLL has developed an innovative model that other corporations can examine to determine how they can utilize the BOP to enhance their bottom line.

Endnotes

1. Economic Intelligence Unit, India Country Indicators, 2003.

2. International Council for the Control of Iodine Deficiency Disorder, *http://www.iccidd.org,* November 2002.

3. World Bank Web site: Nongovernmental Organizations and Civil Society/Overview. *http://wbln0018.worldbank.org/essd/essd.nsf/NGOs/home*, June 8, 2001.

4. E-mail correspondence with Dr. C. S. Pandav, ICCIDD, May 5, 2003.

5. Balu, Rekha, Strategic innovation: Hindustan Lever Ltd., *FastCompany*, 120. June 2001.

6. Kurlansky, Mark, *Salt: A World History*. Penguin USA, New York, NY, 2002.

7. Natural Solutions, *http://www.naturalsolutions.com*.

8. Venkatash, M. G., and Dunn, John, *Salt Iodization for the Elimination of Iodine Deficiency*. International Council for Control of Iodine Deficiency, Ottawa, Canada, 1995.

9. Network for the Sustained Elimination of Iodine Deficiency, *http://www.sph.emory.edu/iodinenetwork/*, 2002.

10. ICCIDD, *http://www.iccidd.org*.

11. Venkatash, M. G., and Dunn, John. op. cit.

12. Pandav, Chandrakant, Prakash, R., and Sundaresan, S., *Universal Salt Iodization in India*. International Council for Control of Iodine Deficiency, Ottawa, Canada, 2000.

13. Interview with Ram Narayan, HLL, March 31, 2003.

14. Interview with Ranjan Sengupta, HLL, April 8, 2003.

15. Ministry of Health and Family Welfare, Notification, September 13, 2000.

16. Kurlansky op. cit., p. 387.

17. HLRC internal document, Dr. Amitava Pramanik, HLL, 2001.

18. HLL internal report, "The benefit of iodine to human beings and Iodine Deficiency Disorder (IDD)," 2001.

19. Ibid.

20. Goindi, Geetanjali, Karmakar, M. G., Kapil, Umesh, and Jagannathan, J., Estimation of losses of iodine during different cooking procedures. *Asia Pacific Journal of Clinical Nutrition*, 4, 225–227, 1995.

21. Interview with Dr. V. G. Kumar, HLL, April 5, 2003.

22. Dandi Salt Web site, *http://www.dandisalt.com*.

23. A Profile: Hindustan Lever Ltd. *http://www.in.biz.yahoo.com/p/hihll.bo.html*, 2000.

24. HLL internal document, Case Study Salt, 2001.

25. Ibid.

26. Interview with Vishal Dhawan, HLL, March 31, 2003.

27. HLL internal document, op. cit.

28. Interview with Vishal Dhawan, HLL, March 31, 2003.

29. Interview with Dr. A. S. Abhiraman, HLL, April 8, 2003.

30. Interview with Dr. Amitava Pramanik, HLL, April 8, 2003.

31. Interview with Ram Narayan, HLL, March 31, 2003.

32. Ibid.

33. Interview with Vishal Dhawan, HLL, April 7, 2003.

34. Interview with Ram Narayan, HLL, April 9, 2003.

35. Ibid.

36. Interview with Ranjan Sengupta, HLL, April 8, 2003.

37. Interview with Gopal Mishra, HLL, April 7, 2003.

38. Ibid.

39. Interview with Vindi Banga, HLL, March 31, 2003.

40. Interview with Sharat Dhall, HLL, April 1, 2003.

41. Ibid.

42. Interview with A. Balasubramanian, April 4, 2003.

43. Ibid.

44. Interview with Sharat Dhall, HLL, April 1, 2003.

45. Interview with A. Balasubramanian, April 3, 2003.

46. Ibid.

47. Interview with Vamshi K, HLL contract employee, April 4, 2003.

48. Interview with A. Balasubramanian, April 4, 2003.

49. Interview with Sharat Dhall, HLL, April 7, 2003.

50. E-mail correspondence from Sharat Dhall, HLL, April 25, 2003.

51. Ibid.

This report was written by Anuja Rajendra and Tej Shah
under the supervision of Professor C. K. Prahalad.
The report is intended to be a catalyst for discussion
and is not intended to illustrate effective
or ineffective strategies.

Selling Health:
Hindustan Lever Limited
and the Soap Market

In the category of infectious diseases, only acute respiratory infections and AIDS kill more people per year than diarrhea, which accounts for 2.2 million deaths annually.[1]

India contributes to 30 percent of all diarrhea deaths in the world.[2]

These statistics outline the pervasiveness of diarrheal disease in the developing world and the tremendous toll it takes on the public health, especially among the poor and children. In India alone, 19.2 percent of the children suffer from diarrhea.[3] At the same time, the preventive measures and cures are relatively simple: access to safe water and sanitation facilities and instruction on better hygiene practices. Yet, in spite of the efforts of nongovernmental organizations (NGOs), developmental agencies, and governments, the problem persists. So what is a viable solution?

THE INNOVATION

The paradox of diarrheal disease is that the solution is known and inexpensive, but it is difficult to reach and educate the poor about the need to wash hands with soap. Hindustan Lever Ltd. (HLL), the largest soap producer in India, helped create a unique approach to public–private partnership as a solution, and made this public health issue an integral part of its business.

This case traces the efforts of HLL, the Indian subsidiary of Unilever, in combatting the health issue of diarrheal disease through innovative methods of marketing a common consumer good—soap.

Diarrheal Disease

Globally, diarrheal disease accounts for more than 2.2 million deaths annually.[4] Children are particularly susceptible due to loss of liquids and dehydration from diarrhea. UNICEF estimates that one child dies every 30 seconds from diarrheal disease,[5] making it the second-largest global "infectious killer" of children under the age of five.[6] In India, national surveys estimate that almost 10 percent of the population suffers from diarrheal disease at any given time,[7] resulting in an estimated 660,000 diarrhea-related deaths per year in India.[8]

What Causes Diarrheal Disease?

Research has proven that human excreta are the main source of diarrheal pathogens.[9] A lack of adequate sanitation facilities for disposal of excreta and poor hygiene practices result in the diarrheal disease pathogens being carried throughout the human environment. There are four key ways in which pathogens are transmitted: through drinking water, from flies and insects, through physical contact with dirt, and from human hands.[10] Flies landing on excreta can carry pathogens to food or surfaces used to prepare food, and feet could track waste into the home. However, "hands are the main vector of diarrheal pathogens, transferring them from surface to surface and person to person."[11] Yuri Jain at HLL describes daily life in India: "Hands feed a child, hands prepare food and in an Indian context people don't typically use knives and forks . . . everything is done with your hands, so that's a transmission mechanism."[12] There is growing evidence that hands are also a main pathway for transmission of acute respiratory track infections (ARIs).[13] Statistics show that at any given time, over 6 percent of the population suffers from ARIs.[14]

A lack of sanitation facilities is widespread throughout India. The majority of India's population is poor, with approximately 83 percent of the population (885 million people) earning a median household income of less than 2,000 rupees (approximately $43) per month.[15] Almost 35 percent of the country is living below the poverty line.[16, 17] Moreover, less than 29 percent of the Indian population has access to modern sanitation facilities, and 64 percent of the population uses the bush or fields as toilets.[18] The number diverges widely by urban and rural populations. As of 2000, 27.7 percent of India's more than 1 billion people lived in urban areas, and 72.3 percent lived live in rural areas.[19] A 1999 sanitation report from the World Health Organization (WHO) and UNICEF revealed that in rural areas, only 16.8 percent of the Indian population use a flush toilet, pit, or latrine, and 81.1 percent have no facility and use the bush or fields as toilets.[20] The same report stated that 60.9 percent of urban Indians own a flush toilet, pit toilet, or latrine, and 19.3 percent have no facility or use the bush or fields as toilets. Handwashing habits also differ in urban and rural areas. Twenty-six percent of urban Indians (173 million) and 74 percent of rural Indians (492 million) do not wash their hands with soap every day.[21]

Handwashing as a Preventive Measure

Research on preventive behaviors for diarrheal disease shows that washing hands with soap could significantly reduce incidences of infection. In 1988, research conducted by the WHO showed that washing hands with soap reduced diarrhea attacks by 48 percent.[22] A evidence review by Valerie Curtis and Sandy Cairncross found handwashing with soap could cut diarrheal disease by 42 percent to 46 percent.[23] Changing behavior to increase the frequency of handwashing could therefore greatly reduce the incidence of diarrheal disease. Washing hands also could be effective in reducing the spread of ARIs.[24]

Currently, handwashing and soap usage are low among most of the Indian population. Although the penetration of soap in Indian households is actually very high, with 95 percent of Indian households owning soap, 665 million Indians do not use soap every day. Of these, 26 percent are urban Indians (173 million) and 74 percent are rural Indians (492 million).[25] "Only 30 percent of soap users uses soap every day."[26] Others use substitute products such as clay, ash, or mud. The International Scientific Forum on Home Hygiene: Rural Study found that after defecating and before and after every meal, 62 percent of the population used water plus ash or mud, 24 percent used water alone, and only 14 percent used soap and water.[27]

The Need for Behavior Change

If a solution to diarrheal disease is simply washing hands with soap, why is this problem still pervasive? Historically, this has been approached as a public health issue that could be solved through large infrastructure projects, a timely and costly proposition for governments in developing countries. In addition, three other reasons are given for the persistent incidence of diarrhea.[28] First, the disease fell into the multiple domains of Ministries of Public Health, Water, or Environment. However, no group ever assumed full responsibility for the disease. Second, attention has been focused on "hot" issues such as HIV that command more public attention, leaving diarrheal disease to be championed by no one. Third, behavior programs to address diarrheal disease are difficult to design and implement.

Changes in consumer beliefs and behavior are especially difficult to engineer in India. First, a deep understanding of the current practices, motivations, and hindrances to the use of soap and handwashing is required. This understanding is difficult to obtain in a country dominated by local cultures. India's 1 billion citizens are spread across 25 states and seven union territories. They speak more than 15 official languages and 325 different dialects, many of which are so different they are only understandable to those in a small geographic area.[29] Second, messages on health and hygiene to create behavior change are difficult to communicate to dispersed populations. Many rural parts of India are "media dark" areas, where citizens have little or no access to mass media channels.[30] Only 22 percent of the population has a TV, and only 42 percent has a radio.[31] This lack of a mass communication venue adds complexities and costs to education campaigns, requiring targeted messages distributed through unconventional means.

A Public Health Issue in the Private Realm

Given these complexities in developing and delivering an effective behavioral change campaign, a multinational corporation (MNC) that serves as a soap manufacturer might be better equipped to reach Indians with health messages to reduce diarrheal disease. This behavior stems out of the belief that water or other substitute products clean as well as soap. Yuri Jain, a general manager at HLL, explains, "We should really think about why a lot of these public programs haven't been as effective as they could have been. When put into the context of handwash and water, a lot of it actually involves changing consumer behavior and that's the crux of the matter. You have a way of doing it, and you change the way of doing it. And who is better placed at changing habits than a large, fast moving, consumer goods company?"[32] MNCs might be in the best position, with the following unique capabilities, to take on the challenge of combating diarrheal disease:

- Deep experience in conducting and analyzing consumer research to identify behaviors and trigger points for behavioral change.

- Marketing expertise to craft communication messages and direct contact programs that can bring about behavioral change.

- Strong brands that can serve as routes for driving behavioral change riding on their consumer equity.

- Experience in adapting their products and messages to meet local conditions, cultures, and traditions.

- Vast distribution networks to deliver products to consumers even in the most rural settings.

- Experience in sharing lessons learned and transferring best practices to increase the efficiency and effectiveness of their operations on a large scale.

- Accountability for achieving results by carefully evaluating investment in projects to ensure success.

- Global reach, with the ability to touch customers in many countries with similar messages and products, and quickly scale projects from local initiatives to regional and global endeavors.

Finally, MNCs sell soap, a product that can address diarrheal disease, and they have a built-in incentive to successfully create the required behavioral changes.

Hindustan Lever Limited

HLL is the largest soap and detergent manufacturer in India, with $2.4 billion in sales in 2001, 40 percent of which is from soaps and detergents.[33] In recent years, HLL's increasing focus on differentiating its products based on a health platform has pushed employees to delve deeper into consumers' needs and behaviors in an effort to find opportunities to make their products imperative to a family's health and safety. One means of making this connection was the tie between diarrheal disease prevention and HLL soap products. Yuri Jain at HLL explains, "When you ask yourself how do you break the transmission of disease with hands, you come up with handwashing with soap. And that clearly suggests there is great business imperative for us to try . . . to make that happen because we are the largest manufacturer of soap. If people start washing their hands with soap more often, the consumption will go up and there is an impact on market size."[34] This clearly could be a "win–win" solution for both the bottom of the pyramid (BOP) consumers and the company.

Not only would this focus on increasing the demand for soap benefit HLL, but it also could benefit Unilever in other parts of the world. In developed countries, the soap market is reaching a point of saturation. However, in developing markets, the opportunity for growth still exists. The opportunity to increase the size of market lies in increasing the frequency of use in India and other developing nations. Moreover, this opportunity to grow sales through health messages exists beyond the soap market and could be used to address other public health issues.

The Largest Soap Manufacturer in India

HLL's mission outlines a broad philosophy of serving all Indians, across all spectrums: wealthy and poor, rural and urban.

Our purpose at Hindustan Lever is to meet the everyday needs of people everywhere—to anticipate the aspirations of our consumers and customers and to respond creatively and competitively with branded products and services, which raise the quality of life.

Our deep roots in local cultures and markets around the world are our unparalleled inheritance and the foundation for our future growth. We will bring our wealth of knowledge and international expertise to the service of local customers.

To meet the needs of such a large and diverse country, HLL has four key profit centers, delivering more than 1,000 stockkeeping units (SKUs) through its more than 30 "power" brands. The largest profit center is Soaps & Detergents, followed by Foods & Beverages, Personal Products, and Specialty Chemicals (see Figure 1).

HLL's Ability to Reach the Masses

HLL has built superior research and development (R&D), distribution, and marketing capabilities to effectively deliver its goods across both urban and rural India. HLL employs more than 100 scientists to develop new consumer goods and pioneer efficiencies in manufacturing. Its investment in R&D resources is returned in cost savings and the ability to price goods affordably to mass markets.

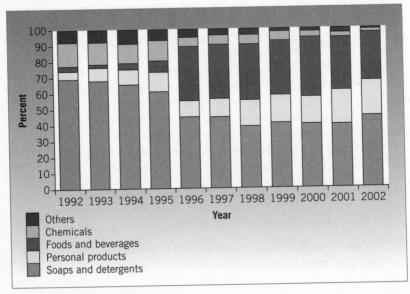

Figure 1   HLL net sales, 1992–2002.[35]

HLL also has assembled the manufacturing and distribution capabilities to provide its products to India. Products are manufactured in almost 100 locations throughout the country. From factories, the products move through a network of central depots to almost 7,500 redistribution stockists. Currently, HLL reaches into all villages with more than 2,000 people[36] and continues to expand its market reach through innovative direct sales programs to distribute products to rural areas. For example, an initiative called Project Shakti employs women to occupy a nontraditional role in commerce, selling HLL's products in their villages. Another initiative, Project Streamline, creates "star sellers" to sell an array of HLL products in rural areas.

To understand consumer behavior along the socioeconomic spectrum, HLL invests a significant portion of its earnings in consumer research and marketing to better position its products in mass markets. Large expenditures on both mass and direct marketing campaigns have made HLL brands such as Lifebuoy soap, Wheel detergent, and Fair and Lovely soap household names across India. HLL also invests in nontraditional and grassroots marketing efforts to reach rural and poor consumers.

HLL's Formula Is Working

HLL's financial performance reflects its success in effectively creating, marketing, and selling its brands. HLL has achieved solid growth with net sales increasing from less than $500 million to over $2.5 billion in the last 10 years (see Figure 2). This growth is due to growing market share as well as acquisitions and mergers.

In 2001, net sales were up over 2000, and net profits increased by over 25 percent despite an overall economic slowdown in India.[37]

Business Opportunity Through Health

The global soap market is increasingly saturated with products, and developing markets hold greater promise for growth opportunities. Currently, the majority of Indian consumers have soap in their homes, but usage is low because consumers don't necessarily associate washing hands with soap as a method for preventing disease. Also, beauty messages dominate ideas about the primary use of toilet soap, and daily washing with soap is not considered necessary for beauty by the Indian consumer. The opening in the competitive landscape, therefore, is to shift the positioning of soap from a beauty platform to a beauty and health platform as a means of increasing consumers' frequency of use.

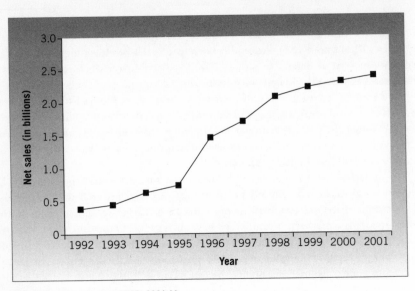

Figure 2 HLL net sales, 1992–2001.[38]

The Worldwide Soap Market

The worldwide soap market in 2000 was worth $88.2 billion (U.S.), and is dominated by a few major global players including Unilever (10.7 percent), Procter and Gamble (7.41 percent), Gillette (7.66 percent), Colgate-Palmolive (4.5 percent), and Johnson & Johnson (4.45 percent).[39] The top 10 industry leaders account for 50.5 percent of the total soap market.[40]

At the global level, however, developed markets are becoming saturated. Market growth has been mainly attributed to new product developments and extensions into antibacterial and moisturizing products, liquid and shower soaps, and products "focusing on added value and convenience."[41] These markets are expected to tighten in the next few years due to increased price competition and consolidation among soap manufacturers, leaving MNCs to seek out new markets in developing countries.[42]

Unilever as a whole is expecting developing markets to comprise approximately 50 percent of its sales over the next 10 years.[43] In emerging markets, the majority of consumers typically buy fewer soap products at lower costs than in the developed world. However, consumers in emerging markets are becoming increasingly value sensitive in their purchases.[44] This is in part due to growing middle classes and increasing customer aspirations in many countries, brought on by the globalization of media messages.

Soap in India

Currently, HLL accounts for 62.8 percent of all soap sales in India. Other large competitors include Nirma with 11.3 percent of the market, Godrej Soaps with 6.2 percent, and Johnson & Johnson with 1.6 percent.[45] Only 5 percent of all soaps come from the small-scale sector. HLL divides the market into several segments, including discount, popular, premium, and super premium, with the discount segment currently the largest segment in India.

The Large Unmet Consumer Need

Given these trends in the Indian soap market, HLL determined it needed to deliver more than beauty benefits and economy. Therefore, HLL focused on three value propositions: economy, beauty, and health. Harpreet Singh Tibb, Activation Manager for the Lifebuoy brand, describes the connection: "If you establish why health is important or why soaps can contribute to reducing germ incidents and perhaps save [consumers] medical bills through long-term associations, I think you have a winner right there."[46] Moreover, health is a meaningful message to consumers across socioeconomic spectrums. As described by Yuri Jain from HLL: "What is hygiene? It's a large, unmet consumer need."[47] Promoting this message presents a large opportunity to help prevent diarrheal disease, but also to leverage health messages as a means of growing sales. Leveraging these new value drivers, HLL sought opportunities to utilize its products, distribution network, and marketing skills and position itself as a "local multinational" to increase its reach and depth into the soap market in India.

Levering Health Messages Through the Global Public-Private Partnership for Handwashing with Soap

HLL sought out initiatives that connect the use of soap to health and hygiene behaviors, including handwashing. In Fall 2000, as part of its research centered around handwashing, HLL learned of a public–private partnership (PPP) being developed among the World Bank and the Water and Sanitation program, with the assistance of the Bank-Netherlands Water Partnership. This group procured the assistance of the London School of Hygiene and Tropical Medicine, UNICEF, U.S. Agency for International Development (USAID), and the Environmental Health Project. They entitled the initiative the Global Public–Private Partnership for Handwashing with Soap (later to become Health in Your Hands—A Public Private Partnership).

The structure for the program was based on the successful Central American Handwashing Initiative, a PPP that united four private corporations (La Popular, Colgate-Palmolive, Unisola [Unilever] and Punto Rojo), USAID, and UNICEF.[48] Before the program was initiated, diarrheal disease caused "19% of under five mortalities in Honduras, 23% in Nicaragua, 20% in El Salvador, and 45% in Guatemala."[49] The Initiative developed handwashing education messages that each private partner incorporated into its own marketing campaigns. The handwashing program resulted in a "30% increase in hygienic handwashing behavior in mothers, and an estimated 1,287,000 fewer days of diarrhea per year for children under five years of age in the two lowest socioeconomic groups."[50] Although the Global Public–Private Partnership for Handwashing with Soap would be similar to the Central American Handwashing Initiative, this campaign would be nonbranded and open to all interested parties. The PPP envisioned reaching 29 million people, the entire population of Kerala, in three years. This type of initiative was well-aligned with HLL's corporate goals of helping to improve the health of a nation. HLL also learned that the Kerala state government and the government of Ghana (two markets in which Unilever had a strong presence) were interested in piloting the initiative. Therefore, HLL committed to the Kerala pilot and, as an early player, was able to help shape the program design and recruit other industry participants.[51]

Partners

To create a pilot of this scale, the PPP needed to leverage the specific competencies of each partner (see Figure 3). First, the program needed scientific credibility and leadership in understanding the fundamentals of handwashing for health and hygiene. Therefore, Dr. Valerie Curtis from the London School of Hygiene and Tropical Medicine teamed with the Centers for Disease Control and the Environmental Health Project (U.S.) to provide credibility regarding the science-based foundation of the program and the monitoring and evaluation functions. This team would help determine the effectiveness of the handwashing campaign in terms of changed behaviors and monetary costs and would disseminate best practices and lessons learned to all participants. Second, the PPP needed expertise in behavior change and marketing. The World Bank and Water and Sanitation Program solicited private sector participation through the Indian Toiletries and Soap Manufacturers Association (ITSMA). HLL as the private sector representative held vast amounts of consumer behavior research as well as significant expertise in program design and communication methodologies in both mass and direct contact media.

Third, to reach the entire population with handwashing communications, the PPP needed government support to utilize existing infrastructure channels, such as schools and clinics, as a way to minimize costs and maximize direct contacts. The government of Kerala viewed this initiative as a welcome alternative to costly infrastructure projects and offered ready access via the governmental machinery. Yuri Jain at HLL described the impact of the PPP being able to work through government channels, "as a company—as Lifebuoy or as HLL—we can only do so much, we can only cover 'X' number of villages. But [in Kerala] we, the public-private partnership, have the government as a partner, which implies access to 10,000 schools, 20,000 social worker centers, 6,000 health centers. We have scale. You multiply that by 30, you get India. When you multiply that by 10, you have the whole world. So it's huge."[52] Finally, The World Bank, in particular the Bank-Netherlands Water Partnership, USAID, UNICEF, and the Water and Sanitation Program provided resource inputs and helped craft funding packages. These groups also had a network of employees experienced in administering large-scale programs. The final funding package was envisioned to leverage a combination of funding from the development agencies, the Kerala government, and the private sector (see Figure 3).

In return for these contributions, each player also expected certain outcomes. The health sector and development agencies sought to leverage additional resources and expertise in designing and implementing education campaigns.

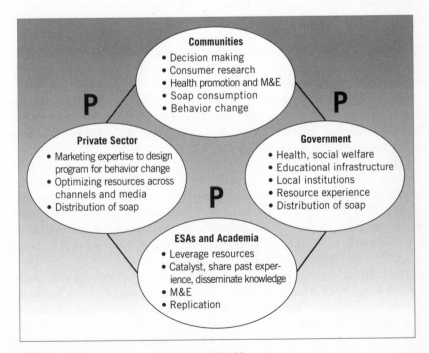

Figure 3 PPP handwashing participants and roles.[53]

The Kerala government sought a less costly solution than large infrastructure projects as a means of reducing diarrheal disease. It also could benefit from the communication expertise of the MNCs. The private sector sought growth in the soap market, increased market reach and visibility, and recognition as a corporate citizen. With the players in line, the PPP hired the Indian Market Research Bureau to conduct studies on handwashing habits in Kerala.

The Kerala Program

Kerala is a well-developed state in India. It has a population of 29 million and a 100-percent literacy rate.[54] Sanitation coverage in Kerala is 51.36 percent in urban areas and 44 percent in rural areas.[53] Despite higher levels of education and sanitation access, research studies in Kerala found that only 42 percent of mothers used soap after using the toilet, 25 percent used soap after cleaning up a child, 11 percent used soap before eating, and 10 percent used soap before preparing food.[55] The Kerala results also showed those who did not wash with soap were five times more likely to have diarrhea than those who washed with soap.

Based on this data, the PPP designed a program that tried to link the handwashing initiative to life-changing events or times when new behaviors are most likely to be adopted (e.g., the arrival of a new baby or vaccination).[56] The complete program was to include four main pieces: a mass media campaign, a direct contact campaign, evaluation, and communications development. The first piece was a direct contact program for women when they visited health or social service institutions. The PPP also designed a direct contact program in schools consisting of four health hygiene education days per year and the creation of a mandatory lunchtime handwashing program for children ages 6 to 11. Finally, the plan included a mass media campaign. The media campaign was to be generic with no company logos.

Calculations for Kerala suggested that through this program, "70% of households would be reached 43 times a year via mass media, and 35% of households would be reached nine times a year through the Direct Contact program."[57] The initial cost estimate for Kerala was a little over $10 million spread over three years to cover the whole state with per-person costs estimated to be $.10 per year.[58] Program administrators estimated that savings in health care costs would cover total program costs after two years.

The Indian government was considering a proposal to fund the mass media campaign, and the Kerala government, World Bank, and UNICEF agreed to pay for the direct contact program.[59] The WHO took charge of the evaluation function, and the private sector agreed to fund the communications research and message development. This allocation of costs among partners allowed each party to achieve a larger objective while bearing only a portion of the costs each year. The private sector committed to take on one-third of the total program costs (see Table 1). These costs were further divided among all participating companies (primarily HLL, Procter & Gamble, and Colgate-Palmolive). HLL agreed to bear the majority of the private-sector costs because it is the largest player in the market. However, this funding model might change. In total, HLL planned to contribute almost $776,000 per year (15 percent of total program costs) or $.027 per head per year.[60]

Table 1   Percentage Contribution per Partner[61]

Participant	Percentage of Costs
Government of India	37%
Government of Kerala/UNICEF	29%
WHO	4%
Private sector	30%
Total	100%

Program design and implementation plans progressed until Spring 2002, when nonprofit groups and political opponents started speaking out against the initiative in Kerala. Environmental and antiglobalization activist Dr. Vedana Shiva, Director of the Research Foundation for Science, Technology, and Natural Resource Policy, wrote:

Kerala has the highest access to safe water, highest knowledge of prevention of diarrhea because of high female literacy and local health practices such as use of jeera water and high use of fluids during diarrhea. The World Bank project is an insult to Kerala's knowledge regarding health and hygiene. It is in fact Kerala from where cleanliness and hygiene should be exported to the rest of the world. People of Kerala do not need a World Bank loan for being taught cleanliness.[62]

Others accused the Kerala government of side-stepping the real problem: proper toilets and sanitation facilities.[63] This opposition soon spread to politicians such as V. S. Achuthanandan, leader of the opposition in the State Assembly, who began speaking out against the initiative.[64] The criticism generated by adverse press began to hinder the PPP's efforts. The World Bank asked the government of Kerala to respond to the criticism, but the state refused. Meanwhile, the state cabinet had not yet approved the proposal, bringing the initiative to a standstill. Final negotiations for the effort are underway, but as an alternative, the PPP has downsized the initiative from $10 million over three years to $2 million for one year.[65]

Despite these difficulties, the PPP and HLL are having successes in other parts of the world. The official launch of the Ghana campaign was in August 2003 and work is well underway in Senegal, Peru, Indonesia, and Nepal. In each country, the program of work will include a similar direct contact and mass media mix, but will be tailored to the individual country's demographics and cultures.

HLL and the PPP

HLL saw the opportunity to benefit from the PPP, whose aim was to stimulate demand for soap through education campaigns. This initiative would leverage each partner's capabilities and expertise to serve the public good and expand the market for soap. However, the problems in Kerala highlighted the complexities and possible downsides of working with numerous partners. Public and international organizations, especially such modern-day political lightning rods as the World Bank, are susceptible to public criticism. The process of building trust and accommodating multiple agendas can also slow down project implementation.

Leveraging Health Messages for Lifebuoy Soap

At the same time HLL was trying to expand the soap market through the PPP, one of its oldest and most successful soap products, Lifebuoy, was losing topline growth at the rate of 15 percent to 20 percent per year, starting in 1999.[66] The Lifebuoy brand team was trying to determine appropriate next steps to revive the ailing brand, and began to look toward handwashing. As a means of countering sales declines, the Lifebuoy brand looked to HLL's work on the PPP for new methods of attracting and winning customers.

The History of Lifebuoy

The Lever Brothers Company created Lifebuoy in 1894 by mixing residue from the manufacturing process for Sunlight detergent with red coloring and cresylic acid to create a strong soap. From the beginning, HLL linked the bright red color and sanitary carbolic smell to "healthy clean." Beginning in the 1960s, the brand messages were reinforced through the use of a sports idiom in Lifebuoy's advertising. An active and energetic sports player needed a strong, effective soap to get truly clean. The Lifebuoy jingle played behind a team sports vignette, "Lifebuoy hai jahan tandurusti hai wahan" or "There's Lifebuoy wherever there is health!" HLL marketed the soap to the Indian male, 18 to 45 years old, with a median household income of less than 2,000 rupees per month or approximately $47. This person was a semiliterate farmer or construction laborer living in a town of 100,000 or less.[67] By 1986, sales exceeded 100,000 tons, with 70 percent of the brand's volume coming from rural areas. By 1992, Lifebuoy sales surpassed sales of any other soap in India.

Beginning in the 1980s, the cheaply priced beauty bar segment began to eat into Lifebuoy profits. As described by Harpreet Singh Tibb, Activation Manager for the brand, "We kept saying health, health, health. And over time, health became synonymous with the base level of cleaning. Every soap over time started speaking about basic health plus something. And the net result was that we were thought to be at the base level of protection. So our health offering became less attractive."[68] He went on to explain that the carbolic fragrance was also outdated, because younger generations and women showed a preference for more floral-type fragrances. At the same time, the enormous brand equity associated with the 107-year old Lifebuoy name, especially in rural India, was something the company could not afford to lose.

Brand Revitalization on a Health Platform

Therefore, the Lifebuoy team decided to revisit its mission. HLL Chairman Manvinder Singh Banga advocated the creation of new opportunities for soap:

If Lifebuoy stands for improving health and is all about germ kill, why is it only a soap, why not a shampoo, talcum powder and so on. Then you begin to think about the ways in which the brand can interface and touch the consumer throughout the day; how can that brand touch the consumer? Today we're only touching the consumer when he or she had a bath, but when you begin to think about it in this framework, you say where are the possible inroads of germs into your day, and where can Lifebuoy play a role? So you get a whole set of growth opportunities that emerge.[69]

With this direction, the marketing team created a new vision and mission for the brand, relevant to all Indians:

Making a billion Indians feel safe and secure wherever they are by focusing on their health and hygiene needs.

The team decided to leverage the historical brand platform of health by tying soap usage to the eradication of family health problems. HLL also linked the data demonstrating how soap can help eliminate common health problems, such as diarrhea, to Lifebuoy, finding that members of families often experience stomach infections (diarrhea), eye infections, and infected sores. As described by Yuri Jain, this results in a significant loss of time and disposable income for an Indian family: "Every time a diarrheal episode takes place, and for a poor family this could be two to six times a year, there are treatment costs; there are medicine costs; there are doctor costs. And so there is a spectrum of savings that is amassed."[70] The team also changed the target audience from men to entire families to expand its audience for the health message and to cater to the increased influence of women on household purchases. HLL hoped this revitalized health platform would create relevance for the new Lifebuoy target consumers and reassure existing customers that it was still a health soap.

Product, Cost, and Marketing Strategy

To address the health needs of one billion Indians, the team created a reformulation that was relevant, accessible, and affordable to the mass market. HLL replaced the carbolic smell with a more fragrant smell to better appeal to families and women. The team also changed the manufacturing process from "hard" soap production to milled soap production, a change that made Lifebuoy longer lasting and produced more lather.[71] Its new positioning was now targeted at the entire family's health.

In addition to these changes, HLL wanted to ensure it could differentiate its product on a health platform. The team decided to add Triclosan, a common antibacterial agent, to strengthen the antibacterial power of the soap. In Europe and the United States, Triclosan has been at the center of the antibacterial controversy. Dr. Laura McMurray at Tufts University School of Medicine found evidence that bacteria could develop resistance to Triclosan and propel the creation of more dangerous forms of bacteria.[72] Despite these criticisms, HLL felt the use of an antibacterial agent was critical in producing the health impact of eradicating and preventing germ regrowth. It named the ingredient Active-B as a cue to the consumer that Lifebuoy provided additional health benefits over other soaps.

The team also had to ensure Lifebuoy was still affordable to its consumers. HLL Chairman Manvinder Singh Banga explained:

> *Lifebuoy is priced to be affordable to the masses. . . . Very often in business you find that people do cost-plus pricing. They figure out what their cost is and then they add a margin and figure that's their selling price. What we have learned is that when you deal with mass markets, you can't work like that. You have to start by saying I'm going to offer this benefit, let's say it's germ kill. Let's say it's Lifebuoy. You have to work out what people are going to pay. That's my price. Now what's my target margin? And that gives you your target cost—or a challenge cost. Then you have to create a business model that delivers that challenge cost.[73]*

The Lifebuoy team had invested its own profits to reformulate the product, and incurred increased production costs from the addition of the Triclosan ingredient. Therefore, the Lifebuoy team reconfigured the product's price and mix to meet the cost challenge and create a viable model to deliver a low-cost, mass-market soap. The team determined the product changes and extra germ-killing ingredient did create additional "value for money" and increased the price from 8.50 to 9.50 rupees. Moreover, the change from a "hard" soap production process to a milled soap process created a longer lasting bar, allowing the team to deliver the same value in a smaller size. The milled soap process was already employed for production of most other HLL soap brands, so the learning curve for adopting the change was minimal, and the changeover was implemented in less than one week.[74] Gurpreet Kohli, a senior product development manager at HLL, recounts this change, "We also engineered [the new Lifebuoy] in such a way that it did not contribute a significant amount on costs either on us or consumers. We changed the mix, the pack size mix, from 150 grams to 125 grams. But it lasts just as long."[75] The team also developed a 60-gram bar priced at 4.50 rupees for consumers who were not able to afford the 9.50-rupee bar.

The team next developed a new series of commercials that linked Lifebuoy to the prevention of diarrhea, eye infections, and infections of cuts and wounds. These commercials would reach customers through mass media channels. However, rural customers, who comprised 70 percent of Lifebuoy sales, often lived in areas without access to mass media. Therefore, HLL needed a special method for reaching its rural customer base.

New Communication Channels: Multicontact Programs and Swasthya Chetna
Health Messages and the Rural Consumer

To reach its rural consumers, HLL first had to understand rural behaviors and preferences. HLL researched hygiene and handwashing practices and the trigger points for using soap. HLL found that although attention to cleanliness has been increasing over time, most customers still associate cleanliness with the absence of dirt as opposed to the eradication of bacteria. For example, focus group and observational interview participants in rural areas often described their hands as being dirty if they were sticky, oily, discolored, or smelled bad. However, if their hands looked and felt clean, then consumers considered their hands to be clean. Through this research, HLL determined the trigger for a consumer to wash his or her hands was to remove unpleasant contaminants, not to kill germs that cause infections. They also found this perception of "visual clean is safe clean" leads to infrequent handwashing and limited use of soap.

Focus group research showed similar results in that only 5 of 13 people washed their hands before eating, and only 10 of 18 washed their hands before preparing food.[76] Moreover, if consumers did wash their hands, they most often used water or a proxy product for soap such as mud or ash. The same study found that after handling cow dung, 5 of 7 interviewees rinsed their hands with water, one washed with mud, and one used soap. Consumers were not using soap because they did not believe they were dirty or did not perceive that soap had added benefits over water or other materials. Therefore, HLL decided it would have to educate customers about germs and the consequences of germs on health to increase soap usage as a means of deterring bacterial infection.

HLL teamed up with the rural India outreach arm of Ogilvy & Mather to design a behavioral-change education campaign focused on uniting the health attributes of Lifebuoy soap with health messages of germ eradication. First, HLL and Ogilvy & Mather brainstormed a way to communicate the negative effects of "invisible" germs in an easily understandable and relevant message to the rural consumer. They also decided to highlight the unique attribute of Lifebuoy soap, Active-B. HLL and Ogilvy & Mather outlined the following key messages:

- Invisible germs are everywhere.
- Germs cause diseases common to rural families including painful stomach, eye, and skin infections.
- Lifebuoy soap with Active-B can protect you from germs.
- Wash your hands with Lifebuoy soap to prevent infection.

HLL next embarked on the creation of a comprehensive program aimed at reaching all members in a rural village to create a sustained behavioral change. Harpreet Singh Tibb of HLL explains:

> If it's going to multiple contacts, it has to be low-cost. It has to be a scalable and sustainable program. It has to be interactive because you're trying to get a behavioral change. And the cost of reaching out to villages in rural India is very, very expensive. I can't keep doing that for ages. So I need to ensure I get the community to own up to this program and get this movement going for ages. And therefore community participation is very important.[77]

HLL titled the program Lifebuoy Swasthya Chetna, or Lifebuoy Glowing Health. HLL hoped to change the trigger for washing hands from "visual clean is safe clean" to a social convention of frequent handwashing.

Program Design: Low-Cost, Scalable, and Sustainable

Although the HLL and Ogilvy & Mather team believed this program could effectively change rural consumer behavior, it also was projected to be costly. Initial plans called for two-person teams from Olgilvy & Mather, to travel in vans equipped with audiovisual equipment, flip charts, interactive games, and a "germ-glow" demo. Costs were estimated to be approximately 4,000 rupees or $87 per visit.[78] These initial expenses proved too costly for the program to scale as needed, especially given that the initiative was funded out of the Lifebuoy marketing budget. Therefore, the team created guiding premises for the model: It needed to be low-cost, scalable, and sustainable.

To maximize expenditures on the program to both HLL and communities, the team decided to hire facilitators from local regions who knew local dialects and could utilize local forms of transportation. In addition, they eliminated the use of costly audiovisual equipment and used only low-cost props. These measures helped reduce costs from an estimated 4,000 to 800 rupees per visit (from roughly \$87 to \$17).[79]

Moreover, because the program could not be rolled out across the entire country at once, HLL systematically chose areas to target with the new program (see Table 2). In this way, HLL maximized its reach to new customers and reassured old customers that the new Lifebuoy formulation was better than the old formulation. First, HLL looked at direct media contact. Second, HLL looked at consumption per state and chose states that had a strong loyalty to the Lifebuoy brand. HLL found that Lifebuoy had solid brand equity in Maharasthra, Bihar, Uttar Pradesh, Karnataka, Jharkhand, Madhya Pradesh, West Bengal, Chhatisgarh, and Orissa. Next, HLL reviewed district data to determine what states had high numbers of infrequent soap users as well as states that contributed a high share to total Lifebuoy sales. HLL then cross-referenced this data against media status. HLL wanted to leverage the Swastya Chetna program in areas that were not accessible by mass communication means. Finally, HLL selected those villages with middle schools so it could gain entrée to the community via the local school system. Harpreet Singh Tibb of

Table 2   Selection Criteria for Villages for Swasthya Chetna Initiative[81]

Process Sheet	Filters	Outputs	Stated Objective
1. Media Reach	Media status	Media grey and dark areas (less than 50 media reach) were selected	Reach those unreachable through mass means
2. State Selection	Lifebuoy rural share and contribution to total Lifebuoy shares	States with high share and contribution were selected	Identify states to increase Lifebuoy consumption
3. SCRs (regions) Selection	% infrequent soap users and soap user potential	SCRs with high infrequent soap users and high soap contribution were selected	Identify potential SCRs to increase frequency of soap usage
	Lifebuoy share of SCRs and their contribution to total Lifebuoy sales	High Lifebuoy shares were selected	Increase Lifebuoy consumption
4. District Selection	Lifebuoy share at district level	Districts with more than 10% share were selected	Increase Lifebuoy consumption
5. Village Selection	2–5K villages with middle schools	Shortlisted 9000 villages with schools	Reach mothers and children

HLL explained the rationale behind this selection: "Principal audiences are the middle school children, ages 7–13. Through them, they are the carriers of change for us. Through them we are reaching out to the mothers, the elders, and their parents, because [the students] are the ones who are the most educated in the family."[80]

In the end, the Lifebuoy team selected 10,000 villages in nine states where HLL stood to gain the most market share as well as educate the most needy communities. This targeted method of selecting villages allowed the Lifebuoy team to capitalize on high-growth regions by providing a direct multiple-contact program that could bring about a lifelong behavioral change, with the hopes of leading to a lifelong increase in soap consumption.

Through Ogilvy & Mather, HLL hired 127 two-person teams to reach an estimated 40 million people in the first year alone. Due to the low cost and ease of implementation, they expanded the program to 70 million people in the second year. The program currently employs 310 teams and estimates the program is reaching 30 percent to 40 percent of the rural population in targeted states. HLL also works to ensure that its products are distributed and available in these sites to ensure it benefits from sales generated by the program.[82]

Creating Behavior Change

The development of Swasthya Chetna relied on a structured communication process for creating behavioral change, as shown in Figure 4.

Each exposure relies on five key communication tactics: education, involvement, shock, reiteration, and reward. These elements were structured into each Lifebuoy Swasthya Chetna visit.

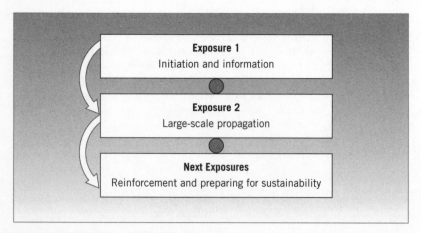

Figure 4 Behavior change methodology.[83]

Contact 1: School and Village Presentation

The first contact session targets schoolchildren ages 5 to 13 and their parents. To begin, the Lifebuoy Swasthya Chetna team presents an interactive flip chart story of Raju, a young schoolboy who uses soap to stay healthy. Through this presentation, the children learn about germs and how they cause stomach, eye, and wound infections. They also learn how soap can reduce infection, and about the five most important times to use soap: after going to the bathroom, before eating, after eating, to bathe, and after playing.

Throughout the session, they also learn about the health benefits of Lifebuoy soap. As explained by Harpreet Singh Tibb at HLL, "In the communication we are just speaking about the category of soaps. We are advocating soap usage, we're not advocating Lifebuoy. But the branding, the elements that we put around it, are all branded with Lifebuoy. We actually categorize the soap as a health soap, because it works better than regular soaps. Health soaps are the ones that actually have active ingredients in them that are twice as effective in preventing germs."[84] To impress on the students the effectiveness of Lifebuoy soap, the facilitators introduce the Lifebuoy Hero, an action character that eradicates germs. The facilitators invite students to share what they have learned in front of their classmates and present them with awards of Lifebuoy soap for correct answers.

Next, the facilitators demonstrate that invisible germs exist and can be eliminated through the use of soap. To convince people that "visual clean is NOT safe clean," the HLL team developed a "germ-glow" demonstration kit, comprised of a bottle of glow-germ powder, a black light, and black viewing box. The glow-germ powder represents germs and how they are affected by soap. The glow-germ powder is applied to the hands of two separate participants. One participant then washes her hands using water and the other uses both soap and water. Once immersed in water, the glow-germ powder becomes invisible, so both pairs of hands appear to be visually clean. However, when both participants' hands are then placed in the black viewing box under the black light, the participant who used only water will have many spots of glow-germ powder residue on her hands compared to the participant who used soap. This innovative demonstration proves to the rural consumer that "visual clean is NOT safe clean," and that washing with soap helps eradicate bacteria and germs.

Following the glow-germ demonstration, the children reiterate the importance of washing by embarking on a parade around their village. Led by the HLL facilitators, the children chant "Swastya Chetna" and "Lifebuoy helps keeps germs away" to raise visibility of the initiative and reinforce prior learning. Finally, the students are given health message stencils about the benefits of Lifebuoy with which to decorate their villages. The children stencil an estimated 200 messages around the village such as "After defecation, use Lifebuoy," or "Before eating, use Lifebuoy," or "Have a bath with Lifebuoy and keep germs away."

At the end of the day, the facilitators tell the students they will return in two to three months for a community-owned program of skits and presentations by students. They work with the local schoolteacher to assign students to skits. This mandates that students work on health issues until the next visit. It also gets parents excited about the prospect of their children presenting in front of the entire village. Finally, facilitators institute a wrapper-redemption program in which students who collect three, four, or five Lifebuoy wrappers before the next visit receive prizes such as small radios or games. The wrapper-redemption program is meant to increase soap usage in homes and benefit Lifebuoy sales.

After school is out, the facilitators meet with the village elders to share similar health and hygiene messages. Elders are often influential parties in guiding village behavior; therefore, education of these individuals early in the process was determined to be a key to gaining the confidence of all villagers.

Contact 2: Lifebuoy Village Health Day

Day 2 is aimed at children ages 5 to 13 and their parents and begins with a health camp. HLL brings a village doctor to speak to participants about the importance of washing with soap. Moreover, the facilitators measure students' height and weight to determine if they fall within healthy norms. Because more than 70 percent of Indian children under four are moderately or severely underweight,[85] HLL gives "Healthy Child" awards to those in the normal range as a method of helping parents understand healthy heights and weights.

In the evening, the children present their health skits and poems to the community as a way to reiterate messages and gain community involvement in the handwashing campaign. During this time, HLL also communicates messages about germs and germ eradication, repeats the germ-glow demonstration, and provides awards for the best presenters.

Contact 3: Diarrhea Management Workshop

The third visit is geared toward young mothers and pregnant women who might not have been involved in the community presentation put on by older schoolchildren. During this session, the facilitators present on the dangers of diarrhea, how it is spread, how it can be prevented, and how it can be treated. They also perform preliminary health checks for the women.

Contact 4: Launch of the Lifebuoy Health Club

On the fourth visit, the HLL facilitators announce the formation of a health club that will include activities centered on hygiene and keeping the village clean. The facilitators will return four to six more times to run health club sessions and maintain active engagement in health and hygiene issues. The club is anticipated to grow through a quarterly newsletter and the Lifebuoy Club activity calendar.

HLL and Lifebuoy Swasthya Chetna

Although the excitement surrounding the program is great, the sales benefits are difficult to quantify. In large part, HLL has undertaken this initiative based on faith that it would have long-term impacts on India's health and the market. Initial data, being collected almost two years after the launch, is just now being reviewed to measure the return on investment and effectiveness of the pilot program. Fortunately, the data indicates the program has resulted in a sustained behavior change. To date, the wrapper-redemption program has had a 30 percent response rate, but little other concrete information on monetary benefits to HLL exists. Harpreet Singh Tibb of HLL explains, "Lifebuoy last year grew by 30%. It's grown across states, across regions. It's very difficult to say what proportion of that can be attributed to this program. But in the geography in which we have this program, Lifebuoy has grown in sales."[86]

Given that initial indications are favorable, HLL also is planning to roll out the initiative in Bangladesh this year with expectations to move to additional countries in the near future. Moreover, the PPP Kerala initiative has borrowed the Swasthya Chetna format for its school visits (although Kerala will be instituting only a three-contact program and will not be participating in the wrapper-redemption program). The ability of other Unilever units to leverage these findings demonstrates the program is transferable and scalable to other markets, countries, and venues.

CONCLUSION

The promise of health is relevant universally.[87]

What Does HLL Gain from
Marketing Public Health Messages about Soap?

Differentiating soap products on the platform of health takes advantage of an opening in the competitive landscape for soap. Providing affordable health soap to the poor achieves product differentiation for a mass-market soap and taps into an opportunity for growth through increased usage. In India, soap is perceived as a beauty product, rather than a preventive health measure. Also, many consumers believe a visual clean is a safe clean, and either don't use soap to wash their hands, use soap infrequently, or use cheaper substitute products that they believe deliver the same benefits. HLL, through its innovative communication campaigns, has been able to link the use of soap to a promise of health as a means of creating behavioral change, and thus has increased sales of its low-cost, mass-market soap. Health is a valuable commodity for the poor and to HLL. By associating Lifebuoy's increased usage with health, HLL can build new habits involving its brand and build loyalty from a group of customers new to the category. A health benefit also creates a higher perceived value for money, increasing a customer's willingness to pay. By raising consumers' level of understanding about illness prevention, HLL is participating in a program that will have a meaningful impact on the Indian population's well-being and fulfill its corporate purpose to "raise the quality of life."

This opportunity for brand differentiation based on health does not just exist in India or in the soap market alone. A snapshot of the world's population, increasingly divided between rich and poor consumers, in developed and developing countries, shows that almost 90 percent of the world's anticipated population growth (from 6.2 billion to 9.1 billion in the next 50 years) will occur in developing markets.[88] Twenty percent alone will occur in India. PPPs are starting to work in these untapped markets, but a huge opportunity still exists for MNCs to spread health messages to other developing countries through branded campaigns.

Moreover, wealthier populations also could benefit from health and hygiene messages. Statistics from the World Bank found that when the Indian population was evenly divided into five socioeconomic quintiles, incidence of diarrheal disease was similar across the quintiles (see Table 3). This suggests that a lack of adequate sanitation facilities in poor and rural populations might not be the primary factor in the spread of diarrheal disease. Handwashing habits might be similar across various populations, which suggests an opportunity to reach out with direct contact campaigns to all socioeconomic populations to transform handwashing behavior and greatly increase the frequency of handwashing and soap sales.

Table 3   Incidence of Diarrhea by Socioeconomic Quintiles[89]

Prevalence of Diarrhea (% ill in the preceding 2 weeks)	Poorest	Second	Middle	Fourth	Richest	Population Average
Total	10.2	10.4	10.2	10.1	8.5	9.9
Urban	4.9	12.0	9.0	9.5	8.0	
Rural	10.3	10.2	10.4	10.3	10.2	

This opportunity might also exist in developed nations. The Economist reported that in England, fewer than one-half of British mothers washed their hands after changing their children's diapers.[90] By reinforcing health messages to low-use populations, MNCs stand to benefit globally.

In addition to reaching low-use populations, MNCs have an opportunity to provide solutions for other health problems of the poor. The growing populations in developing countries are at risk from many of the same basic health issues stemming from poverty and its accompaniments of poor sanitation infrastructure, lack of access to health resources, and inability to buy affordable preventive measures. By creating affordable products that meet basic needs like preventing disease, MNCs could capitalize on large untapped markets. According to HLL, the poor can be just as discriminating as the rich when it comes to brand consciousness. Keki Dadiseth of HLL is quoted in a Fast Company article as saying, "Everybody wants brands. And there are a lot more poor people in the world than rich people. To be a global business and to have a global market share, you have to participate in all segments."[91] As HLL builds brand equity around its ability to offer a better quality of life through health, it will find ways to scale its lessons learned from the soap market to other product offerings and markets around the world.

Methods for Increasing Market Sales

To date, HLL has helped create two initiatives to spread health and hygiene messages and expand the soap market. Are there lessons that can be drawn from the first few years of working in these different models? Are these programs scalable, low-cost, and impactful?

Scalability

Both the PPP and Swasthya Chetna initiatives aim to reach large populations in short time frames. The PPP is initially reaching a smaller number of people than Swastya Chetna; it aims to reach 49 million people in its first year of operation, whereas Swasthya Chetna will reach over 70 million people by the end of this year (see Table 4).

Moreover, Swasthya Chetna has been able to design and implement its program more quickly—it already operates in nine Indian states, whereas the PPP is still in the planning stages in Kerala. At the same time, the network and resources of the PPP have allowed it to immediately expand globally with project planning already underway in five other nations. This is on a much greater scale than Swasthya Chetna's planned expansion to Bangladesh. In addition, the PPP is targeting all socioeconomic groups in the population,

Table 4 Comparison Between the PPP and Swasthya Chetna

	"Health in Your Hands" PPP	Lifebuoy Swasthya Chetna
HLL Visibility	Not branded	Branded
Scope	Whole population, all segments	Targeted population Rural Media dark Strong Lifebuoy brand support Low per capita soap consumption Use of schools for program access
Methods	3 contacts with school children Daily contact with school hand wash Contacts with young mothers through social work and health care system	7 contacts with school children 1 contact with community 1 contact with young mothers
Partners	Local government health care system Local government school system Development agencies Other MNCs	Local government school system
Total Program Costs (*in India*)		
2002*	$3,493,333.33	$695,652.17
2003**(Revised due to Kerala slowdown)	$2,000,000.00	$1,043,478.26
Program Costs per Head		
2002	$.120	$.017
2003	$.069	$.010
HLL Total Program Costs (Revised due to Kerala slowdown)***	$444,444.44	$8.26

*PPP estimates based upon $10.4M for 3 years of implementation as estimated by the Water and Sanitation Program.[1] Swastya Chetna estimates based upon 800-rupee cost per village.

**PPP estimates based upon $2M for scaled-back Kerala initiative. Swastya Chetna estimates based upon 80-rupee cost per village

***HLL assumed to bear 2/3 of total program costs for PPP.

[1]Water and Sanitation Program. "Hand Wash India presentation," *http://www.wsp.org/english/activities/handwashing/vbehal.pdf*, April 28, 2003.

Table 4 Continued

	"Health in Your Hands" PPP	Lifebuoy Swasthya Chetna
HLL Costs per Head (Revised due to Kerala slowdown)	$.015	$.010
Timeline		
2001	1st meeting of members	Preparation for launch
2002	Preparation for launch	40m in 10,000 villages in 9 states across India
2003	Total: 49.2m Ghana (20.2m) Maybe Kerala (29m) Preparation for launch in Senegal, Peru, Nepal, Indonesia	Total: 100m 100m in 15,000 villages in 9 states across India Preparation for launch in Bangladesh
2004	Total: 272.1m Senegal 9.9m Peru 26.7m Nepal 23.9m Indonesia 211.6m Each continent to learn cultural lessons and align program to each region	Total: 100m India (11 states) 100m Bangladesh (number TBD) Each HLL office to learn from best practices and spread it to that region
Benefits	Scales quickly Can support programs in countries where desired	Branded Targeted to largest growth segment Fewer partners, so greater autonomy and program discretion Slightly lower costs per head
Disadvantages	Not featuring HLL brand names Complications may occur due to many partners (i.e., slower pace in Kerala) Slightly higher cost per head	Funded by brand P&L, so restrictive growth

meaning that it could potentially have a greater effect on overall soap market sales than the Swasthya Chetna campaign that is targeted to Lifebuoy's main customer segment.

Impact on Behavior Change and Soap Sales

Although scalability seems to be greater with the PPP, direct benefits to corporate sales lie with Swasthya Chetna. Through strategic selection of villages, Swasthya Chetna has maximized use of limited funds to reach targeted demographics to increase Lifebuoy sales. This not only results in cost savings and efficiencies, but also might be more effective than an unbranded campaign in creating behavior change. Research shows that use of a brand can help strengthen the health messages being delivered by conveying quality, increasing consumer confidence, and ensuring that messages are delivered in a nonpatronizing tone.[92] By reaching out to poor populations with strong brands and building habits involving their brands, HLL can create an unshakable hold on consumers' wallets. Conversely, the PPP seeks overall market sales, which might or might not directly benefit HLL.

At the same time, promotion of a branded product can leave the company open to criticism. Therefore, it's important the campaigns have a solid science-based foundation and are transparent. The Lifebuoy Swasthya Chetna campaign has done both. As explained by Harpreet Singh Tibb at HLL:

> We're not shying away from the fact that Lifebuoy is going to benefit or we're trying to get soap consumption up. We're being up-front about it. But we're also telling them that we're doing something for the good of the community and it's there for you to see yourself. And that's the reason we're actually going into schools and schools are giving us permission to go in. Because they believe that what we're saying is actually making sense. I'm trying to develop the category because I believe soaps can reduce diarrheal incidents by 40%. And if you believe it's true, there's no reason why you should dispute this program.[93]

Developing the Expertise to Sell Health

HLL will undoubtedly continue to evaluate the advantages and disadvantages of both programs to promote hygiene and soap usage as it moves forward. To date, both the PPP and the branded direct marketing campaign have proven to be innovative and viable models for expanding markets while helping improve the quality of life for the poor. Both programs combine partnerships (the PPP with NGOs and governments and Swasthya Chetna with schools), health education campaigns, and low-cost products to successfully translate improved hygiene behavior into increased sales in a scalable way.

A central challenge in "selling" health is the development of successful partnerships between private business and public health offices and organizations. Both groups need to invest together to create the market for a product. Private organizations contribute competencies around behavior change and delivery of low-cost products, whereas public organizations provide access to consumers, in effect, the channels to deliver messages and extend product reach. Both groups are investing in and addressing a common problem, but are evaluated on producing two different results: NGOs and governments are interested in an improved quality of life, whereas private businesses seek increased earnings.

These different motivations produce an inherent tension in the PPP model. This tension is apparent in the status of the highly publicized Global Handwashing Initiative PPP, where political roadblocks have slowed down the program and thus impacted HLL's plans to deliver health education and expand the soap market. Yet, these lessons have helped HLL to transfer knowledge from the Global Handwashing Initiative PPP to improve its own branded health education program, Swasthya Chetna. Working with more localized partners—in this case, village schools—HLL is rapidly scaling its program throughout rural India. By learning how to build partnerships and work in PPPs, even if toward seemingly different ends, HLL has gained a competitive advantage. HLL can leverage its experience accessing public health channels to sell products as health solutions, while increasing its market share both in India and abroad.

Endnotes

1. Curtis, Valerie. October 2002. "Health in Your Hands: Lessons from Building Public-Private Partnerships for Washing Hands with Soap." *http://globalhandwashing.org/Publications/Lessons_learntPart1.htm*.

2. UNICEF, as quoted in Water and Sanitation Program. "Hand Wash India Presentation," *http://www.wsp.org/english/activities/handwashing/vbehal.pdf*, April 28, 2003.

3. National Health Survey 1998–1999, as cited in Water and Sanitation Program. "Hand Wash India presentation," *http://www.wsp.org/english/activities/handwashing/vbehal.pdf*, April 28, 2003.

4. Curtis, Valerie. Op. cit.

5. Water and Sanitation Program. "Hand Wash India Presentation," *http://www.wsp.org/english/activities/handwashing/vbehal.pdf*, April 28, 2003.

6. Curtis, Valerie. Op. cit.

7. Gwatkin, Davidson R., et al. May 2000. *Socio-Economic Difference in Health, Nutrition, and Population in India*. HNP/Poverty Thematic Group of the World Bank.

8. Water and Sanitation Program. Op. cit.; the number of deaths (660,000) was derived by multiplying 2.2 million diarrheal deaths annually by India's percentage contribution of 30% as estimated by UNICEF.

9. Curtis, Valerie. Op. cit.

10. Water and Sanitation Program. Op. cit.

11. Curtis, Valerie. Op. cit.

12. Interview with Yuri Jain, HLL, March 26, 2003.

13. Curtis, Valerie. Op. cit.

14. Gwatkin, Davidson R., et al. Op. cit.

15. Water and Sanitation Program. Op. cit.

16. The World Bank. 1997. *India: Achievements and Challenges in Reducing Poverty.* Washington, D.C.

17. This World Bank study defines someone living below the poverty line as anyone with a per-capita monthly expenditure lower than 49 rupees (rural) and 57 rupees (urban) at 1973–74 all-India prices. This corresponds to a per-capita expenditure sufficient to provide basic nonfood items and a caloric intake of 2,400 calories per day for rural Indians and 2,100 calories per day for urban Indians.

18. WHO/UNICEF Joint Monitoring Programme for Water Supply and Sanitation Coverage Estimates, 1980–2000. "Access to Improved Sanitation: India." September 2001.

19. United Nations Population Division. 2003. *World Population Prospects: The 2002 Revision Population Database. http://www.un.org/popin/data.html.*

20. WHO/UNICEF Joint Monitoring Programme for Water Supply and Sanitation Coverage Estimates, 1980–2000. Op cit.

21. Water and Sanitation Program. Op. cit.

22. WHO, 1998, as cited in Handwash India presentation, *http://www.wsp.org/english/activities/handwashing/vbehal.pdf*, April 28, 2003.

23. Curtis, Valerie. Op. cit.

24. "How to Save 1m Children a Year." *The Economist.* July 6, 2002.

25. Water and Sanitation Program. Op. cit.

26. Ibid.

27. Ibid.

28. Curtis, Valerie. Op. cit.

29. Kolanad, Gitanjali. 2001. *Culture Shock! India.* Graphic Arts Center Publishing Agency.

30. Water and Sanitation Program. Op. cit.

31. Gwatkin, Davidson R., et al. Op. cit.

32. Interview with Yuri Jain, HLL, March 26, 2003.

33. HLL, Annual Report, 2001. All figures have been converted from rupees to U.S. dollars based on an exchange rate where $1 is equal to 46 rupees.

34. Interview with Yuri Jain, HLL, March 26, 2003.

35. HLL, Annual Report, 2002.

36. HLL. Undated. "A Profile."

37. HLL, Annual Report, 2001.

38. HLL, Annual Report, 2001. All figures have been converted from rupees to U.S. dollars based on an exchange rate where $1 is equal to 46 rupees.

39. Euromonitor 2000 as cited in The London School of Hygiene and Tropical Medicine. (undated). "The Global Market for Soaps, A Market Research Report for the Public-Private Partnership on Handwashing with Soap," *http://www.wsp.org/english/activities/handwashing/globalmarketsoap.pdf.*

40. Ibid.

41. Ibid.

42. Ibid.

43. HLL. (undated). "A Profile."

44. Interview with C.R. Viney, Lowe Advertising, March 24, 2003.

45. HLL, Michigan Mkt. Contruct Retail Sales Data, Email from Govind Rajan, April 29, 2003.

46. Interview with Harpreet Singh Tibb, HLL, March 26, 2003.

47. Interview with Yuri Jain, HLL, March 26, 2003.

48. "Public-Private Partnerships: Mobilizing Resources to Achieve Public Health Goals. The Central American Handwashing Initiative Points the Way," *http://globalhandwashing.org/Publications/BASICS.htm#private,* April 28, 2003.

49. Ibid.

50. Ibid.

51. Interview with Yuri Jain, HLL, March 26, 2003.

52. Ibid.

53. Ibid.

54. "PPP for Handwashing Initiative—Kerala." *http://www.worldbank.org/watsan/forum2001/2001_kerala_ppt.pdf,* June 4, 2003.

55. Curtis, Valerie. Op. cit.

56. Ibid.

57. Ibid.

58. Ibid.

59. "Clean Hands, Clean State. Kerala 'Handwash with Soap' Program." *http://www.wsp.org/english/activities/handwashing/kerala.pdf,* January 2002.

60. This figure is calculated by dividing total project costs of $10.48 million by three years to get an annual cost per year of $3.49 million. This figure is then divided by three to ascertain private-sector costs. The resulting $1.16 million is multiplied by two-thirds to get an estimated annual cost per year for HLL of

$776,000. The original $10.48 million figure is from the Handwash India presentation, *http://www.wsp.org/english/activities/handwashing/vbehal.pdf*, April 28, 2003.

61. "Clean Hands, Clean State. Kerala 'Handwash with Soap' Program." *http://www.wsp.org/english/activities/handwashing/kerala.pdf*, January 2002.

62. Shiva, Vandana. "Saving Lives or Destroying Lives? World Bank Sells Synthetic Soap & Cleanliness to Kerala: The Land of Health and Hygiene." *AgBioIndia*, September 23, 2002.

63. Sharma, Devinder. "So(a)ps for Unilever." *Indeconomist, http://www.indeconomist. com/301002_health.html*, October 30, 2002.

64. Kurian, Vinson. "'Hand Wash' Campaign in Kerala Raises a Stink." *Business Line.*, *http://www.blonnet.com/2002/11/06/stories/2002110601771700.htm*, November 6, 2002.

65. London School of Tropical Medicine and Hygiene. "Health in Your Hands: PPP-HW. LSHTM Progress Report. August 26, 2002–June 30, 2003." *http://www.globalhandwashing.org/Global%20activities/Attachments/lshtmreportyear2.pd f 10*, December 2003.

66. Interview with Aasif Maalbari, March 26, 2003.

67. HLL. "Brand Fact Book: Lifebuoy." Undated presentation.

68. Interview with Harpreet Singh Tibb, HLL, March 26, 2003.

69. Interview with HLL Chairman Manvinder Singh Banga, HLL, March 29, 2003.

70. Interview with Yuri Jain, HLL, March 26, 2003.

71. Interview with Gurpreet Kohli, HLL, March 27, 2003.

72. Fox, Maggie. "Common Disinfectant Could Breed Superbugs." *http://www.nutriteam.com/triclo.htm*, August 19, 1998.

73. Interview with HLL Chairman Manvinder Singh Banga, HLL, March 29, 2003.

74. Interview with Ajai Mittal, HLL, March 29, 2003.

75. Interview with Gurpreet Kohli, HLL, March 27, 2003.

76. Probe Quality Research. Undated. "Project Glove: A Triggers and Barriers Study on Handwash Habits." Prepared for HLL.

77. Interview with Harpreet Singh Tibb, HLL, March 26, 2003.

78. Ibid.

79. Ibid.

80. Ibid.

81. HLL February 2003. "Rural Prioritization Strategy-2-03." Presentation.

82. Interview with Harpreet Singh Tibb, HLL, March 26, 2003.

83. HLL, Lifebuoy Swasthya Chetna: Press Conference, May 2002.

84. Interview with Harpreet Singh Tibb, HLL, March 26, 2003.

85. Gwatkin, Davidson R., et al. Op. cit.

86. Interview with Harpreet Singh Tibb, HLL, March 26, 2003.

87. Interview with Govind Rajan, HLL, March 27, 2003.

88. Population Reference Bureau. "PRB 2002 World Population Data Sheet-2002." *http://www.prb.org/pdf/WorldPopulationDS02_Eng.pdf*, April 28, 2003.

89. Gwatkin, Davidson R., et al. Op. cit.

90. "How to Save 1m Children a Year." *The Economist.* July 6, 2002.

91. Balu, Rekha. "Strategic Innovation: Hindustan Lever Ltd." Fast Company, June 2001, p. 120. *http://www.fastcompany.com/magazine/47/hindustan.html*.

92. Harvey, P. 1999. *Let Every Child Be Wanted: How Social Marketing Is Revolutionizing Contraceptive Use Around the World.* Westport, CT: Greenwood.

93. Interview with Harpreet Singh Tibb, HLL, March 26, 2003.

This report was written by Mindy Murch and Kate Reeder, under the supervision of Professor C. K. Prahalad. The report is intended to be a catalyst for discussion and is not intended to illustrate effective or ineffective strategies.

SECTION III

Known Problems and Unique Solutions

The problems at the BOP are not new. However, they represent a new challenge. They demand innovations in how these traditional problems are addressed. For example, the solutions must be affordable. That means dramatic cost reductions from the solutions available to the top of the pyramid consumers in developed countries. Second, BOP consumers have unique demands based on the circumstances of their lives—poor infrastructure, lack of trained manpower, and lack of access to raw materials. Further, the poor educational attainment of BOP customers can also limit the solutions that are suitable for them, as we illustrate next.

The loss of a limb is not a new problem. This has often been a result of wars, accidents, and disease. Fitting a prosthesis—below or above the knee—has been a standard part of medical care. Significant progress has been made in the West on prosthetics, but a typical lower knee prosthesis can cost up to $8,000 in the United States. This is prohibitive for a BOP customer. Further, poor farmers and workers in India have unique functional requirements. Most of them need to squat on the floor and sit cross-legged. They have to walk on uneven ground and often walk barefoot. These are not among the requirements of a patient in the West. The BOP consumers in India also have to be concerned about how long it takes to get a customized prosthesis. They cannot afford multiple days for multiple fittings; it must be done in one day. Further, skill levels being what they are in India, the entire process of providing customized prosthesis must be "deskilled." As a result, the BOP consumer in India needs, compared to a consumer in the United States, a prosthesis with higher levels of functionality, at a fraction of the cost and fitted in a very short time. It is this task that Jaipur Foot addresses.

Jaipur Foot is the world's largest prosthesis provider, with more than 16,000 prosthetic fittings per year. The charity BMVSS (Bhagwan Makaueer Viklang Sahayata Samiti) serves more than 60,000 by providing calipers, appliances, and other aids. The functionality of the Jaipur foot, measured against what is available in the United States along more than 20 dimensions, is equal or better. However, the Jaipur Foot costs less than $30 compared to $8,000 for a comparable prosthesis in the United States. In fact, the Jaipur Foot is given free to all. Jaipur Foot is now in 16 countries where BOP patients exist, such as

Afghanistan, Angola, Somalia, Iraq, Mozambique, Cambodia, Vietnam, and Croatia.

Similarly, the Aravind Eye Care System operates out of its home base in Madurai, India, with several satellite branches across Tamil Nadu. Aravind performs more than 200,000 cataract operations per year. By fundamentally altering the process by which patients needing eye care are identified (using more than 1,500 eye camps) to the process by which the surgery is performed to counseling, Aravind has revolutionized eye care. The productivity of doctor–nurse teams is six times higher than it is in the rest of India and considerably higher than anything in the United States. The quality levels are above the gold standard. The cost per operation is less than $50-100 compared to $2,600 to $3,000 in the United States. Aravind also manufactures its own interocular lens (IOL) and sells it for $5 compared to a cost of $200 in the United States. The Aravind complex has now grown to include research, manufacturing of supplies, training, and telemedicine.

Jaipur Foot and the Aravind Eye Care System represent two examples of innovative solutions that result in serving the BOP. Both these groups are driven by a strong vision of their leaders, who are dedicated to bring world-class solutions to the BOP. Both are highly focused on one problem—prosthetics and eye care, respectively. They are not general hospitals. This forces innovations in care delivery processes. Both of them focus on scale. They are extremely cost-conscious and focus on making the treatment accessible to all and delivering it free. Aravind provides free care to 60 percent of its patients. The rest of them pay a nominal amount given the quality of care.

Escort Hospital is specializing in cardiac care. Last year it performed more than 6,000 cardiac surgeries of various kinds in one location. Its costs are about US $3,000 compared to $XXXX in the United States and $XXXX in the United Kingdom. As a result, the National Health Service in the United Kingdom is discussing the possibility of sending patients from the United Kingdom for cardiac surgeries in India to save costs and reduce the wait time in their own country.[1]

As a result, we find a dramatic difference in costs of care:

Advantage over U.S. Costs

- Jaipur Foot (Prosthetics)   200x
- Aravind (Eye care)   100x
- Escorts (Cardiac care)   10x

The lessons from these cases are simple. Focusing on the BOP consumers and enabling them to get access to world-class quality forces innovations that can dramatically alter the cost structure and build a global opportunity.

---

[1] Data from an Escorts case.

Jaipur Foot: Challenging Convention

At age 14, Ms. Sudha Chandran, an aspiring dancer, lost her lower right leg in a car accident. Convinced she would never walk, let alone dance again, she spent several months on crutches and prepared for a life as an amputee. Then one day in 1984, she read about Jaipur Foot. Fitted with a replacement leg for free from Jaipur Foot, Ms. Chandran was able to resume her training as a classical dancer and later become a film star.

There are 5.5 million amputees in India. An additional 25,000 people lose their limbs annually to diseases, accidents, or other hazards.[1] The majority of these people live well below the poverty line and cannot afford health care or medical services. In a world where prosthetics is a complicated and expensive industry, there is an operation of impressive scope that offers hope to the some of the most impoverished citizens of India and maybe even the world. It offers these handicapped citizens a chance to return to their livelihoods and pursue their dreams. This operation is called Jaipur Foot.

THE INNOVATION

A prosthetic foot in the United States costs $8,000 on average. The Jaipur Foot is tailored to the active lifestyles of the poor and costs only about $30. It is provided and serviced for free to impoverished handicapped citizens in India.

Developed in 1968, the Jaipur Foot is a predominantly hand-made artificial foot and lower limb prosthesis. It has revolutionized life for tens of thousands of amputees around the world. This foot was originally designed to meet the needs of a developing country lifestyle such as squatting, walking (barefoot), and sitting (cross-legged). Primarily fabricated and fitted by Bhagwan Mahaveer Viklang Sahayata Samiti (BMVSS), a nongovernmental, nonreligious, and nonprofit organization, the Jaipur Foot is fitted on approximately 16,000 patients annually. BMVSS services approximately 60,000 patients each year by providing the Jaipur Foot, calipers, and other aids and appliances. There are seven centers throughout India and a number of mobile camps held every year in various parts of the country. With the help of BMVSS, Jaipur Foot camps also have been held in 19 countries, including Afghanistan, Bangladesh, the Dominican Republic, Honduras, Indonesia, Malawi, Nigeria, Nepal, Nairobi, Panama, Philippines, Papua New Guinea, Rwanda, Somalia, Trinidad, Vietnam, Zimbabwe, and Sudan. With innovations in technology and management, as well as an understanding of the needs of its patients, BMVSS developed a unique business model.

The Nature and Scope of the Problem

Global Amputees

There are anywhere from 10 million to 25 million amputees in the world, with an additional 250,000 added each year. Causes of amputation vary greatly, but in countries with a recent history of warfare and civil unrest, amputation is largely due to trauma and landmine accidents.[2] In the more developed countries of the world like the United States, the causes are more often related to accidents, circulatory diseases, and cancer. Regardless, prosthetics in both developing and developed nations is expensive and complicated, leaving a sizable number of amputees unable to afford adequate prosthetic care.[3]

Developed World

According to a 1996 National Center for Health Statistics study, there are more than 4 million amputees in the United States and approximately 200,000 new amputees every year, of which approximately 70 percent are lower limb amputees[4]. According to the World Health Report in 1998, amputation resulting from diabetes will more than double globally from 143 million cases in 1997 to 300 million by 2025.[5] The most common causes of amputation of lower extremities are disease (70 percent), trauma (22 percent), congenital or birth defects (4 percent), and tumors (4 percent). Upper extremity amputation usually is due to trauma or birth defect. The cost of a prosthesis is very high in the United States, leaving many without appropriate care. According to Mark Taylor, from the University of Michigan Prosthetics Department, due to insurance company policies and high costs, only 50 percent of U.S. patients receive the prosthetic medical care they require.

Developing World

In the developing countries of Asia and Africa, landmines have left millions of people limbless. According to the U.S. Centers for Disease Control, approximately 300,000 children are severely disabled because of landmines, with an additional 15,000 to 20,000 new victims each year.[6] Most victims are not soldiers, but women and children who happen to live in areas that were once war zones (see Table 1). By some estimates, there are more than 100 million landmines buried all over the world. In many poor nations, most amputees have to settle for a lifetime on crutches. In Vietnam alone, landmines injure more than 2,000 people each year.[7] It costs approximately $300 to provide a high-quality artificial leg in Vietnam.[8]

Table 1 Countries with the Most Landmines

Country	No. of Landmines
Afghanistan	9,500,000
Angola	9,000,000
Iraq	7,500,000
Kuwait	5,000,000
Cambodia	5,500,000
Western Sahara	1,500,000
Mozambique	1,500,000
Somalia	1,000,000
Bosnia-Herzegovina	1,000,000
Croatia	1,000,000

Source: United Nations data.

In Afghanistan, there are approximately 10 million landmines and at least 50,000 amputees.[9] In Cambodia, there are 25,000 to 40,000 amputees, or one amputee per 300 inhabitants. There are nearly as many landmines in Cambodia as people. Government hospitals are so severely under-resourced that patients, including the very poor, are forced to pay for services or drugs, leaving many without care.[10] In Kosovo, the World Health Organization (WHO) estimated the 1999 landmine injury rate at 10 in 100,000, exceeding the rates of both Afghanistan and Mozambique. In India, there are 5.5 million people suffering from locomotor disabilities. Of these, about 1 million have lost their limbs and 4 million suffer from polio. Due to the increase in road accidents, diseases, and other hazards, 25,000 new cases are added to the population of amputees every year.

Treatment Costs

Developed World

Table 2 shows the costs for prosthetics in the United States in the developed world.

Table 2 Prosthetic Costs in the United States

Below the Knee Limb			
Legs	$4,009–¢5,000 (Low End)	$7,000–$9,000 (Mid End)	$10,000–$25,000 (High End)	
Prosthetic Socket	$3,450 (Replacement Socket)	$650 (Replacement Cover)		
Prosthetic Foot	$250–$12,000			
Prosthetic Sock	$19 (Sheath)	$80 (Sheath w/Gel)	$25 (Wool Socks)	$9 (Single Ply) $50 (Shrinked)

Above the Knee Legs			
Legs	$8,765 (Low End)	$12,265 (High End without Knees and Feet)		
Prosthetic Socket	$4,300 (Replacement Socket)	$900 (Replacement Cover)		
Prosthetic Foot	$700–$5,400			
Prosthetic Sock	$25 (Sheath)	$80 (Sheath w/Gel)	$25 (Wool Socks)	$10 (Single Ply) $80 (Shrinked)

Source: The Open Roads Team. Reprinted with appreciation to the Open Roads Team.

Developing World

OpenRoads, a U.S.-based nongovernmental organization (NGO), will be shipping 100 prosthetics every year to each site. Table 3 shows their estimated costs of providing limbs, based on the assumption that buying in bulk will reduce overall costs. With prosthetic care as expensive as it is today, it leaves many patients, in both the developing and developed world, without the care they need. A fast, dependable solution at a cost people can afford (in the developing world, this cost is nothing) is not only necessary but also imminent. Innovative business models, such as the Jaipur Foot, already have started to accomplish this successfully.

History of Prosthetics

The history of prosthetics begins at the very dawning of human medical thought. Its historical twists and turns parallel the development of medical science, culture, and civilization itself. The prostheses of ancient cultures began as simple crutches or wooden and leather cups depicted in Moche pottery. An open socket peg leg had cloth rags to soften the distal tibia and fibula and allow a wide range of motion. These prostheses were very functional and incorporated many basic prosthetic principles.

Table 3 OpenRoad Cost Estimates for Providing Prosthetic Care Globally

Year	Location	Number of People Served	Cost per Site
1	Kosovo	50	$15,000
	Rwanda	50	15,000
2	Kosovo	100	30,000
	Rwanda	50	15,000
3	Kosovo	100	20,000
	Rwanda	100	20,000
	Afghanistan	50	10,000
4	Kosovo	100	15,000
	Rwanda	100	15,000
	Afghanistan	100	15,000
	Mozanbique	50	7,500
5	Kosovo	100	15,000
	Rwanda	100	15,000
	Mozanbique	100	15,000
	Afghanistan	100	15,000
Total		1250	$237,500

Source: The Open Roads Team. Reprinted with appreciation to the Open Roads Team.

An artificial leg invented by Pare in 1561 for individuals amputated above the knee was constructed of iron and was the first artificial leg known to employ articulated joints. Major advances have been made in the field of prosthetic rehabilitation, stimulated in part by wars that increased the number of individuals who lost limbs. During the American Civil War (1861–1865), interest in artificial limbs and amputation surgery increased in the United States, with the government paying for artificial limbs for veterans. In 1862, the U.S. government enacted the first law providing free prostheses to people who lost limbs in warfare. In 1870, Congress passed a law that entitled war amputees to receive prostheses every five years.

World War II spurred further developments. Dissatisfaction with heavy, uncomfortable artificial limbs gave impetus to prosthetic research. The American Orthotic and Prosthetic Association was established in 1949 and developed educational criteria and examinations to certify prosthetists and orthotists. In 1945, the National Academy of Sciences set up a Committee on Artificial Limbs (CAL) to develop design criteria that would improve their functions. CAL influenced development of modern prosthetics from 1947 to 1976. During this period, plastic replaced wood as the material of choice, socket designs followed physiological principles of function, lighter-weight components were developed, and more cosmetic alternatives were fabricated.

In 1956, the biomechanics laboratory at the University of California (Berkeley) introduced the solid ankle cushion heel (SACH) foot, which became the most popular prosthetic foot. In the 1960s, hydraulic knee mechanisms became more prevalent, and 1970 marked the inaugural year for the International Society for Prosthetics and Orthotics. In 1971, Otto Bock introduced endoskeletal prostheses.

Modern times are characterized by the emergence of prosthetics as a science as well as an art. Research into human movement, new materials, and new technology have led to the creation of very light and functional components. Gel liners provide a shock-absorbing interface between residual limb and hard socket. Research is attempting to find a method to bring sensation into the prosthetic limb.[11]

Lower Limb Anatomy

To fully understand the innovation behind the Jaipur Foot, it is important to know something about the lower limb anatomy. The limbs must bear weight, provide a means for locomotion, and maintain equilibrium. Bipedalism is the process by which we are able to stand upright and to move about on two limbs. It imparts three unique functions on the lower limbs.

The ankle joint is a hinge-type joint that participates in movement and is involved in lower limb stability. Dorsiflexion and plantar flexion movements take place at the ankle. Dorsiflexion is necessary to have the foot contact the ground heel first and to allow the foot to clear the ground during the swing phase of gait. Plantar flexion provides the propulsive force necessary to lift the limb off the ground and start it swinging forward during the toe-off portion of the gait. The foot plays an important role in supporting the weight of the entire body and in locomotion. The bones of the foot are arched longitudinally to help facilitate the support function. The transverse arch helps with movements of the foot. These movements help keep the sole in contact with the ground despite the unevenness of the ground surface. They also work in concert with the ankle joint to help propel the foot off the ground during the toe-off portion of gait.

Gait Cycle

The rhythmic alternating movements of the two lower extremities comprise the gait cycle, which results in forward movement of the body. Simply stated, it is the manner in which we walk. Gait cycle is the activity that occurs between the heel strike of one limb and the subsequent heel strike of that same limb.

Stance begins when the heel of the forward limb makes contact with the ground and ends when the toe of the same limb leaves the ground. It consists of the following actions:

- *Heel strike.* Heel of foot touches the ground.
- *Midstance.* Foot is flat on the ground and the weight of the body is directly over the limb.
- *Toe off.* Only the big toe of the limb is in contact with the ground.
- *Swing.* It begins when the foot is no longer in contact with the ground. The limb is free to move.
- *Acceleration.* Swinging limb catches up to and passes the torso.
- *Deceleration.* Forward movement of the limb is slowed down to position the foot for heel strike.
- *Double support.* Both limbs are in contact with the ground simultaneously.

Lower Limb Prosthesis:
An Attempt to Simulate Natural Limb's Functions

People with limb loss (acquired amputation) or limb absence (congenital deficiency) use prosthetic limbs to restore or imbue some of the function and cosmetics of an anatomical limb. Solutions differ in the way they mimic the natural foot's functionality, or a part thereof.

Development of the Jaipur Foot

Ram Chandra, born into a family of master artisans, is commonly recognized as one of Jaipur City's finest sculptors. Growing up, Chandra saw that local people who were amputated were fitted with artificial limbs, either imported from abroad or locally made, that were not flexible enough and did not allow for a normal range of motion. The prosthesis did not facilitate postures common in India such as squatting or sitting cross-legged. Further, the shoes attached to the limb were made of heavy sponge, which made the prosthesis useless for farmers working in the rain or irrigated fields. This led to a high rejection rate of the prosthesis by the local amputee population.

While watching these patients, Chandra came up with an idea of creating an artificial limb that more closely resembled a natural foot, was lighter, and was tailored for local conditions. He took his ideas to doctors at the city hospital and learned about human foot anatomy. Equipped with this knowledge, Chandra experimented with locally available materials such as willow, sponges, and aluminum molds to create an artificial limb.[12]

One of many defining moments came one day when Chandra suffered a flat tire while riding his bicycle. According to Chandra, he went to a roadside stall whose owner was retreading a tire with vulcanized rubber. Once his bicycle was fixed, Chandra rushed to doctors to determine if this material could be used for a limb. Later he returned to the tire shop accompanied by an amputee and a foot cast, and asked the owner to make a rubber foot. The foot had the mobility and durability that Chandra sought, although it had to undergo numerous refinements. Working further with Dr. P. K. Sethi, an orthopedic surgeon, Dr. S. C. Kasliwal, and Dr. Mahesh Udawat, Chandra refined and improved the design to eventually create what is now known as the Jaipur Foot. To facilitate the spread of the foot, its creators decided not to patent the Jaipur Foot.

Step 1: Design Considerations

The Jaipur Foot was designed to simulate normal foot movements and provide a quality solution for the masses. For those poor in India who had lost their limbs, continuing to earn a livelihood was the biggest concern. In the absence of an efficient social security system, being able to work was essential for their survival. It necessitated a prosthesis that supported their work and lifestyles. Jaipur Foot's design process emphasized the activities listed in Table 4, which are commonly practiced by India's working poor.

Step 2: Overcoming Constraints

However, the technical demands were not the only demands by the creators of the Jaipur Foot. In addition, they faced the constraints listed in Table 5.

Table 4 Considerations in the Jaipur Foot Design Process

Activity	Mechanical Requirement
Squatting	Need for dorsiflexion
Sitting cross-legged	Need for transverse rotation of the foot
Walking on uneven ground	Need for inversion and eversion in the foot so that varying terrain is not transmitted to stump
Barefoot walking	Cosmetically similar to natural foot

Table 5 Constraints of Development for the Jaipur Foot

Constraints	Implication
Poverty	The vast majority of local amputees were poor. Lower cost of prosthesis with the possibility for alignment and adjustments would facilitate a specialized yet equally functional solution.
Closed economy	Limited import of foreign materials in India meant the foot had to be fabricated from readily available local materials.
Work lifestyle	Most amputees worked hard for long hours. The ability to walk on uneven ground was essential for their work. India was largely an agricultural economy, and days spent without limbs threatened their livelihood and in many cases sustenance. This led to a need for accessible prostheses that could be fitted quickly.
Limited trained manpower	Lack of skilled labor relative to the huge demand for prostheses necessitated a simplified manufacturing process, which could be performed with limited training.

Step 3: Deviation from Traditional Design

The design of the Jaipur Foot was initially based on the SACH foot design.[13] However, the design divorced from the SACH foot due to problems such as weight and nonsuitability to local conditions. The endoskeletal design was pursued, and a new knee-joint design evolved. Distortions were introduced in the sockets so that adequate pressure was put only on those tissues, which could resist them. Total contact sockets also were introduced.

The Jaipur Foot is made of three blocks simulating the anatomy of a normal foot. The forefoot and heel blocks are made of sponge rubber and the ankle block consists of light wood. The three components are bound together, enclosed in a rubber shell, and vulcanized in a mold to give it the shape and cosmetic appearance of a natural foot.

Below-knee as well as above-knee prosthetic products are indigenously designed and fabricated from locally available and durable high-density polyethylene pipes and a Jaipur Foot. These are rapid-fit limbs with low fabrication times. Fitting and fabrication times vary from one hour for below-knee prostheses to about five to six hours for above-knee prostheses. Functionality of the prosthesis mirrors that of a natural human limb, and it permits amputees to run, squat, sit cross-legged, climb trees, and jump from heights. The Jaipur Foot is waterproof and does not require maintenance after it is fitted. Barefoot walking is possible, an amputee can work in wet and muddy fields, and the foot is suitable for any type of terrain. The patient also can wear shoes. Biomechanically, it is based on the standard *patella-tendon-bearing* prosthesis and scientifically fabricated to meet its weight distribution requirements for maximum comfort. Average weight of the prosthesis is 3.11 kg; the weight of a 55-kg person's lower limb is 3.36 kg.

Step 4: Materials Sourcing

BMUSS, generally known as "the Society," produces the prosthesis with readily available and inexpensive components to limit the cost of procurement as well as the cost of the prosthesis itself. A typical Jaipur Foot, shank, and simulated knee joint are constructed with the materials listed in Table 6.

Table 6   Cost Analysis of Above-Knee Limbs with Plastic Knee Joint

S. No.	Name of Material	Quantity	Rate	Amount
1.	Jaipur Foot	1	120.25 each	120.25
2.	HDPE pipe 90 MM	0.60 RMT	146.16/Mtr.	87.70
3.	HDPE pipe 110 MM	0.60 RMT	219.25/Mtr.	131.55
4.	Plastic knee joint	1 set	100/set	100.00
5.	Plaster of Paris	4 kg	4/kg	16.00
6.	Stockinatte 2"	150 gm	115/kg	17.25
7.	Stockinatte 4"	200 gm	115/kg	23.00
8.	A.K. belt	1	39 each	39.00
9.	Elastic belt	1	10 each	10.00
10.	Cotton bandages	3	4 each	12.00
11.	Dunlop solution	20 gm	90.8/kg	1.81
12.	Steel screw	4	0.13 each	0.52
13.	Press buttons	4	0.06 each	0.24
14.	Soapstone powder	50 gm	2/kg	0.10
15.	Loctite	1/4 tube	0	5.00
	Total material cost			564.42

Note. 1 $US = Rs. 45.

The estimated US$12.54 cost of materials outlined in Table 6 includes the cost of the components of the Jaipur Foot itself as well as the simulated joints for an above-knee limb. Each material is locally sourced and does not require special procurement agreements. Most are virtual commodities. Furthermore, most of the materials can be sourced locally if necessary when the Jaipur Foot is manufactured in other developing nations.

Step 5: Production Equipment

The Jaipur Foot, as well as the calipers and other portions of the prosthesis ultimately fitted on the patient, is constructed with very basic tools. Most of the fabrication process is completed with the tools of an ordinary artisan. The most specialized piece of equipment consists of the foot-shaped die used to mold the shape of the foot. However, its cost is not significant enough to even warrant listing on a fixed asset schedule. The most expensive piece of equipment is the vacuum-forming machine used to get an exact replica of the mold. This is used when heated HDPE sheet or pipe is draped over the mold of the patient's remaining limb (stump). The machine costs approximately 200,000 Rupees, or roughly US$4,000. For heating pipe and sheets, a machine is used that resembles an ordinary oven. The machine is commonly found throughout India and the rest of the developing world. The Jaipur location of the Society requires two vacuum-forming machines to serve an estimated 60 patients per day. Each machine lasts from five to seven years.

Step 6: Labor

Fabrication of the Jaipur Foot, as well as the process by which a patient is fitted, is a very labor-intensive process. This process capitalizes on the large supply of skilled artisans in India and their manageable labor rates. A Jaipur Foot artisan is a craftsman with several years of experience who is further trained for several more years to mold, sculpt, and form the Jaipur Foot. The Society typically schedules 70 trained technicians and artisans each day to achieve a one-to-one patient-to-employee ratio. Artisans and technicians, who are more experienced artisans, operate in a supervisory capacity and are paid by the hour plus overtime. A typical artisan earns 5,000 Rupees per month, or roughly US$100 including benefits. The estimated US$1,200 annual income of an artisan is approximately twice that of the per-capita income in India.

An on-site doctor supervises the entire fabrication and fitting process. The Society has one doctor on the payroll full-time. In addition, other local doctors either volunteer their time or work on a part-time basis to ensure that a certified physician approves a patient's final prosthesis and fitting.

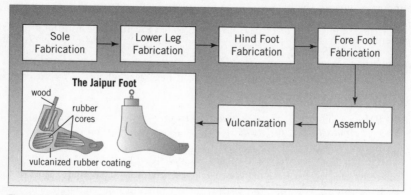

Figure 1   Jaipur Foot fabrication process. *Source:* Copyright ©2004 Hesperian Foundation. www.hesperian.org.

Step 7: Fabrication

Fabrication of the Jaipur Foot is a fast and simple process (see Figure 1). The foot incorporates locally available materials and equipment. These include a die, tread rubber compound, sponge rubber, cosmetic rubber, nylon cords, a vulcanizer, wood, and scissors. The foot and ankle assembly is made of a vulcanized rubber compound. An aluminum die is used to cast a normal foot shape. The die consists of four sections, which can be bolted together. This allows for ease of setting up different material components. The process thus involves several stages with serial sequences of plaster mold-die in four sections. The position of the undersurface of the foot and toes is slightly rocketed with the toes slightly off the ground to achieve the rolling action. The heel is kept slightly off the ground to accommodate the heel when worn in the shoe. This complements the "rocker" action of the foot. Figure 1 illustrates the Jaipur Foot fabrication process.

Step 8: Fitting of the Jaipur Foot

Nearly 60 patients each day obtain prostheses from Jaipur Foot's main facility in Jaipur, India. Remarkably, unless other medical conditions intervene, each patient is custom-fitted with a prosthesis in one day—usually within three hours. The goal is to return the patient to his or her profession and an independent life after the patient's first visit to the clinic.

However, the Society's desire to accommodate the social requirements of India's poor does not consist solely of the speed of service. The Society's operating process also attends to the psychological needs of its patients. The Society provides on-site meals and overnight accommodations to patients at no cost. These services are shared with other patients to provide an immediate support group for the patients and to develop a sense of community within the facility. Additionally, free meals and accommodations are provided to the patient's family members. This permits family members to affordably travel with patients and provide on-site support and comfort. A typical patient experience to receive a Jaipur Foot might proceed as follows:

Monday

1:00 PM	The patient catches a train from New Delhi to Jaipur, India. The patient's husband and child accompany her on the journey.
6:00 PM	The family arrives at the front gate of the Society in the heart of Jaipur. A guard at the gate of the one-story facility admits the family inside.
6:30 PM	The family joins other patients and family members at a communal dinner prepared by the Society's food service employee.
9:00 PM	The family sleeps on mattresses in a large room within the facility's modest housing wing.

Tuesday

8:00 AM	The family shares breakfast with other patients and families at the facility.
8:30 AM	The patient joins the line forming in the Society's inner courtyard and awaits registration.
9:00 AM	A doctor checks the patient and outlines the prosthesis that is required. The patient will keep the card until it is given to a technician.
9:10 AM	The patient is prepared for a cast.
9:30 AM	A trained artisan wraps a cast around the limb, forms it tightly around the limb, and removes it.
9:45 AM	The patient is ushered back to the inner courtyard where she waits. The artisan pours a mold into the cast, lets it dry, and then carves it into the limb's specifications under the supervision of a technician.
10:15 AM	A common HDPE sheet is heated in a oven, is removed, and is stretched over the mold of the patient's remaining limb with the help of a vacuum-forming machine.
11:00 AM	A prefabricated Jaipur Foot is attached to the prosthesis.
NOON	The on-site doctor supervises as the patient tests the new prosthesis in the courtyard. The patient describes some modest discomfort as she walks around a separate inner courtyard.
12:15 PM	Adjustments are made to the prosthesis to make it more comfortable.

12:30 PM   The patient and her family share lunch at the facility.
2:00 PM   The family catches a train back to New Delhi.
7:30 PM   The family returns home to resume a life similar to their lives
             before the loss of patient's limb.

Competitive Benchmarking

The Jaipur Foot supports developing country lifestyles (e.g., squatting, sitting cross-legged, walking on uneven surfaces, and barefoot walking), whereas a conventional SACH foot does not. Table 7 details a comparison of the Jaipur Foot with VariFlex (Ossur) and TrueStep (College Park Industries), two leading prostheses in the developed world. Table 7 compares the prostheses for range of motion and general attributes, such as cost, activities supported, and quality standards to which they adhere.

The Jaipur Foot provides for an excellent range of dorsiflexion movement. As Table 7 demonstrates, although not explicitly superior to the Western prostheses shown, the Jaipur Foot possesses technical characteristics that make it a comparable product. The clear differentiating features are the respective prices and the years of introduction of the products. The Jaipur Foot presents an interesting comparison to the Western prostheses on a price performance basis despite being introduced nearly two decades before its Western counterparts. Furthermore, the Jaipur Foot compares favorably on the activities for which it was designed, especially walking barefoot, working in wet fields, walking on uneven ground, and climbing trees.

Community Outreach: Providing Access
BMVSS

The designers of the Jaipur Foot quickly discovered that designing a prosthesis that could withstand the rigorous use of India's poor was only the beginning. The next challenge was to construct an organization and operating system which could make the Jaipur Foot available to as many amputees as possible. The expectation was that nearly all prospective amputees would fall below the poverty line. Subsequently, Jaipur Foot's custodians focused their attention on the financial and social needs of India's working poor. Their efforts eventually took the form of the nonprofit society BMVSS, generally referred to as "the Society."

BMVSS was established in March 1975 by Mr. D. R. Mehta. In the first seven years after the development of the Jaipur Foot in 1968, hardly 50 limbs were fitted. In the first year after the formation of the society, 59 limbs were fitted. Now, the number of limbs fitted every year approaches 16,000. During the time from March 1975 (when BMVSS was established) to March 2003, BMVSS

Table 7 Comparison of Prostheses

Feature/ Function	Variflex (Since 1990)	College Park Foot (Since 1991)	Jaipur Foot (Since 1968)
Range of Motion			
Dorsiflexion	Limited dynamics	250	400
Plantar Flexion	Limited dynamics	250	00
Inversion	120 (split toe version)	120	100
Eversion	120 (split toe version)	120	100
Supination	Not applicable	200	70
Pronation	Not applicable	200	50
Attributes			
Cost (foot piece) Indian Rs.)	$1,400	$1,059	$5 (240
Average cost (including prosthesis & fitting)[a]	$3,700	$2,700	$30 (1500 Indian Rs.)
Fitting/fabrication time	1–2 hours	1–2 hours	2 hours
Foot piece weight	240g	510 g	850 g
Size/weight rating	Up to 166 kg	Up to 160 kg	Not rated
Adjust for heel height change	Low/high heel options	No	No
Warranty	30 months	36 months	None
Maintenance requirements None		None	Limited
Average life	2–3 years	3 years	2.5–3.0 years
Activities supported			
Work in wet fields	Yes	Not recommended	Yes
Walk barefoot	Special sole required	Yes	Yes
Sit on floor	Yes	Yes	Yes
Squat	Yes	Yes	Yes
Drive a car	Yes	Yes	Yes
Ride a bike	Yes	Yes	Yes
Walk on uneven ground	Yes (split toe version)	Yes	Yes
Climb trees	Yes (with limitations)	Yes (with limitations)	Yes
Hike	Yes	Yes	Yes
Swim	Yes	Not recommended	Yes
Run	Yes	Yes	Yes
Quality standards			
CE marked	Yes	Yes	No
Additional	ISO 10328 standard		Internal quality standards

[a]This is the average cost for a complete solution, which might involve multiple clinic visits. Actual costs will vary depending on options chosen.

successfully fitted 236,717 limbs in India and 14,070 around the world (see Tables 8 and 9). If not for the value system and patient-centric management practices followed by BMVSS, Jaipur Foot might have remained on the shelf and in limbo. BMVSS emphasizes a holistic approach to addressing the problems of amputees. The society focuses on not only the medical problems of the underprivileged, but also the financial and social problems.

The society has laid down extremely simple procedures for reception, admission, measurement taking, manufacturing, fitting, and discharge of patients. Unlike in medical centers all over the world, patients are admitted as they arrive without regard to the time of day. Further, patients are given boarding and lodging facilities at the centers of BMVSS until they are provided with limbs, calipers, or other aids. In most orthopedic centers, patients must come back several times for a custom fit. This process could take several weeks. Such a system would be unsuitable for the poor patients who find it extremely difficult, both in physical and financial terms, to come back a second time from long distances. The Jaipur Foot is custom-fitted on the same day—in fact, in less than four hours. Most significantly, the prosthesis, orthotics, and other aids and appliances are provided totally free of charge to the handicapped. If not for this policy, more than

Table 8   Number of Artificial Limbs and Other Aids Distributed by BMVSS in India

Artificial limbs	219,450
Calipers	152,165
Tricycles	36,941
Crutches and other aids	225,492
Hearing aids	6,666
Polio surgery	3,860

Source: Jaipur Foot (BMVSS).

Table 9   Number of Artificial Limbs and Other Aids Distributed by BMVSS Throughout the World

Afghanistan	1,355	Panama	400
Bangladesh	1,000	Philippines	3,000
Dominican Republic	500	Papua New Guinea	170
Honduras	400	Rwanda	500
Indonesia	600	Somalia	1,000
Malawi	250	Trinidad	200
Nigeria	500	Vietnam	600
Nepal	200	Zimbabwe	250
Nairobi	500	Sudan	1,800
		Total	13,225

Source: Jaipur Foot (BMVSS).

90 percent of the patients would have remained deprived of artificial limbs, calipers, and other aids and appliances. The setting up of a patient-oriented value and management system was an equally important innovation.

BMVSS has 10 branches in India. In addition, there are approximately 60 workshops that fabricate or fit the Jaipur Foot in India. The Society also has aided the establishment of several centers abroad. Funded by the Indian government and philanthropic groups, BMVSS and similar organizations offer medical care, room, board, and a prosthetic at no cost to the patient. It also has helped launch free clinics in more than a dozen countries.

Jaipur Foot: Filling a Social Need

The determination was made at the outset that the Jaipur Foot prosthesis would be provided free by means of a nonprofit framework. The prospect of no additional funds realized for additional prostheses fitted forced administrators to focus on containing costs. In particular, emphasis was placed on the cost of the materials used to construct the Jaipur Foot, the capital equipment required to fabricate the foot, and the method by which the foot was fitted to a patient to make the prosthesis widely available.

Jaipur Foot Operations

The result is an organization that spends nearly 74 percent of its expenses on the materials, labor, and services necessary to fit amputees with a prosthetic limb. Figure 2 estimates the cost components of providing each Jaipur Foot.

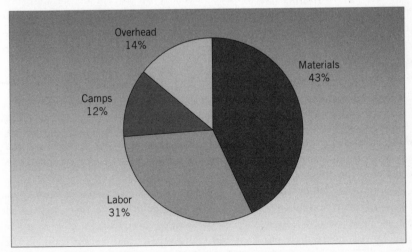

Figure 2   Cost of typical Jaipur Foot below-knee limb. *Source:* BMVSS Adjusted Cost Report.

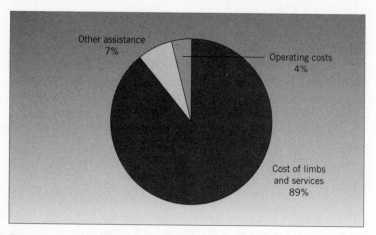

Figure 3   Jaipur Foot 2002 expenses by classification. Overhead costs of camps are included in costs of limbs and services. *Source:* BMVSS Adjusted Cost Report.

Only 14 percent of the cost of a typical Jaipur Foot goes toward meeting overhead and administrative costs. The remaining cost goes toward the materials used in the foot, the labor employed to manufacture and fit the limb, and the cost of running, camps which reach the poor throughout India and beyond. This cost efficiency is also reflected in the Jaipur Foot's annual expenses, shown in Figure 3.

Jaipur Foot's expense breakdown for the 2002 fiscal year underscores the efficiency of expense and underpins the Society's effort to serve as many patients as possible given its financial resources. Nearly 90 percent of the company's expenses in the 2002 fiscal year was directly related to the cost of producing and fitting prostheses for the poor. Another 7 percent of expenses went toward other forms of charitable assistance. Only 4 percent of its expenditures went toward administrative and overhead expenses.

Comparison with Ossur

The Society's (BMVSS) cost structure differs significantly from that of Ossur, an Iceland-based publicly traded company that manufactures, markets, and sells prostheses throughout Europe and North America. Ossur is the second-largest producer of prostheses in the world.

As Figure 4 demonstrates, just over half of Ossur's annual expenses goes toward administrative and operating costs and the other half goes toward the cost of producing prostheses. A more detailed examination of the annual financial statements of Jaipur Foot and Ossur reveals that a significant portion of Ossur's expenditures are related to sales and marketing (21 percent) and

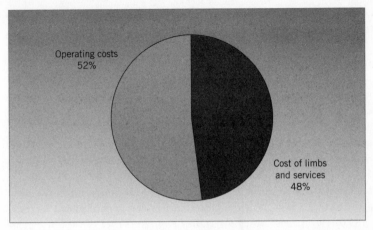

Figure 4   Ossur 2002 expenses by classification. *Source:* Ossur 2002 Annual Report.

research and development (9 percent). Although this disparity in part underscores the different competitive environments, regulatory environments, and organizational goals that separate the two organizations, it also provides a framework that underscores the Society's ability to funnel its resources directly to patients.

Scalability

Camps

The Society's current method of expanding the reach of the Jaipur Foot to more remote areas of India and beyond is the camp system. Administrators, doctors, technicians, and artisans from the Society's Jaipur location travel to a predetermined site and set up a temporary facility referred to as a camp. A camp is typically funded by another private organization or government that has invited the Society to the location. A camp can last from just a few days to several weeks depending on the number of amputees to be fitted with prostheses.

A BMVSS physician supervises the camps. It takes about one day to set up and a half-day to close. The sponsoring organization pays the Society's employees a travel allowance and a per diem while on site. In general, the camp requires one artisan for every two patients expected per day. Although most of the components of a typical Jaipur Foot and caliper can be locally sourced, the Society usually travels with the expected required materials. Likewise, employees travel with the equipment necessary to fabricate the prostheses, including a vacuum-forming machine, the largest and most expensive piece of equipment required for fabrication. Any material shortages are usually covered with locally purchased goods. The sponsoring organization takes responsibility for promoting the camp and for any transportation of amputees.

New Locations

The Society also facilitates the establishment of new permanent locations to fabricate and fit the Jaipur Foot. Although the Society itself supports several locations in India, including New Delhi and Mumbai (Bombay), the Society encourages other charitable organizations to run clinics. The Society is active in assisting the new organization in determining the feasibility of clinic location, training employees, and making the Jaipur Foot available to the clinic.

The Society, in conjunction with a new organization, studies the number of amputees near the new location and estimates the ongoing need for the Jaipur Foot prosthesis. A new location requires a modest level of capital expenditure. The most significant piece of equipment is the vacuum-forming machine at an estimated cost of US$4,000. Additional equipment and tools generally cost another US$2,000. Artisans are trained at the Jaipur facility for up to six months. Virtually all this training takes place with patients and under the supervision of technicians and doctors. The Society maintains and updates a manual, which outlines the fabrication and fitting of the Jaipur Foot to assist in this process.

After the new location is staffed, its employees are trained, and the new clinic is ready to fit patients, the Society sends a technician to supervise and support the clinic's initial operations. The number of artisans and technicians at the new facility depends on the expected patient load. Additionally, each clinic retains a doctor to supervise the treatment and fitting of patients. The Society makes the process to fabricate the Jaipur Foot available to the new clinic, or the Society simply produces the required number of prostheses and supplies them to the new clinic free of charge.

Future of Jaipur Foot

Jaipur Foot Technical Improvements

BMVSS collaborates with hospitals, but is also involved in its own R&D to further improve the limb design. R&D at BMVSS is led by Ram Chandra, and Dr. M. K. Mathur, a trained orthopedic surgeon and former head of physical medicine and rehabilitation at a leading hospital, heads the medical and technical effort. Its staff includes doctors, technicians, and social workers.

BMVSS/Jaipur Foot has made several changes in the design and manufacture of lower limb prostheses to keep pace with increases in human understanding of biomechanics and advances in material technology. High-strength plastics are now being used instead of aluminum. Total contact sockets also have been incorporated in the design. However, the custodians of BMVSS have targeted other areas for improvement. The Jaipur Foot currently is being hand-designed, which raises the issues of inconsistency and its impacts on quality and reliability.

Furthermore, at 850 grams, the current foot piece is heavy compared to other solutions. Jaipur Foot has not been tested or certified for any well-known international standard. It also has not yet received regulatory approvals for usage in certain developed countries such as the United States (such an approval has not yet been sought).

Collaboration with Space Research Organization

BMVSS has signed an agreement with the Indian Space Research Organization (ISRO) to receive ISRO's polyurethane technology.[14] ISRO, established in 1969, is one of the premier space research organizations in the world. Its activities include space research, design, development, and launch of satellites and other space vehicles.

The polyurethane technology developed by ISRO is born out of ISRO's pioneering R&D of various polymeric materials to ensure the reliability and quality of launch vehicles and satellites. Polyurethane is a versatile polymer that can be produced in various forms like adhesives, coating materials, and in flexible or rigid forms. ISRO has developed polyurethane polymer and its advanced derivatives, which are being extensively used in propellants, cryogenic insulation, thermal insulation pads, structural damping, acoustic insulation, and other lightweight structural materials for vibration control, shock absorption liners, and adhesives.

This collaboration is expected to reduce the cost of manufacturing a Jaipur Foot. The cost of each foot will be reduced by about 40 percent to Rs. 140. The foot piece also will become lighter by approximately 60 percent to 350 grams.

The technology transferred to BMVSS will help produce a more durable and comfortable artificial foot in large numbers. Average foot fabrication time will be reduced from three hours to about 40 minutes. Polyurethane foot prostheses would be biomechanically advantageous from a comfort perspective. The slip resistance of the polyurethane foot is much higher than rubber and allied materials used in conventional artificial foot prostheses. Amputees using the polyurethane foot prostheses could walk more safely on any surface because its abrasion resistance is higher. In addition, the polyurethane foot lasts longer.

The polyurethane foam foot molded with cosmetically attractive skin covers has been found to be more acceptable to amputees. The new polyurethane foot has been subjected to accelerated flex fatigue tests, and several amputees have been successfully fitted with such prostheses produced under the technology transferred by ISRO. Field trials have been encouraging.

Endnotes

1. *www.jaipurfoot.org.*

2. *http://www.mossresourcenet.org/amputa.htm.*

3. *http://www.limbsforlife.org/about.htm.*

4. *http://www.ottobockus.com/products/op_lower_cleg1.asp.*

5. *http://www.newbeginnings2000.org/facts.html.*

6. *http://www.openroads.org/.*

7. *http://www.pofsea.org/Outreach/Outreach.html.*

8. *http://www.pofsea.org/Help.html.*

9. *http://www.dpa.org.sg/DPA/publication/dpipub/spring97/dpi18.htm.*

10. *http://telebody.com/sihanouk/AboutTheHospital/about-the-Hospital.html.*

11. *www.nupoc.northwestern.edu/prosHistory.html.*

12. Interview with Ramchandra Sharma, BMVSS.

13. Interview with M. K. Mathur, BMVSS.

14. *The Hindu Business Line.* (July 30, 2002).

This report was written by Scott Macke, Ruchi Misra and Ajay
Sharma under the supervision of Professor C.K.Prahalad.
The reports are intended to be catalysts for discussion and are not
intended to illustrate effective or ineffective strategies.

The Aravind Eye Care System: Delivering the Most Precious Gift

Unlike most people who retire to a quiet life, Padmashree Dr. G. Venkataswamy,[1] affectionately referred to as "Dr. V," saw his leaving the Government Medical College, Madurai[2] as the head of the Department of Ophthalmology, in 1976, as an opportunity to face a challenge that personally troubled him: For an estimated 45 million people worldwide, and 9 million in India, the precious gift of sight had been snatched away, most often needlessly. His vision was simple, yet grand: Eradicate needless blindness at least in Tamil Nadu, his home state, if not in the entire nation of India.

THE INNOVATION. . .

Motivated by the vision to eradicate all needless blindness in India, Aravind Eye Care System embarked on a series of innovations to bring world-class eye care to the poorest people in rural and urban India. Focusing on innovations in the organization of workflow—from patient identification to postoperative care—Aravind has built the world's premier eye care institution. It is the largest eye care system in the world. It is also the most productive, and boasts world-class outcome rates.

Beginning in 1976 with a modest 11-bed private clinic in Dr. V's brother's house in Madurai, with a mission of eradicating needless blindness, his dream, by 2003, had grown into The Aravind Eye Care System. It was not merely a chain of hospitals, but an eye care system consisting of a center for manufacturing synthetic lenses, sutures, and pharmaceuticals related to eye care; an institute for training; an institute for research; an international eye bank; a women and child

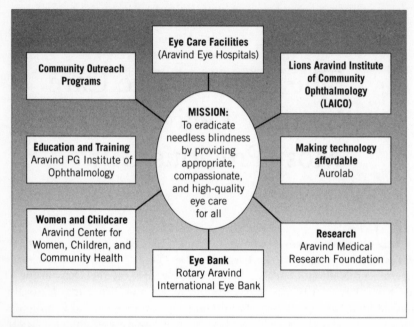

Figure 1   Aravind Eye Care System

care center; a postgraduate institute of ophthalmology awarding MS degrees and offering fellowship programs; and a center for community outreach programs (see Figure 1). The Aravind Eye Hospital (AEH) at Madurai had grown to a 1,500-bed hospital performing nearly 95,000 eye surgeries every year. In addition to Madurai, there are four more AEHs located at Tirunelveli, Coimbatore, Theni, and Pondicherry. The five hospitals together perform a total of 190,000 surgeries every year, or nearly 45 percent of all eye surgeries performed in the state of Tamil Nadu and 5 percent of the total in India.

Organization of Aravind Eye Care

The system began and continues to work under a nonprofit trust named Govel Trust, of which Dr. V[3] is the Chairman. Dr. Namperumalsamy ("Dr. Nam") is the director of this trust, and Dr. G. Natchiar, Dr. V's sister and Dr. Nam's wife, is the joint director. Dr. Nam also serves as the director of the hospitals and is responsible for all senior medical officers, heads of different clinics, residents, and fellows. The medical officers are permanent employees of the hospital. The nursing and other paramedical staff work under the joint director. The various other units, such as the Lions Aravind Institute of Community Ophthalmology (LAICO), have their own heads who report to Dr. Nam.

The organization is very open and transparent. All information on operational details is freely shared with those interested. The leadership style of Dr. V and many others is that of leading by doing. The overall culture at the AEH is one of service, humility, kindness, and equality.

AEH has only full-time doctors; no part-time or visiting doctors are employed, unlike in many large hospitals, which give facilities and time slots to doctors who would come and see the patients. Private practice is not allowed for any of the doctors. "We do not think part-time or external doctors can develop institutional loyalties. They also may not develop the skills we need," said Dr. V.

Broadly, on average, medical officers do 60 percent clinical work, 20 percent teaching, and 20 percent research. However, this varies considerably among doctors. Doctors are encouraged to teach at LAICO and also do research. There is no compromise on the surgical work expected from the doctors, but they can take time off from outpatient treatment if they are pursuing research. Doctors can initiate projects on their own and get support from the Aravind Eye Care System through the Aravind Medical Research Foundation. They can also send proposals to outside funding agencies for research support.

The staff of the AEH, Madurai, as of February 2003, numbered 762. For about 113 doctors, there were 307 nurses, 38 counselors, and 304 other staff. The pattern of staffing in other units was broadly similar (see Table 1).

Table 1 Composition of Staff Strength in Different Units of Aravind Eye Hospitals

Category	Madurai	Theni	Tirunelveli	Coimbatore
Medical officers	43	2	13	18
Fellows and PGs	70	3	18	18
Paramedics	307	19	70	134
Counselors	38	3	15	20
Others	304	21	78	84
Total	762	48	194	274

Source: Data supplied by Aravind Eye Care System.

The driving mission of the AEH is sustained by a combination of the following elements:

■ **Purpose.** Dr. V: "Despite all our efforts, so many people with problems with their vision have still no access to hospitals. Much of the blindness can be corrected through surgery. But they are afraid of operations. So we have to increase the awareness of the causes of blindness and the need for early treatment. Even in villages where we conduct eye camps, only 7 percent of people having eye problems turn up. We have to do more to create demand. Most of this blindness is needless and curable. We have to eradicate all needless blindness."

- **Volume.** Dr. Nam: "At present we do about 3.6 million eye surgeries in India. If this can be increased to 5 million, needless blindness can be eradicated. We do about 2,600 surgeries per doctor per year in our Aravind Eye Hospitals. The national average is about 400. It is possible for other hospitals to come to our level of productivity. We are willing to help them to do so."

- **Systematic approach.** Dr. Natchiar: "All our systems are oriented towards enabling the doctors to be at their productive best. We support them through well-trained paramedical staff. Community outreach programs are central to our mission, since most of the blind are poor and are in rural areas."

- **Technique and training.** Dr. Nam: "We perform 95 percent of our cataract surgeries with insertion of intraocular lenses (IOLs).[4] The national average of IOL surgeries is only 60 percent, and in some states like Bihar, it is only 30 percent. We have to bring up this percentage through training of doctors."

Financial Self-Sustainability

Despite having a majority of patients as free patients, the Aravind Eye Care System had always been financially self-supporting. Even from the beginning, it did not depend on government grants or donations (except for the support given by the government for eye camp patients), and until now it had not applied for any other government grants for service delivery. Table 2 gives the income and expenditures (before depreciation) from 1997–1998 through 2001–2002.

The Finance and Accounts function is managed by Mr. G. Srinivasan, an engineer by profession, and the brother of Dr. V. He is also the Founder-Secretary of the Govel Trust. In the initial years, the Govel Trust borrowed some money from the State Bank of India by pledging the properties of the trustees. Neither the hospital nor the trust resorts to any organized fundraising through donations. The Madurai hospital was self-supporting for all recurring expenditures from the beginning, and after five years it had accumulated adequate surplus for its own

Table 2 Income and Expenditures, 1997–1998 to 2001–2002 (in Rs. Million)

Year	Income	Expenditures	Surplus
1997–1998	180.3	81.7	98.6
1998–1999	239.5	123.2	116.3
1999–2000	276.3	143.2	133.1
2000–2001	340.4	156.6	183.8
2001–2002	388.0	177.5	210.5

Source: Data supplied by Aravind Eye Care System.

development and the establishment of new hospitals at Theni, Tirunelveli, Coimbatore, and Pondicherry. Each of these branch hospitals is also meeting all of its operational costs through patient revenues and generating a surplus to contribute to the development of subsequent hospitals. Although donations are accepted and welcome, the hospital consciously chose to remain financially viable essentially through patient revenues for its core activities of patient care, community work, and training. "Tight financial control and on-time accounting, coupled with appropriate pricing and transparency, are the reasons for this financial success," said Srinivasan.

Dr. V and Dr. Nam make the point that not only is the Aravind Eye Care System self-sufficient in terms of operational income and expenditures, but it also takes care of capital expenditure for all expansion and new units. Said Dr. V, "You management people will tell me, why don't you go to the banks, take loans and grow faster? Cost of debt is low. But we, as a policy, will not go to the banks for loans, since it will compromise our freedom." The building of the system's next hospital will, according to Dr. V, not happen until further surplus is accumulated. Dr. V does not see any conflict between eradicating blindness as quickly as possible and this policy of gradual growth. There are large areas in Tamil Nadu not covered by any hospital, including the areas of North Arcot and Dharmapuri. Dr. V said, "We feel it is important to preserve our financial self-sufficiency. Also there is a limit to the rate at which we can grow effectively without compromising on the basic values of the organization."

The rates charged by Aravind, both for operations and for stays, are quite moderate. Paying patients have a choice of the type of surgery and the quality of accommodations they want, ranging from an air-conditioned private room to a nonprivate room. There are five categories of accommodation and five categories of elective surgery available to them. The total cost, including surgery and a typical two-day stay at the hospital, would range from a basic charge of $50 (cataract operation without IOL and in regular accommodations, now a rarely performed procedure) to $330 (Phaco with acrylic foldable IOL with air-conditioned deluxe accommodations). The range of prices and the choices available to patients are shown in Table 3.

Table 3 Costs for Procedures and Accommodations

Type of Surgery	Price Range in Rs.	Price Range in U.S.$
Cataract without IOL	2,100–5,900	45–133
Cataract with IOL	3,800–8,700	84–193
Phaco with IOL	5,700–8,900	127–198
Phaco with foldable IOL	9,500–11,900	210–265
3-piece IOL	12,500–14,900	278–331

Source: Data supplied by Aravind Eye Care System. Price range is based on the quality of accommodations selected by patients.

Recruitment and Training

AEH laid great stress on the kind of people it recruits. Said Dr. Natchiar, who is in charge of training of paramedical staff:

We have a ratio of about one-to-six between doctors and nurses. We have also about 40 counselors. We have about 900 girls between our four hospitals and Aurolab. We recruit girls from rural backgrounds; generally we do not prefer urban girls. We take them between ages 17 and 19, very rarely more than 19. We look for girls from large families, probably farmers' families, with the right attitudes. Knowledge and skills are important, but not so much as the right attitude. We never advertise. Usually, once a year, we put up a notice in our hospitals indicating our intention to recruit, and word of mouth carries the news. Between the selection cycles about 400 to 500 applications are received. We take about 60 to 100 girls per year. Selection for all the hospitals is done only in Madurai and Tirunelveli. I along with Dr. Usha (a younger ophthalmologist and a member of the family who was being groomed to head recruitment and training of nurses) and the head nurse are involved in all selections. Parents are always called for the interview as well. We look for the right kind of person. We give no consideration to any letters of recommendation from anyone. After recruitment, we give them two years' training. The training is considered to be excellent and is recognized in the U.S.A., and the government of India is considering adopting our training syllabus for nurses' training. During the training period, we rotate them among all our different hospital units.

The ophthalmic assistants in the first four months are trained in basic sciences and details about human anatomy and physiology. By the end of the first four months, the trainers and Dr. Usha, who heads the training of nurses, select the ophthalmic assistants for the different tasks, such as outpatient department, operation theater, counseling, and so on. The criteria for making such decisions are not very clearly articulated, but are clearly understood by the team. In the next eight months the assistants receive special training for the department for which they were chosen. The next six months are then spent in apprenticeship with a trainer nurse working in the same department. There is one-on-one training at each step. During the last six months they work on their own with some guidance from senior nurses and doctors. The training for the nurses is essentially in Tamil (the vernacular language spoken in the state); they are also taught some basic medical terminology in English and trained in basic conversational English.

This training was designed after the training program for ophthalmic assistants that Dr. V coordinated in 1973 for rehabilitation work funded by the United States Agency for International Development (USAID). As of now, the training program does not lead to a degree for the ophthalmic assistants. The training modules are being formalized and written up with the help of qualified volunteers from the United States. Dr. Natchiar noted that, "At the end of two years, we ask the parents to allow the girls who would like to be absorbed permanently. Parents' consent is always taken. In our experience, 99 percent of the trainees stay on with us. Those who we consider to be unsuitable, mainly due to their attitude, are not given job offers."

During the three years of their service as permanent employees, the ophthalmic assistants are also given training in cooking, housekeeping, tailoring, and so on. This helps prepare them to become good housewives in the future. The cost for these programs is borne by the Aravind Eye Care System. Voluntary bhajan (devotional songs) and yoga sessions are also organized in the evening. The nurses are encouraged to be kind to the patients at all times and approach them with thankfulness for providing them an opportunity to serve. The nurses are asked to save a part of their salary in a bank account in their name, so that they have a sizable sum saved for their marriage.

As for what the nurses find good in this hospital, Dr. Natchiar said, "More than salaries, it is the recognition that they get in society. They get a lot of respect. Then they also get very good training and experience here. Opportunity to go abroad, even for short periods, is also seen as a positive factor." The nurses feel very proud to work at AEH. One of the senior nurses said, "I work more than the government hospital nurses do; I get paid a little less or at par with them, but I get much more respect in the society. When I go in the bus, someone will recognize that I work in AEH and offer me a seat or be nice to me. I really feel happy about it." Dr. Usha said, "The ophthalmic assistants are at the core of our success. They add so much to the Aravind Eye Care System." Dr. V said, "The senior nurses appreciate the atmosphere of peace and quiet efficiency and set an example for the junior staff."

Doctors are crucial at AEH. Most are inducted as residents. The Residency Program leads to a master's degree in surgery (MS) and lasts for three years, during which participants are given a stipend. An MS degree is almost essential for further practice. AEH takes about 30 residents every year in its various training programs. During residency, the residents are given full exposure and training in all branches of ophthalmic surgery. At the end of training, many are offered jobs as permanent medical officers in the AEHs. Most of the residents accept the offer.

In addition to the Residency Program, AEH has a Fellowship Program as well. Fellows are those who already have an MS degree but who want to specialize in a particular branch (e.g., retina-vitreous, cornea, pediatric ophthalmology, glaucoma, uvea, or orbit). Fellowships usually last for 18 months and do not lead to any degree. During their fellowship, the candidates get a stipend. There are 40 fellows in Aravind in various specializations. Said one fellow, "I already have an MS degree. But we did not get adequate exposure to surgery in our course. Also here we have a large number of specializations not available elsewhere easily." Said another, "We did not get adequate surgical exposure in MS. This is usually the case in many colleges, especially North India. I get exposed to different kinds of IOL surgeries as well as plastic surgery. In Delhi, where I studied, we did not have so many cases of varied nature. They did not have a phaco machine there. There we did about one or two cases of surgery per month; here we do some 30 cases per day!" Most of the fellows do not join AEH after completion of their training, because they are from different parts of India and come to AEH for training in particular specialties. Those who join are largely from the local area.

There is also a focus on the professional growth of all the doctors. Attendance in "Journal Rounds" for all medical officers and fellows is a must. At this forum, a medical officer or fellow selects an article of interest from a journal and presents it to all others. There are also the "Grand Rounds," in which doctors of all the units of AEH discuss predecided topics through teleconferencing.

There is a strict monitoring of quality. Morbidity meetings are organized every week in a nonthreatening manner. Complication rates of individual surgeons as well as that of the hospital are calculated every month. Dr. V and others stress the quality of eye care provided at AEH. Dr. Nam said, "Our destination is 'good sight.' We provide our doctors with the best that is available in the world. We train them through exchange programs with prestigious medical schools all around the world. With several universities we have set up very rewarding collaborative research programs."

The quality of eye care at AEH is as good as or better than that at the best centers for eye care in the world. For example, Table 4 shows a comparison of medical complications at the Coimbatore AEH compared to the standards obtained in the United Kingdom as documented by a national survey by The Royal College of Ophthalmologists in the United Kingdom.

One of the residents from Harvard Medical School who was in Madurai said, "Here I get more clinical experience than any of my classmates at Harvard. I also get to see many instances of rare eye diseases. In Harvard, I would only read about them. Here I see them." A medical officer said:

> I see the following plus points here. I am at my home place. We get a very good exposure to the latest surgical techniques. We also get opportunities to practice telemedicine with eminent people.[5] If you want to be abreast of the latest techniques in ophthalmology, this is the best. We get opportunities to do research, attend international conferences, and present papers. We can attend one or even more than one conference each year. I am in charge of the newly set up Vision Rehabilitation Centre. My long-term mission will be to develop this center, using new techniques such as magnifying devices and developing skills for the visually handicapped to improve the quality of their life. I plan to set up similar rehabilitation centers in other hospitals, too.

Table 4 Aravind Eye Care System Compared with The Royal College of Ophthalmologists

Adverse Events During Surgery			Adverse Events Within 48 Hours of Surgery		
Event	Aravind, Coimbatore (N = 22,912)	U.K. National Survey (N = 18,472)	Event	Aravind, Coimbatore (N = 22,912)	U.K. National Survey (N = 17,257)
Capsule rupture and vitreous loss	2.0%	4.4%	Corneal edema	8.0%	9.0%
Incomplete cortical cleanup	0.75%	1.00%	Uveitis more than Expected	5.0%	5.6%
Iris trauma	0.3%	0.7%	Periocular bruising and edema more than expected	1.0%	1.4%
Persistent iris prolapse	0.01%	0.07%	Weak leak/rupture	0.67%	1.2%
Anterior chamber collapse	0.3%	0.5%	Hyphaema	0.9%	1.1%
Loss of nuclear fragment into vitreous	0.2%	0.3%	Retained lens material	0.87%	1.1%
Wounds	0.30%	0.25%	Vitreous to section	0.1%	0.3%
Choroidal hemorrhage	—	0.07%	Endoph-thamitis	0.05%	0.03%
Loss of IOL into vitreous	0.01%	0.16%	Hypopyon	0.04%	0.02%
			Other*	0.7%	1.5%

*Other includes iris abnormality, intraocular lens dislocation, cystoid acula oedema, choroiditis, optic neuropathy, and capsule opacity.

Sources: Aravind Hospital, Coimbatore: Aravind Eye Care System. The Royal College of Ophthalmology, Cataract Surgery Guidelines, Outcome of Cataract Surgery, U.K. National Survey, 2001.

Asked whether he found time for research in the midst of all these activities, he said, "Time is not a problem. Those interested can find the time." However, this was not the view of another: "It is all right to say you have a lot of opportunities to do research. But after a long day of 12 or 13 hours, how many can find the energy to do research? We have full days here." Said another doctor:

We do commit ourselves totally to the cause of eradication of avoidable blindness. That means we have to do a certain number of surgeries every day. But subject to this, we have quite a lot of flexibility. We have a unique culture based on service. All the doctors speak softly to patients and nurses. No shouting here. If a doctor behaves in an unacceptable manner, word goes around the hospital in no time, and the doctor will be in trouble. We believe in mutual respect as a core value.

Going to camps together with ophthalmic assistants and other administrative staff of the hospital also increases camaraderie and understanding among the different categories of staff.

Said Mr. Thulasiraj, who had an MBA from the Indian Institute of Management, Calcutta, and who left a lucrative job in the private sector to serve as the administrative officer in Aravind Hospital, Madurai (now in charge of LAICO), "Doctor turnover is a problem. The retention is only for about three to four years. Every year we lose 20 to 25 doctors. India produces about 800 ophthalmologists per year. Can we get from that pool? We have also the fellow pool, about 25 or so." Thulasiraj stated (this was confirmed by Dr. Nam) that although in the earlier years doctors were paid less than market rates, now this is not so. Doctors' salaries are at par with what they could get elsewhere. Of course, with private practice people could make much more money. Said Thulasiraj, "What we can offer is a good work environment, a good name, and a status based on our high integrity. We also offer good salaries and opportunities for personal growth. But we should be able to retain enough doctors, all the same."

AEHs Workflow

Outpatient Departments

The workflow in the outpatient (OP) departments of the different units of AEHs, whether at the paying or free sections, is essentially the same. Patients start gathering much earlier than the starting hour of 7 A.M. and wait in the designated waiting areas. At 7 A.M. sharp, the first patient registers in the reception area. The computerized registration takes only about a minute per patient, after which the patient moves on to the case sheet counter located adjacent to the waiting hall. With the counters generated through computers, the case sheet and the patients are escorted to the doctors by the staff. Three computers are used for new cases, and one for old cases; they can handle 200 cases per hour. Trained paramedical staff members do the preliminary checks on the patients and trained refractionists rather than doctors do basic refraction tests. The patients then meet the resident doctors at the examination stations (usually four to five), who record their diagnoses and recommendations. The final disposal of the cases is always done by a medical officer, a permanent doctor of the hospital. The whole process takes about two hours for a patient, but this varies depending on the tests needed. The paying OP staff members examine 1,000 patients per day, six days a week.

Many patients are advised to wear glasses after the refraction tests. After the glasses are prescribed, they can (but are not obliged to) go to one of the spectacle shops located in the hospital. These shops are run as a separate profit center. These shops sell spectacles at less than what they would cost in an outside optical shop. There are separate shops in the free and paying hospitals, but the prices of similar spectacles are the same in all the shops. The grinding and fitting of the glasses is done in house while the patients wait, rather than having them come back after one or two days, as is the practice with most of the optical shops in India. The system at Aravind thus saves time for patients. This enables patients to leave the hospital with glasses within three to four hours.

Those needing surgery are admitted immediately (subject to room availability), or the patients can choose a later date. In the case of paying patients, they can also choose the type of surgery (with the type of lenses preferred—rigid, foldable, etc.—and whether they preferred phaco surgery) and the type of rooms. They can also indicate whether they want a particular doctor to perform the surgery.[6] All these requests are processed on the computer, and an admission or reservation slip is generated and given to the patient.[7] The entire process of helping the patients to make their choices is carried out by a set of counselors (paramedical staff) who explain the alternatives, the type of surgeries that can be performed, the aftercare needed, the likely time to get full vision, and the costs. The rate card showing rates for different types of surgeries and different categories of rooms is shown to the patients to help in their choice. Pictures of the alternative rooms are also shown, along with the facilities available. Dr. Aravind Srinivasan said:

In many hospitals, many of these functions (especially refraction testing) are carried out by doctors. We seek to maximize the doctors' contribution by helping them to devote their time mainly to medical advising. Tests that can be done by paramedical staff are done by paramedical staff only. Our counselors are highly trained to help the patients to make informed decisions, so that doctors are not required to spend their time on such matters.

Patients move smoothly from place to place. They are always given clear directions where to go next; no one has to inquire where to go or where a facility is located. This leads to a lack of crowding in the waiting hall, quite unusual in a hospital of this size. There are paramedical personnel stationed at critical places for directing people to avoid confusion and crowding.

The doctors doing surgery do so only in the morning and attend the OP department in the afternoon. The doctors are rotated between free and paying hospitals, so that both categories of patients receive similar-quality medical attention.

Surgical Wards

The workflow in the surgical wards at Madurai is equally smooth and efficient. At 7 A.M., the doctors are in their surgical gowns and masks. The names of patients to be operated on during the day in each theater are put up. This scheduling is done using software, which incorporates all the preferences expressed by patients at the time of their registration, including preferences for particular doctors. The nursing staff arrives at 6:30 A.M., and the patients for the day are moved to a ward adjacent to the operating theaters. The patients to be operated on soon are given local anesthetic injections and their eyes are washed and disinfected. By 7:15 A.M., two patients are on two adjacent operating tables. In general, in many hospitals, two operating tables are not kept in an operation theater because of the presumed risk of infections. However, AEH has been following the system of having more than one table in an operation theater from its inception and has not had any problems, because all eye patients are otherwise healthy and the chance of cross-infection is considered to be very small. This is vindicated by the low rates of postoperative complications experienced.

The operation theater has four operating tables, laid out side by side. Two doctors operate, each on two adjacent tables. By the time the first operation is over, the second patient is ready with the microscope focused on the eye to be operated on. The first patient is bandaged by the nurses and moved out. The third patient, who has in the meanwhile been moved in (they usually walk in on their own), is sitting on a bench in the theater. As soon as the first patient moves out, the third patient is put on the first table and prepared for the operation. As soon as the second patient is finished, the doctor moves back to the first table, with virtually no loss of time. He is constantly moving between the two tables, with hardly any break. In the same way, another doctor operates on the third and fourth tables. As Dr. Aravind said:

> *I work like this the entire morning from 7 A.M. until 1 P.M. or 1.30 P.M., or even later if there is a large number to be attended. Most doctors take a break for breakfast and a brief tea break maybe for five to ten minutes. Usually I do about 25 surgeries in a half-day session. Most do this number.*

Usually no surgeries are done in the afternoon. The theaters are scrubbed and cleaned and instruments are sterilized. The patients who have already been operated on are moved back to their wards.

The procedures in other hospitals in Theni and Coimbatore are the same. The Coimbatore hospital is a newer, integrated, well-designed hospital with all the specialties and also the facilities for training for the Dip NB (equivalent to MS) program. It also conducts short-term specialized programs for doctors from other developing countries. The basic workflow for the outpatients and the surgeries is the same as in Madurai. The Theni hospital is smaller and does not do pediatric and retinal surgeries.

Table 5 gives the details of the number of surgeries done and the outpatients attended to from 1997 by all the hospitals under the Aravind Eye Care System. Even in a small hospital like Theni, the three doctors stationed there perform 6,000 operations every year. In most eye hospitals in India, each surgeon does about 400 surgeries per year, whereas in Aravind hospitals this number is about 2,600 surgeries per year.

Table 5   Surgeries Done and Outpatient Visits, 1997–2002

Year	Paying		Free Including Camp		Total	
	OP Visits	Surgery	OP Visits	Surgery	OP Visits	Surgery
1997	401,518	42,808	574,350	80,287	975,868	123,095
1998	465,496	49,275	697,649	108,552	1,163,145	157,827
1999	530,253	55,460	752,819	127,708	1,283,072	183,168
2000	567,105	58,267	763,888	134,498	1,330,993	192,765
2001	603,800	63,265	725,210	127,893	1,329,070	191,158
2002	650,047	68,055	749,324	128,384	1,399,371	196,425

Note. These figures are for all the hospitals of the Aravind Eye Care System.

Source: Data supplied by Aravind Eye Care.

Table 6 gives the details of OP visits and major surgeries done in each hospital unit of the Aravind Eye Care System.

Said Dr. Aravind, "We work like this for six days a week. Most of the Sundays we go out to the eye camps, and spend at least half a day testing the patients. Sometimes if one is lucky, one may get one Sunday off in a month. Besides surgery, we do OP work, and many do research as well. To us, this hospital is our life. We have dedicated our lives for this one mission."

The paying wards have regular beds on cots, but the free wards have "beds" in the form of mats on the floor. Two types of mats are used to distinguish the eye camp patients from the walk-in free patients. The use of mats enables better utilization of floor space; about 30 patients can be accommodated in one room.

The Aravind Eye Hospital in Madurai has an excellent information technology system that keeps track of all the patients. The system generates daily schedules, taking into account the load on that day, patients' preferences for doctors, and the pending work. This enables the hospital administration to keep track of the workload in different units. The details of complications in terms of categories of patients and the surgeons are maintained. The abstracts of medical records of patients are entered into the system, including past clinical visits. This enables a history sheet to be generated for a returning patient quickly.

Table 6 Patient Statistics for Different Units of the Aravind Eye Care System, 2002

	Madurai	Tirunelveli	Theni	Coimbatore	Total
Outpatient visits					
Paying	276,548	132,272	40,149	201,078	650,047
Free (direct and camp)	328,651	138,425	41,685	240,653	749,324
Of the above:					
Hospital OP visits	409,755	182,356	60,035	285,463	937,609
Eye camp OP visits	195,144	88,341	21,799	156,178	461,762
Total	605,199	270,697	81,834	441,641	1,399,371
No. of eye camps	591	364	132	463	1,550
Surgery					
Paying	34,510	12,107	1,863	19,575	68,055
Free (direct and camp)	66,363	19,719	5,273	37,029	128,384
Total	100,873	31,826	7,136	56,604	196,439
Some major types of surgeries					
ECCE without IOL	1,257	1,862	99	1,259	4,447
ECCE with IOL	40,962	4,383	6,084	9,651	61,080
ECCE IOL with phaco	9,900	3,569	262	7,626	21,357
Small incision cataract surgery	27,503	14,984	0	24,797	67,284
Laser photo-coagulation	6,652	1,995	209	3,423	12,279

Source: Data supplied by Aravind Eye Care System.

The AEHs are very particular about the quality of the surgeries done, as revealed by their low complication rates. Although some of it is beyond the control of the hospitals, the Aravind management keeps very close track of the intraoperative and postoperative complication rates. The major complications are very much under control and are considered highly satisfactory, according to the doctors at Aravind. All the same, each complication is traced to the operating team that performed it, and the reasons are identified. Corrective action, including training of whomever is found deficient, is undertaken.

Community Outreach Programs
Eye Camps

For some time one of the primary types of outreach effort in India has been that of eye camps. Usually sponsored locally by nongovernmental organizations (NGOs), such as the Rotary or Lions Clubs, or local industrialists, businessmen, or philanthropists, these camps would gather patients, test them, and conduct the needed surgeries at the camp site itself. Although this is a good way to reach out to people, maintaining AEH's high standard of sanitation was always a concern in these camps. By 2002, the official position of the government of India was to discourage such camps. This fortunately came at a time where there were more Aravind hospitals to accommodate a wider geographic mix of patients. Aravind conducts all its surgeries only in its base hospitals, where conditions are under full control. Aravind organizes about 1,500 eye camps per year, with the travel expenses of the doctors (medical officers and postgraduate residents) paid for by the AEH Diabetic Retinopathy Management Project

Started in 2000, this project aims at creating awareness about diabetic retinopathy in communities. It consists of examining people for diabetes and then screening all diabetics for retinal disorders. In 2002, 46 eye camps were organized in which 11,644 persons were examined. Of these, 3,443 were diabetics, all of whom were screened for retinopathy. Of the persons screened, 533 turned out to have retinopathy. Patients needing surgery are so advised. Extensive campaigns are also conducted through leaflets, posters, and booklets on diabetes and its effects on the retina.

Community-Based Rehabilitation Project

This is a project undertaken by the Theni unit since 1996 and supported by Sight Savers International that aims at rehabilitating incurably blind persons through community-based support. House-to-house identification of eye problems and screening camps are organized and patients with eye problems are treated. Rehabilitation consisted of teaching the incurably blind people skills in orientation, mobility, and activities of daily living. Some were economically rehabilitated through building of appropriate skills.

Eye Screening of School Children

This is another program aimed at screening school children for eye defects and taking corrective measures early. Teachers are trained to measure visual acuity and identify signs of squint and vitamin deficiency and screen the children. The identified children were then tested by ophthalmic assistants and later by ophthalmologists. In 2002, 68,528 children in 80 schools were screened and 3,075 were given glasses to correct refractive errors.

Refraction Camps

Detection and correction of refractive errors through spectacle lenses has been identified as one of the priorities for reducing avoidable blindness by the global initiative "Vision 2020: The Right to Sight," launched in 1999 by the World Health Organization (WHO). Recognizing this, Aravind started conducting refraction camps in industries, offices, and so on. In these refraction camps, patients receive an eye examination and a prescription for glasses if one is indicated. The patient can decide to purchase the spectacles at the camp itself. He or she selects a frame and the dispensing is done on the spot for more than 85 percent of the orders. Such on-the-spot dispensing of glasses has now been integrated with the eye camps and school screening camps as well.

Use of IT Kiosks for Teleadvice

This initiative was launched with the help of the Indian Institute of Technology (IIT), Chennai. Under the guidance of Dr. Ashok Jhunjhunwala, a professor at IIT, Chennai, a number of IT kiosks were put up all over Tamil Nadu by a company called n-Logue. In one cluster of villages near Melur, about 40 kilometers from Madurai, the IT kiosks were provided with Web cameras that enable patients to take a picture of their eyes and send them as e-mail attachments along with a voice description of the problem to doctors at AEH, Madurai. One doctor is nominated to take care of these e-mails. The doctor makes the diagnosis based on the description given by the patient and the picture sent, and gives advice to the patient. This is not, however, an online service.

Other Units and Activities of the Aravind Eye Care System

Aurolab

The cost of surgery has always been a central concern at AEH. As noted earlier, AEH decided on the IOL technique as the standard technique to be adopted in all cases, except where this could not be done. However, in the 1980s, the cost of IOL lenses, all of which were imported, was very high (about $80–$100), and this made the cost of surgery quite high. Hence in 1991, AEH set up a facility to manufacture lenses. Named Aurolab, this was set up as a separate nonprofit trust with the mission of achieving "local production at an appropriate cost." Some of the members of the Aurolab Board were common with Govel Trust. The technology was obtained from IOL International, Florida, USA, with a one-time fee paid to the company for technology transfer. This venture was also supported by Seva Foundation, Sight Savers International, the Combat Blindness Foundation USA, Canadian International Development Agency (CIDA) through Seva Service Society, and Mr. David Green, an Ashoka Fellow and Executive Director of Project Impact, Inc., in California.

Aurolab employs 220 people, of whom 10 percent are diploma or graduate engineers, pharmacists, and marketing personnel, and 90 percent are specially trained women. High school girls with 12 years of formal education from rural areas are selected along with the selection of the ophthalmic assistants for AEH. For six months they receive the same training as the ophthalmic assistants, and in the next 18 months specific training is given for the manufacturing of lenses.

Raw material for the lenses is imported from the United States and the United Kingdom. The rigid IOL are produced for less than U.S.$5 at Aurolab. In 2002, Aurolab produced about one-fifth of the total number of low-cost lenses produced in the world. However, it also produced rigid and foldable lenses as well as superior categories, such as acrylic lenses. Aurolab had been able to get the CE Mark (a mark of quality) and ISO 9002 certification. As of 2003, Aurolab produced about 700,000 lenses per year (with a single shift working). Large NGOs such as Christoffel Blinden Mission, USA, and Sight Savers International, UK, also buy IOL lenses from Aurolab and supply them to various eye hospitals all over the world. This increased sales worldwide and 33 percent of the IOLs produced were exported. Of the 67 percent consumed domestically, 20 to 25 percent were used by AEH and the rest were sold on the open market. Since inception, Aurolab has supplied more than 2 million lenses to nonprofit organizations in India and 85 to 90 countries.

In 1998 Aurolab diversified into the manufacturing of sutures used in the IOL surgery. The sutures are made from silk and nylon and come attached to a tiny stainless steel needle. The cost of the sutures at Aurolab was one-fourth of the price of imported sutures. The Managing Director of Aurolab, Dr. Balakrishnan, said, "Aurolab was responsible in driving down the prices of IOL all around the world. Our lenses are high quality, low price, and take us nearer to our goal of eliminating needless blindness."

Over the years, Aurolab has been organized into four distinct divisions: the IOL Division, the Sutures Division (both described earlier), a Pharmaceutical Division, and a Spectacle Lens Division.

The Pharmaceutical Division of Aurolab produces pharmaceuticals used in cataract surgery and for other eye-related needs at a reasonable cost. They are usually those items not easily available or available at a high cost. The total number of drugs formulated by Aurolab was 25 in 2002. It is the sole Indian manufacturer for Econazole, Coltrimazole, and Prednisolone Sodium Phosphate eye drops.[8] Aurolab pharmaceuticals and suture needles are covered under the Indian Drug Control Act and are WHO-GMP-certified. The international certification also makes it possible to sell these formulations on the international market.

The Spectacle Lens Division provides technical support services for the production, quality control, and training for optical shops located inside the AEHs. The Spectacle Lens Division was set up in 1999 to improve the prescription and provision of spectacles. A laboratory with plastic lens surfacing and computerized edging facility was established to research and refine the process. Lens-edging facilities were established close to the optical shops for quicker delivery. Technologies for a scratch-resistant coating system to provide hard coating on both sides and color tints to satisfy the needs of low-vision patients had also been acquired and are being used to produce the needed lenses.

LAICO

In the early 1990s, Aravind started collaborating with Lions Club International Foundation, a voluntary organization for community service. LAICO was established in 1992 with the support of Lions Club International Sight First Program and Seva Sight Program. The objective of LAICO was to improve the planning, efficiency, and effectiveness of eye hospitals with a special focus in the developing countries. LAICO contributes to eye care through teaching, training, research, and consultancy. LAICO offers long-term courses in hospital management as well as short skill development courses in the area of community outreach, social marketing, and instruments maintenance. These courses are offered at very reasonable prices. LAICO has already worked with 149 eye hospitals in India, Africa, and Southeast Asia. It is Asia's first international training facility for blindness prevention workers from India and other parts of the world.

LAICO also works closely with identified eye hospitals in their capacity building. The AEH staff first visits the hospitals requesting such support to understand "the ground realities" regarding their problems, bottlenecks, and constraints. Then it invites some personnel from the hospitals for training at LAICO. The training consists of visiting the Aravind hospitals and its outreach camps to study the workflow. At the end of the training, a full action plan has to be made and the progress is assessed after six to nine months.

LAICO has made interventions in Uttar Pradesh, West Bengal, Orissa, Delhi, and a few other states in India. It has also made interventions abroad in different countries, including Malawi, Kenya, Zimbabwe, and Zambia. In some countries, in addition to the training of doctors, the nurses from Aravind were sent for a month to impart rigorous training. In most interventions, quite dramatic improvements have been recorded. Relating the experience in Chitrakoot, Madhya Pradesh, Mr. Saravanan, a LAICO faculty member, said:

> In Chitrakoot, they were doing 20,000 to 25,000 surgeries per year. Ninety percent of this was done in a three-month period. Of the surgeries, 70 to 80 percent were non-IOL surgeries. Only in slack periods would they take up IOL. After our intervention, they were able to do 25,000 to 30,000 surgeries per year, all IOL. Our aim in such interventions was to enhance not only their capabilities but also their skills.

LAICO, in collaboration with the International Agency for Prevention of Blindness (IAPB), has committed to achieving the "Vision 2020: The Right to Sight" global initiative. Thulasiraj is the regional chairman of IAPB, Southeast Asia Region, and is thus able to be involved in policymaking for eradicating blindness at both the international and the national levels.

Aravind Medical Research Foundation

A number of clinical, population-based studies and social and health systems research are conducted using the data readily available in the hospitals and the community outreach programs. The Aravind Medical Research Foundation coordinates the research needs. Many of these research projects are supported by different agencies, and some by AEH itself. The research covers a variety of fields such as clinical trials to evaluate alternate surgical techniques and drug therapies, impact of vitamin supplements on morbidity and mortality of infants and children, beneficiary assessment, impact assessment of cataract intervention, barriers experienced by patients in accessing eye care sources, and infrastructure utilization in eye care. Dr. VR. Muthukkaruppan, previously a professor of immunology at the Madurai Kamaraj University and a former Vice Chancellor of Bharathidasan University, Tiruchirapalli, has been appointed to provide leadership to the research efforts of the Aravind Medical Research Foundation.

Aravind Center for Women, Children, and Community Health (ACWCCH)

This center, started in 1984, aimed at reducing nutrition-related blindness in children through programs of preventive health care. It works with government public health programs of immunization, education programs on nutrition, and training programs to create awareness under the leadership of Dr. Lakshmi Rahmathulah. It conducts regular village health programs and training programs for village health care workers.

Rotary Aravind International Eye Bank

This eye bank, established in 1998, is one of the four eye banks in the country affiliated with the International Federation of Eye Banks. By 2003, the bank had processed 4,383 eyes, and the hospitals had conducted 2,181 transplants.

Aravind Postgraduate Institute of Ophthalmology

As part of its efforts to train ophthalmologists, AEH introduced the Residency (postgraduate) Program in 1982 and with this the name of Aravind Hospital, Madurai was changed to Aravind Eye Hospital & Postgraduate Institute of Ophthalmology (AEH&PGIO). AEH&PGIO admitted around 30 resident doctors as of 2003. All admissions are strictly based on merit and no admission or capitation fee is collected, whereas the going rate in 2003 was about Rs. 1.5 million to 2 million at other private teaching hospitals. Affiliated with Dr. MGR Medical University, Chennai, it offers the Diploma in Ophthalmology (DO), and the MS in Ophthalmology (MS). Eight candidates earned their DO and four graduated with an MS in 2001; in 2002, six graduated with the DO and four with an MS. In affiliation with the National Board of Examination, New Delhi, the Aravind Eye Care System offered the Diplomate of the National Board. Nine students qualified in 2001 and 13 in 2002. In affiliation with The Royal College of Ophthalmologists, London, membership in the Royal College of Ophthalmologists (MRCOpth) and FRCS was offered. Four candidates passed Part 1 of the MRCOpth in 2002[9] and four candidates received their FRCS. It also takes fellows for further "super" specialization in such fields as retina-vitreous, cornea, pediatric ophthalmology, glaucoma, anterior chamber, and uvea. In addition, it conducts programs on various short-term courses for practicing ophthalmologists and many areas generally connected to ophthalmology.

Aravind Eye Care System: Future Directions

Dr. V is not satisfied with his achievements; he is thirsting for more. His vision is no longer focused on the AEHs, but on the larger issue of how to make an impact on blindness and its cure. Said Dr. V:

> *I am now seriously wondering how to develop sustainable systems. Only by strengthening existing hospitals can do this. I feel existing doctors in the country are heavily underutilized. They are engaged in many items of work not necessary to be done by them. We have to bring up the way of working with hospitals to bring up the productivity of doctors. Despite all our efforts, only about seven percent of the target populations are coming to the camps. We have to increase this percentage. We have to upgrade the skills of doctors to perform IOL surgeries. This will make a huge difference in the recuperation time and subsequent ability to earn one's living. Postoperative care has to be improved; counseling is to be improved. It is in these areas that we at Aravind hope to make a difference.*

Dr. Nam's vision is this:

Keeping the mission of reducing needless blindness, Aravind would like to venture into other specialities with all its available expertise, skill, management capabilities, and community involvement in ophthalmology, in addition to cataract care in the future. Just like we have established a model for cataract intervention, which is recognized by all, we would like to put into action all programs under Vision 2020 of the World Health Organization. Research to prevent blindness will also form an integral part of the system in the future.

Said Thulasiraj:

I can see many management issues coming up. There is going to be a need to restructure ourselves. There is considerable geographical spread as well as functional diversity. How should we restructure? We are still too centralized in our decisions. Too many decisions are taken here at Madurai. We also have to broad base our leadership. Too much energy is coming from Madurai. How do we stimulate similar efforts from other units? A lot of our strength comes from what I call "unconscious competence" Our strength is really not our technical skills or equipment. This can be easily replicated. Values are our unique strength. Values are the real reason for efficiency. We must find ways of sustaining and strengthening our values and culture. Integrating the culture of all our units is very important. Integrity is a hallmark of this place. We never give commissions to other doctors, chemists or other hospitals for special tests. We tell other diagnostic facilities what they should charge a poor patient sent from Aravind for a particular test (e.g., MRI or CT scan) and they oblige. We have been able to have our way. We should be able to keep this integrity intact.

Dr. Aravind also said:

One of our key strategic future steps is to develop dual specialties among our doctors. We would like to retain and get the best out of our doctors. One way may be to provide more meaning to their work. We are trying to help doctors to develop at least one other specialty. We can then also involve them in the running of the Aravind Eye Care System. We also need to find resources to fund our research projects. We need to build more linkages with other eye care institutions all over the world.

Endnotes

1. Awarded in 1972 by the Government of India. Padmashree is one of the top civilian honors conferred by the government every year for outstanding work in different fields.

2. Madurai is a famous temple city and is the third largest city in the state of Tamil Nadu, South India.

3. Dr. V celebrated his 85th birthday in 2003.

4. An intra-ocular lens (IOL) is a tiny artificial lens inserted into the eye after removal of the natural lens affected by cataract. Earlier, after the removal of the natural lens, a thick positive-powered glass (known as aphakic glass) was required to be worn by the patient. IOL obviated this need.

5. Telemedicine was done in the Aravind network through video conferencing sessions. In such sessions, where the administrative problems of different units were discussed, the doctors in other units could consult senior people on particular problems and cases. They could also show the patient through videoconference to get the opinion of other doctors.

6. Free patients cannot choose their doctors. The actual exercising of this option, even by paying patients, is not very common.

7. For free patients, phaco surgeries are not available. Of course, all except those contraindicated are given IOLs, but free patients are given only rigid lenses.

8. Information taken from the 2001 Activities Report.

9. In 2002, 11 candidates appeared from India, 5 of whom were from Aravind. Of the 7 candidates who cleared that year, 4 were from Aravind.

Compiled by C. K. Prahalad from a more detailed case study
prepared by S. Manikutty and Neharika Vohra of the
Indian Institute of Management, Ahmedabad, 2003.

Known Problems and Systemwide Reform

Many of the problems at the BOP require systemwide reform not piecemeal solutions. Government departments and firms tend to focus on subsystems with which they are familiar or have control over. In this section we examine several examples of firms approaching systemwide reform.

The movement of grain from the farm to the table in India, with its subsistence farmers, an archaic system of logistics and trading renders the agricultural processing system very inefficient. Farmers take their produce to a mandi, a government-sanctioned auction market. The traders in the mandi are the intermediaries who buy the grain, aggregate it, and sell it to processors both large and small. The system of movement of grain from the individual farm to the processing plants is complex and also different for different grains. The ITC eChoupal case story describes the traditional system for soybeans as well as the changes made to the system by ITC. ITC, the food processing firm, decided to change the system by going directly to the villages, providing the village with a PC and training the lead farmer (sanchalak) to operate the PC. The farmers are able to check the prices at various mandis (as opposed to the one closest to their village or the one to which they happen to go), and decide when and how much to sell. They are able to realize better prices for their crop. Further, they are now able to dialogue with the company and ask for advice on better seeds, fertilizers, and pesticides. They get paid promptly and their grain is weighed accurately. From the company point of view, they now have a direct link to the farmers (producers), are able to dramatically reduce the costs of aggregation of soybean crops from multiple farmers and villages, and are ensured of good supply. The efficiencies of the system reduce the total cost per ton by as much as 8 percent. The farmer gets a better price, and the company gets a better supply at lower costs.

Now that ITC e-Choupal has built a network, the network can accommodate other providers of farm inputs, such as financing, crop and rain insurance, better seeds, and farm equipment, to flow through the same system. The farmers are able to use the Internet connections to evaluate their positions. One farmer started to check the prices of soybeans on the Chicago Board of Trade and based his pricing on that information. Farmers learned to connect to the rest of the world seamlessly. The entire process of agricultural inputs, origination, trading, aggregation, logistics, and processing had to be streamlined.

EID Agriline is also a case of the same process, in this case, oriented toward sugar cane. The two examples—ITC e-Choupal in the northern part of India in soybeans and EID Parry Agriline in the southern part of India in sugar cane—are both efforts in changing the total crop-specific agricultural system.

ICICI is involved in a similar attempt to change the system in the area of access to credit for the BOP customers. BOP customers typically had to depend on local money lenders to give them access to credit. The interest rates charged were usurious (as high as 400–500 percent per year). Further, local money lenders could not give them access to modern financial systems. The question is how a large bank accesses BOP consumers and at the same time provides them with cost-effective service. ICICI decided to go through village-level self-help groups (SHGs), which they help organize. Each SHG consists of 20 women from the village, who are taught the disciplines of saving, holding meetings, discussing priorities, and investing. Based on their track record of saving, the bank lends money to the SHG (not to the individuals). The SHGs then disburse the money among their membership, based on their needs and an evaluation of projects. The SHGs become an extension of the bank. They act as evaluators of credit, evaluators of viability of projects, providers of loans, and collectors of dues. The experienced leaders of SHGs became the promoters of other such groups in the neighboring villages. In a very short period of time, ICICI has been able to spread its distribution to 10,000 SHGs. The new systems of distribution totally changed the traditional systems and created a level of transparency and access that would have been impossible in the traditional system.

In all these cases—ITC e-Choupal, EID Parry Agriline, and ICICI's rural initiative—the goal is to understand the existing system and create an alternative system that is more cost-efficient. More important, these systems provide the BOP consumers the tools for them to be better informed and thus able to better negotiate. The new system allows for dialogue among the communities of peers—SHGs and sanchalaks from multiple villages. This also allows the communities and the individuals to decide the level of risk they are willing to take on.

ICICI Bank: Innovations in Finance

The number of people living on less than $1 per day in India is significantly greater than the entire population of the United States. From a social perspective, this is a humanitarian pandemic. From an economic perspective, these people represent the bottom of the pyramid (BOP). From a commercial perspective, these individuals are not considered a viable market given their miniscule purchasing power. Do the poor of India represent an opportunity for a large, organized financial services company?

THE INNOVATION...

Can lending to the very poor be financially viable for banks? Should leadership training precede access to saving and credit offered by the organized financial sector? Are there alternate models of credit evaluation, contract enforcement, and building trust in large institutions among the poor consumers? The ICICI experience provides insights on how formal banking can convert the poor into customers, at the same time empowering the poor.

ICICI Bank, the second-largest banking institution in India, sees the poor as a lucrative customer class critical to the future of the company. "I think we have to recognize a whole lot of potential is going to come out of the Bottom of the Pyramid,"[1] stated Chanda Kochhar, the Executive Director of Retail Banking for ICICI Bank. ICICI deems the nearly 400 million impoverished people of India as a huge market with real economic potential and commercial viability.

In fact, the mission statement of the Social Initiatives Group within ICICI Bank is "to identify and support initiatives designed to improve the capacities of the poorest of the poor to participate in the larger economy."[2] Also, there is a widespread belief within ICICI "that the poor do pay for the services rendered to them and they ought to be viewed as consumers rather than passive beneficiaries."[3] With this idea engrained as a core belief, ICICI Bank has focused its resources and creative thinking toward innovatively serving the bottom of the economic pyramid.

The Nature of the Market in India

Banking in India is very focused on the upper income groups. The breakdown of banking access by income category is shown in Figure 1.

The government of India has been extremely sensitive to this asymmetric access to banking. "Of the 428 million deposit bank accounts in the country, 30% are in the rural areas. With a rural population of 741.6 million, the rural penetration of banks . . . is as low as 18%."[4] India has instituted policies to address the rural poor due to the traditionally ineffective banking penetration.

The Reserve Bank of India (RBI), which is the Central Bank and the regulatory arm, has been deeply concerned about access to banking among the rural poor. RBI has a Rural Planning and Credit Department (RPCD) that is directly responsible for encouraging flow of credit to rural, agricultural, and small-scale industries' sectors, drafting policies on lending to priority sectors, and tracking implementation of poverty alleviation schemes.[5] The RBI also has

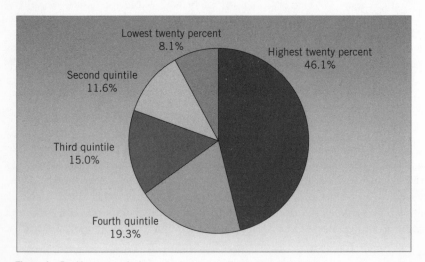

Figure 1 Banking access by income category. *Source:* http://www.hokenson.biz.

a fully owned subsidiary named the National Bank for Agriculture and Rural Development (NABARD), which works to provide credit to farmers, encourage the proliferation of rural banking, and coordinate the financing of rural development projects.

The RBI, through the RPCD and NABARD, has instituted several policies to encourage rural banking and the extension of credit to the rural hinterlands. The first was an initiative that required banks to open one rural branch for every three urban branches opened. As stipulated in Section 22 of the Banking Regulations act of 1949, "Private sector banks . . . are required to open a minimum of 25% of their total branches in rural, semi-urban areas as a condition of the license issued to them."[6] Another initiative required that 40 percent of the net bank credit that commercial banks provide must be allocated to priority sectors (housing, agriculture, rural development, etc.). Eighteen percent of the net bank credit must be allocated toward agriculture-related areas, 13.5 percent of which must be direct to farmers, and the remaining 4.5 percent to agriculture-related areas (tractor companies, seed banks, pesticide factories, etc.).

The RBI, also through NABARD, started a pilot project in 1991 for purveying micro credit to the rural poor by linking selfhelp groups (SHGs) with banks. "A healthy microfinance sector leads to a healthy finance sector in general. This mutual link has to be established by the microfinance institutions/NGOs and realized by the policymakers."[7] This pilot project was initiated because, despite having 150,000 rural banking outlets, a 1981 RBI survey found that 36 percent of the rural poor still utilized informal sources of credit. The project, the SHG-Bank Linkage Program (see Table 1), encouraged state banks with rural branches to give loans directly to SHGs as opposed to leaving the onus of BOP credit to MFIs (microfinance institutions). As of March 31, 2002, "the number of SHGs linked to banks aggregated 461,478. This translates into an estimated 7.87 million very poor families brought within the fold of formal banking services."[8] The fact that RBI and NABARD are "devoting significant time, energy and financial resources on microfinance is an indication of the reckoning of the sector."[9]

Table 1 SHG-Bank Linkage Program Cumulative Progress, 1992–2002

Up to end March	No. of SHGs financed by banks	Bank Loans (Rs. millions)	Refinance from NABARD (Rs. millions)
1999	32,995	571	571
2000	114,775	1,930	1,501
2001	263,825	4,809	4,007
2002	461,478	10,263	7,965

Source: http://www.nabard.org/roles/mcid/nbmf20021.pdf.

These initiatives, although great for the development of the Indian countryside, were viewed by most banks as developmental and, thus, nonprofitable. Providing credit to poor farmers and opening costly rural branches was seen as a loss-making or a break-even proposition at best. ICICI, however, viewed these reforms as an opportunity. K. V. Kamath, CEO and Managing Director of ICICI Bank, stressed that ICICI "wants to lend in a sustainable way to rural India."[10] ICICI took a proactive approach when entering the retail banking sector not only to satisfy the RBI regulations but also to go above and beyond. "In the true ICICI style, we said if we have now acquired this initiative, let us see in what way we can actually make this initiative truly scalable."[11] With the entrenched corporate philosophy that the rural market is to become the engine for future growth, ICICI began looking at how rural banking could be done profitably.

History of Microfinance

Microfinance, even in the formal sector, has a long history. However, it has usually been characterized by its nonsustainable donor-led model. The primary focus of MFIs has been access to credit, a very capital-intensive process. The other plank of banking, namely, savings, has been primarily ignored by MFIs. Also, the majority of its lending occurs to segments who do not qualify for the BOP or poorest of the poor.

Despite these hindrances to sustainability, MFIs remain vitally important as a financial gateway to the poor. Access to credit and participation in trustworthy financial institutions are two of the most important steps in securing basic services of everyday life. The poor need these services to save small amounts in a secure manner, to invest in their business or home, to cover large expenditures, and to ensure against risk.

Poor households around the world have demonstrated their ability to use and pay for financial services through longstanding informal agreements such as savings clubs, rotating savings and credit associations, and mutual insurance societies. In India, there are numerous ways in which the poor can access credit through informal and semiformal institutions. The poor, in the absence of formal institutions, often must resort to the informal sector, which is characterized by monopolistic practices and exorbitant interest rates—at times even in the form of human capital. In a paper published by the ICICI Social Initiative Group, Bikram Duggal and Anit Singhal wrote, "Informal systems may be inefficient and even exploitive due to their monopoly power. Interest rates in the informal market vary from 3 to 10 percent a month. Vegetable vendors are known to borrow at even 10 percent *a day* to finance their daily working capital needs."[12]

In trying to estimate the degree of dependency the poor in India have on the informal sector, data from the All India Debt and Investment Survey of 1992 estimated, "the share of the non-institutional agencies (informal sector) in the outstanding cash dues of the rural households is as high as 36%. The data further reveal the credit dependence on the informal sources was higher in the case of lower asset groups. The dependence on the informal sector was as high as 58% for households with assets lower than Rs. 5,000."[13] In other words, a majority of the extremely poor are reliant on extortionist money lenders for living capital.

Yet formal financial intermediaries, such as commercial banks, typically do not serve poor households. The reasons include the high cost of small transactions, the lack of traditional collateral, geographic isolation, and simple social prejudice. "According to Mahajan,[14] the transaction costs of savings in formal institutions were as high as 10% for the rural poor. This was because of the small average size of transactions and distance of the branches from the villages." Even those institutions that provide financial services to the poor are limited in scale. With more than 400 million poor people and participation rates in formal institutions around 30%, demand far outstrips supply.

Early efforts to provide financial services to the poor tied those services to specific economic activities that were perceived as more financially sound. For example, between the 1950s and 1970s governments and donors focused on providing subsidized agricultural credit to small and marginal farmers in hopes of raising productivity and incomes. During the 1980s, micro-enterprise credit expanded by providing loans to poor women to invest in tiny businesses, enabling them to generate and accumulate assets and raise household income and welfare. The proof that women are more able partners for MFIs is well-documented and rests on a few simple principles. Because women are in charge of the household, the benefits of the money lent are more likely to filter into the family. Therefore, by lending to one woman the bank is helping the lives of at least four or five people. Also, women are more likely to respond to the pressure of the social collateral, which many of the MFIs depend on for repayment.

The world of MFIs is diverse—they exist in various legal forms, including nongovernmental organizations (NGOs), credit unions, nonbank financial intermediaries, and commercial banks. In the most recent meeting of the Micro-Credit Summit in November 2002, there were more than 2,100 MFI entities in various forms that provided information on loans to more than 54 million clients. Their success has shown that poor people can be valuable clients of specially designed financial services.

In 1997, the Micro-Credit Summit was formed to exchange ideas and start a global campaign dedicated to reaching 100 million of the world's poorest families by 2005. Worldwide, there are more than 7,000 MFIs. Of these, fewer than 100 claim financial self-sufficiency. Each type of MFI faces unique constraints that prohibit its financial sustainability. In the NGO model, they typically lack the resources to build permanent support structures of microlending, such as access to savings institutions. In addition, they face constraints of the scalability of their operation, and thus individual transactions become too costly.

Most of the problems with MFIs are due to the fact their primary focus has been on access to credit. With such small loans (and thus meager interest payments) the key to sustainability becomes scale. If an MFI could achieve a large volume of loans, then the aggregate interest payments would suffice to cover operating costs. Achieving such scale is very labor-intensive and takes many years. However, the experience with SHGs in India has shown that lending can be profitable without massive scale and without donor dependency as long as it is coupled with saving requirements. The experience with SHGs has shown that savings must precede credit.

ICICI Bank and the BOP

Although most banks struggled to appease the minimum standards of the government regulations, ICICI Bank, the recently developed commercial/retail subsidiary of ICICI Limited, saw this as an opportunity to expand and grow. As a commercial entity with shareholders to satisfy, ICICI Bank could not enter this market aggressively unless it was convinced it could be done profitably. "At the ICICI Bank we were very clear we would not restrict this initiative to be a mere marginal experiment. We decided we wanted to actually develop a model that not only is scalable, but is low-cost and commercially viable."[15] Thus, the management of ICICI entered this market fully convinced it could be a profit-making venture. With this market in mind, ICICI outlined three strategic goals: to increase banking penetration in rural areas through innovative ways of defining distribution points, to prepare rather than react to the increasingly important rural market, and to support the downtrodden as a good corporate citizen.[16] All these goals were aimed toward enabling the poorest of the poor to "become active and informed participants in socioeconomic processes as opposed to passive observers."[17]

ICICI was well-situated to take the lead in rural banking as a universal bank providing a wide range of banking services that was technologically driven. For example, ICICI was the first bank in India to launch a Web site (1996), the first bank to launch Internet banking (1997), the first bank to launch online bill payment (1999), and the only bank in India with more than 1 million online customers. ICICI's channel usage reflects this technological approach toward banking (see Figure 2).

"If you are going to gain sustainable competitive edge, you have to leverage technology in a big way. Our aim was to move from physical branch banking to virtual banking. Block by block we slowly built up a clicks-and-mortar strategy."[18] This progressive and imaginative use of technology was a vital key to ICICI's ability to serve the BOP profitably.

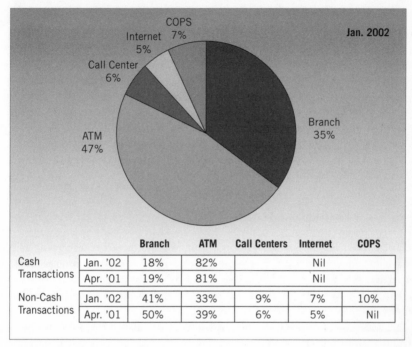

		Branch	ATM	Call Centers	Internet	COPS
Cash Transactions	Jan. '02	18%	82%		Nil	
	Apr. '01	19%	81%		Nil	
Non-Cash Transactions	Jan. '02	41%	33%	9%	7%	10%
	Apr. '01	50%	39%	6%	5%	Nil

Figure 2 ICICI's channel usage. *Source:* http://r0.unctad.org/ecommerce/event_docs/monterey/mor-icici-india-EFfD.ppt.

ICICI also was a new entrant to retail banking. ICICI started retail banking under a new and changing regulatory regime that was decidedly more market-based than before. As a new player in this environment, ICICI was not burdened with legacy thinking and could attack the issue with fresh ideas. Additionally, ICICI was not hampered with a large physical branch network, and thus was well-positioned to introduce low-cost banking channels. For comparison, the State Bank of India, one of the oldest and largest banks in the country, had to financially support a network of more than 13,000 branches.[19]

As ICICI oriented the banking operations toward the BOP (see Figure 3), it began looking at entering the microfinance field because there certainly was and still is a vast unmet demand for credit in rural areas. "In rural areas, only one million households have received access to microcredit from MFIs."[20] Yet the competitive situation was relatively crowded. "India currently boasts more than 500 microfinance institutions."[21] However, the incumbents in this space were all struggling to turn profits because they were used to working as donor-funded and supported institutions. This dependence often affects scalability and sustainability. Additionally, these MFIs were experiencing low savings to credit ratios, liquidity problems, high capacity-building costs and general

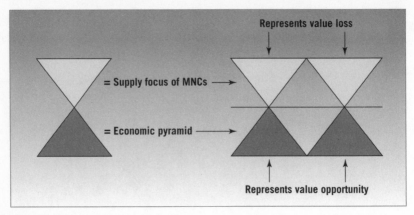

Figure 3   Value opportunity and value loss.

inefficiencies. ICICI saw a real opportunity in this area because many of the problems and risks with microfinance could be alleviated by the capital, expertise, scale, and reach of a major bank. By entering the microfinance field, ICICI has taken on the role of social mobilization as well as financial intermediation.

In addition to looking at microfinance, ICICI also wanted to increase its banking presence in rural areas. To do this, the bank needed to rapidly proliferate its points-of-presence or distribution points. However, the traditional brick-and-mortar approach to expansion is prohibitively expensive given the vast and varied landscape of India. Additionally, it is very difficult to staff rural branches with competent bankers either because educated urbanites do not want to live in these areas or there is a paucity of qualified locals. To minimize the costs associated with expanding rapidly and to gain qualified rural staff, ICICI decided to partner with NGOs and MFIs currently in the field. By "piggybacking" on the established network of these rural-oriented players, ICICI can gain knowledge about the market they intend to serve and eventually increase its banking presence. ICICI has combined the social mobilization strength of NGOs and MFIs with the financial strength of the bank.

ICICI has thus identified two innovative models toward serving the BOP:

1. The *direct access, bank-led model*, which was catalyzed by the merger with the rural banking institution, Bank of Madura, utilizes the power of ICICI to promote and grow SHGs and to dramatically increase the scope and scale of rural savings and lending.
2. The *indirect channels partnership model* leverages the relationships, knowledge, and rural network of organizations in the field to avoid the costly brick-and-mortar expansion process and thus helps efficiently cultivate ICICI's banking presence.

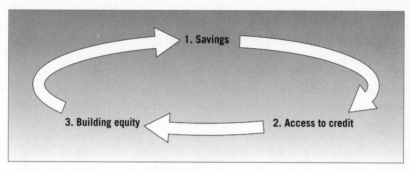

Figure 4   Financial cycle in the developing world.

These models are aimed at "facilitating the participation of the poor in the larger economy," which can "lead to the creation of a virtuous demand-led growth cycle."[22] ICICI is implementing these models to serve the BOP throughout their financial lifecycle (see Figure 4).

The Indian banking system has three distinct tiers. The first tier, where ICICI competes, consists of commercial banks, of which there are approximately 80. In the next tier are regional rural banks, which operate in approximately 200 rural command areas. The last tier consists of cooperative and special-purpose rural banks. There are more than 350 central cooperative banks, 20 land development banks, and a number of primary agricultural credit societies.[23] India certainly has an extensive and wide-reaching banking system. Yet "despite fairly broad banking coverage nationwide, the financial system remains inaccessible to the poorest people in India."[24]

ICICI is now the second-largest bank in India with total assets of about 1 trillion rupees (approximately US$22 billion). With heavy competition among both domestic (State Bank of India, HDFC, Canara Bank) and international banks (HSBC, Standard Chartered, Citibank) for the assets of the urban Indian elite, ICICI executives see the rural hinterlands as the true engine of growth in India and are positioning the bank, through increased distribution points, to be the pre-eminent banking presence in those areas.

Direct Access, Bank-Led Model

The direct access, bank-led model is one of the approaches ICICI is taking toward serving the BOP. This model is aimed at proliferating the points of presence of ICICI through the creation of savings programs for and provision of direct microloans to SHGs. The purchase of the Bank of Madura truly catalyzed this model. Then, ICICI has added a number of innovative layers to what the Bank of Madura had already implemented.

History of the Bank of Madura:
The Rural Development Initiative

The Bank of Madura, established in 1943, was one of the premier private-sector banks. However, the least profitable area for the bank was its presence in the rural sector, mostly in the southern Indian state of Tamil Nadu. Presence in the rural sector was important to the RBI, and various stipulations were enforced to ensure banks followed this directive. The government required a certain number of employees, guards, and support personnel to operate in addition to scheduled audits to monitor activity and performance. The overhead and the administrative costs were too high given the low level of banking activity per branch.

Under the leadership of Dr. K. M. Thiagarajan, who assumed the position of Chairman in 1993, the Bank of Madura reoriented its focus toward increasing deposits and consolidating unprofitable branches. The Bank of Madura escaped many of the waves of reform and liberalization due to its small size, which allowed the bank much more flexibility to act without costly bureaucratic impediments. Of its 270 brick-and-mortar branches, approximately one-third were located in rural areas (a branch was considered rural when it was located within a village surrounded by a cluster of hamlets with a population of 1,000 to 3,000 people). To reduce the unprofitable operations, 103 rural branches were reduced to 77. Also, the Bank of Madura became the most automated old private-sector bank in the country by implementing a number of technological improvements, which allowed the bank to eliminate overhead and increase the customer base. With the branch consolidation and technological changes, Bank of Madura deposits had increased to 37 million rupees (US$740,000); the bank was showing profits just prior to the merger with ICICI Bank in 2001. Rural branches tended to be neglected. It was difficult to attract talented, educated, and motivated personnel. Managers were incredibly reluctant to move to these rural areas because of the poor lifestyle. Originally, tenure of about two years in a rural branch became part of the career track for a manager eligible for promotion. Even with the incentive of eventual promotion, Bank of Madura found it difficult to attract managers.

The Bank of Madura's executive team began to realize there were many more issues than just the low level of economic activity in these rural areas that prevented the branches from reaching profitability and extending their presence in the communities. The low level of economic activity was in fact misleading. The informal and semiformal money-lending sectors were incredibly active and used by many families in the villages, especially in southern India where people inherently believed in implicit contracts. Although the high interest rates precluded the possibility of true economic development for the recipients, the informal and semiformal sectors were well-established and formidable. In addition, the banks had difficulty establishing a trusting relationship with the communities and stimulating new economic activity. Dr. Thiagarajan felt that to increase profitability in these rural branches, the banks would first have to establish a reputation of trustworthiness and credibility to stimulate more economic activity. Integral to this mission was being able to attract personnel who had an interest in working with the economically impoverished, not only in their financial standing but also with issues of education, health, civil, and social rights.

Thiagarajan became familiar with the Grameen Bank model started in Bangladesh, providing small loans to clients below the poverty line. Executives at the Bank of Madura felt the efforts in Bangladesh could be replicated in India. In 1995, they developed and implemented the Rural Development Initiative, focused on economic empowerment of the poor in rural areas. To begin, they had to find the right people. Word spread quickly throughout the organization of the new and prestigious program. Thiagarajan reversed the negative perception of the rural managerial positions by creating a lengthy interview process for what was previously deemed a marginal job. Applicants were turned down if they expressed the slightest hesitation about the demands of the job or the time window the post might require. In addition, existing personnel in the rural branches were reviewed, and those who did not match the profile were weeded out. The applicants had to have the desire to help the poor and become personally involved with their economic development.

The interview process produced a team of 325 individuals and a core executive team of 15. The bank also initiated a new policy that stipulated that any individual working in the rural sector could request a transfer at any time. This was a perk for the rural field agents and added to the allure of the position. Next the team had to learn the intricacies of microfinance and how to make it successful. It began a serious study of microfinance with experts around the country, because many NGOs and academics were already active in this area in India.

After a number of consultations with outside experts, the core team held its own two-day retreat and decided on the strategic and organizational directions the bank would take next. Some limits the program was placed under were that there were to be no additional expenditures, including new staff. The operational costs were to remain the same. Over the course of the retreat, the team had decided that the clients, bank, and program would be better served with its own unique program. Of course, the team members drew on many important lessons they had seen in the field from other players; however, with the financial backing of the savings institution they represented, they saw a new opportunity for themselves. The essential strategic design of their program was to form, train, and initiate small groups of women into formal savings, banking, and lending. The vehicle conceived for this was the SHG. The Bank of Madura's conception of the SHG was as follows:

1. A group of 20 women from the same village whose individual annual incomes placed them below the poverty line. Multiple groups could be formed in the same village.

2. The members did not participate, as of yet, in the formal banking sector.

3. Leaders should be selected from within the group to bear responsibility for collecting the savings, keeping the accounts, and running the monthly meetings.

4. On formation of the group, the bank will undertake to educate these women with the basic concepts of banking and encourage them to begin a savings program for themselves, thereby creating new customers for the bank.

5. After one year of training and monitoring the regularity of meetings, loans were dispersed to the group in the average size of 10,000 rupees (US$200) per member. This was a considerable loan, above the amount normally given for consumption purposes, to begin a small business or expand an existing operation in agriculture, for instance.

6. The loans would be given based on need, not in ratio to existing savings deposits.

The Bank of Madura's SHG vehicle allowed for many other positive intangible changes in the women's self-esteem and confidence to decide on and influence events in their own homes and villages. The maturation of an SHG followed the general pattern shown in Figure 5.

At the time of the merger in 2000, there were 1,200 SHGs formed; a social vehicle had been created with considerable power. Women participating in the SHGs found themselves becoming more articulate, more confident, and empowered. The focus of the SHG movement was on the maturation of the

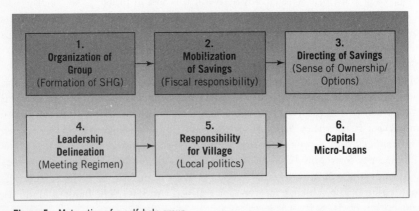

Figure 5 Maturation of a self-help group.

individual and thus the group as a whole by enforcing a strict meeting schedule and savings regimen. Ultimately, federations were formed, representing large numbers of SHGs that included thousands of members. The rapid spread was due in part to the training structure the Bank of Madura provided.

The greatest difficulties the SHG program would have to face first were intangible. How would a bank raise the confidence and motivation of a group of women without familial relation, without incentive to trust one another, and without any formal participation in the financial sector? Further, there was a stigma attached to formal banking as an untrustworthy institution. This mistrust was based on prior experiences some of the women had with bank loan officers, who demanded bribes and wrapped the entire savings-and-loan process in obscurity to confuse the locals.

The potential candidates for the SHGs, of course, understood their needs very well but had not been actively seeking alternatives. The answer to developing the group dynamic lay in the composition of the groups, so that a feeling of mutual dependence was immediately created, not merely financial but also psychological. Additionally, the framework that created a joint guarantee for the loan of all the members was also vital. This forced a rapid development of interaction between women who formerly would not have had any or very little reason to engage with one another. Eventually, a small number of groups began forming and the members soon felt the benefits initially in the form of increased confidence, the mutual benefit of cooperation, and other externalities of a diverse and established support network. Concepts of citizenship were developed where members began to recognize their duty to the communal setting in which they played a role. With the passing of time, established groups and their most proactive members were trained to form new groups, which spread the SHG movement at an accelerating pace.

To date, there have been many instances of total transformation, not only of the individual's self-confidence, but also of village politics, ethics, and social norms. The SHG units began to develop a fierce identity both for themselves and within the context of the larger SHG network. Members of the SHGs adopted a certain color and style sari to demonstrate their solidarity. The hustle and bustle at the local bank offices has become a flurry of blue, maroon, and yellow robes as the women go about their daily business. Songs and ceremonies have emerged, celebrating the SHG unit. These songs are offered at the commencement of each meeting to bring the members together in thought and act.

Merger with Bank of Madura

As they entered the new millennium, ICICI's executive team identified three areas as the next sectors of growth: international, urban retail, and rural retail. With the rural sector targeted as an important driver of growth, Executive

Director of Retail Banking Chanda Kochhar began looking for a suitable partner to help avoid the time and cost of Greenfield expansion. They identified the Bank of Madura as a profitable, well-capitalized, private-sector commercial bank in operation for 57 years. The main advantages for ICICI were the addition of 1.2 million customers and the Bank of Madura's rural branch network. The Bank of Madura's most significant presence was in the southern states, with 77 branches in the rural area of Tamil Nadu. The Bank of Madura was especially strong in small- and medium-sized corporate banking, which would help ICICI expand its corporate business. An additional strength was the Bank of Madura's microfinance initiative. ICICI made it clear it intended to aggressively develop this initiative. P. H. Ravikumar, Senior Executive Vice President of ICICI Bank, stated that in "the area of micro-credit lending they also have a strong presence, especially in those areas where the lending is to self-help groups involved with handicrafts, weaving, etc. We will evaluate the micro-credit areas and wherever possible will try to grow them."[25] The merger was approved on March 10, 2001, by the RBI. With the merger, ICICI Bank Limited became one of India's largest private-sector banks with total deposits of Rs. 13,460 crores. After the merger, ICICI became the most visible bank in the state of Tamil Nadu with activity in 23 of the 28 districts.

Scaling SHGs

When ICICI inherited the Rural Development Initiative from the Bank of Madura, the SHG program was still not financially sustainable. To reach profitability, the number of SHGs had to expand exponentially without increasing ICICI's costs of managing these groups. ICICI developed a simple three-tier system. Under this system, the highest level was a bank employee called a *project manager*. The project manager oversaw the activities of six *coordinators*, approved loan applications for the area manager, and helped with the development of the SHGs. The coordinator was herself an SHG member who had a contractual relationship with the bank. She was overlooking the actions of six *promoters*. The promoters' primary responsibility was the formation of new groups. Within a year of election to promoter, the woman then becomes a *social service consultant* (SSC) and must form 20 groups within 12 months. If the groups are formed, she is financially compensated by the bank and becomes part of the pyramid structure of creating and monitoring the SHGs.

Under the ICICI model, SHGs form and expand in a pyramid structure. In early 2001, at the time of the merger, there were 1,200 SHGs that had been formed under the Bank of Madura structure. By March 2003, more than 8,000 SHGs had been formed. The acceleration and success of the program depended on the training and empowerment of the women participating in the existing SHGs. At a certain degree of maturity, existing members who have demonstrated leadership ability are trained by the bank to become SSCs. The SSC's primary responsibility is to form new SHGs in neighboring villages and thus expand the SHG network. ICICI provides a small financial incentive of 100 rupees for each new group formed, and the SSCs must fulfill certain quotas to retain their status. The SSC must travel to villages within a 15-kilometer radius and form five new groups within two months and 20 groups within 12 months. ICICI has set strict guidelines for the member formation:

- All members are from the same village.
- They are all married to ensure there is a family that receives the benefits as well.
- Members are between the ages of 20 and 50.
- SHGs must focus on the illiterate and those existing below the poverty line.

NABARD created a list of questions that determine the poverty level of a certain family and tries to assess its eligibility for SHG participation:

- Is there only one source of income for the family?
- Are there any permanently ill members of the family?
- Do you regularly borrow from money lenders?
- How far is your drinking water source?
- Do you belong to a scheduled caste or scheduled tribe?[26]

If they answer "yes" to three or four of the questions, they are considered good candidates for the SHG. After a series of visits with multiple families, plans for group formation begin. The most successful groups have members who share some sort of similarity, whether they are from the same caste or have had a similar experience of poverty. Before the first SHG meeting, the SSC meets again with the village elders and gets their permission to work on a more significant level with the village to aid its development.

NABARD estimates that the process of group formation can take five to six months. In the first few meetings, it is not unusual for members to leave and new members to arrive. Once a core set of members has been established, a leader must be selected along with two animators. These three women are agreed on by all members and will share in the duties of running the group and keeping the accounts. The animators keep the minutes book, which details the proceedings of the meetings, the savings and loan register, the weekly register, and the members' passbooks. Proper documentation of the activities, especially of the internal lending, will help the approval process from the bank. The preliminary meetings also include Basic Awareness Training (BAT) given by an

SSC, coordinator, or project manager. The SHG also must agree on the meeting times, penalties for missed meetings, and repayment habits.

The motto of the SHG becomes "Savings first, credit later." The members are taught that the savings habit is crucial to their rise out of poverty by reducing their vulnerability to consumption and medical emergencies. Once the group has gone through training and begins to gather its own momentum, the SSC will leave to go form new groups, yet will still be responsible for a certain degree of monitoring and assistance in training. After the SSC has formed 20 groups, she will have earned 2,000 rupees (US$40) from ICICI Bank and will then become a promoter. During this process, she will have reported her activities to the coordinator, who is responsible for multiple SSCs.

In the SHG hierarchy, a coordinator overlooks the activities of six SSCs or promoters who have fulfilled their quota of forming 20 groups within one year. Similar to the SSCs, the promoters are selected on the basis of talent and skill. With each promoter in charge of 20 groups, the coordinators are overlooking the activities of 120 groups. ICICI provides them with an annual salary of 2,400 rupees (US$48) for the 120 groups or some proportional piece thereof, depending on how many are formed. The coordinators and the promoters work closely with the bank personnel who support their efforts. They are not considered official employees of the bank but rather like contracted agents that perform a very particular function. These women have passed through various levels of election and are considered to be the most talented and motivated members. They, of course, began as members within a particular SHG and continue with their duties to that original vehicle. Within the official hierarchy of ICICI, there are managerial positions that support the efforts of the SHGs and their various executives (see Figure 6).

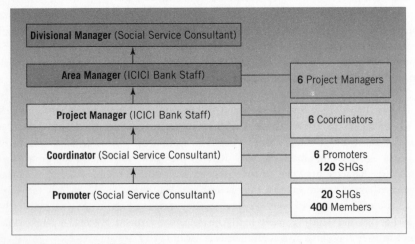

Figure 6   Structure for SHG promotion.

Learning to be Financially Smart

The SHG process is oriented toward building new disciplines and capabilities. Collective responsibility and group pressure act as social collateral. Toward this end, the process has three essential steps:

1. Learn to save.
2. Learn to lend what you have saved.
3. Learn to borrow responsibly.

Beginning with the first monthly meeting, each member must bring 50 rupees (US$1) to each meeting to contribute to a joint savings account with the other members. The leader and representatives are responsible for collecting this money and opening up the savings account for the group. Instructions have been issued by the RBI to all commercial banks to allow registered and unregistered SHGs to open savings accounts in their group's name. It is imperative that each woman contributes and participates each month. This begins to build the momentum of savings that ICICI believes is essential for greater economic independence.

After six months, they have amassed 6,000 rupees (US$120) plus interest. At this point, the idea that they are contributing to something that is able to expand beyond their individual means is evident. The savings are converted into a fund. The group can access this fund and use it for emergency lending to an individual within the group. This marks the first step in a transition into formal lending and a departure from the dependence on the local money lender. Emergency lending can be defined as immediate payment of a medical emergency, short-term borrowing for consumption purposes, or other health reasons. This emergency loan is very short term, and the women pay an interest rate of 24 percent per annum to the account. The members know, even if they have little or no education, that this is desirable compared to dealing with money lenders. They compare the internal rate of the SHGs with the informal rate, which can be as high as 10 percent a day.

Often, monthly meetings take on a completely different agenda. Here, the activity revolves around the needs of the village and other concerns of women. In Tamil Nadu, water availability and purification, transportation, and electricity were the most highly debated topics. The SHG allows women to stand together as thousands, and local politicians take them very seriously . Chanda Kochhar, the Executive Director of Retail Banking at ICICI, related stories of women who rarely stepped out of their homes before joining the SHG. Through working with their peers, they gained such a degree of confidence and esteem that they were debating with local politicians on such issues as the construction of a dam and the digging of a well. The group also focuses on literacy training.

One year after formation of the SHG, the group is ready to submit a loan proposal to the bank manager. The proposal process is relatively paper-intense. There are certain key supportive documents in the process, including loan agreements signed by each member of the SHG, an updated family survey, a No Due certificate that guarantees that there are no outstanding loans owed by any member, and a Letter of Sanction approved by the area manager. The size of the total loan to the SHG is 250,000 rupees (US$5,000) with a distribution of 12,500 rupees (US$250) to each member. Activities that can be funded with this amount would include purchase of livestock, leasing of land for agricultural purposes, the opening of a small tea shop, candle manufacturing, and the purchase of a home. These loans are noncollateralized. The savings account cannot be held as collateral against the loan because the bank wants to continue encouraging the internal lending process. However, the SHG as a whole is responsible for each member's loan, which builds a strong degree of social collateral. This social collateral has proved able enough to achieve a repayment rate of 99.99 percent, making the rural sector one of the most credit-worthy in the banking industry. To fulfill the repayment terms, each member must pay 400 rupees (US$8) to the bank for 43 months, an effective annual interest rate of 18 percent. Within India this is higher than most home loans, which are in the area of 9 percent, and other commercial lending at 12 percent. ICICI charges this rate to cover the training costs and salaries of the promoters and coordinators who make this operation sustainable.

The NABARD journal published for bank managers described the steps to successfully deal with the SHGs from the institution's perspective.[27] An assessment by the bank is encouraged. NABARD has assembled several checklists that correlate with high repayment rates and characteristics of the SHGs. These include the following:

- Is the group size between 15 and 20 members?
- Are all members considered very poor?
- Was there a fixed amount of savings collected each month?
- Is there more than 20 percent literacy?
- Have they used their savings for internal lending purposes?
- Have the members kept a high level of attendance?

If the SHG meets a certain number of these criteria, the loan officer is instructed to grant the loan immediately. If the SHG is lacking in many areas, the loan application is suspended, and the group is granted four to six months to improve its operation. The officer is also encouraged to examine the books of the SHG and determine their accuracy and appropriate depth of content. Although the accounts are relatively small, these small savings of many SHGs grow into valuable large accounts. Cost savings occur because, although the savings account and loan represents 20 people, only the three elected officers interact directly with the bank officers, saving time and labor of the bank. In addition, because there is internal monitoring for repayment, the bank incurs very little cost in appraisal and monitoring of the loan. Further, the bank's reputation increases its social base of recognition within the village and attracts more business within other sectors.

In a continuation of the first monthly meetings, individual members report progress on the various business enterprises to the group. The members also bring their personal monthly loan payment. These payments are collected by the animators, recorded in each member's passbook, and brought to the bank the next business day. If a member misses a payment, a penalty is assessed by the SHG, which is added to the shared savings account. If the first round of lending is successful, the SHGs can approach the bank for a second round with an increased credit line of 15,000 rupees (US$300) per member.

Far from just creating a financial partnership with the women involved with the SHGs, ICICI Bank also sponsors additional activities and annual events that celebrate the progress of their direct access, bank-led model. A yearly celebration called Women's Day is held each spring. Here, many SHGs participate in singing and sporting activities, representing their groups with their dedicated saris and original songs. ICICI awards 5,000 rupees (US$100) to the group with the highest literacy rate. The bank also has partnered with the Aravind Eye Hospital to hold medical eye clinics for cataract surgery. The bank pays the traveling expenses of the surgeons and their staff, and Aravind performs the necessary surgeries free of charge for the villagers. To date, ICICI has been involved with 70 eye clinics, and Aravind doctors have tested 68,000 villagers and performed 4,000 surgeries. Veterinary camps also have been conducted.

In addition to the hierarchical structure of the coordinators, promoters, and SHGs, there have been additional affiliations formed to monitor the growing complexity of lending, economic progress, and social development. The federation of the joint meeting committees (JMCs) represent tens of thousands of women and is chiefly responsible for the handling of the emergency funds. Each single JMC is run by three female officers and is comprised of 20 SHGs from 10 to 20 villages within the same area. These three women meet once every three months to monitor the internal lending activities of the 200 to 400 women. This internal fund is created by each member contributing 10 rupees (US$.20) and is available as petty cash even when the bank is closed. The loan is typically used for emergency medical purposes. The size of the loan must not exceed 300 rupees (US$6). Terms of the loan are a monthly interest rate of 2 percent and a short-term length of about 10 days. If payment is late, there is a 1-rupee (US$.02) daily penalty for every 100 rupees (US$2) borrowed. The JMC also is responsible for the creation of and maintenance of an information booth erected in one of the central villages. The information booth displays events

Table 2 Total SHG and WFS Deposits

Deposits of the SHGs at the Business as of 01/01/2003 (thousands of rupees)	
Savings Bank	26750
Recurring Deposit	7628
Fixed Deposit	17582

Deposit in Women Dev. Trust at Achampathu Br. (Welfare Fund)	
Savings Bank	649
Recurring Deposit	15429
Fixed Deposit	68038

such as births and deaths in the villages and world news. The booth costs 1,000 rupees (US$20) to create and is also monitored in part by the promoter and coordinator assigned to that area. The executive officers also report on the progress and state of the JMC to the area coordinator and project manager.

Rural India continues to demonstrate a low life expectancy of 63 years by developed nations' standards. To combat the uncertainty in this situation and protect the respective members of the group, SHGs have become sophisticated to the point of developing their own welfare fund scheme (WFS) as a form of life insurance. Its purpose is to cover the remaining principal of an outstanding loan on the death of a member and to help the family pay for the funeral expenses. The SHG as a single entity becomes eligible for the WFS after 11 months of formation and must decide to participate as a whole. Each member contributes 310 rupees (US$6.20) to a common fund held in a fixed deposit account at ICICI. Currently, the aggregate of WFSs represents 2,873 SHGs with more than 54,000 members and 15.7 million rupees (US$314,000) in deposits (see Table 2). The interest this account collects is paid to a member's family in case of death to assist with funeral arrangements and other adjustments. The WFS is run by seven elected trustees who oversee the application process. As of March 2003, they received 74 applications for disbursement from the WFS and paid out more than 510,000 rupees (US$10,200).

ICICI's unique approach has been successful in accelerating the growth of the SHGs in the Tamil Nadu area as seen in Figure 7. ICICI's mission is to extend this program to other needy areas of India and reinterpret microfinance in a wider context to include savings, insurance, banking services, and derivatives. "The momentum of the SHG movement in the country really needs to be accelerated in order to bring about lasting changes in the rural economy and the lives of the poor."[28]

Many bank loans are used for agricultural purposes. In one instance that illustrates the impact of a loan to enable an agricultural practice, Ms. Pundiselvi in the Nahramalaiphur village used the loan to lease a small parcel of land to

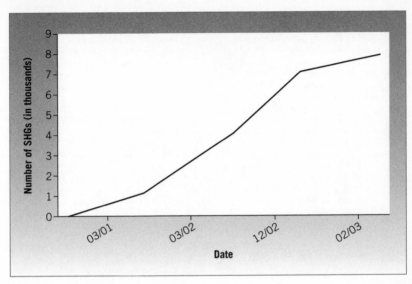

Figure 7 Growth of SHGs under ICICI Bank.

raise chilis for cooking and flowers for decorative purposes. The cost of the land was 10,000 rupees (US$200) for the season, and the seed inputs cost a few thousand rupees. Currently, Ms. Pundiselvi has paid back 7,000 rupees (US$140) or 70 percent of the loan due to the produce generated from her land. In the same village, Ms. Saraswathi owned and operated a small grocery shop with a small inventory and limited selection of goods. With the 10,000-rupee (US$200) loan, she expanded her existing shop and now enjoys an increased monthly income. Ms. Saraswathi has never missed a monthly payment and has paid back 6,000 rupees (US$120) or 60 percent of her loan. One enterprising woman pooled the money from the loan with other family assets and dug a new well for her village. She charges other farmers and villagers 25 rupees (US$.50) per hour to pump water for irrigation purposes. The irrigation system the pump fed also increased the yield of her own nearby fields.

The tangible impacts on asset value of the household, income development, working days, and the share of the loan amount by a particular agency have been carefully monitored and measured by NABARD. In a comprehensive study released in 2002, NABARD studied the effects of SHGs and bank linkages of more than 560 member households belonging to 220 SHGs across 11 states. The report favors the view that microlending has significant positive impact on income levels and income-generating activities. It also reports that the involvement of the members in SHG activities has contributed to their self-confidence and communication skills. Figure 8 includes several charts assembled by NABARD that speak to these points.

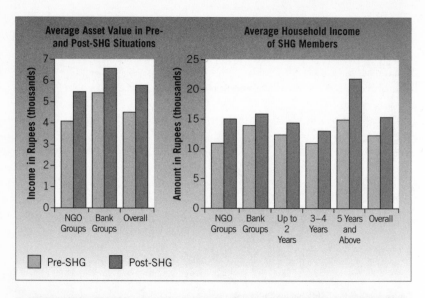

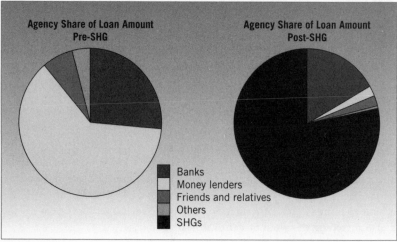

Figure 8   Benefits of self-help groups. *Source:* Badatya, K. C., & Puhazhendi, V. (2002). SHG-Bank linkage programme for rural India: An impact assessment. NABARD 27, 33, and 39.

ICICI's dedication to the SHG program has a dual inspiration. The first is that ICICI believes the rural sector will be the next area of growth for India and that the SHG movement, if properly scaled and managed, makes good business sense. The bank expands its customer base and receives new deposits while reducing the cost of single transactions with the use of the animators and SHG leaders. The second positive aspect of the SHG program comes from ICICI's sense of corporate social commitment to the development and enabling of the rural poor. The NABARD research concluded that SHG participation had significant impact on various aspects of confidence, communication, and decision-making. One of the most important objectives for the SHG program is to improve the assertiveness of the SHG members, which NABARD measured in a survey published in their series on microfinance.

The study conducted by NABARD questioned 115 members on their experience with certain psychological aspects and social ills associated with poverty, such as domestic violence, gambling, and drinking. They saw a noteworthy reduction in these social evils, as measured in Table 3. Other positive indicators of change in confidence, freedom of communication, and the woman's role in decision making for the household also showed considerable gain. "There have been cases where the ladies were not even stepping out of their houses. But today they have the confidence of not only sitting in groups but actually debating on some of the social and economic issues of the village: whether a dam should be constructed or not, whether water should be allowed, whether electricity should be allowed. That is the movement in the confidence levels we see."[29] In Table 3, the left column is the indicator of change. The numbered columns show the percentage of SHG members responding affirmatively to the psychological benefit.[30]

Table 3 Positive Effects of Self-Help Groups

Indicator of Change	Pre-SHG %	Post-SHG %
Self-confidence and self-worth		
Respondent exudes confidence	21	78
Can confidently meet financial crisis	33	85
Respectful treatment from family members	40	89
Comes out to help neighbors/others	51	95
Decision-making		
Joint decision-making on purchase of household assets	39	74
Makes joint decisions on social matters such as education of children and marriage	42	69
Communication skills		
Speaking out freely	23	65
Talks only if asked	40	9
Behavioral changes		
Protests drinking and gambling	37	81
Protests wife-beating by husbands	52	78
Domestic violence	67	49
Increased mobility	45	75

The impact of the ICICI microfinance program has been to fundamentally change the lives of the SHG members with long-lasting economic solutions while achieving break-even costs in the operation at its present scale. ICICI's plan is to continue the accelerated growth with the proliferation of its pyramid model and its three main constituents: the area manager, the coordinator, and the promoter.

Indirect Channels Partnership Model

"Our vision is to attain national outreach. To reach out to rural areas where we do not have branches, we have developed the partnership model. Our aim is to combine the social mobilization strength of NGOs and MFIs with the financial strength of the bank. The partnership model helps overcome the constraints faced by NGOs and MFIs in scaling up their activities."[31]

The indirect channel partnership model is another approach being taken by ICICI Bank in its effort to increase distribution points and to cost-effectively serve the BOP. The model looks to leverage the current infrastructure and relationships that microfinance institutions and NGOs have in place to deliver banking services to the rural poor. By piggybacking on this network, ICICI does not have to implement a costly brick-and-mortar expansion model. Also, ICICI can learn from these organizations, whose sole focus is to serve this customer class, thus minimizing their learning curve costs.

Microfinance Institutions

ICICI originally began the indirect channel partnership model in a catalytic role. The bank began giving grants and loans to MFIs to spur their credit activities to the rural poor. However, the role as a donor organization and passive lender did not truly fit into ICICI's goal to be a leader in rural banking. Thus, ICICI created a unique lending scheme that attempts to create a more sustainable economic situation for these MFIs and encourages a more commercial approach. "The partnership model essentially is looking at microfinance as a viable business activity, but with the financial institution playing the catalytic role of providing cash flow funding for the initial three years to the service provider."[32] ICICI now provides these MFIs with a line of credit to meet their cash flow deficit for three years. In the fourth year, the MFI will then begin to repay the loan within two to three years. Additionally, ICICI wanted to go further by actively developing rural programs with their partners in the field, making equity investments in these partners, creating technologies that would help penetrate the rural areas, and utilizing their corporate network to funnel resources toward the rural effort.

The first steps in this indirect channel partnership model were taken with the DHAN Foundation (Development of Humane Action) in Karnataka, PRADAN (Professional Assistance for Development Action) in Jharkhand, and CASHPOR (Credit and Savings for the Hardcore Poor) in Uttar Pradesh. ICICI worked with the DHAN Foundation, a regional NGO that assists the poor in microcredit, in researching the idea of kiosks and in looking at "rural information and communication technology (ICT) projects that seek to bring emerging technologies like low-cost computing and Internet access to rural households."[33] ICICI also partnered with PRADAN to take advantage of their deep knowledge of SHGs. ICICI provided loans to PRADAN so they could expand their SHG lending and, in the process, learned about setting up women's savings and credit groups. CASHPOR is an association of Grameen Bank Replications in Asia, with SHARE being the CASHPOR representative in India. ICICI partnered with CASHPOR and SHARE, in the form of an equity investment, to catalyze the MFI movement in India and to learn from the innovative Grameen model. Each partnership is designed to build on the unique strengths of each organization and on the context in which they are working.

Rural Kiosks

ICICI has now set up additional partnerships with EID Parry, n-Logue, ITC e-Choupal, and BASIX to take advantage of the rural kiosk network they each have established. Each partnership is designed to build on the unique strengths of each organization and to truly leverage their experience and relationships. These partner organizations receive in return the backing of the second-largest bank in India to help expand their kiosk network. ICICI envisions setting up many more partnerships with MFIs and NGOs that have the expertise and passion for serving the rural poor.

Future Initiatives

Although ICICI has already made a significant impact in providing credit to the BOP, their effort is still in its nascent stages. ICICI is constantly striving to cost-efficiently serve this customer class by developing innovative technologies and novel distribution models. With new initiatives such as rain insurance, venture capital, mobile ATMs, and derivatives, ICICI is always testing, rolling out, and then scaling up innovative ways to profitably serve the BOP.

The rural ATM machine, to be placed in the kiosks, is a simplified version of a regular ATM. With a simple interface and multiple languages, the rural ATM will be accessible by all and will be the conduit through which ICICI delivers banking services to the remote Indian countryside. It is currently in development in the lab of Dr. Ashok Jhunjhunwala and is expected to cost a mere 3,000 rupees or US$600 versus the 80,000 rupees or US$16,000 that it costs for a normal ATM machine. As stated earlier, ICICI envisions placing this rural ATM in the kiosks their partners have already implemented.

ICICI also is investigating the possibility of building a mobile ATM. The ATM machine would be installed in an ICICI-branded truck that would circulate through a number of villages on a specified, predetermined route. Rural villagers would know when the ATM was coming to their village and would be able to take care of their banking needs on that day. With the mobile ATM, ICICI could serve a number of villages with limited capital outlay.

ICICI is constantly investigating other ways to proliferate their banking presence. In fact, one of the key challenges for the future is how to create more convenient and low-cost access points for rural customers. Some ideas include partnering with the Indian postal service to place ATMs within their extensive infrastructure and integrating ATMs with vending machines.

ICICI is also researching the possibility of implementing a smart-card-based payment system to eliminate the costs associated with cash handling. "The two key challenges that must be overcome to extend banking to the rural and poor population are elimination/reduction of cash handling and innovation of low-cost delivery channels."[34] Smart cards effectively harness the technology advances of the new economy and apply it to the old economy. "By combining the features of a handy credit/debit card with the advantages of . . . storage capacity . . . the smart card provides secure identification, a store of value and an ability to function off line while maintaining an audit trail of all the transactions."[35] Smart cards were launched in October 2000 by ICICI at the Infosys Campus in Bangalore and at Manipal Academy of Higher Education (MAHE) to create a cashless economy.

However, many problems exist with smart cards, such as high cost and lack of technological infrastructure for widespread adoption. The high cost is especially amplified at the rural level. However, ICICI is watching closely what BASIX is doing currently with smart card technology to see if it is cost-effective and viable. Figure 9 shows how the smart card system would work with Farmer Service Centers or MFIs.

Insurance is another product ICICI Bank is investigating for the poor. The high probability of being exposed to risk and thus the vulnerability of the poor leads ICICI to believe that insurance is a crucial product that the BOP will pay for. "Vulnerability is predominantly economic."[36] By utilizing insurance to manage risk and "..counter structural, market and life-cycle related risks,"[37] ICICI can help to create more of a stable life for the poor. Therefore, ICICI Bank is looking at creating an insurance product that would pool, price, and trade the risks of the poor. One unique product in this class is rain insurance, which would allow farmers to collect money during droughts and protect them from fluctuations in the weather.

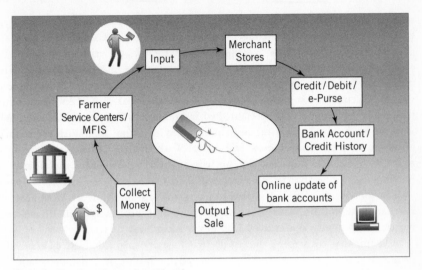

Figure 9 How the smart card would work.

ICICI Bank is also looking at venture capital to share in the risk with the enterprising poor in ventures with the possibility of high return. To break the poor out of the cycle of credit, ICICI envisions implementing a venture capital model that would invest in promising businesses and would hopefully bring "investors' interest—and with it the promise of professional management—to the management of the enterprise."[38] Venture capital would "enable the poor to invest in long-term assets."[39] This model would spur economic activity and tap into the creative minds of the BOP.

Derivatives are another instrument that ICICI is looking at for the poor. Agricultural crops are a perfect underlying asset on which a derivative could be structured. "The principles of a derivative contract appear to have relevance in the context of commodity markets and indices based on weather and other variables that have a bearing on the livelihoods of the poor."[40] In fact, many rural villagers already engage in informal derivative deals by buying and selling crop futures. ICICI is looking at formalizing and institutionalizing this process.

Conclusion

ICICI has made profitable inroads into serving the BOP. "Banking with the poor has undergone a paradigm shift. It is no longer viewed as a mere social obligation. It is financially viable as well."[41] ICICI's efforts at growing the microfinance model and of partnering with MFIs and NGOs in the field have been successful. As part of the bank-led model, ICICI has increased the number of SHGs from around 1,500 to more than 8,000 within the two years since their purchase of the Bank of Madura. Through this model, ICICI has utilized its creative thinking to create a strong growth model and utilized its financial expertise to fashion a model that is economically viable. Additionally, ICICI has created an innovative method of mobilizing rural savings that also acts as a great risk-mitigating factor when eventually providing credit. ICICI's partnership model has led to fruitful partnerships with more than 10 major NGOs and MFIs who all have strong physical presence within the rural areas. This model is poised to take off as the kiosks proliferate. With that said, there is much work to be done. ICICI, however, has positioned itself as a pioneer and leader in looking at creative approaches to serving the BOP.

The innovation that ICICI is exhibiting toward the BOP has a number of ancillary benefits. By focusing on serving the BOP profitably, ICICI developed radical technologies and created whole new strategies.

Additionally, by serving the BOP, ICICI has positioned itself as a socially conscious corporate citizen. This is looked on highly by customers and by investors in the stock market. Such a position also helps ICICI's bargaining power with the Reserve Bank of India and other government institutions.

Endnotes

1. Interview with Chanda Kochhar, Executive Director of ICICI Bank, March 27, 2003.

2. *http://www.icicisocialinitiatives.org.*

3. Bhatt, Ela. National workshop, Microfinance for Infrastructure: Recent Experiences, p. 9. August 31, 2000.

4. Duggal, Bikram, and Singhal, Amit. 2002. *Extending banking to the poor in India.* ICICI Social Initiatives Group, p. 12.

5. *http://www.rbi.org.in/personalised/personalisation.asp?filename=rbiprofile.html&secid=.*

6. Master Circular on Branch Licensing, Reserve Bank of India. *http://www.rbi.org.in/index.dll/14?opensection?fromdate=&todate=&s1secid=1001&s2sec id=1001&storyno=0&archivemode=0.*

7. Bhatt, Ela. National workshop, Microfinance for Infrastructure: Recent Experiences, p. 4. August 31, 2000.

8. *http://www.rbi.org.in/index.dll/18636?OpenStory?fromdate=11/22/02&todate= 11/22/02&s1secid=0&s2secid=0&secid=.*

9. Sriram, M. S., and Upadhyayuala, Rajesh S. *The Transformation of Microfinance in India: Experiences, Options and Outure*, p. 5. Indian Institute of Management. Ahmedabadi, Research and Publication Dept. December 1, 2002.

10. Interview with K. V. Kamath, CEO/ Managing Director of ICICI Bank, March 27, 2003.

11. Interview with Chanda Kochhar, Executive Director of ICICI Bank, March 27, 2003.

12. Duggal & Singhal, op. cit., p. 2.

13. Ibid., p. 1.

14. Ibid., p. 5.

15. Interview with Chanda Kochhar, Executive Director of ICICI Bank, March 27, 2003.

16. Interview with M. N. Gopinath, General Manager of ROG & RMBG, March 17, 2003.

17. http://www.icicisocialinitiatives.org.

18. http://www.openfinancemag.com/spring03/story9.html.

19. http://www.tcs.com/0_downloads/source/press_releases/200210oct/sbi_ctf.pdf.

20. http://www.digitalpartners.org/planet.html.

21. http://www.digitalpartners.org/planet.html.

22. Ananth, Bindu, Duggal, Bikram, and Saboo, Kartikeya. 2002. *Micro Finance: Building the Capacities of the Poor to Participate in the Larger Economy*, p. 1. ICICI Social Initiatives.org.

23. http://finance.indiamart.com/investment_in_india/banks.html.

24. Ibid.

25. http://www.indiainfoline.com/view/221200a.html.

26. NABARD, *A Handbook on Forming Self-Help Groups*, p. 4. January 4, 1993.

27. NABARD, *Banking with Self-Help Groups: How and Why?* p. 5. January 4, 1993.

28. Interview with Chanda Kochhar, Executive Director of ICICI Bank, March 17, 2003.

29. Interview with Chanda Kochhar, Executive Director of ICICI Bank, March 17, 2003.

30. Badatya, K. C., and Puhazhendi, V. 2002. *Self-Help Group-Bank Linkage Programme for Rural India: An Impact Assessment*. NABARD, p. 45.

31. Interview with M. N. Gopinath, General Manager of ROG & RMBG, March 17, 2003.

32. Interview with M. N. Gopinath, General Manager of ROG & RMBG, March 17, 2003.

33. http://edev.media.mit.edu/SARI/papers/CommunityNetworking.pdf.

34. Duggal and Singhal., op. cit., p. 4.

35. Ibid., p. 5.

36. Ananth, Duggal, and Saboo., op. cit., p. 5.

37. *Social Initiatives Group*, ICICI Bank, p. 13.

38. Ananth, Duggal, and Saboo., op. cit., p. 25.

39. Ibid., p. 25.

40. Ibid., p. 25.

41. NABARD. *Self-Help Group–Bank Linkage Program*, p. *1.10*.

This report was written by Todd J. Markson and Michael Hokenson under the supervision of Professor C. K. Prahalad. The report is intended to be a catalyst for discussion and is not intended to illustrate effective or ineffective strategies.

The ITC e-Choupal Story: Profitable Rural Transformation

Rural India is a difficult location for business. Transport, power, and information infrastructures are inadequate. Business practices are underdeveloped. Lack of access to modern resources has resulted in an undertrained workforce. Rural society is structured around subsistence incomes. These and a litany of other constraints dissuade most companies from taking on the challenge of rural commerce. Yet, such an engagement can result in a win–win agenda. It can bridge rural isolation and the resulting disparity of incomes and opportunity for the poor while creating a new profit opportunity for firms willing to tackle the inefficiencies. The question is how modern resources and methods can be practically deployed commercially to overcome rural constraints. If done well, what are the social impacts of such an engagement?

THE INNOVATION

The e-Choupals, information centers linked to the Internet, represent an approach to seamlessly connect subsistence farmers with large firms, current agricultural research, and global markets. The network of these, each operated by a local farmer in each community called the *sanchalak*, allow for a virtual integration of the supply chain and significant efficiencies in the traditional system. The farmers benefit by realizing better prices for their crops, better yield through better practices, and a sense of dignity and confidence in being connected with the rest of the world.

ITC's e-Choupal initiative began by deploying technology to re-engineer procurement of soya from rural India. The effort holds valuable lessons in rural engagement and demonstrates the magnitude of the opportunity for private-sector firms. It also illustrates the social impact of bringing global resources and farm and business practices to the Indian farmer.

The Paradox of Indian Agriculture

Agriculture is economically, nutritionally, and socially vital to India. It contributes 23 percent of the gross domestic product (GDP), feeds a billion people, and employs 66 percent of the workforce. A fuller understanding of the sector requires a review of the paradoxes that beset it.

Economically Vital Yet Archaically Regulated

Agriculture's share of GDP has shrunken steadily, but at 23 percent it remains a critical component of the economy (see Table 1). The forecast for the upcoming monsoon is still considered a predictor of economic performance in India.

Table 1 GDP by Sector

Macroeconomic Indicators	1993	1998	1999	2000	2001	2002	2007
Nominal GDP (US$)	273.93	414.32	444.35	450.68	481.42	500.99	695.78
Agriculture (% of GDP)	28.16	25.42	23.85	22.74	22.76	23.15	19.60
Industry (% of GDP)	23.88	24.33	23.53	24.23	23.59	26.35	30.60
Services (% of GDP)	38.90	42.05	43.59	44.16	44.85	50.50	49.90

Source. Copyright 2003, The Economic Intelligence Unit.

Until recently, agriculture was heavily regulated. Legislation, a remnant of government intervention in days of production shortfalls, controlled land ownership, input pricing, and all aspects of product marketing. Produce could be sold only in government-recognized locations to authorized agents. Processing capacities, private storage, forward trading, and transport were restricted. The result was corrupt, ineffectual, and archaic systems. At one end, routine starvation existed alongside granaries overflowing with food-stocks of over 60 million metric tons. At the other end, the unprofessional business environment made the sector uninviting to most modern companies.

High Production Yet Impoverished Producers

Suboptimal farming practices and vicarious weather patterns left post-Independence India with an underperforming agricultural sector and acute food shortages. The goal of self-sufficiency in food brought agriculture into the mainstream of political and social consciousness. The ensuing "green revolution" has made great strides in agricultural productivity in India. Starting post-Independence (1947) as a food importer, the green revolution in the 1960s made India a net exporter of most food grains by the mid-1970s. The Indian farmer did not progress accordingly. After independence, the government parceled and redistributed larger land holdings to correct historical inequities and entrust ownership to end cultivators, thus encouraging productivity. In subsequent years, ownership ceilings were legislated and inherited land was partitioned into smaller lots. The combined result is that the Indian farm is a very small-scale operation measured in fractions of acres. The obvious result is that the typical Indian farmer is very poor.

As can be seen from Figure 1,[1] in 1993, agricultural laborers in most states made barely enough to keep a three-person family above the poverty line.

Proportion of GDP to Employment

The economy is growing far more rapidly in nonagricultural areas. The recent growth spurt in the Indian GDP has been led by the service sector. This is where the new and better jobs are. While 66% of the Indian population earns its livelihood through agriculture, it makes up only 23% to the Indian GDP. Most of the agrarian workforce is based in rural India. There is a vast disparity in access to education and opportunities between urban and rural India. This means the farmer rarely knows of nonagricultural opportunities. A subsistence existence means he does not have the resources to pursue opportunities even when he knows about them. Denying two-thirds of India a place in the emerging economy will result in inequitable and therefore unsustainable growth, even as agriculture runs out of viable employment for rural India.

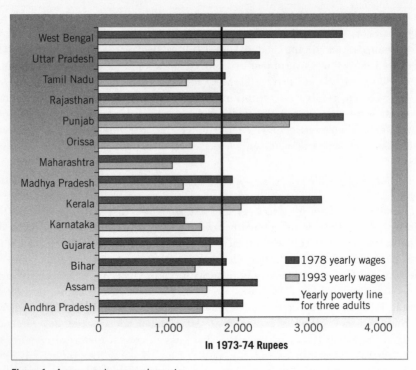

Figure 1   Average real wage and poverty.

Solution Essentials

Any remedy for the asymmetry of opportunity must provide rural India with both the knowledge of opportunities and the ability to pursue them. Sustainable commercial engagement in rural India is a channel that can serve as a foundation for the greater social agenda. Such an interchange can bring global resources, practices, and opportunities to the Indian villages while better compensating the farmer and helping alleviate his subsistent myopia. Pioneering engagements also can create a commercial environment where many more enterprises enter and operate.

In this context, we study an experiment in change in rural areas of central India.

The Oilseed Complex[2]

Edible oil from vegetarian sources is a fundamental part of the Indian diet. *Oilseed complex* is the term used to refer to the class of crops from which edible oils are extracted. The complex is further classified into traditional (groundnut, rapeseed–mustard seed, safflower) and nontraditional (e.g., sunflower, soya, cottonseed). The process of oil extraction varies by oilseed. At a high level, the process consists of two stages. The crushing stage involves the mechanical pressing of seeds to extract oils, leaving behind cakes with varying residual oil content depending on the efficiency of extraction. The solvent extraction phase consists of the extraction of the remaining oil content using an organic solvent. The residue, called deoiled cake (DOC) is sold as animal feed. Because of its low oil content, soya-oil extraction is done almost exclusively by the solvent extraction process. The extraction is carried out by the crushing industry. The oil is sold locally in India, and the DOC is exported.

Oilseed production was stagnating in the 1970s with demand outstripping supply, so that by 1979–1980, imports accounted for 32 percent of the domestic supply. Heavy reliance on imports was considered undesirable from a food security and price management perspective. Following the green revolution in wheat and rice, the Indian government turned regulatory attention in the early 1980s to oilseeds. The protectionism brought substantial gains on the production side by doubling oilseed output to 21 million metric tons in 1993–1994. Equally vital from a food security perspective, variability in oilseed production had been reduced, thereby increasing reliability of supply. Forty percent of the increased output was attributable to the introduction of new crops (soya and sunflower). Soya therefore represents an important innovation in the Indian oilseed complex that is resulting in better utilization of scarce resources and greater cropping intensity. Soya was exempted from the Small Scale Industries Act in its crushing sector to allow for processing in large-scale, modern facilities.

Marketing Prior to the e-Choupal

It is essential to note that the system described in Figure 2 varies in details among states, crops, and even districts. Also, the percentage of produce going through the channel depends on the state and crop in question. The only norm is that 90 percent of the produce went through traders and *mandis* (government-mandated marketplaces).

There are three commercial channels for the products: mandis, traders for eventual resale to crushers, and producer-run cooperative societies for crushing in cooperative mills. The farmers traditionally keep a small amount for their personal consumption and get the produce processed in a small-scale job-shop crushing-plant called a *ghani*.

The Mandi

The mandi is central to the functioning of the marketing channel. The Agricultural Products Marketing Act legislated the creation of mandis to enable

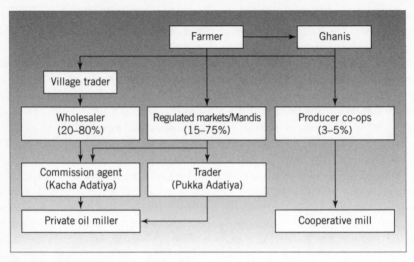

Figure 2 Marketing prior to the e-Choupal.

a more equitable distribution of the gains from agriculture among the producer, consumer, and traders. The mandi acts as a delivery point where farmers bring produce for sale to traders. The area served by a mandi varies by state. In the soya-growing areas of Madhya Pradesh, the average area served by a mandi is around 700 square kilometers. A large portion of traditional grains is used by the farmer or bartered for different crops. Soya, however, is not native to the Indian palate. Its major outlet is the crushing plant. Thus, nearly the entire crop must be marketed. This makes the mandi a vital part of the soya chain.

The Commission Agents

Mandi trading is conducted by commission agents called *adatiyas* (brokers who buy and sell produce). They are of two types: kachha adatiyas and pukka adatiyas. *Kachha adatiyas* are pure purchasing agents and buy only on behalf of others. *Pukka adatiyas*, on the other hand, finance the trade as representatives of distant buyers and sometimes even procure on their own account. All the adatiyas belong to the Agarwal and Jain community, which manages grain trade across the entire country, an amazing fact considering the vast cultural and social diversity across the nation. It challenges the assertion that rural India is culturally unfathomable. An adatiya is as distinct from most rural farmers as any executive.

The lack of professional competition combined with the communal stranglehold on rural trading has made commission agents extremely wealthy. The commission agent we spoke with belonged to a medium-sized mandi. He talked casually of assets and incomes in crores of rupees (millions of dollars). This is counter to the notion that there is no money in rural India. The adatiyas established the soya industry and expanded it on the basis of familial and community trust, not professional norms. Buying and selling were based on oral agreements, mutual understanding, and community norms. Their network within this industry and their financial might made them a formidable presence.

Mandi Operations

Figure 3 shows the process of how the mandi operates.

Inbound Logistics

Based on local information within the village, the farmer will decide which of the nearby mandis to sell in. The crop is taken to mandis in trolleys drawn by animals or tractors. Very often, to avoid peak-season crowds, the farmer will go to the mandi the night before. Peak-season mandi volume can be around 2,000 to 5,000 metric tons per day.

Sources of Inefficiency

- The farmer does not have the resources to analyze or exploit price trends. The timing of the sale is therefore not optimal.

- The selling decision is not always geographically efficient. The actual price of his produce will be determined only at the auction. The selection of mandi is based on often dated and unreliable information as opposed to a quoted price. By the time the farmer gets his price, it is too late to change his selection of mandis.

- The overnight stay costs the farmer.

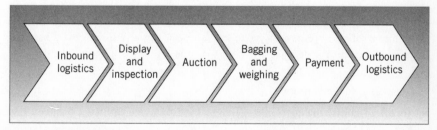

Figure 3 Mandi operations.

Display and Inspection

When the mandi opens in the morning, farmers bring their trolleys to display areas within the mandi. The inspection by buyers is by sight. There is no formal method of grading the produce, and the only instrument used is the moisture meter. Formal testing for oil content is not performed and global safety checks are not performed in the mandi.

Sources of Inefficiency

- Most crops are displayed in the open. Very few covered areas are available for lease by the farmers. As a result, displayed crops are subject to the elements.

- Sight inspection is unscientific and arbitrary, to say the least. The evaluation tends to favor the informed and wealthy buyer, not the poor farmer. Crops are judged on moisture content and presence of foreign matter such as stones or husks.

- The lack of scientific grading does not reward the farmer for better produce generated by investment in better seeds or agricultural practices. Ground conversations indicate that wide differences in quality are rewarded; however, subtle and less detectable differences are not recognized. The farmer therefore does not have an incentive for improving quality. These differences in quality of inputs impact the processors of soya.

Auction

Once potential buyers have inspected the produce, a mandi employee conducts the auction, where commission agents place bids. The auctions we observed were open oral auctions with incremental bidding. The auction offers a stark contrast in perspectives. On one hand, the farmer sees the auction as the assessment of six months of investment and labor. The auction represents the payday for the farmer, maybe one of two per year. His eyes reveal the emotion of the 30 seconds in which the price for his lot is judged. On the other hand is the commission agent, whose margin is ensured regardless of the price. He has many more lots (trolleys of produce) yet to buy and can casually mishandle a handful of grain and comment derogatorily about its quality and laugh while he does so.

Sources of Inefficiency

- By all accounts, the auction is efficient with no overt collusion between the buyers. However, the farmers we spoke to had a largely negative opinion of the auction for nonfinancial reasons. They felt a systematic loss of dignity in the auctioning process. The very fact that their life work is auctioned off is seen as an insult. They also felt belittled by having to stand by and watch agents raise bids in increments of 25 or 50 paise per quintal (we saw chana (chick peas) being auctioned in increments of Rs. 1, but this can vary between crops). The final indignity is that the farmer cannot refuse the sale at the auctioned price.

- The agents clearly belonged to a close-knit community that is socially and economically distinct from the farmers. Although they might not collude in pricing, they do collude in establishing the practices of the trade. These practices uniformly exploit the farmer's situation. Not surprisingly, the farmers we spoke to did not view the commission agents charitably and felt that all commission agents were the same.

Bagging and Weighing

Once the price per quintal has been established by the auction, the farmer moves the trolley to the weighing area run by the buying commission agent. In most cases, the weighing area is in the mandi complex. In some cases, especially if the mandi is small, the weighing area might be at the commission agent's home near the mandi. Here, the produce is transferred from the trolley into individual sacks. The sacks are then weighed, one at a time, on a manual scale.

Sources of Inefficiency

- The farmer bears the cost of bagging (Rs. 3 per bag at Mandideep mandi).
- Mandi laborers do the bagging and weighing. A traditional compensation for these laborers is the sale of spilled produce. They will therefore ensure that some portion of the produce is spilled in the weighing area. They gather and sell this grain at the end of the day. Estimates of the amount vary, but farmers at Peepalrava suggested that it was 1 to 3 kgs per quintal. The assessment at Khasrod was a minimum of 2 kgs per quintal.
- The weighing, managed by workers called *tulavatis* (weighers), is another source of discontent. Farmers feel tulavatis consistently underweigh their produce by applying practiced and timely nudges to the scale. Historical intimidation and long queues waiting behind them dissuade the farmers from protesting (according to a farmer from Khasrod, any complaints were met by a retort that this was not gold being weighed on the scale). One commission agent we spoke to readily acknowledged the systematic underweighing that every agent did. However, he felt the agent community as a whole was being discredited by the excessive greed of a few. He himself would be content with a few hundred grams a quintal.

Payment

After weighing, the full value of the grain is calculated. The farmer goes to the agent's office to collect a cash payment. The agent pays a mandi fee (1 percent of purchase value in Madhya Pradesh) to the mandi.

Sources of Inefficiencies

- The exploitative tone of the interaction also runs through the payment process. The farmer is never paid in full at once. The payments are stretched over time. This must be understood in the context that the farmer often travels many hours to get to a mandi. Repeating the trip costs him time and money. By this time, the farmer is also at the agent's mercy because the grain has already been delivered.

- Apart from the multiple trips to the agent's office, the farmer gets no interest for the delayed payment and bears the cost of the time and travel. Agents, on the other hand, charge crushers usurious rates for the privilege of delayed payments.

Outbound Logistics

The bagged produce is then loaded onto the end buyer's trucks and transported.

Sources of Inefficiency

- Along with the legal loss of value to taxes, there is an unofficial trade estimate of 1.5 percent to 2 percent of the product value being lost in tax evasion. Not all the value lost to tax evasion is illegal. Some of it is incurred when processors move plants to poorly developed zones for government-sponsored tax incentives.

- Multiple points of handling in the supply chain require the seeds to be bagged, a source of inefficiency in the unloading operation at the processing plant. Bulk (unbagged) seeds can be unloaded four to fives times faster than bagged seeds.

Other Sources of Market Inefficiency and Their Impact

- Limited storage levels mean traders do not have the luxury of storing and managing different qualities and grades of produce. Different grades are mixed.

- National pricing information is unreliable or unavailable. Prices are set dynamically in mandis. Publication and statistical analysis are made only for prices at a few major centers. For the most part, there is no information available about local pricing levels and trends. This means pricing is localized and lack of information reduces arbitrage opportunity and leads to market inefficiency.

- Arbitrage restrictions also arise from forward trading restrictions. The 11-day-forward trading restriction implies that for an arbitrage opportunity to be consummated, the product must actually be sold, shipped, and delivered within this window. Thus, arbitrage is limited to a small geographic proximity of the original mandi.

ITC: IBD and the Soya Business

The ITC group is one of India's foremost private-sector companies with a market capitalization of around $4 billion and revenues of $2 billion. ITC has a diversified presence in tobacco, hotels, paperboards, specialty papers, packaging, agribusiness, branded apparel, packaged foods, and other FMCG products. Spurred by India's need to generate foreign exchange, ITC's International Business Division (IBD) was created in 1990 as an agritrading company aiming to "offer the world the best of India's produce." Today, IBD is a $150-million company that trades in commodities such as feed ingredients, food grains, coffee, black pepper, edible nuts, marine products, and processed fruits.

When ITC entered this industry, produce was bought and crushed by small crushers who were also traders. ITC began with buying and exporting DOC. In a year, it realized it needed greater presence in the chain to better understand product dynamics. ITC then began renting processing plant time and buying soya from mandis. ITC's procurement has grown rapidly since, and its initiative has seen the introduction of professional practices, transparency, and formal contractual relationships between agents and buyers. ITC's reputation (as corroborated by an agent in Sonkach) is that of being trustworthy, true to its word, prompt with payments, and interested in only high-quality produce.

A unique set of tactical, strategic, and social imperatives drove ITC to conceive the e-Choupals and re-engineer the entire value chain by deploying them.

The Tactical Imperative

The mandi was not an optimal procurement channel. At first sight, agent commissions would seem to be a source of inefficiency, but this sum is comparable to the salary paid to an employee for rendering similar services. The real sources of inefficiency are the price and quality distortions caused by the agents' stranglehold on the market and ITC's distance from the farmer. Some examples of this are as follows:

- *Distance from farmer.* ITC had no direct interaction with the farmer. This gap created a range of supply-chain issues. ITC's knowledge of its crops, supplier, and therefore supply risks was limited. ITC's ability to improve the quality and quantity of its supply by bringing modern agricultural practices to the farmers was also limited.

- *Daily price inflation.* The agent purchased grain on ITC's behalf. Some produce of good quality would command a premium. Some of poor quality would sell at a discount. The agent purchased a range of qualities through the day at a range of prices. He mixed them at the end of the day and charged ITC a single price near the higher end of the spectrum.

- *Seasonal price inflation.* A corollary effect was that high-quality produce was used to make an entire lot of lower quality produce acceptable. Agents therefore paid an inflated premium for high-quality produce. This drove up the high mandi price for the day. Very few farmers actually got this price, but this price acted as the benchmark for the next day's pricing, thereby inflating the mandi price over a length of time. This created a distortion that inflated the overall seasonal procurement prices for ITC.

- *Capture of intraday price shifts.* Mandi prices were fluid and varied within the day. ITC provided the agent a price range for the day to buy within. If the agent's average buy price within the day was lower than the ITC price, the agent sold the grain to ITC at the ITC price and pocketed the difference. If the average buy price was higher than the ITC price, the agent would still buy the produce, but tell ITC that because its price was not high enough, no grain could be bought. He would then store the grain and sell it to ITC the next day when ITC raised its price to make up for the previous day's procurement shortfall. Commission agents therefore captured the entire benefit of intraday price shifts.

The agent never lost. Officially the agent's commission is 1 percent of ITC's price. In reality, ITC estimated the agent's operating margin at around 2.5 percent to 3 percent. The other insight is that the auction process is transparent in name only. The market is created, manipulated, and managed by the agents. The e-Choupal is an ideal vehicle to communicate directly with the farmer and thereby bypass the inefficiencies arising out of the agents' intermediation.

The Strategic Imperative

Whereas the inefficiency in the supply channel was causing ITC to look inward, a changing landscape was forcing it to look outward. The agricultural commodity trading business was small compared to international players. By

1996, the opening up of the Indian market had brought in international competition. These established, large companies had better margin-to-risk ratios because of wider options for risk management and arbitrage. To replicate their operating model would require a massive expansion of horizontal and vertical presence. The investments for this would be better spent in other sectors of India's liberalizing economy. After exploring sale, merger, and closure in 1998, ITC decided to retain the business. The chairman of ITC challenged IBD to use information technology (IT) to change the game and create a competitive business that did not need a massive asset base. ITC needed to address the following advantages its competitors enjoyed:

- *Horizontal spread.* Presence in dozens of countries allows customer proximity and a diversified supply base.

- *Vertical presence.* Integration allows companies to extract value-chain efficiencies.

- *Old and family-owned.* An intimately managed company has deep knowledge and trading methods developed over the years that enable profitability in commodity markets with otherwise thin margins.

- *Risk management.* Operating in countries where financial and logistical institutions to manage risk (to allow futures trading, etc.) lowers the cost of bearing risk.

ITC devised a strategy to systematically deploy IT to change the game in each area. The horizontal integration deficiency was addressed through customer relationship management (CRM)-based solutions that were used to identify and provide for the nonstandard needs of customers in an industry where the basic services had been standardized. Customized IT application and realignment of business goals and processes were deployed to manage risk and build the organization's knowledge base.

The e-Choupal network was conceived to achieve virtual vertical integration by extending ITC's engagement all the way to the farmer in the field.

The Social Imperative

The social agenda is an integral part of ITC's philosophy. ITC is widely recognized as dedicated to the cause of nation-building. Chairman Y. C. Deveshwar noted, "ITC believes its aspiration to create enduring value for the nation provides the force to sustain growing shareholder value."

This vibrant view of social conscience allowed ITC to recognize the unique opportunity of blending shareholder value creation with social development. The social impact of the e-Choupals as envisioned by ITC ranges from the short-term provision of Internet access to the long-term development of rural India as a competitive supplier (and buyer) of a range of goods and services to and from the global economy. The sustainability of the engagement comes from the commitment that neither the corporate nor social agendas will be subordinated in favor of the other.

e-Choupal: Vision and Planning

Implementing and managing e-Choupals is a significant departure from commodities trading practices in India. Trading is not capital-intensive because processing is outsourced and commodities are traded for margins that come through arbitrage of knowledge, time, or location. On the other hand, the e-Choupal model required significant capital outlays. Getting concurrence from the ITC Board for such a venture, as well as the diligent management of its progress, required clarity of vision and an understanding of revenue streams and operations. Through its tobacco business, ITC has dealt for decades with every aspect of Indian agriculture, from research to distribution. ITC's translation of its strategic, tactical, and social imperatives into a business model demonstrates a deep understanding of both agrarian systems and modern management methods. Some of the guiding management principles are listed in the following sections.

Re-engineer as Opposed to Reconstruct

The conventional view of transforming established business systems begins with the failure of the current system and the means to change it. ITC looked at what was good with the current system and therefore what it could build on. ITC not only kept efficient providers from the existing system but also created roles for some inefficient providers from the previous system. This philosophy has two benefits. First, it avoids reinventing the wheel in areas where ITC would not be able to add value through its presence. Second, it co-opts members of the rural landscape, thereby making their expertise available to ITC and foreclosing the same from ITC's competition. A good example of this in action is the role created for the commission agents, as discussed later.

Address the Whole, Not Just a Part

The farmer's universe consists of many activities, ranging from procuring inputs to selling produce. Today the village trader services the spectrum of the farmer's needs. He is a centralized provider of cash, seeds, fertilizers, pesticides, and marketing. In doing so, the trader enjoys two competitive benefits. First, his intimate knowledge of the farmer and of village dynamics allows him to accurately assess and manage risk. Second, he reduces overall transaction costs by aggregating services.

The linked transactions reduce the farmer's overall cost in the short term, but create a cycle of exploitive dependency in the long term. Rural development efforts thus far have focused only on individual pieces rather than entire needs. Cooperatives have tried to provide agricultural inputs, rural banks have tried to provide credit, and mandis have tried to create a better marketing channel. These efforts cannot compete against the trader's bundled offer. Functioning as a viable procurement alternative therefore requires one to eventually address the gamut of needs, not just marketing.

An IT-Driven Solution

From the conception of the model, an IT-centric solution was recognized as fundamental to optimizing effectiveness, scalability, and cost. IT is 20 percent of all the effort of the business model, but it is deemed the most crucial 20 percent. The two goals envisioned for IT were the following:

- Delivery of real-time information independent of the transaction. In the mandi system, delivery, pricing, and sale happen synchronously, thus binding the farmer to an agent. The PC was seen as a medium of delivering ITC and other rates prior to the trip to the mandi, allowing the farmer to make an empowered choice.

- Facilitation of collaboration among the many parties required to fulfill the spectrum of farmer needs. This goal follows from the need to address the whole, not just the part.

It is a tribute to ITC's understanding of rural value systems that it did not hesitate in installing expensive IT infrastructure in places where most people would not. It is a tribute to rural value systems that not a single case of theft, misappropriation, or misuse has been reported among the almost 2,000 e-Choupals.

Clarity of Payback Streams

Profitable re-engineering requires the unambiguous understanding of value provided, the circumstances in which they are applicable, and the revenues they are capable of generating. Three sources of payback were expected:

- *Crop-specific intervention.* ITC recognized that agrarian systems vary by crop. This means the sources of inefficiency in the supply chain, the correction required from the e-Choupal, and the magnitude and timing of the resulting efficiencies will differ by crop. For example, the systems and consequently the e-Choupal models and payback streams for coffee and shrimp are very different from that of soya. ITC's goals for the soya intervention reflected this nuanced analysis, and the project was targeted with recovering the entire cost of infrastructure from procurement savings. This is in contrast with the coffee and shrimp efforts, where the source of e-Choupal value is such that the investment recovery horizon is much longer.

- *Low-cost last mile.* The same system of physical and information exchange that brings produce from the village can be used to transfer goods to the villages. Because infrastructure has already been paid for by procurement, it is available at marginal cost for distribution. This ties in nicely with ITC's larger goal of transforming the e-Choupal network into a distribution superhighway. ITC's current channels reach areas with populations of 5,000 and above. The e-Choupals allow penetration into areas with populations less than this. We saw products such as herbicides, seeds, fertilizers, insurance policies, and soil testing services being sold through e-Choupals.

- *Intelligent first mile.* Once the notion of consumerism and service has been established in the minds of the village farmers, their creativity and intimate knowledge of rural needs can be used to conceive the next product to be sold in villages. Thus the farmers are transformed from consumers into participants in the process of product design. This helps broaden the ITC offering and further bolster payback.

Modularity of Investments in Size and Scope

ITC managed its investments modularly along the scope and scale axes in what it terms "rollout-fixit-scale up" and "pilot-critical mass-saturation." This incremental control of investment levels along with the clarity of revenue streams and the social import were critical in getting board approval for the initiative.

Risk Assessment and Mitigation

ITC identified the following risks as it worked out the business model:

- Radical shifts in computing access will break community-based business models.
- The sanchalaks are ITC's partners in the community. As their power and numbers increase, there is a threat of their unionizing and extracting rents.

■ The scope of the operation, the diversity of activities required of every operative, and the speed of expansion create real threats to the management of execution.

Managing Bureaucracy

When the e-Choupals were conceived, they faced a fundamental regulatory obstacle. The Agricultural Produce Marketing Act, under the aegis of which mandis were established, prohibits procurements outside the mandi. ITC took the government through the spirit of the Act as opposed to the letter and convinced them that e-Choupal procurement was in line with the goals of the Act. Because ITC would not be using the mandi infrastructure for its procurement and they would have to incur their own costs on the e-Choupal infrastructure, the government offered to waive the mandi tax on the produce procured through the e-Choupal. ITC recognized the tax was a major source of revenue for the government and local mandis. Also, as ITC's competition was also subject to it, the tax itself was not making ITC uncompetitive. ITC, therefore, chose to continue paying the tax rather than risking relationships with the government and the mandi.

e-Choupal Operations: Participants and Processes

The model is centered on a network of e-Choupals, which are information centers armed with a computer connected to the Internet. The name is derived from the Hindi word *choupal* meaning a traditional village gathering place. The e-Choupals were meant to act as an e-commerce hub as well as a social gathering place. A local farmer called the *sanchalak* (coordinator) runs the village e-Choupal. The commission agent has been incorporated into this process as the provider of logistical support. He is known as the *samyojak* (collaborator).

The e-Choupal

The e-Choupal, which physically consists only of a computer with an Internet connection, is established in a village. It resides in the local sanchalak's living room. In keeping with the philosophy of modular increments based on proven results, ITC experimented with a variety of village conditions before developing a checklist for attributes it looks for in selected villages. ITC is working to saturate its operating areas so that a farmer has to travel no more than 5 kilometers to get to an e-Choupal. ITC expects each e-Choupal to serve about five to seven villages in this 5-km radius. Today e-Choupal services reach out to more than a million farmers in nearly 11,000 villages through 2,000 kiosks across four states (Madhya Pradesh, Karnataka, Andhra Pradesh, and Uttar Pradesh). Of the e-Choupals we visited in Madhya Pradesh, the one in Khasrod services about 500 to 700 farmers in 10 villages and another one in Dahod services 5,000 farmers in 10 villages. The average seems to be around 1,000 farmers per e-Choupal.

The e-Choupals were initially rolled out as just gathering spots where agrarian information would be made available to farmers while familiarity and trust were developed for the ITC brand. The fear at this time was that the village was not ready to accept IT.

Within three months, a farmer asked how long ITC expected its representatives to do this in person and said he had heard of something called the computer that could be used to achieve this purpose. This triggered the rollout of IT and the scale-up of e-Choupals.

The Sanchalak

ITC manages the geographical and cultural breadth of its network by channeling communication through a local farmer called the sanchalak. Recruiting a farmer from the community served several purposes:

- For generations, institutions, individuals, and often the weather have betrayed the Indian farmer. Trust is the most valuable commodity in rural India. No transaction will happen without trust, regardless of the strength of the contract. The sanchalak is selected to provide this vital ingredient to ITC's message.
- ITC did not have to invest in building and securing a physical infrastructure such as a kiosk for housing the computer.
- The sanchalak is trained in computer operation and can act as a familiar and therefore approachable human interface for the often illiterate farmers and other villagers.
- ITC expects to leverage the power of the small-scale entrepreneur.

The sanchalak receives a commission for every transaction processed through the e-Choupal. Working as a sanchalak also boosts his social status. This is a very important aspect of rural Indian life.

Maintaining Village Trust

ITC insists that at no time should the sanchalaks give up farming, for this would compromise the trust the sanchalak commands. The fact that the sanchalak works on commission could undermine his credibility. ITC mitigates this by projecting the role as a public office as opposed to a profitable venture. This is one reason he holds a title (sanchalak). This image is reinforced by a public oath-taking ceremony where, in the presence of a gathering of the local villagers, the sanchalak takes an oath to serve the farming community through the e-Choupal.

Picking and Training Sanchalaks

Although ITC was an agricultural company, its reach ended at the mandi. It did not extend into the villages beyond. ITC used its relationships with the commission agents to help identify farmers. Villagers then were contacted to determine the ground reaction to the nominee. Care was taken to ensure the polled villagers were representative of a cross-section of the farmers. Like the identification of villages, initial decisions involved mainly trial and error. In the initial trial, six individuals with very different characteristics of age, wealth, status, education levels, and village sizes were selected. Performance was measured; hypotheses regarding critical attributes were established and tested on the next wave of sanchalaks. ITC's field operatives readily acknowledge that successful sanchalaks demonstrate a wide variety of demographic attributes and a large part of the selection is subjective. A few attributes have emerged as widely prevalent among successful sanchalaks:

- Must make his living from farming.
- Progressive and willing to try something new.
- Ambitious and have aspirations of earning additional income through the e-Choupal.
- Of median wealth and status. If he is too poor, he will not command respect and therefore not be heeded; if he is too rich, he would not be approachable.
- Must be able to read and write.
- Must be part of an extended family large enough to find among themselves time enough to service the e-Choupal. (In Dahod, the e-Choupal is run by the son of the sanchalak.)

The sanchalak undergoes a training program at the nearest ITC plant. He is trained on basic computer usage and the functions within the e-Choupal Web site. He is trained on the basic business skills needed to function as a sanchalak. He is also trained on quality inspection and pricing. For the sale of products through the e-Choupal, the sanchalak receives product training directly from the manufacturer, with ITC involving itself only in product design and facilitation. In reality, the sanchalak gets most of his training on the job. This makes selecting sanchalaks with a natural drive all the more important.

Performance and Motivation

The sanchalaks we spoke to indicated three equally weighted motivations:

- They saw it as a means to help society.
- They saw it as a profitable business.
- They saw it as a means of getting access to a functional computer (as opposed to just a computer, which they would have trouble making functional, as discussed later).

Selecting the sanchalak is not the end of the story. Most do not have retailing experience and some might be satisfied only with the prestige of association. One motivation technique is a ceremony during which sanchalaks are given their annual commission checks with public announcements of earnings and stories of what sanchalaks have done with past commissions. This demonstrates the income potential and spurs nonperformers to work. The zeal to perform sometimes leads to territorial disputes, but ITC does not interfere in their resolution because it encourages sanchalaks to better service their customer bases.

Sustaining Commercial Volume

Virtual vertical integration can work only if there is a continuous flow of information between the e-Choupals and ITC. Because of the number and spread of the e-Choupals, this communication must be initiated by the sanchalaks. If their motivation to communicate with ITC diminishes, the channel will still function for procurement, but will lack the vitality to manage supply risk, distribution, or product design. Maintaining continuous commercial flow keeps the sanchalak motivated to spend time and money calling the ITC representative to ask about new products, convey village demand, and provide local updates. An example of the power of local information was seen early in e-Choupal implementation. A competitor tried to divert produce coming to the ITC factories by stationing motorcycle-riding representatives on the roads leading up to the plant. This person would stop farmers and offer them a premium over the ITC rate to divert their trolleys to the competitor's plants. Information about this came to ITC from alert sanchalaks, and ITC was able to take necessary measures.

ITC maintains commercial volumes and therefore keeps commission checks flowing through e-Choupals by intelligently sequencing procurement and sales year-round. Purchases and sales have been arranged so that kharif (cropping season coinciding with India's monsoon from July to October) procurement, rabi (winter cropping season in irrigated areas) inputs, rabi procurement, and kharif inputs sequentially maintain a steady stream of revenue for sanchalaks.

The Samyojak

The commission agents earned profit from two sources. The first was through provision of value-added logistical services that substituted for the lack of rural infrastructure. The second was by blocking information flow and market signals on the trading transactions. Complete disintermediation would result in the loss of a legitimate and essential service in the rural context. The goal was selective disintermediation so that agents would participate, but only as providers of essential services, not as principals in a trading transaction. In this incarnation, the agent was christened the samyojak.

The samyojak's collaboration began right from the selection of the first sanchalaks. Because of their long association with the business, samyojaks knew village dynamics. They knew who grew soya, what kind of families they had, what their financial situation was, and who was seen as acceptable in the villages. There is no other source with such information on rural India. As part of the ongoing operations, ITC is strongly committed to involving samyojaks in every element of their operation and allowing them revenue streams through providing services such as management of cash, bagging, and labor in remote ITC procurement hubs, handling of mandi paperwork for ITC procurement, as licensed principals for retail transaction of the e-Choupal, and as licensed suppliers of fertilizers sold through the e-Choupals.

Why Did the Samyojaks Help?

ITC hid nothing from the samyojaks. They were transparent about the goals and the future of the e-Choupals. The samyojaks realized that by introducing ITC to the sanchalaks, they were setting into motion an initiative that would reduce their commissions; yet they cooperated with ITC for the following reasons:

- ITC's communications with the samyojaks carried two clear messages. First, any e-Choupal procurement would happen over and above the volumes ITC would procure in the mandis, thereby protecting their commission earnings. Second, samyojaks would be involved with all new revenue streams arising from the e-Choupals. The trust ITC had built in the mandi made this statement believable.

- A conscious effort was and is made to divert revenue to samyojaks. As far as possible, mandi procurement is maintained.

- Every effort was made to maintain the level of samyojaks' trust. All communication with the sanchalaks happens in the presence of samyojaks. ITC never permitted any negative communication regarding the existing model, the mandi, or the commission agents. Samyojaks were always acknowledged as the enablers of the entire concept.

Conversations with a samyojak in Sonkach indicated that despite the best of intentions, the agent's procurement revenue has fallen by 50 percent. Because the mandi is not near an ITC hub, he provides no other services and therefore has no other revenue streams. This man had more pragmatic reasons for cooperating:

- The samyojaks are fragmented. There is the fear that if one does not help, another commission agent would help ITC and walk away with the promised e-Choupal revenues and the mandi revenues. Interestingly, revenue streams were mightier than the sense of community in this case.

- The samyojaks feel that if pushed into a corner, ITC could go it alone. The process would be slower, but it would eventually achieve the desired results.

- The samyojaks see the opportunity to develop good will and networks in the villages.

- Finally, the samyojak said that he saw globalization as an irresistible trend. Although he saw loss of revenue in the short term, his long-term interest lay in cooperating with an international company.

The Transformation of the Traditional System: e-Choupal Processes

The re-engineered value chain looks very different from the existing system and contains the stages shown in Figure 4.

Price Setting and Dissemination

The previous day's mandi closing price is used to determine the benchmark fair average quality (FAQ) price at the e-Choupal. The benchmark price is static for a given day. This information and the previous day's mandi prices are communicated to the sanchalak through the e-Choupal portal. The commission agents at the mandi are responsible for feeding daily mandi prices to e-Choupal. The reality is that in the large majority of the e-Choupals where the VSAT (Very Small Aperture Terminal) has not been installed, the Internet connection cannot be relied on. In this case, the sanchalak calls an ITC field representative. This situation is changing rapidly as VSAT penetration is increasing.

The farmer brings a sample of his produce to the e-Choupal. The sanchalak inspects the produce and based on his assessment of the quality makes appropriate deductions (if any) to the benchmark price and gives the farmer a conditional quote. The sanchalak performs the quality tests right in front of the farmer and has to rationalize any deductions to the farmer. The benchmark price represents the upper limit on the price a sanchalak can quote. These are simple

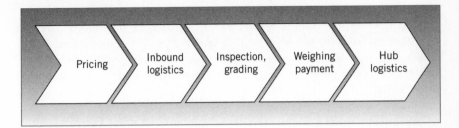

Figure 4   The new value chain.

checks and balances to ensure transparency in a process where quality testing and pricing happen at multiple levels.

If the farmer chooses to sell his beans to ITC, the sanchalak gives him a note including his name, the village, particulars about the quality tests (foreign matter and moisture content), approximate quantity, and the conditional price.

Inbound Logistics

The farmer takes the note from the sanchalak and proceeds to the nearest ITC procurement hub, ITC's point for collection of produce and distribution of inputs sold into rural areas. Some procurement hubs are simply ITC factories that also act as collection points. Others are purely warehousing operations. ITC's goal is to have a processing center within a 30- to 40-km radius of its farmers. There are currently 16 buying locations; there will eventually be 35 in the state of Madhya Pradesh.

Inspection and Grading

The first point of inspection is the e-Choupal. When the farmer brings a sample in, the sanchalak visually inspects the produce for foreign matter and determines the moisture content in the soybean using his moisture meter. The initial, conditional pricing is based on this inspection. At the ITC procurement hub, a sample of the farmer's produce is taken and set aside for laboratory tests. The chemist visually inspects the soybean and verifies the assessment of the sanchalak. It is important to note that this test is the only assessment before the sale. Laboratory testing of the sample for oil content, and so on, is performed after the sale and does not alter the price. The reasoning for this is that a farmer cannot comprehend the results of a laboratory test and will not trust its merits. Therefore, pricing is based solely on tests that the farmer can understand. The farmer accepts foreign matter deductions based on the visual comparison of his produce with his neighbor's for the presence of stones or hay. He will accept moisture content deductions based on the comparative softness of his produce when he bites it.

ITC is working toward changing farmer attitudes on this count. It is developing an appreciation of better quality by using the subsequent lab tests to reward farmers with bonus points if their quality exceeds expectation. At the end of the year, farmers can redeem their accumulated bonus points for e-Choupal purchases such as farm inputs (or in the future use it toward insurance premiums).

Weighing and Payment

After the inspection, the farmer's trolley is weighed in its entirety on an electronic weighbridge, first with the produce and then without. The difference is used to determine the weight of his produce. He then collects his payment in full at the cash counter and returns to his village. The farmer is also reimbursed for his freight expenses. Every stage of the process is accompanied by appropriate documentation. The farmer is given a copy of lab reports, agreed rates, and receipts for his records. Samyojaks, who are adept at handling large amounts of cash, are entrusted with the responsibility of handling cash (this is not true at procurement centers near large ITC operations where ITC is capable of handling cash itself). Through their social network, samyojaks can also get cash at short notice.

Logistics and Storage

The farmer transports the produce in his trolley from the farm to the nearest processing center or storage hub. The farmer bears the risk of transportation until it is delivered and the sale is completed. The transportation costs he incurs are reimbursed by ITC. This reimbursement was initially based on the distance of the issuing e-Choupal from the processing center. This gave farmers the incentive to travel to a faraway e-Choupal with their samples to get a higher transport reimbursement. ITC therefore did away with differential compensation and replaced it with a system of uniform compensation. Much of the procurement hub-related logistics are managed by the samyojaks. Their responsibilities include the following:

- Labor management at the hub
- Bagging and baggage handling
- Storage management
- Transportation from the hub to processing factories
- Payment processing and cash management
- Handling mandi paperwork for the grain procured at the hub

For his services in the procurement process, the samyojak is paid a 0.5 percent commission.

Farmer Gains

- Better information content. Prior to the e-Choupal, the farmer's information was incomplete or inaccurate. The only sources of information were the village grapevine and the commission agent. The e-Choupal allows farmers access to prices at several nearby outlets. Some e-Choupal sanchalaks have taken this a level further. They have begun accessing external pricing indicators such as prices on the Chicago Board of Trade Web site to track global trends and determine the optimum timing of their sale.

- Better information timing. An indicative price was available only when the farmer traveled to the mandi, incurring costs that he could ill afford. The final price of the transaction was available to the farmer only on the completion of the auction, at which time there was no backing out of the transaction. At the e-Choupal, the farmer has access to price choice prior to his trip.

Both factors work together to provide the farmer with a better price for his crop.

- *Transportation cost.* The farmer bears the cost of transporting the crop to the mandi for a sale. ITC compensates its sellers for their transportation costs.

- *Transaction duration.* The mandi process can stretch over several days from arrival to full payment. Most farmers have traveled long distances to come to the mandi and incur costs of overnight stays or multiple trips. The sale to ITC takes no more than a few hours. (ITC targets two hours, and farmers spoke of two to three hours; our observation was that it probably takes two to three hours, possibly more in the peak season, but far less than a day.) Both factors result in a lower logistic cost for the farmer.

- *Weighing accuracy.* The mandis' manual scales are inherently inaccurate, easily manipulated, and subject to manual errors. ITC's electronic weighing scales are accurate and impartial.

- *Granularity of weighing.* The manual scales require that the produce be first transferred into bags. This intermediate bagging results in pilfering and loss of produce and the compounding of manual weighing errors over the entire load. The single weighing of the entire trolley at ITC eliminates these losses.

Both factors contribute to lower transaction loss.

■ *Professionalism and dignity.* The ITC procurement center is a well-maintained, professionally run operation where the farmer is treated with respect and actually serviced as a customer. The farmers we spoke with evinced great emotion for the dignity accorded to them by a professional process. Farmers mentioned simple touches such as a shaded area with chairs to await their paperwork as indicators of ITC's respect for them and their produce.

Even though intangible in the short term, the self-confidence created by the professional treatment is changing the way farmers conduct themselves. Sanchalaks and even a commission agent noted this change in farmer attitudes.

ITC Gains

■ *Disintermediation savings.* The commissions paid to the agents were not excessive, but the true cost of intermediation, including the rent seeking, was between 2.5 percent and 3 percent of procurement costs. A 0.5 percent commission to the sanchalak has replaced this.

■ *Freight costs.* Direct reimbursement of transport costs to the farmer is estimated to be half of what ITC used to pay the commission agents for transport to their factory.

■ *Quality control.* Removal of intermediary manipulation of quality and the ability to directly educate and reward quality in the customer base results in higher levels of quality in e-Choupal procurement. This results in higher oil yields.

■ Risk management. The e-Choupal allows ITC to develop long-term supplier relationships with its farmers and attain some modicum of supply security over time. Risk is also managed in the e-Choupal world by far stronger information infrastructure. Sanchalaks and samyojaks working on behalf of ITC provide excellent ground information on pricing, product quality, soil conditions, and expected yields. This allows ITC to better plan future operations.

e-Choupal Procurement Savings in Numerical Terms

In the mandi system, there was a markup of 7 percent to 8 percent on the price of soybeans from the farm gate to the factory gate. Of this markup, 2.5 percent was borne by the farmer and ITC had to swallow 5 percent. ITC's costs

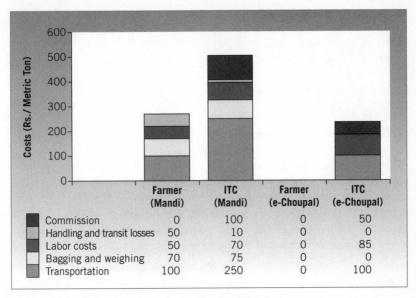

	Farmer (Mandi)	ITC (Mandi)	Farmer (e-Choupal)	ITC (e-Choupal)
Commission	0	100	0	50
Handling and transit losses	50	10	0	0
Labor costs	50	70	0	85
Bagging and weighing	70	75	0	0
Transportation	100	250	0	100

Figure 5 Cost comparison between the mandi and e-Choupal.

are now down to 2.5 percent. Figure 5 shows the breakdown of the transaction costs incurred by the farmer and ITC per metric ton of soyabeans procured in the mandi and e-Choupal.

Compared to the mandi operation, the farmer gained Rs. 270 per metric ton. ITC gained also Rs. 270 per metric ton. The total system efficiency is Rs. 540 per ton. This is a win–win situation for both. There are additional sources of benefits that can accrue over time to both the farmers and ITC as they learn to leverage the e-Choupal network.

The Social Impact of e-Choupals

One of the most exciting aspects about the e-Choupal model is that it profitably provides an inaccessible village with a window to the world. The e-Choupal computer is the first and only PC in most of these villages. This, coupled with the higher remuneration and appreciation of the professional transaction, is causing several shifts in the social fabric. These changes can be categorized into the following broad areas:

- Improved agriculture
- Better lifestyles
- Brighter futures

Improved Agriculture

The impact of the e-Choupal on agriculture extends through the lifecycle of the crop. The improvements are attributable to three areas:

- Bridging the information gap
- Cheaper and smarter agricultural inputs
- Farmer as a source of innovation

Their collective impact can be gauged by the fact that prior to the e-Choupal, soya cultivation was on the decline. Productivity was stagnant and farmers saw no future in it. In Khasrod, we were told that from a high of 100 percent of the farmers planting soya, it had come down to 50 percent and was expected to decline further. Since ITC's involvement, soya is seen as profitable again, and nearly 90 percent of the farmers are planting soya.

Bridging the Information Gap

Agricultural research centers (e.g., the Indian Council for Agricultural Research), universities, and other agencies in India have developed several practices and technologies to improve productivity and quality. The impediment has been access to a system for large-scale, low-cost dissemination of knowledge. E-Choupals leverage technology to reach out to a wide base literally at the click of a mouse. The constant presence of the sanchalak, who is himself a farmer who applies these techniques, ensures that the practices actually make their way from the Web site to the field. Some areas about which information is provided by the e-Choupal Web site are the following:

- *Weather.* This is a very popular section on the Web site because it provides localized weather information at the district level. Other public sources generally provide only aggregated statewide weather information. The weather information is intelligently coupled with advice on the activities in the agricultural lifecycle. One farmer observed that prior to the e-Choupal, unreliable weather information would result in prematurely planted seeds that would be washed out by early rains. The recent access of accurate rain information has stemmed over half this loss.

- *Agricultural best practices.* Scientific practices organized by the crop in question are available on the Web site. Additional questions are answered through frequently asked questions and access to experts who respond to e-mails from the villages. An example we encountered in the villages was soil testing, which never happened prior to e-Choupal operation.

- *Customized quality solutions.* After the sale is completed, ITC performs laboratory testing of the sample collected. Based on these results, the farmer is given customized feedback on how he can improve the quality and yield of his crop.

Cheaper and Smarter Agricultural Inputs

The market for agricultural inputs is estimated to be Rs.175,000 crore. However, the rural market is serviced by an unorganized and inefficient informal sector. The lack of physical infrastructure makes the cost of establishing and managing a distribution channel extremely expensive. Many companies could not market their products and services to rural areas in a cost-effective manner. ITC is able to use information to drive demand of inputs and fulfill them through the e-Choupal.

- *Low-cost last mile.* With the infrastructure cost recovered through procurement, the channel is available to distribution at only the incremental marginal cost. The fixed cost overhead applied to distributed commodities is therefore very low. Hubs, transportation, organization, and communication infrastructure are all shared. One sanchalak spoke of an herbicide, Pursuit, that ITC made available at 20 percent below market price.
- *Demand aggregation.* The informational atmosphere of the e-Choupal and the trust engendered by ITC drive demand for inputs. The sanchalak is in an ideal position to aggregate village demand, place a single order, and optimize logistics costs for ITC.
- *Intelligent product deployment.* Inputs such as fertilizers and pesticides are not generic in their application. The optimal deployment is subject to the soil and crop. Determining these parameters themselves requires services such as soil testing to be performed. Past providers brought inputs but not the information and services required to make them effective. ITC's full-service approach corrects for this by coupling the input sale to the information on the Web site and services such as soil testing.

Farmer as a Source of Innovation

The global resources, practices, and remunerations the e-Choupal brings to the farmer have unshackled the farmers' innovation and given them an avenue to see their ideas realized. This fits in perfectly with the ITC vision of using the e-Choupal as the "intelligent first mile." Farmers are now coming up with products and services that ITC could provide to further improve their operations. We heard farmers demand that ITC certify and make available the

Samrat variety of seeds that is preferred to the currently certified JS300 variety. Some farmers wanted ITC to bring its resources to bear on the onion and potato crops. They had information to the effect that the Indian onion crop was regarded as inferior to the Chinese crop in the world market. This is caused by the lack of availability of seeds and information. They have approached ITC with this suggestion, saying it would be mutually profitable to make these resources available.

Better Lifestyles

The realization of e-Choupal as a distribution channel begins in agriculture but extends well into consumer goods and services. In the traditional channel, the farmer lacks the resources to make informed purchasing decisions. This channel is comprised of mobile traders and cycle-based distributors. More often than not, they did not understand the farmers' issues and ended up selling them products and services that did not satisfy their needs. With companies hesitating to serve the rural market, a farmer often didn't have many choices. He had to buy what was available. This lack of choice also meant he had to pay a premium for the products that were available.

Orchestrating the Network

ITC's objective is not to be a platform provider for sale of third-party products and services but a network choreographer that orchestrates bidirectional demand and supply of goods through a collaborative business model. ITC intends to differentiate itself by serving only those products and services to which they can add value. The strengths that sustain this business model are the following:

- *Knowledge of customer.* ITC's core asset is its knowledge of the customer. By transforming the value chain and setting up a platform for procuring commodities from them directly, they now have a foundation for forging a close relationship with the farmers. This relationship leads to a better understanding of the issues that worry farmers. This is critical to serving their needs.

- *Physical assets (deployed infrastructure).* In its e-Choupals, hubs, and processing centers, ITC has a ready infrastructure that is needed to implement an alternative channel for distribution of goods and services into rural India. Its e-Choupals can double as storefronts and the hubs as centers for stocking inventory.

- *Information and communication infrastructure.* The information infrastructure implemented by ITC can be used to enhance its business decision-making, better manage risk, and identify opportunities for cross-selling and upselling. It can leverage detailed transactional data and transform them into actionable knowledge. Data mining and data warehousing will help them better understand the behavior of their customers, identify unfulfilled needs, and realize ways to serve them efficiently. The communication infrastructure compensates for the lack of physical infrastructure needed for marketing products and services in rural India. Some of the functions it can enable are as follows:

  - Rapid, low-cost information dissemination, thus allowing the farmer an informed choice and minimizing the need for a traveling sales force.

  - Online ordering and order management, eliminating the need for physical storefronts.

  - Customer intelligence, maximizing customer satisfaction and profitability.

- *Process benefits.* Having set up a streamlined process for bringing products out of rural India, ITC can now leverage that to take products into rural India. For instance, the samyojak network can be employed to efficiently distribute the products to the e-Choupals. The sanchalaks, through their community presence, can pick up market signals and consumer information first and transmit them back to the distribution channel.

- *Reputation of ITC.* Another factor that enhances this channel is ITC's reputation for transparency. Products sold through this channel will have instant credibility by virtue of their association with ITC. Also, by establishing its primary objective as procurement from this channel, ITC has demonstrated it has no vested interests in promoting this channel for distribution of products.

Sources of Efficiency

There are several differences between this channel and existing channels. These differences also represent sources of efficiency for ITC, farmers, and intermediaries.

- *Access to market intelligence leading to a better fulfillment channel.* Sanchalaks, through their close relationships with farmers, have the potential to pick up market signals and consumer information and transmit them back to the distribution channel. They can gain specific information about the community's needs and preferences, thus giving ITC the unique ability to customize products and provide superior fulfillment. Such information is not otherwise available. Market information was previously gathered from agents located at the mandis. Although the agents interacted with the farmers, they were not one of them and did not understand the needs of the community. ITC can now aggregate reliable pieces of information logged from a large number of villages, lending a competitive edge to its trading decisions. Access to information also lets ITC keep a finger on the pulse of the demand and thus helps manage inventories and create an efficient supply chain for the rural market.

- *Pull-based marketing.* This channel is also different from the traditional channel in which inputs were sold mainly by pushing it to the end customers through dealers. The fundamental premise of this strategy is that farmers educated in best practices understand exactly what inputs they need and why they need them. This eliminates the need to spend time and advertising outlay to convince the farmer.

- *Demand aggregation leading to scale economies.* Sanchalaks aggregate demands from individual farmers. In an environment where physical infrastructure is inadequate, the scale economies allowed by aggregation are crucial for keeping down logistics costs.

- *Supply aggregation leading to customization.* At the other end of the network, ITC aggregates products and services from several sources to provide the total solutions.

Status of Operation

Product distribution has been operating in two ways. The first is by using the e-Choupal as the storefront where products are delivered directly by ITC or through a samyojak. The second is by using the hub as the storefront, where ITC sells goods at the produce receiving point. In this case, the samyojak handles the logistics. After completing the sale of his produce, the farmer can conveniently buy products right there and take them on his empty trolley back to the village. The way in which a particular product is delivered depends on the nature of the product. For instance, a fertilizer with a strong odor cannot be sold from the e-Choupal (which is actually part of the sanchalak's residence).

E-Choupals ensure quality in delivering products and services through several product- and service-specific partnerships with the leaders in the respective fields. ITC gives the participating company direct access to the customer through e-Choupal in return for a commission. Participating companies often place samples with the sanchalaks. The sanchalaks aggregate demands from farmers and place the order with the supplier. The sanchalak earns a commission of 2 to 3 percent for every sale he makes. The samyojak serves as a distribution point for the sanchalaks in his region. For his services, he gets a 1 to 3 percent commission.

Brighter Futures

The e-Choupals impact the future of the villages in which they operate through three channels:

- Knowledge of the world
- Access to credit
- Insurance and risk management

Knowledge of the World

Computers are bringing the same resources to rural villages as they brought to urban India. Their impact is no less dramatic. Some of the stories we gathered from the villages are summarized here:

- Children use computers for schoolwork and games. A particularly poignant story is that of Khasrod, where 2,000 local students printed their mark-sheets from the local e-Choupal, saving them days of waiting and a long trip.
- Sanchalaks chat (over the Internet) extensively among themselves about the status of operations and agriculture in their villages.
- Villagers access global resources to learn about agriculture in other parts of the world and take action to compete in the world outside, not merely at the local mandi.
- Youngsters in the village use computers to investigate the latest movies, cell-phone models, and cricket news. One young sanchalak said that some of his friends had aspirations for their future and used the e-Choupal to learn about the computer.

Access to Credit

The farmer's low income and difficulty accessing credit severely limit his capacity to pursue opportunities within and outside agriculture. Access to credit has long been considered a major poverty alleviation strategy in India.

Demand for rural credit is estimated at Rs. 143,000 crore. The government has implemented a variety of credit-linked programs supplemented by subsidies. Among them, the Integrated Rural Development Program (IRDP) started in 1978–79 was a major national rural poverty alleviation program with a large credit component. Under this program, nearly 53 million families were assisted with bank credit of Rs. 31 billion and subsidy of Rs. 10.5 billion. However, its impact had not matched the resources spent. The loans were not tailored to meet individual needs and lacked the support systems necessary to help farmers.

Many financial institutions stay away from rural India due to the following reasons:

- Lack of accessibility to credit history
- High delivery, transaction, and administration costs
- Poor financial disclosure on account of tax issues
- Informal sector that lacks access to capital markets
- A perception of high risk leading to high borrowing costs

ITC proposes to address these problems through e-Choupals and partnerships with financial institutions:

- *Accessibility to credit history*. Farmers in rural India borrow money from local money lenders, through government incentive schemes, friends, relatives, or traders. Local money lenders and intermediates are aware of the creditworthiness of the farmers and are therefore willing to loan money, albeit at a higher rate. With the e-Choupal, ITC now has the capability to manage credit risk through its sanchalak network. The sanchalak network can be used not only to verify the creditworthiness of an individual farmer, but also to continuously monitor credit risk. In the future, ITC can create a consolidated farmers' database with all information pertaining to their holdings and transactions. This database can be used as a source of creditworthiness profiles of the farmers.
- *Transaction and administration costs*. For major financial institutions, transaction costs in servicing the rural market have been high because of the difficulty in reaching the market. By leveraging the IT infrastructure and the sanchalak network, administrative costs can also be reduced.
- *Status of operation*. ITC is set to link with banks such as ICICI and design products tailored to rural India. Some of the products being designed include the following:

- Noncash loans for farm inputs: Instead of giving cash to the farmer directly, the financial institutions will purchase farm inputs on behalf of the farmer. The farmer is expected to pay back the loan to the financial institution.

- Loans to sanchalaks: Instead of giving loans directly to the farmer, loans will be given to the sanchalak, who in turn loans it to the farmer. With better access to the farmer, the sanchalak can manage the credit risk better than the financial institution.

- Direct loans to farmers based on sanchalak recommendation: In this case, the sanchalak's commission is based on the loan recovery and therefore he has the incentive to monitor the risk on a continuous basis.

Insurance and Risk Management Services

Insurance is an excellent example of how ITC brings its knowledge of rural dynamics to bear on product design. Insurance in rural India suffered from several problems. Some characteristics of this effort are as follows:

- Products have been designed to deal with rural cash cycles. There is recognition that in bad years farmers might not be able to pay premiums. Rather than penalize the farmer with a lapsed policy as current products do, ITC's offerings allow for correction in later years or only diminish the final payout.

- ITC uses the e-Choupal Web infrastructure to set up and issue electronic reminders for premium payment. This addresses a major limitation of the current products. The agents currently selling insurance have little incentive to encourage renewals and the policy lapse rates are high.

- A system of interlocking instruments has been set up so that insurance premiums can be credited with quality bonus points from the farmer's soya sale.

- The sanchalak is assisted in making the sales pitch by informational Webcasts and video presentations.

Detractors, Risks, and Limitations

In the net sum, the change brought about by the e-Choupal is overwhelmingly positive. It is, however, important to note the parties who are adversely affected in the short term.

Detractors

Diversion of produce to e-Choupals has caused soya volumes to shrink by 50 percent at mandis we visited. Most people who have lost money are closely connected to the mandi. They include the following:

- *Commission agents.* Despite ITC's best efforts to maintain the mandi volumes and compensate the commission agents for lost income, there is little doubt that on the whole they have lower incomes after the e-Choupal than before.
- *Mandi laborers.* The workers in the mandi who weighed and bagged the produce have been severely impacted by the drop in volume. ITC's long-term vision is to employ many of these people in the hubs in much the same functions as they perform in the mandi. The Sonkach mandi has 28 tulavatis and 300 laborers.
- *Bazaars near the mandi.* When farmers sold produce in the mandi, they would also make purchases of a variety of commodities at the local bazaars. This revenue has now been diverted to shops near the ITC hubs. This in itself is more a diversion of revenue than its elimination.
- *Some mandi operations.* ITC still pays mandi tax for all the grain procured through e-Choupals but it now pays the tax to the mandi nearest to the procurement center. As a result, tax is being diverted from several mandis to the few mandis near procurement hubs. The result of this is that regional mandis have lost taxes that contribute to maintaining their infrastructure.
- *Competing processors.* Even before the advent of the e-Choupal, the soya crushing industry suffered from severe overcapacity (half of all capacity was excess). The efficiency pressures imposed by the e-Choupal have spurred industry consolidation.

Risks and Limitations

Apart from the risks identified by ITC, there are some additional areas that bear watching and could require active intervention.

Subversion of Samyojaks Toward Competitive Entry

ITC's relationship with the samyojaks seems to be uneasy. It seems ITC could easily manage internally most of the services provide by the samyojaks. The one samyojak we spoke with indicated that past relationships and the promise of future business keep him loyal to ITC despite deep reduction in procurement business. The primary barriers to competitive entry are scale of operations, a trusted network, and rural know-how. Multinationals with the financial muscle to invest for the scale can use discontented samyojaks as collaborators.

Farmers and Customer Service

ITC has awakened farmers' aspirations. If they do not keep up with these aspirations, the farmers will look elsewhere to satisfy them. As an example, in the conversation where the sanchalak asked us about Indian onions in the global market, he also knew what the solution was. He half-complained that he had told ITC several times to begin sales of better onion seeds, but he had not heard back from them.

Social Impact Limited by Stratification

The computer in the village is no doubt revolutionary, but there is also no doubt the villages we saw were stratified to the point where not everybody can walk up to the sanchalak and ask to be shown the computer. There are clearly people at lower income levels and the entire adult female population who do not have access to the computer (we have used only masculine pronouns in this case study because that is the reality of the society we visited). The innate power of the computer to drive social change will not be able to transcend this barrier unaided. This is by no means a reflection on ITC; it is a reflection on the nature of the underlying society in rural Madhya Pradesh.

The solution might lie in observing where the system has driven social change. Village farmers belong to many social and economic strata. Yet the sanchalaks are servicing all of them equally. In this case, the potential for commerce has broken a barrier that society has built. Similarly, engagement with the isolated demographics, especially women, might be possible through the active procurement and distribution through the e-Choupal of products tailored specifically to them.

e-Choupals: Future Generations

ITC recognizes the limitations of today's e-Choupals in their manifestation as vehicles of procurement efficiency. Not every crop lends itself to such an intervention. With crops such as soya, where value is to be had, followers will soon imitate ITC and eliminate the competitive advantage. ITC's vision for the e-Choupals extends many generations as the e-Choupal evolves into a full-fledged orchestrator of a two-way exchange of goods and services between rural India and the world. The soya choupal is Wave 1, with several more to follow:

- *Wave 2*. The source of value in this generation will be preservation of identity through the chain. This is a significant source of value in crops such as wheat, where the grade of the grain determines its end use and the ability to separate different grades from field to consumer will command a price premium. E-Choupals in Uttar Pradesh have already started wheat procurement.

- *Wave 3*. This wave takes identity a step further by building the concept of traceability into the supply chain. This is vital in perishables where traceability allows ITC to address food safety concerns and once again provide a value that the customer is willing to pay for. Shrimp is a good example of a crop where Wave 3 will apply. ITC's intervention in such products will actually be at the level of production. ITC will define standards that producers must adhere to and work with farmers to ensure product quality. Farmers in turn will get the best prices from ITC because ITC commands the traceability premium.

- *Wave 4*. The first three waves fill institutional voids; Wave 4 creates institutions. The first three waves apply to environments where ITC was the sole buyer in the e-Choupal channel. For commodities where the underlying markets have reached a high degree of efficiency, such basic sources of value will not exist. For crops such as these, the e-Choupal will serve as the marketplace where multiple buyers and sellers execute a range of transactions. A good example of this is coffee. ITC's source of value will be the sunk cost of the IT infrastructure and the transaction fees.

- *Wave 5*. Whereas the first four waves related to the sourcing from rural India, the fifth wave elaborates the rural marketing and distribution strategy. This is not the same as the rudimentary distribution of agricultural inputs that is being done today. ITC plans to bring together knowledge of the customer, knowledge of the business, deployed infrastructure, its reputation, experience gained over the first four waves, and an organization of people, processes, and partners. This base will allow ITC to bring value-added products and services to bear on rural India.

- *Wave 6*. After the sourcing of goods from rural India, ITC's last wave has the ambitious vision of eventually sourcing IT-enabled services from rural India. Telemedicine, ecotourism, traditional medicine, and traditional crafts are some of the services that can be sourced from rural India. Although some time off, it is an agenda that inspires because of the scale of the vision and the potential impact.

Endnotes

1. "Poverty Dynamics in Rural India"—IMF Working Paper, Revised November 6, 2002.

2. A major source for this section is World Bank Report #15677-IN: India the Oilseed Complex: Capturing Market Opportunities, July 1997.

This report was written by Kuttayan Annamalai and Sachin Rao, under the supervision of Professor C. K. Prahalad. This report is intended to be a catalyst for discussion and is not intended to illustrate effective or ineffective strategies.

SECTION V

Scaling Innovations

Civil society organizations and startups account for a disproportionate number of experiments to improve the lot of the BOP consumers. However, their reach is limited. Their orientation is local and they do not have the resources or the managerial skills for scaling up, much less taking it global.

One of the pressing problems at the BOP is access to clean, good-quality energy. The poor spend a disproportionate amount of their income on expensive and inefficient sources of energy—batteries, oil, and candles. Grid-based electricity does not reach most of them. E+Co is a pioneer in developing alternative energy sources, such as solar and wind, and experimenting with them in remote parts of the world, be it in Latin America, Africa, India, and other such places. They have active projects in countries as varied as Nicaragua to India. They have acted as an "angel and seed fund" group enabling local entrepreneurs to build viable commercial businesses and, at the same time, bring good-quality energy to the isolated populations. The portfolio of projects has all the desirable ingredients: private sector initiatives, commercial viability, success in harnessing renewable sources of energy, and aid for BOP consumers in isolated regions of the world. Given this track record, however, E+Co finds it hard to raise money for scaling up the effort.

A similar but less difficult situation exists for Voxiva, a startup that is a pioneer in the surveillance of emerging public health crises. Voxiva started by developing a system that allows for public health workers in remote regions of Peru to monitor the outbreak of infectious diseases and communicate relevant information to the central public health administrators in the capital of Lima.

The system accommodates a wide variety of devices—regular telephones, wireless, and PCs—to communicate. The system takes the structured information and converts it into a database that can be readily viewed by authorities. This is a real-time, low-cost, effective surveillance system. Voxiva successfully demonstrated it in Peru. Voxiva also had to raise funds to expand.

The company found that the competencies it had developed in converting inputs from a variety of devices, particularly voice messages, into a real-time monitoring system, might have applications in other parts of the world and in other sectors as well. The Voxiva system found applications in the U.S. Department of Defense as it inoculated soldiers for smallpox (a dispersed population with few skills in medical diagnosis). The soldiers could just call in their condition and the central monitoring stations could identify infections. The blood supply in the United States was the next target of opportunity. The situation in Iraq and the threat of SARS in Southeast Asia gave Voxiva a way to leverage its innovations in developed and other developing countries. With this track record, Voxiva was able to raise the modest but adequate capital it needed for expansion.

E+Co and Voxiva illustrate how startups can demonstrate the development of fundamentally new solutions to age-old problems, be it access to energy in isolated rural populations or providing public health access to and warning of latent outbreaks of disease in remote areas. Both bring new skills and technology and elegant, cost-effective solutions. The solutions of Voxiva also have applications in developed markets, such as the United States. These startups need access to funding to scale up. Funding sources, including private equity, are hesitant to back ventures that go against the grain. Non-grid-based electricity or a surveillance system that is not PC-based (but PC-compatible) find it that much harder to attract investments. If access to funding is not solved, ventures such as E+Co and Voxiva will have to seek adoption of these initiatives by multinational corporations that have the scale and resources required.

The Voxiva Story

Over the last two decades the spread of new diseases such as Acquired Immune Deficiency Syndrome (AIDS) and Severe Acute Respiratory Syndrome (SARS) has generated a renewed awareness of the threats posed by infectious diseases. Indeed, infectious diseases, such as cholera, meningococcal disease, and measles, cause 63 percent of all childhood deaths and 48 percent of premature deaths, and at least 300 million people have acute cases of malaria, 90 percent of them in sub-Saharan Africa.[1]

THE INNOVATION...

Controlling the threat of infectious diseases demands early detection of outbreaks and immediate response. Without timely information and effective two-way communication, health authorities cannot hope to manage the spread of diseases such as SARS. In rural areas of the developing world, where many new outbreaks occur, a pay phone is often a community's only link to the outside world. Voxiva's technology turns a village pay phone into a communications device on par with that of a computer. By calling into Voxiva's system and pushing buttons on the phone, rural health workers can report new cases of disease systematically and in real time. Health authorities can see the information immediately via the Internet, analyze the data, and use the system's communication and messaging tools to respond. By leveraging the world's 2.5 billion phones, as well as the Internet, Voxiva's solutions have a much wider reach than Internet-only solutions. Although Voxiva's technology was developed for the developing world—and pioneered in Peru—its simplicity and practicality have created great demand in the United States and developed world markets. Voxiva's systems are now used by U.S. government agencies—from the Food and Drug Administration (FDA) to the Department of Defense to the San Diego County Health Department—as well as by private health providers. In the developing world, Voxiva has deployed health solutions in Latin America, Africa, Iraq, and India.

Continuing threats of emergent diseases, such as SARS, threaten state and regional economies. In a report issued by the Asian Development Bank (ADB) in the spring of 2003, it was estimated that the SARS outbreak will, in addition to the loss of life, cost Asia approximately $7 billion in forecast economic output while the region as a whole could lose up to $28 billion.[2] However, disease detection and communication can inhibit the spread of infectious diseases. According to the World Health Organization (WHO), reporting systems are the intelligence network that underpins disease control and prevention. Without this framework in place, it is impossible to track where disease is occurring, measure progress in disease control targets, or provide an early warning system for outbreaks and the emergence of new diseases.[3]

There are three key ingredients of an effective system for disease surveillance and response:

- Real-time collection of critical information from a distributed network of people, in this case, health workers with new cases of disease to report.
- Rapid analysis of data to drive decision-making and allocation of resources.
- Communication back to the field to coordinate response.

Voxiva's solutions are designed to address all three: real-time data collection for early detection of outbreaks, rapid analysis, and communications for response. Although Voxiva's system was developed initially to support disease response, the fundamental problem that Voxiva solves is universal and applicable to a range of problems, from monitoring of patients to crime reporting to tracking commercial orders and distribution. Although solutions to these problems might seem obvious in the developed world where people have ready access to the Internet, Voxiva primarily targets rural areas, where 70 percent of the world's poor live with limited access to telecommunications.[4]

So how does Voxiva bridge this communications gap? Why is it targeting make under $2 a day? Their value added is socially admirable, but is it profitable? In this case Voxiva challenges a basic assumption held by many: Computers must proliferate in rural communities to connect the poor to real-time information systems. In bypassing this assumption, Voxiva rejects previous notions of cost structure by leveraging existing infrastructure: the billions of phones already in place. By creating an account for rural health workers and letting them access robust information systems from any phone or a computer, Voxiva connects marginalized communities to the health system in a systematic and meaningful way.

The Founders of Voxiva

Before co-founding Voxiva in March 2001, Paul Meyer founded IPKO, the first and largest Internet service provider in Kosovo. Started in the weeks after the 1999 war, IPKO was hailed by the United Nations Secretary General as "a model for future humanitarian emergencies," and is today one of the largest businesses in Kosovo. Before IPKO, Meyer wrote speeches for President Clinton, graduated from Yale Law School, and deployed IT systems to help reunite refugee children separated from their families in West Africa and the Balkans. After returning from Kosovo, Meyer was a Senior Fellow of the Markle Foundation, where he studied efforts to "bridge the digital divide"—projects using information and communications technologies (ICTs) to support development. He summarized his findings in three general points:

1. Most projects were deployed on a pilot basis and were fundamentally not scalable. Making a system work in one village in India is very different from making it work in 600,000 villages in India.
2. Projects were overwhelmingly focused on connectivity and devices—building out networks or putting computers in schools—rather than on applications that addressed critical information flow challenges. There was much greater emphasis on machines and data networks and not enough thinking about people and the human networks.
3. There was too much focus on the Internet and computers as a solution, particularly given the challenges of electricity, hardware and maintenance costs, training, and literacy.

Above all, Meyer observed that people were ignoring the fact there are a lot more telephones in the world—2.5 billion at last count—and deduced that telephones are a much more accessible, practical tool for most people in the world.

Dr. Pamela Johnson, a PhD in medical anthropology, is co-founder and Executive Vice President of Business Development at Voxiva. She provides insight into the marriage among government, technology, and public health that serves to define the company. Previously, she was the coordinator for child survival at the U.S. Agency for International Development (USAID), overseeing public health programs in 50 countries, and subsequently helped lead the U.S. government's eGovernment Initiative at the White House. Johnson said, "To me the real potential of technology in the developing world is to try to make better use of scarce resources."

Dr. Anand Narasimhan, Voxiva's third co-founder, provided the technological vision for the company. Before joining Voxiva, he was the founding Chief Technology Officer of J2 Global Communications, the largest unified messaging company in the world, and spent many years at IBM.

Voxiva: A Social Venture

Voxiva was founded to deliver practical technology solutions to important problems in the developing world. Voxiva sought to extend the reach of software applications to people and communities without access to the Internet and to connect them in a systematic and meaningful way to promote health and development. Although Voxiva's solutions create significant social value, the company balances its social vision with its clear mandate to create strong returns for investors. Meyer contemplated starting Voxiva as a nonprofit organization but concluded that only by creating a powerful economic model that leverages Voxiva's technology and infrastructure across many applications and customers could the company scale and realize the full potential of its founding vision.

Voxiva's initial investment came from socially minded sources: Ben Cohen of Ben & Jerry's Ice Cream ($250,000) and the Markle Foundation[5] ($500,000). The funding for Voxiva's first deployment, the Alerta disease surveillance system in Peru, came from the World Bank's InfoDev[6] program for innovative uses of technology in economic development. Meyer noted, "We were able to get started because we raised money from people who thought what we were doing was important to the world and also believed in our business model. For the early investors, it was probably more the former than the latter." Voxiva has since raised more than $8 million from socially minded angel investors and top-tier investment firms like Allen & Company in New York.

Beyond helping it raise the initial capital, Voxiva's social vision and mission have helped the company enormously in winning customers and attracting dedicated employees. Because of Voxiva's track record in the developing world and deep understanding of the public health sector, customers trust Voxiva and are more comfortable working with Voxiva than with a more traditional software company. In addition, Voxiva has been able to attract, retain, and motivate exceptional employees by appealing to their hearts as well as their wallets. According to Meyer, the ideal Voxiva employee is part McKinsey consultant, part Microsoft engineer, and part Peace Corps volunteer.

Voxiva in Peru

Voxiva first deployed its technology in Peru to facilitate real-time disease surveillance from rural health workers. The project was funded with a $250,000 grant from the World Bank's InfoDev program. Officials from the Gates Foundation and the WHO suggested Peru as a good place to pilot the system because the country had established a strong paper-based disease surveillance system in the aftermath of a devastating cholera outbreak in 1991. Voxiva wanted to work with a pilot customer who would actively manage the information collected by the system and use the system to respond to disease outbreaks in real time, a role filled by Peru's Department of Epidemiology (OGE). As Johnson emphasized, "The head of the OGE not only understood the role of information technology, but could see the power behind it. We like to work with people who are really hungry for information and actually want to do something with it. We don't believe in collecting data to end up in annual reports. We believe in collecting data for action."

Voxiva also wanted a pilot country where the telecommunications infrastructure had sufficient reach into rural areas. By 2002, telephones had reached more than 6,000 communities in Peru, with Internet access reaching 900. Karen Lynch, Director of the Markle Foundation's Global Digital Opportunity Project, said, "Markle's interest was that [the project] be done in a developing country that showed some critical success factors, such as in-country leadership and an enabling environment, and Peru filled that bill—among other reasons because its president was showing a strong interest in information technology and Peru had put considerable work into its health care administration."

Peru's Ministry of Health

Problem Definition

The fundamental challenge faced by Peru's Ministry of Health was to monitor new cases of disease from more than 6,000 health clinics spread across

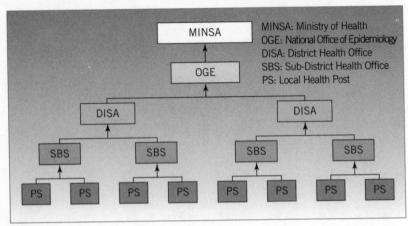

Figure 1 Hierarchical information flow in epidemiologic surveillance from rural clinics to the Ministry of Health of Peru. Data flows up gradually with a paper-based system but no information flows back to health workers in the field.

the country and respond in time to stem new outbreaks. Peru's existing surveillance system collected weekly disease outbreak reports from every health clinic in the country. However, because the reports were collected on paper and recompiled at each level of the Ministry of Health's (MINSA) hierarchy (see Figure 1), weeks or months could pass before Ministry of Health officials in Lima learned of outbreaks and were able to respond.

"Previously you couldn't transmit data and therefore couldn't administer data," said Dr. Luis Botton, IT Director at the District Level within the Health System.

Moreover, information rarely, if ever, flowed back to health workers in the field. More than 90 percent of rural health workers reported receiving health alerts "never," rarely," or "less than once a month."

Voxiva's Alerta disease surveillance application was designed to allow for information to flow directly from health clinics into a national-level system so that information is accessible to those at all levels simultaneously. Moreover, the system allows health authorities at higher levels to view the incoming data on a map, analyze it, and use the system's communication and notification tools to provide feedback to the field and coordinate the response.

How It Works

Voxiva designed Alerta to address the needs of Peru's dispersed rural health workers. Alerta allows front-line health workers to submit disease reports in real time from any phone or Internet-connected device. Users receive an account

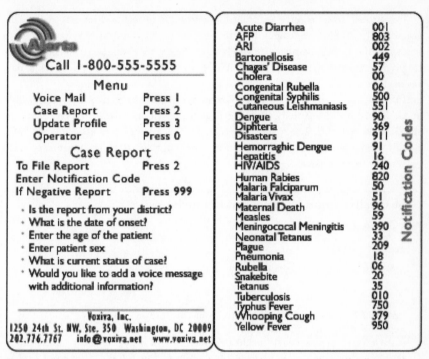

Figure 2 Alerta user cards. Health workers enter numeric codes corresponding to the diseases they must report.

number, personal identification number (PIN) and a plastic card with simple instructions and codes for all the diseases they need to report (see Figure 2). From a phone, they dial a toll-free number to access the system. From the Web, they go to Voxiva's Web site.

Authorized users log on and follow instructions on a wallet-sized card or a simple voice-prompted menu and enter digital information about cases of disease and disaster incidents. They can attach additional information in voice files. Each user also has a voice mail account, which can be accessed when he or she logs on. Thus, rural health professionals are able to send and receive voice messages, even if they do not own a telephone. Users are also able to receive health alerts, information about diseases, vaccination programs, training opportunities, natural disastors, and so on.

Health authorities can monitor incoming cases through a Web interface. Individual disease reports arrive in real time with full case details. Authorities can also listen to voice files recorded by the remote health workers. Data are available immediately, and health officials can export data to various programs for analysis and presentation. Geographic information systems can also be used to view data using dynamic maps.

Designated users receive automatic notification of selected reports via e-mail, voice mail, or SMS message. Health officials can communicate with remote health professionals using voice mails as if they were e-mails, to individuals or to predetermined groups of users. The system is operational 24 hours a day, seven days a week.

Information is entered into the Voxiva system directly, making it accessible at all levels simultaneously. Because health posts enter data directly, errors in the data are reduced. The system provides feedback to users at all levels via SMS, e-mail, and voice mail. Health workers use voice mail to communicate with each other peer to peer.

Medically remote, but not out of touch

The Houston Chronicle

March 6, 2004

http://www.chron.com/cs/CDA/ssistory.mpl/business/2436493

Associated Press

PACARAN, Peru — Beyond the reach of the Internet and paved roads, this quiet town in the Andean foothills is typical of much of rural Peru, where isolation can hinder timely medical reporting and health officials' ability to respond. But when villagers from the hamlet of Picamaran, a five-hour hike away, started showing up in Pacaran with symptoms of sometimes-deadly bartonellosis three years ago, nurse Malena Rivas turned to her new "computer"—a cell phone.

Using a pilot program set up by Voxiva, Rivas dialed a toll-free number and, through a several-step menu system, punched in the data on her patients. Within minutes, the Health Ministry had the data. And only days later, university physicians arrived to contain an epidemic of bartonellosis, also named La Oroya Fever after the Peruvian smelter town where an 1871 outbreak killed more than 7,000. The disease, which is transmitted by sand fly bites, can cause fever, chills, aches, seizures and death.

The Alerta Pilot

The Alerta pilot connected approximately 204,000 individuals in two sparsely populated districts south of Lima to the national health surveillance system: Chilca-Mala with 15 residents per square kilometer and Cañete with 24 inhabitants per square kilometer. The system incorporated 76 health clinics, health centers, and district centers (SBS) that are part of the four levels of the Ministry of Health. In total Peru has more than 6,000 health posts (PS); 53 SBSs; 34 state-level health centers (DISA), which play a vital role in outbreak management; along with the Department of Epidemiology (OGE) and the Ministry of Health (MINSA) located in the capital, Lima.

The initial pilot ran from March 2002 through early September 2002. After a short orientation, health professionals began to use available telephones and the Internet (whichever was available) to submit real-time, electronic reports of mandated diseases and disasters. Of the participating health posts, 68.4 percent had easy access to a phone. Another 17.1 percent reported via high-frequency radio link to a nearby clinic. Only 14 percent of facilities had no access to technology and reported using the traditional paper methods.

Prior to Alerta's installation, 28 health posts reported on a weekly basis and 22 reported on a monthly basis to the Chilca-Mala SBS. Although MINSA required that health posts and centers report on a weekly basis, due to the cumbersome process of transporting the reports, many reported only monthly. After Alerta's deployment, 12 of the 22 that had previously reported on a monthly basis began reporting on a weekly basis because of access to a telephone in their village. Of the posts with access to a phone or radio, 86.5 percent reported regularly.

A total of 26,264 cases was reported during the pilot with more than 4,167 calls. Altogether, 204 users, including front-line health workers and management, utilized the program during the pilot. A survey conducted in August 2002 revealed that 90 percent of the respondents who used the system believed the faster responses from supervisors were a primary benefit of the system, and 70 percent of the users cited the increased communication with their colleagues and supervisors as another key benefit of the system.

Cost–Benefit

An evaluation of the pilot by San Marcos University in Peru found that, as compared with the traditional system, Alerta required a substantially lower allocation of resources, lower operating costs, and resulted in a threefold increase in reporting coverage. Overall, the Alerta system required 40 percent lower costs of operations than the traditional paper system. The study also concluded that the use of voice mail for communications was 7.8 times less expensive than written communication.

Alerta's benefits, based on the pilot, can be summarized as follows: (see Table 1).

1. It is intuitive to use and accessible, even from very remote regions of Peru.
2. It allows for quicker, better informed decision-making by health authorities and better allocation of scarce resources.
3. It fosters better data quality because data is entered directly by users in the field and validated at the source.
4. It allows for rapid feedback of information to the field and can be used to reinforce the skills and knowledge of health workers in the field.

Table 1 Alerta Pilot Scorecard

Goals	Grade	Comments
Technically Appropriate and Feasible	B+	Voxiva reaches the lowest common denominator of technology: the village phone. Its system has even incorporated reports from clinics that report via high-frequency radio. Because most users interact with the system via the phone and respond to voice prompts, they do not have to be literate to use the system. On the other hand, many end users who work at health posts are not familiar with the use of IVR and voice mail, so ongoing training is required.
Cost-Effective	A+	It had a clear and rapid benefit demonstration because deployment was fast. Compared to other IT applications, startup costs were low due to piggybacking on the existing telecom infrastructure. Also, the fact that it is an open system makes integration with the existing IT health system used by the Ministry of Health possible and relatively simple. Voxiva provides an "appropriate" IT solution in an environment with not only limited (but growing) telecom infrastructure, but it's also appropriate in a resource-strapped country like Peru.
Can Be Maintained with Local Skills and Resources	A-	Because Voxiva relies on existing infrastructure, the phone and data networks are maintained by telecommunications companies like Telefonica in Peru. As an application service provider, Voxiva's in-country team worries about keeping the application up and running, allowing the customer to focus on managing the information. Since it is so intuitive for end users, the system requires very little training for most users. Higher level users who manage the information require better skills and more extensive training.
Accepted by Clients and Providers	A-	High score from all end users. More important, it had multilateral and private-sector participation and alignment with national planning to strengthen the disease prevention system. There is avid dedication in both quality and intensity of use. For example, the Navy had 100 percent reporting from participating naval bases. The only vulnerability is due to the frequent turnover in the Ministry of Health. In three years working in Peru, Voxiva has interacted with six Ministers of Health.

Table 1 Continued

Goals	Grade	Comments
Result in Favorable Effects on Health	N/A	At this point health impact has not been assessed. The goals of the project were not measured in health objectives, but rather by efficiency within the process and overall medical administration.

Source: Rodrigues, R. J. (2000). *Telemedicine and the transformation of healthcare practice in the information age.* In Speakers' Book of the International Telecommunication Union (ITU) Telecom Americas 2000; Telecom Development Symposium, Session TDS.2; Rio de Janeiro, April 10–15, 2000, p. 9.

5. It reduces the paperwork burden on health workers in the field.
6. It promotes transparency and accountability by making information available at multiple levels simultaneously.
7. It is cost-effective relative to the current system and other IT rollouts because it leverages the existing telecommunications infrastructure and has an open structure to seamlessly link to legacy systems.

In the words of Dr. Jaime Levano, an Alerta user in Cañete, Peru, "We can see the information instantaneously . . . now everyone is informed about a case and the disease and the appropriate measures can be taken according to the case . . . it is truly an important benefit . . . it could help eradicate diseases."

Alerta Deployed for the Peruvian Navy

In October 2002, Alerta was expanded to support the disease surveillance efforts of the Peruvian Navy (DISAMAR), with support from the U.S. Navy's Global Emerging Infections System (GEIS).

After 15 months of operations, the results of the deployment were presented to the American Society of Tropical Medicine and Hygiene. "The introduction of Alerta has led to early outbreak identification/response, timely case management, and increased review of clinical procedures within reporting units." Compliance with the system reached a sustained 100 percent within six months of its launch. The study concluded that:

Alerta represents a fully functional alternative for cost-effective real-time disease surveillance in countries at all stages of technological development. The investment required is small compared to alternative approaches to building disease surveillance capabilities, particularly in terms of infrastructure and maintenance expenses. The combination of scalable technology, accurate and close monitoring of performance, controlled growth, and effective mechanisms for information sharing, feedback and data-driven decision making has turned this pilot project into a highly innovative, cost-effective and replicable surveillance model.

Beyond Health Care in Peru

Although Voxiva's efforts have been directed primarily at delivering health care solutions, because of the flexibility of the technology platform, the company has begun to deploy solutions in additional vertical markets. In the summer of 2003, Voxiva deployed its second application—Citizen's Alert in Lima, Peru—to allow citizens to report crime to municipal authorities in real time and for authorities to track the location of police and dispatch them accordingly. The system was first deployed for the Miraflores municipality in Lima and has since been expanded to four additional municipalities. Like all its applications, Voxiva hosts the solution and charges on a per–citizen, per-month basis.

Application in Developed Countries: From Peru to the Developed World

Although Voxiva's systems were originally developed to serve developing world markets, the simplicity and practicality of the solutions have created demand for the systems in the United States. In the spring of 2002, in the wake of the anthrax letters and broader fears over bioterrorism, Voxiva's board directed the company to explore opportunities in the United States.

Voxiva's first customer in the United States was the FDA. The FDA had developed a Web-based system for monitoring blood shortages but soon discovered that 40 percent of the nation's blood centers did not have ready access to the Internet. In fact, according to a study conducted by the Pew Foundation in April 2003, 42 percent of Americans have not used the Internet, nor do they plan to do so.[7] Because Voxiva's systems are accessible from the phone as well as the Web, the FDA was able to deploy a much more accessible system to track blood shortages (see Figure 3).

Voxiva's other U.S. deployments include disease surveillance systems for Washington, DC, and San Diego County and a smallpox vaccination monitoring system for the U.S. Department of Defense.

Smallpox Vaccination Program: U.S. Department of Defense

CHALLENGE: Concern about weaponized smallpox led the Department of Defense to vaccinate military personnel against the disease. Because data on the effects of the smallpox vaccine were more than 30 years old and because of changing demography and health status of the U.S. population, the Department of Defense wanted to monitor the early recipients of the vaccine closely.

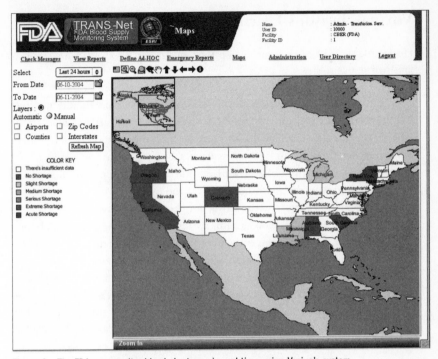

Figure 3   The FDA can monitor blood shortages in real time using Voxiva's system.

SOLUTION: Voxiva deployed SAFEVAX, an electronic diary, for the Department's Smallpox Vaccination Program. Vaccinees, using secure IDs and passwords, report on their symptoms on a daily basis using toll-free telephone access or the Internet. If vaccinees miss a report, they receive a reminder call from a call center operator who can help them submit their data. Vaccinees can access their own diary after logging into the Web site. SAFEVAX facilitates rapid identification of reactions; analysis of reaction patterns and trends; and automatic alert and notification. The Department of Defense can specify criteria based on symptoms (i.e., fever of over 103 degrees) that result in an automatic telephone or e-mail notification to the appropriate person.

Even as Voxiva continues to win business related to bioterrorism preparedness and homeland defense, it has discovered even greater opportunity for its technology in providing patient monitoring systems for leading disease management companies and home health agencies in the U.S. and U.K. markets. Voxiva has also found a market for its crime reporting system in the United States. In spring 2004, it signed its first contracts to deploy the service for several university campuses.

Voxiva's Lessons Learned

Having deployed health solutions on five continents, Voxiva summarized its lessons learned as follows:

1. Foster two-way information flows. Information systems should not just collect data, but also provide feedback and support to health workers in the field. Too often systems are put in place for monitoring and evaluation with information flowing upward to managers but providing no value to the health workers in the field. A well-designed information system supports and contributes to the performance of all the users.

2. Leverage existing infrastructure. It is not necessary to have PCs everywhere to have a robust information system. By leveraging phones, mobile phones, handheld devices and faxes, as well as PCs and the Internet, it is possible to deploy a health information system much more quickly and cost-effectively than systems that require the up-front purchase, installation, and maintenance of a widespread network of expensive hardware or devices

3. Avoid stovepipes. Information systems should be integrated across programs. With paper reporting systems currently in place, health workers are overburdened with different forms for each program they interact with. In some countries, health workers spend as much as 40 percent of their time filling out forms, compiling data, and copying data. The danger is that those paper stovepipes get replicated with technology and health workers have to use a different system (and perhaps even a different device) for each program they report to (e.g., tuberculosis, malaria, HIV/AIDS, etc.).

4. Software is not a system. Deploying PCs and clinic-level software does not produce an integrated national system. What is needed is a robust, scalable, integrated information system that connects health professionals from the local to the national level and provides them with the information and support they each need. What is needed is more analogous to a sophisticated phone and Web banking system than to Microsoft Excel. This requires a different technology architecture and different approach.

5. Technology alone will fail. Change management and capacity building are key. Most public health agencies in the developing world are not accustomed to real-time information. Helping decision-makers incorporate better information and use it for strategic decision-making and response is critical to the success. This requires considerable change management, training, and capacity-building efforts that dovetail with the deployment of an information system.

Voxiva's Global Rollout

Although Voxiva's detour through the U.S. market delayed its international expansion, the credibility Voxiva earned from serving customers such as the FDA and Department of Defense has served it well in its subsequent expansion in the Middle East, Africa, and Asia. Customers in new countries seem much more comfortable with technology that is "good enough" for the U.S. market.

Iraq

In Spring 2003, the company won a $1.3-million contract to deploy the national disease surveillance system for postwar Iraq. The contract was part of a larger $43-million contract awarded by USAID to Abt Associates to strengthen the Iraqi health care system. Voxiva's first task order from this contract was to design a platform and database architecture for a facilities-based, real-time Iraqi health information system to strengthen health service delivery and support project monitoring and evaluation, with rapid prototype deployment of a disease surveillance module in Basra. Voxiva deployed the Alerta system— renamed "SMART" by Iraqi Ministry of Health officials—in January 2004. The company had to expand its standard training to include a new module, "How to use a cell phone," because cell phones had been outlawed under Saddam Hussein and few health officials had even seen one.

HIV/AIDS in Africa

In Fall 2003, Voxiva turned its attentions to the challenges of combating HIV/AIDS in Africa. In his 2003 State of the Union address, President Bush committed $15 billion over five years to fight AIDS in Africa under the President's Emergency Plan for AIDS Relief (PEPFAR). Voxiva believed its solutions were perfectly suited to supporting the huge challenges involved in scaling up and managing the delivery of care and antiretroviral treatment (ART) to millions of people in some of the poorest countries in the world. These were countries where many health clinics lack even electricity, health personnel are limited in number and skills, and information systems are rudimentary.

In December 2003, Voxiva CEO Paul Meyer was invited to accompany U.S. Secretary of Health and Human Services Tommy Thompson, WHO Director J.W. Lee, PEPFAR Director Randall Tobias, the directors of the Centers for Disease Control, National Institutes of Health, Global Fund for AIDS, and the CEOs of Pfizer, Merck, and Bristol-Myers on a weeklong delegation visit to four countries in Africa to plan the PEPFAR implementation. The fact that Voxiva was the only software company on the trip was testament to its rising profile in the arena of global public health.

Based on that visit and on lessons learned from Voxiva's previous experiences, the company proposed a system that would assist clinicians, managers, and decision-makers to:

- Monitor key indicators of a national HIV/AIDS program with accurate, current data for national and global reporting requirements.
- Carefully manage ART to reduce the spread of viral resistance.
- Coordinate services and programs across multiple facilities and levels.
- Provide for the information needs of PEPFAR in a way that is sustainable and strengthens underlying health information and infrastructure.

The system was also designed to improve management of programs by allowing countries to:

- Clinically manage chronic illnesses (HIV/AIDS and opportunistic infections), including complex treatment regimes.
- Train, support, and supervise health personnel.
- Assure reliable distribution and tracking of pharmaceuticals.
- Promote transparency and accountability at all levels.

The company's efforts have been rewarded. In February, Voxiva won an initial contract under PEPFAR to deploy the national HIV/AIDS information system for Rwanda. In addition, Voxiva was part of a consortium led by Catholic Relief Services that was awarded a five-year, $335-million contract to deliver HIV/AIDS care in ten countries and another consortium led by Columbia University that was awarded a five-year, $125-million contract for eight countries. At printing, the company was also bidding on contracts in South Africa, Nigeria, Madagascar, and Uganda.

India

Voxiva launched its operation in India on February 1, 2004, and won its first contract—to deploy a surveillance system for Japanese encephalitis—within a month. To launch Voxiva India, Voxiva recruited Madhu Krishna from her post directing the Bill & Melinda Gates Child Vaccine Program in India. Krishna says she joined the company "because Voxiva has the potential to transform public health." Meyer is bullish on the company's prospects in India: "I think that India is the market where Voxiva will reach its fullest potential. All the conditions are there: the fixed-phone network reaches into the most rural areas. Mobile networks are building like crazy. The cost of calls has dropped fifty-fold in the last three years. Most importantly, there are a billion people, very few of whom are connected to the health system in a meaningful and systematic way. We intend to change that."

Voxiva's Challenges

- Voxiva seems to have hit on a solution to a universal problem: allowing organizations to collect data from and communicate with dispersed populations in a timely and systematic way by leveraging existing infrastructure. Although the opportunities in front of the company are vast, Voxiva faces a range of challenges as it grows; namelt to continue to build the Voxiva brand and reinforce its social capital. Voxiva has benefited enormously from its brand recognition as a provider of practical technology solutions and a socially minded venture. That brand positioning has yielded great advantage for the company in terms of its ability to raise capital; hire, motivate, and retain employees; and attract customers who feel more comfortable working with a company that understands their problems and shares their values.

- Ensure that its capacity to win new business does not outpace its ability to deliver quality services. With operations on five continents, the company will be challenged to maintain the quality of its services. The company cannot afford to let its delivery slip.

- Focus on key opportunities and avoiding distraction. Clearly there is a market for Voxiva's solutions across a range of geographies and sectors. Focus and prioritization are keys. "Saying no to opportunities is a huge challenge," admits Meyer. He constantly finds himself weighing the business opportunities versus the social benefits; short-term results over long-term impact; and fighting the inclination to grow all at once into different sectors.

- Deal with the challenges and long sales cycles of selling services to governments and international development agencies. Voxiva seems to have solved this problem by partnering with officially approved contractors, from Northrop Grumman to Abt Associates to CARE, who subcontract the provision of data collection and communications systems to Voxiva.

- Develop recurring revenue business models that generate revenue from local economies. Voxiva has benefited greatly from its ability to win large, externally funded contracts to enter countries. Without the grant from the

World Bank to launch Alerta, for example, it would never have had the resources to enter Peru. However, to build a lasting scalable business, it must develop more solutions like Citizen's Alert in Peru and its patient-monitoring applications in the United States that generate stable recurring revenues.

■ Manage a diverse team and foster continuing innovation. One of Voxiva's strengths has been to bring together a team with a diverse background. Voxiva employs medical doctors, software engineers, social scientists, development experts, telecom specialists, change management consultants, and financial analysts. Meyer strongly believes that innovation comes from bringing together people with diverse perspectives and "forcing their brains to work together. It isn't always easy, but it's where the magical insights come from."

Conclusion

Three years after Voxiva's founding, Voxiva is operating on five continents. Meyer still relentlessly challenges his employees to create innovative applications that deliver on two bottom lines: social and financial.

Endnotes

1. WHO Report on Global Surveillance of Epidemic-Prone Infectious Diseases. WHO/CDS/CSR/ISR/2000.1, *http://www.who/int/emc-documents/surveillance/docs/ whocdscsrisr2001.pdf/Introduction.pdf*, May 2002. Note: Cancers, cardiovascular, and respiratory and digestive deaths also can be caused by infections and raise the percentage of deaths due to infectious diseases even higher.

2. Economic Impact of SARS—From Asian Development Bank, May 9, 2003, *http://www.abd.org/Documents/News/2003/nr2003065.pdf*.

3. WHO Report on Global Surveillance of Epidemic-Prone Infectious Diseases. WHO/CDS/CSR/ISR/2000.1. *http://www.who/int/emc-documents/surveillance/docs/wh ocdscsrisr2001.pdf/Introduction.pdf*, May 2002.

4. The World Bank's Agriculture and Development Home Page: *http://lnweb18.worldbank.org/ESSD/ardext.nsf/11ByDocName/AgricultureRuralDevelop ment*, October 2, 2003.

5. The Markle Foundation focuses its work in the program areas of policy for network society and information technologies for better health. The overarching goal of the Markle health program is to accelerate the rate at which information

technology enables consumers and the health system that supports them to improve health and *health care.* *http://www.markle.org/*, February 2004.

6. InfoDev was founded in September 1995, and is a global grant program managed by the World Bank to promote innovative projects in the use of information and communication technologies (ICTs) for economic and social development, with a special emphasis on the needs of the poor in developing countries. *http://www.infodev.org/*, February 2004.

7. Pew Internet and American Life. "The Ever Shifting Internet Population: A New Look at Internet Access and the Digital Divide." *http://www.pewinternet.org/reports/toc.asp?Report=88*, April 16, 2003.

This report was written by Cynthia Casas and William C. Lajoie under the supervision of Professor C. K. Prahalad. This report is intended to be a catalyst for discussion and is not intended to illustrate effective or ineffective strategies.

Biographies

Ruchi Misra

Ruchi Misra is from Montville, New Jersey. After graduating from Barnard College, Columbia University, in 1997, she became a financial analyst for Salomon Smith Barney's Equity Capital Markets Group in both the New York and Hong Kong offices. Two years later, she was promoted to Associate at Freeman & Co., a financial services management consulting firm in New York City. There she focused on mergers and acquisitions, strategy for asset management, and investment banking clientele. In 2004, Ruchi will earn her MBA from the Michigan Business School as well as an MS in Environmental Science from the University of Michigan School of Natural Resources. At Michigan, Ruchi has focused on corporate social responsibility and making the business case for sustainability.

Jeff Phillips

Jeff Phillips is from Olathe, Kansas. He graduated from the United States Air Force Academy in 1997 and served five years on active duty in the Air Force. At the Michigan Business School he concentrated on Corporate Strategy and International Business. After graduating in April 2004, Jeff began working for the management consultancy Booz Allen Hamilton in Cleveland, Ohio. What amazed him most about this experience was being able to create knowledge that will fundamentally alter the way companies view emerging economies. He hopes one day to own and operate a business incubator in a developing country.

Michael Hokenson

Michael Hokenson is currently a second-year CEMP student, earning an MBA and an MS in environmental science from the University of Michigan. He was raised in New Jersey and received his undergraduate degree from St. John's College in Santa Fe, New Mexico, majoring in philosophy and mathematics. After traveling extensively in Asia in 1997, he founded MINLAM, Inc., a fair trade manufacturing firm designing handicraft products in Nepal in cooperation with the NGO Rugmark. Michael has worked in various entrepreneurial ventures, including the launch of Kinetix LLC in 2001, a consulting firm based in New York City whose mission it is to assist businesses in the profitable alignment of financial goals with ethical and ecological principles. Michael believes the landscape of development currently taking place in emerging economies is transforming because of the need to balance development with environmental considerations. After graduation, Michael plans to focus on serving the capital and conservation management needs of small and medium-sized enterprises in emerging economies.

Sachin Rao

Sachin Rao grew up in Mumbai, India, and holds an undergraduate degree in software engineering. He spent seven years executing, managing, and selling offshore software solutions for clients around the world before coming to the Michigan Business School to get his MBA. At Michigan, his focus has been on Corporate Strategy, International Business, and watching his son, Dhruva, grow. Sachin's most enduring lesson from the experience is that at the BOP, social consciousness enables rather than compromises shareholder return.

Tej Shah

Tej Shah has a strong background in health care after spending three years at Deloitte Consulting. In 2004, Tej will earn his MBA from the Michigan Business School, where he has concentrated on Marketing and Corporate Strategy. Tej became interested in emerging markets after developing grant applications for an HIV/AIDS nonprofit organization in Harare, Zimbabwe, in 2002. Working on this book allowed him to experience firsthand the power of an underserved community. Following graduation in 2004, Tej will return to Deloitte in their Chicago office as a Senior Consultant.

Todd Markson

Todd Markson is from Concord, Massachusetts. He graduated from Brown University in 1997 with a BA in political science and economics, having studied abroad for one semester at Yonsei University in Seoul, South Korea. After Brown, Todd entered the Peace Corps in Mali, West Africa, as a Small Enterprise Development volunteer, working with native entrepreneurs in starting new ventures and attracting the flow of microfinance to underdeveloped communities. After returning to the United States, he was part of the founding team of two startups in the Bay Area of California, one a contact updating software company and the other an entrepreneurial incubator still in existence. Todd received his MBA with Distinction in April 2004 from the Michigan Business School with concentrations in Corporate Strategy, International Business, and Finance. Todd will be a Senior Associate at DiamondCluster, a strategy consulting firm, out of their London, England, office. The most intriguing aspect of this research is the realization that with business model modifications and innovative application of technology, vast new markets open up. Multinational companies can profitably expand their reach while providing individuals at the bottom of the economic pyramid with products and services that they need and desire.

Kate Reeder

Kate Reeder is from Providence, Rhode Island. She earned her MBA in April 2004 from the Michigan Business School, where she focused on Marketing and Corporate Strategy. Prior to graduate school, Kate lived in San Francisco, California, and worked on a variety of projects as a creative services consultant for Sapient Corporation, a technology consultancy. She holds a BA in political science from Brown University.

Ajit Sharma

Ajit Sharma's native state, Bihar, is at the bottom of the pyramid in India, the poorest state in the nation. Paradoxically, it is the richest state in terms of natural resources. It has a glorious past, being the birthplace of two religions (Buddhism and Jainism), the place from where Ashoka ruled over India, the place where the first university (Nalanda) was established, and the place from where Gandhi started his fight for India's independence. Ajit believes that the BOP paradigm opens up new possibilities for the development of regions, like Bihar, caught in the downward spiral of poverty. For this reason, the concept is very close to his heart and he hopes to use it someday for the development of his state. Ajit earned his B. Tech. in Manufacturing Engineering from National Institute of Foundry and Forge Technology (NIFFT), Ranchi; and his masters from NITIE, Mumbai. He will complete his MBA from the University of Michigan in 2005. Ajit would like to express his gratitude to his parents, Shri Balram and Smt. Sushma, his brother Amit, and his wife Pratibha for their unconditional love and support.

Praveen Suthrum

Praveen Suthrum, from Hyderabad, India, cofounded the XMAP program at the University of Michigan Business School. He obtained his BS in electrical engineering from the Mangalore University. Praveen then worked for six years with Satyam Computer Services, India's IT outsourcing leader, in various capacities, and more recently as a business manager serving Fortune 100 clients. In 2003, he adapted the eGovernance model, developed as part of the XMAP program, to aid reconstruction efforts in Iraq and presented the model to key dignitaries, including former Secretary of State Madeleine Albright and the Prime Minister of Iraqi Kurdistan, Dr. Barham Salih. Additionally, Praveen consulted with the U.S. Institute of Peace on the feasibility of eGovernance in Iraq. At the Michigan Business School, he has focused his studies on corporate strategy and emerging markets.

Andrew Wilson

Andrew Wilson received his undergraduate degree in business from Southern Methodist University and spent more than five years with Deloitte Consulting as an Associate Consultant focused on the energy sector. In 2004, Andrew will earn his MBA from the University of Michigan Business School, where he has concentrated in strategy and general management. What impressed him most about his experience with Casas Bahia was management's hands-on role in changing the lives of customers. He is excited that the group's collective work is helping to shape global development.

Mindy Murch

Mindy Murch graduated from the Corporate Environmental Management Program, a dual masters program between the University of Michigan's School of Natural Resources & Environment and Business

School in 2004. Prior to graduate school, Mindy worked for PricewaterhouseCoopers Management Consulting Service and the U.S. Department of Agriculture Forest Service in Washington, DC. Mindy holds a BA in Russian Language and Literature from Bowdoin College.

Kuttayan Annamalai

Kuttayan Annamalai is from Tamil Nadu, India. He earned his bachelors degree in engineering from Birla Institute of Technology and Science, Pilani, India, in 1995. In 2004, Kuttayan will earn his MBA from the University of Michigan Business School, with emphases in strategy and finance. Prior to his MBA, Kuttayan was a consultant at a technology services company, where he led initiatives to solve strategic technology issues for Fortune 500 clients. The bottom of the pyramid project was an eye-opener for him, as he explored innovative business models that not only catalyzed rural transformation but also redefined corporate social responsibility.

Sami Foguel

Sami Foguel is from Salvador, Bahia, Brazil. He received his undergraduate degree in engineering from Universidade Estadual de Campinas in 1998 and worked for McKinsey and Company as a consultant mainly focused on financial institutions. In 2004, Sami will earn his MBA from the University of Michigan Business School, where he has concentrated in General Management and Finance. After graduation, Sami will return to McKinsey and Company in their São Paulo office. What impressed him most about his experience with Casas Bahia was management's ability to understand and fulfill the untapped financing needs of the poor population in Brazil.

Anuja Rajendra

Anuja Rajendra grew up in Patiala, India, and Okemos, Michigan, a paradoxical combination that invoked her passion for global economic development. After earning a BS in Industrial and Operations Engineering from the University of Michigan, Anuja worked in business development for American Power Conversion Corporation, where she was promoted three times in 18 months, becoming the Regional Sales Support Manager for the Northern United States. In 1997, the tragic death of her sister, Rachana, in an automobile accident motivated Anuja to start Moon-baked Creations Contemporary Art Lounge and Café in Okemos, Michigan. She later became the Director of Strategic Partnerships for a technology startup and then the Director of Development for a $1.5-million nonprofit organization. As a 2004 MBA candidate at the University of Michigan Business School, Anuja is focused on global social entrepreneurship and hopes to start a business that will serve the bottom of the pyramid.

Scott Baron

Scott Baron graduated in May 2004 from the University of Michigan and will earn his MS from the School of Natural Resources & Environment and his MBA from the Michigan Business School. Scott's focus is on renewable energy, particularly wind and hybrid power systems. Working with C. K. Prahalad for the past year, he was inspired to start his own business implementing renewable energy projects in bottom-of-the-pyramid markets. This venture won numerous distinctions at business plan competitions around the country, including Best Social Return on Investment at the Global Social Venture Competition. Prior to coming to Michigan, Scott worked in the field of climate change, where he helped start the Chicago Climate Exchange, a voluntary market for the trading of greenhouse gases. Scott is from Chicago and graduated from Northwestern University with a BS in economics and environmental policy.

George Weinmann

George Weinmann grew up in New Orleans, Louisiana. He graduated from the University of Virginia with a BS in aerospace engineering before working for the Boeing Company for five years, where he helped organize Boeing Ventures and led several new businesses in energy and telecommunications. At the Michigan Business School, George concentrated on entrepreneurship, strategy, and international business and was a student member of the Wolverine Venture Fund. After graduation in 2004, George is pursuing a career in international business. For George this project impressed on him the power of entrepreneurship and investment to solve critical societal needs.

Scott Macke

Scott Macke is from Marshalltown, Iowa, and graduated from Butler University in Indianapolis, Indiana, in 1996 with a degree in accounting. He worked in auditing and tax for an Indianapolis-based accounting firm for three years and then worked for two years conducting privately held business valuations for a regional CPA firm in Denver, Colorado. Scott is concentrating on Finance and Corporate Strategy at the Michigan Business School and will work for Robert W. Baird in equity research after graduation.

Ajay Sharma

Ajay Sharma is from Jaipur, India. After receiving a BTech in electrical engineering from the Institute of Technology in Varanasi, Ajay joined Infosys Technologies (India), where he provided IT solutions to Fortune 500 clients. He later worked in the Management Consulting Services group of PriceWaterhouseCoopers (USA) as Principal Consultant. In 2004, he will earn his MBA from the Michigan Business School, where he has focused on Corporate Strategy and International Business. From the bottom of the pyramid project, Ajay developed amazing insight into how developed economies can learn from innovations created in resource-constrained emerging economies.

Sharmilee Mohan

Sharmilee Mohan, a Class of 2003 MBA graduate, participated in the Cemex project focusing on understanding Mexican society and Cemex's (and competitors) strategy to provide housing for the poor profitably. She traveled to Guadalajara, Mexico, with no Spanish-speaking skills or a Spanish–English translator. She considered her one-week trip to Guadalajara an adventure and a huge success from an academic and cultural standpoint. She learned a lot about Mexican society, especially the poor, firsthand. As an Indian citizen, she is no stranger to a wide range of issues surrounding emerging economies today such as poverty, gross domestic product growth, abundance of educated and/or semiskilled labor, corruption, globalization, exploding consumerism, outsourcing, and so on. Nevertheless, her experience in Guadalajara was an eye-opener when she approached the same issues and challenges that shroud emerging economies from a business perspective. Currently, she works for a management consulting firm in New York focusing on strategy and operations.

William LaJoie

William LaJoie is from Denver, Colorado, and his primary interests are the underlying factors that drive exponential growth. After obtaining his BA in English literature from the University of Notre Dame, he spent two years volunteering at the Working Boys' Center, a school for the working poor, in Quito, Ecuador, teaching in the elementary school, high school, and adult literacy program. After returning to the United States, William worked as a Program Manager for LinkShare Corporation, a provider of Internet-based affiliate solutions, where his clients included Dell and Ford. In 2004, William will earn his MBA from the University of Michigan Business School, where he has combined his interest in Marketing, Technology, and Emerging Economies. He is pursuing a career in market research and is looking forward to living happily ever after with his fiancée, Dana.

Cynthia Casas

Cynthia Casas, who cofounded the XMAP program with Praveen Suthrum, is a first-generation American of Mexican descent from El Paso, Texas. After obtaining her BS in International Business from American University in 1994, she worked for GE Capital in London and then IBM in Singapore. In 1996, Cynthia embarked on a new career path, first at an environmental nonprofit organization in the United States and then at the World Bank, where she worked in the Corporate Strategy Group and External Affairs departments. In 2004, Cynthia will earn her MBA from the University of Michigan Business School, where she has brought together her backgrounds in business and economic development to bear on defining the role of the business sector in poverty alleviation. Through her work with C. K. Prahalad, she has had the chance to study profitable companies that seek to improve the economic viability of the regions and communities in which they operate. Copresident of the Emerging Markets Club and member of Net Impact while at Michigan, she is passionate about discovering and initiating business practices in developing countries that are both socially and environmentally sustainable.

Index